Ecodynamics

Ecodynamics

A New Theory of
Societal Evolution

by
Kenneth E. Boulding

A Sage View Edition

SAGE PUBLICATIONS   Beverly Hills   London

Copyright © 1978 by Sage Publications, Inc.

For information address:

SAGE PUBLICATIONS, INC.
275 South Beverly Drive
Beverly Hills, California 90212

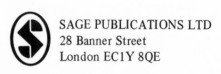

SAGE PUBLICATIONS LTD
28 Banner Street
London EC1Y 8QE

Printed in the United States of America

Library of Congress Cataloging in Publication Data

Boulding, Kenneth Ewart, 1910-
  Ecodynamics

    1. Social evolution.   2. Social structure.
3. Evolution.   I. Title.
HM106.B57   301.4   77-27282
ISBN 0-8039-0945-4

FIRST SAGEVIEW PRINTING

CONTENTS

PREFACE

This is a work of ideas rather than of scholarship. The ideas have been generated in my own mind as the result of an immensely complex process of input from outside and self-generated input from within. My debt to the producers of the input from outside is enormous, and I cannot identify consciously more than a very small number of them. For the debts that I cannot acknowledge, I must beg to be forgiven. The inputs have been through a very large selective process, out of which emerges the output which is this volume. I am sure I have filtered out some things that should be in, and left in some things that should be out. But I do judge, as objectively as I can, that what has emerged is a synthesis which, if somebody else had done it, I would not hesitate to describe as "important." Whether this judgment is correct, only the future can tell.

A selective synthesis is another name for a textbook, and this is one of the things that this volume is intended to be. I have used it myself as a teacher in a class of college students, mostly on the sophomore and upper-class levels at the University of Colorado in the spring semester of 1976, in a course entitled "General Social Dynamics." I learned a great deal from the students and also from some colleagues who attended the course. To judge from the examinations and the student response, the book at least taught them something about the universe in which they find themselves. I hope others will see it as equally useful.

This book has developed in many stages over a considerable number of years. Perhaps it began with some lectures I gave at the International Christian University in Tokyo in the spring of 1964, published a few years later as *A Primer on Social Dynamics* (New York: Free Press, 1970). The ideas were further refined in the Patten Lectures I gave at Indiana University in Bloomington, Indiana, in 1973; in further lectures at Cornell University in the fall of

1974 as an Andrew D. White Professor-at-Large; and in my three Mies van der Rohe Lectures at the Illinois Institute of Technology in March 1975. The first draft of the work was essentially completed at my summer cabin near Boulder in the summer of 1975, and I tried out some of the ideas on a little group at Wellesley College, where I was lecturing in the fall of 1975. In all these places, I received help from considerable numbers of people. I have also benefited much from correspondence, and from the comments of a number of people who read the manuscript in various stages. I am particularly grateful to Professor Richard Adams of the University of Texas at Austin; and to my wife, Elise Boulding, without whose penetrating criticisms the book would probably have been finished sooner—and who, I think, still does not agree with a good deal of it.

Special thanks are due to the University of Colorado and its Institute of Behavioral Science, which has provided me with ideal conditions for work. Special thanks are also due to the Ford Foundation, for a grant which has greatly facilitated my work. I am particularly grateful to my administrative secretary and colleague, Vivian Wilson, without whose constant help and valuable criticism I doubt if the manuscript would have ever been finished.

—K.E.B.

INTRODUCTION
What This Book is All About

EVOLUTION AS A PATTERN OF THE UNIVERSE

Be warned at the outset that this is a book about the universe, or at least about an image of it in the mind of the writer. It is therefore bound to be highly inaccurate, for even what all human beings taken together know about the universe is likely to be a very sketchy representation of it, partly because the universe itself is bigger than the capacity of the human nervous system and partly because our image of it is derived from a very small and biased sample of time and space. All images of the universe must be accepted as imperfect and subject to constant revision. Furthermore, my expertise is primarily in the social sciences, and the social systems of planet Earth represent an extremely small fraction of the universe.

Still, it is *our* fraction. We have largely created it, and we can hardly be blamed for being unusually interested in it. The descriptions in this book of the universe at large, and even of that very small portion of it that constitutes the history of earth's biosphere, are the work of an amateur and must be taken as suggestive rather than as definitive. One of the objectives of the work, however, is to look at the history of the social system, which the human race has created, in the larger setting of the universe as it extends in time and space.

The book is about evolution, the pattern that can be perceived in the structure of the universe in space and time. The human mind seems to have a rage for pattern, sometimes to the point of falling into superstition, which is the perception of patterns where there are none. When we talk about evolution, however, we are not talking about the mere description of the history and geography of the universe as a four-dimensional space-time object, something which is quite inaccessible to us in any completeness. We are looking for patterns within this structure. It is one of the principal contentions of this work that evolution itself evolves. That is, it is not a single pattern, but a succession of patterns, this succession itself having a pattern of its own. From the point of view of our own planet, we detect three major evolutionary patterns—physical, biological, and societal. The evolution of the physical world I have also called "pre-biological evolution," although it continues after living organisms and humans have appeared. It is the evolution of elements, molecules, compounds, stars, planets, rocks, land forms on this planet, water, and air. This process follows a phase pattern. That is, environments change, and existing structures become unstable and are transformed into new structures that are stable in the new environment. A very familiar example is water, which is solid below a temperature of zero degrees Centigrade, liquid between zero and 100 degrees Centigrade, and gas above 100 degrees at our own atmospheric pressure.

The origin of the universe, or even whether the universe had an origin, is still a deep mystery to us. There is much evidence that the universe is expanding, which suggests that it began with a "big bang." After that, whatever it was, we detect two processes that seem to have directionality in time—a time's arrow—pointing toward irreversible change. One is the famous second law of thermodynamics, that entropy increases in any process. The other is the law of evolution, that complexity increases in terms of differentiation and structure. These may seem at first contradictory. The second law of thermodynamics points toward exhaustion, decay, loss of structure and uniformity, with the universe returning to chaos, a structureless homogeneity in which nothing more can happen. Evolution seems to point in the opposite direction, toward differentiation into structures of increasing complexity. The paradox may perhaps be resolved by looking at evolution as the segregation of entropy, the building up of little islands of order and complexity at the cost of still more disorder elsewhere. The entropy concept is an unfortunate one, something like phlogiston (which turned out to be negative oxygen), in the sense that entropy is negative potential. We can generalize the second law in the form of a law of diminishing potential rather than of increasing entropy, stated in the form: If anything happens, it is because there was a potential for it happening, and after it has happened that potential has been used up. This form of stating the law opens up the possibility that potential might be re-created in particular forms. An example would be the biological potential of the fertilized egg for producing the life history of the corresponding organism. This potential is gradually used up as the organism ages; finally it is exhausted and the organism dies. If, however, in the process the organism fertilizes another egg, the biological potential is re-created, though never of course in exactly the same form.

In terms of physical evolution, it looks as if it is the expansion of the universe that brings about the increase in complexity of physical structure, oddly enough, through the dilution of energy. What the ultimate stuff or building blocks of the universe is we do not know. Perhaps it does not have any. The distinction between energy and matter is certainly a very convenient one and corresponds to a great deal of our experience, even though we know now that energy and matter can be transformed one into the other. When energy levels are very high, there is not much material structure. As the universe expands, however, energy presumably becomes more diffuse in space, temperatures fall, and material structure becomes more complex. Protons and electrons combine to form atoms; the elements evolve in the stars, first in gaseous form, then as energy becomes still more diffuse and matter becomes cooler, into liquid and solid forms. Elements combine into compounds of increasing complexity as the energy environment permits. Ordinarily we think of the phase rule in terms of pressure and temperature, but perhaps both of these are manifestations of something more fundamental in terms of energy density. There is much here that we do not understand.

DEFINITIONS, SPECIES, AND POPULATIONS

Perhaps the most fundamental concept of the universe is that of a species or a population. A species is a set of individuals or objects each of which conforms to a common definition. The objects are not necessarily identical; indeed, in an important sense, no two objects can be identical because each occupies a different position in space-time. The definition identifies characteristics of an object that are similar enough to merit classification as a species. This is taxonomy—the division of the universe into a partition of sets of objects, each of which constitutes a species. The definition is a kind of fence that includes all things in the species and excludes all things that are not. Every definition divides the universe into two parts: those things which conform to it and those things which do not. Taxonomy is part of our image of the universe, and it may be incorrect, in the sense that the species defined by the taxonomic definitions are too heterogeneous to be a really interesting pattern. Thus, the medieval elements of earth, air, fire, and water were too heterogeneous to be really useful in chemistry, and the chemical elements present a taxonomy that certainly increases the productive power of the human race over what could be done with the medieval elements. Similarly, I am arguing that the classical economic taxonomy of factors of production into land, labor, and capital is also too heterogeneous to be useful and that know-how, energy, and materials are a much more useful taxonomy in understanding productive processes. It must be emphasized that taxonomy is probably more a pattern of the human mind than it is of the universe itself.

A population is simply the number of individuals or elements in a species. Thus, the universe has a population of hydrogen atoms, of water molecules, of human beings, and of automobiles. The population concept itself is capable of degrees of complexity. At the simplest level, we have species consisting of a fixed number of elements and individuals without additions or subtractions. Anything that is conserved in the universe represents a species of this kind, but we are not quite sure what is conserved. At the second level of complexity, we have a species consisting of a population of individuals to which, over time, some are added and from which some are subtracted. A third level of population complexity consists of individuals who are not only added to and subtracted from but who "age"; that is, in whom the time interval between the "birth" or addition and the present is in some sense significant. Age has very little significance in physical and chemical populations, though it may have some significance for radioactive elements, which is perhaps the first appearance of something like "aging" in the universe, and in a sense a star ages as it passes through successive stages of development. In biological populations, of course, aging is very significant. There are only certain ages at which organisms are fertile and the probability of death is in almost all species a rising function with age.

PRODUCTION AND ECOLOGICAL
INTERACTION AS A GENERAL PATTERN

There are patterns that emerge in biological and societal evolution which are present only in a primitive form in physical evolution. One of these is the distinction between the genotype and the phenotype and the pattern of "production," which is the process by which the genotype produces the phenotype. This is very clear in biological systems, fairly clear in social systems, much less clear in purely physical systems. Production, whether of the chicken from the egg or a house from a blueprint, involves three essential factors: know-how, energy, and materials. Genetic structure or *know-how*, whether this is coded in DNA patterns of the biological genes or in human knowledge and the blueprints of the production of human artifacts, must be able to direct *energy*, to sustain appropriate temperatures, and to transport and transform selected *materials* into the improbable structures of the phenotype (the chicken or the automobile). In physical systems, the closest parallel is catalysis, in which the catalyst acts as a template that is able to impose its structure on the otherwise formless molecules of its environment. How important catalysis has been in physical evolution, I simply do not know. It clearly cannot be important until a solid state is reached.

Another concept of great importance in biological and societal evolution is that of an ecosystem of interacting populations of different species. In an ecosystem a species grows if the additions to it (births) exceed the subtractions from it (deaths), and declines if the subtractions exceed the additions. We suppose that these additions and subtractions are a function of the size of all relevant populations in the environment of the species, including its own population. Mutation consists essentially in changes in the parameters of these functions. Any change is likely to favor some species and to diminish others. With a given set of parameters we can postulate an equilibrium system in which each species is stationary in population, with additions equal to subtractions. This equilibrium population is the "niche" of the species. If the niche of any species declines to zero, the population will become extinct. Any ecosystem will have "empty niches"; that is, a potential species, which would have a positive population in the system, if it existed. Biological and societal evolution consist mainly in the filling of empty niches by mutation. On the other hand, the probability that such a niche will be filled in a given time is certainly less than one, and as time goes on other mutations may close the niche before it has been filled. If this happens, the subsequent course of evolution is different from what it would have been if the niche had been filled. Evolution, therefore, is a system with strong elements of indeterminacy in it, in the sense that the time at which an event of probability of less than one actually happens is important in determining the course of the system. In this sense, evolution is very different from simple dynamic systems, such as celestial mechanics, which have predictability only because their evolution has largely ceased and they have essentially reached equilibrium in space-time.

There are certain parallels to ecosystems in purely physical and chemical dynamics. Each chemical molecule or compound could be considered as a species. When, for instance, hydrogen burns in oxygen, hydrogen molecules and oxygen molecules "die" and water molecules are "born"; the populations of hydrogen and oxygen molecules diminish and that of water molecules increases. Under given environmental conditions, chemical reactions tend to produce an equilibrium population of the different chemical species much as an ecosystem does, each population remaining constant because the births into it equal the deaths out of it.

EVOLUTION AS A PROCESS IN "KNOW-HOW"
OR GENETIC STRUCTURE

A major thesis of this work is that evolution is primarily a process in genetic structure, which I have called "know-how." It is more than the "information" of information theory. It involves not only improbability of structure, but the structure's ability to "instruct"; that is, to be a code of selection according to a program. The fertilized egg "knows how" to produce a chicken in much the same way a potter knows how to make a pot or General Motors knows how to make an automobile. As we move down into the physical-chemical universe, the know-how concept becomes more tenuous. Nevertheless, in a certain sense, helium "knows how" to have two electrons and hydrogen knows only how to have one. Chemical valency is a principle of selection, a precursor of evaluation in the biological and social spheres. It is only stretching the metaphor a little to say that carbon "prefers" to hold onto four hydrogens rather than three, and that CH_3 is a "radical"; that is, an unsatisfied structure.

As we move into biological evolution, we find two different modes of genetic structure. There is what might be called "biogenetics," which is the genetic structure of the gene and of DNA, a program for producing the corresponding organism or phenotype and for producing the nervous system, which impels or at least predisposes toward certain types of behavior. Once we have reasonably complex nervous systems produced by biogenetics, however, another process emerges, which might be called "noogenetics." This is the structure within the nervous system which the individual organism has to learn, often of course from its parents, but also from its other environments. No one really knows when learning began in the biosphere. It is certainly important in all species that have parental care of offspring. The possibility of learning from the general environment, even in quite primitive species, should also not be overlooked. Certainly many species of birds have to learn at least part of their birdsong, kittens learn a good deal about how to be a cat from their mothers, and a kitten raised by a dog can have peculiar behavior patterns. When we get to the human race, of course, noogenetic patterns predominate. Biogenetics produces an extremely unstructured human nervous system with fantastic potential for learning. We really know very little about the biogenetics of the human nervous system. It certainly can possess biogenetic defects, and biogenetic origins may produce structures that make some learning processes easier than others, but on the whole the noogenetic element is overwhelmingly dominant. If nobody spoke to children, if all schools and universities were shut down for as little as one or two generations, the human race would be virtually identical biologically to what we are now, but its culture would, if it survived at all, revert to the Stone Age.

HUMAN HISTORY AS THE "NOOGENETIC" EVOLUTION OF HUMAN ARTIFACTS

The main thrust of this work is toward human history and the perception of patterns in it. We do not know much about the process by which the human race actually evolved in the last two million years, and it is certainly puzzling how an organ which seems to be as redundant as the human brain could have been developed by natural selection. Once we have Adam and Eve, however (or whatever they may have called themselves), with the genetic structure of Homo Sapiens, evolution passed into a new phase and a "higher gear" in terms of human artifacts and accelerated markedly. These artifacts are species created by noogenetic production processes rather than by biogenetic processes. They are of three major kinds: material artifacts—from first eoliths and flint instruments to the space shuttle—which have been produced in a fantastic variety far exceeding the variety of biological species. Then there are organizational artifacts, which usually involve a complex of supporting material artifacts plus behavioral and role patterns, and mental images. They stretch from the original hunting-gathering band through General Motors, the United Nations, and NASA. Then there are personal artifacts— that is, humans themselves insofar as they have been produced by other human beings and by themselves. This species includes the knowledge and evaluation structure of our brains and the skills of our body, the language that we speak and write, and the almost infinite variety of reactions to our physical, biological, and human environment. My blue-grey eyes are a biological artifact; they were the only eyes that my genes knew how to make. The English language which I speak and am writing, however, is a social artifact produced by noogenetic processes by very large numbers of other human beings stretching back many hundreds or even thousands of years. All these human artifacts—Things, Organizations, and People—have been and continue to be produced in a vast worldwide drama, which I have called, rather playfully, the "TOP" saga.

The production of all these artifacts involves the three essential factors of production: know-how, energy, and materials. These processes of production, as we have seen, are highly similar to the processes of biological production, but there is one important difference. Biological evolution never got beyond two sexes, with some possible exceptions in recombinant DNA. Each biological species constantly rearranges its own gene pool—the genetic patterns contained in all its members—into new organisms, but it cannot draw on any other gene pool. In the production of human artifacts, however, the genetic structure can extend to the whole "noosphere" of the human race, and such artifacts are multiparental, being produced by the cooperation of very large numbers of other artifacts and of persons having very different know-how and skills. It is this property of societal evolution that has made it so rapid by comparison with biological evolution. Within biological evolution itself, the development of sexual reproduction almost certainly speeded up the rate of evolution by increasing the production of new species because it increased the capacity for variation. Again somewhat playfully, I have called this the great drama of production by which Know-how guides Energy to select, transport, and rearrange Materials into the improbable structures of the phenotypes the "KEM" saga, a pattern that stretches over both biological and societal evolution.

THREAT, INTEGRATIVE, AND EXCHANGE SYSTEMS

Because of the capacity for language, and therefore for images that extend far beyond immediate personal experience, the human race has developed a group of genetic organizers for which there is practically no parallel in biology, although perhaps there is a certain parallel in the enzymes, hormones, and chemical messengers by which the genetic structure organizes the production of the organism. In the human race, communication by means of language, other symbols, behavioral signs, and so on becomes a process of complex mutuality and feedback among numbers of individuals that leads to the development of organizations, institutions, and other social structures which affect behavior and material and personal products. There seem to be three major groups of these organizers, which I have identified as the Threat system, the Integrative system, and the Exchange system. This is a recurring thread in the great drama of human life and history, and I call it the "TIE" saga, for these relationships do indeed tie us together into organizational structures, thereby enormously increasing the capacity of the human race for making both material and personal artifacts. The threat system begins with a communication of the type, "You do something I want or I'll do something you don't want," usually with some evidence of the capability of the latter, that can be followed by submission, defiance, flight, or counterthreat. The first produces empires, states, armies, and so on. The second produces war. The third produces dispersion of the human race, though dispersion may also have other sources. The fourth produces deterrence, which also leads to war. The threat system undoubtedly produced civilization. It has been an essential part of every known human society, but it also has very deep pathologies in terms of violence, destruction, war, unhappy families, and disturbed personalities.

Integrative systems also begin very early in human history. They involve such things as love and hate, benevolence and malevolence, affection, altruism, community, legitimacy, and so on. This is perhaps more heterogeneous than the threat or the exchange system, but it undergirds both, and neither can develop very far without it. Both threats and exchange must be legitimated and placed in some kind of framework of community before they can become very extensive. Illegitimate threat—as in the bandit, for instance—can only produce a very small, temporary relationship. Threat must be legitimated in the form of the tax collector, the policeman, or recognized authority before it can organize states and empires. Similarly, exchange with strangers must be legitimated before the system of exchange can become very extensive. A vital element in integrative structures is the concept of identity, for a person's image of identity is a very important determinant of behavior and of other people's responses. Identity, however, is closely bound up with community. One's identity, indeed, can almost be defined as the group with which one identifies, whether family, religious, occupational, national, or political.

Exchange in any extended sense probably comes later than the other two, but once it develops it is very powerful in organizing the division of labor and in expanding the quantity and the number of species of human artifacts, especially material artifacts in the form of commodities. Exchange is based on invitations rather than threats—"You do something for me and I'll do something for you." It tends to be a positive sum game, beneficial to both parties, and a powerful source of human learning through specialization. It has to be legitimated, however, through some kind of integrative structure, and its legitimation always seems to be a little precarious, perhaps because the identity of an exchanger is a weak one. It implies *property*, for you cannot exchange what is not yours. The property can either be privately or publicly owned, by an individual or by an organization or community of some kind.

No human relation seems to exist that does not exhibit all three of these organizing relationships in various proportions. Each has pathologies of its own. The threat system may be the most pathological, but exchange systems can lead into unemployment, maldistribution, and overemphasis on monetary values. Integrative systems can lead into tyrannies of persuasion, unduly demanding parents or children, religious intolerance and persecution and xenophobia, and without integrative systems the threat system would never lead to organized warfare.

NICHE EXPANSION IN HUMAN HISTORY

Human history is characterized by a phenomenon that is virtually unknown in prehuman biological systems: niche expansion through the production of artifacts. Even during the paleolithic period, there must have been a slow expansion of the niche of the human race through the development of improved knives, arrowheads, slingshots, fire, artificial shelters, clothing, and other human artifacts. Societal evolution in this period seems to have been surprisingly slow in view of the fact that these humans were biologically virtually indistinguishable from ourselves. Unfortunately, the record is so imperfect that we know very little about the evolution of language, and it seems to take a very long time to learn to form communities beyond the small band. The development of agriculture and the domestication of animals in the neolithic period enormously expanded the human niche, from perhaps ten million to hundreds of millions. Metallurgy almost certainly expanded it further, although by improving weaponry this may also have led to civilization and war, two things which oddly enough seem to go together. How much war has contributed to diminishing the human niche is hard to say. One suspects that its impact may be much less than one would judge from the history books, simply because it is dramatic and spectacular, whereas it is the dull, humdrum things like plowing, reaping, and producing that really expand the human niche.

The rise of science in the last five hundred years has expanded the human niche still further, though how far is uncertain—and we are still in the middle of the process. Part of the expansion of the last hundred years has been the result of the discovery of new lands, rich ores, and fossil fuels. With the exhaustion of these resources, the human niche might conceivably shrink, a very painful process. On the other hand, the rapid advance of knowledge continues and it would not be surprising if this growth continued to expand the human niche. There is even a possibility that the human race might begin the colonization of space and expand beyond its original planet, though extraterrestrial environments would have to be highly artificial and probably very expensive. Yet the low energy requirements in space might well offset the absence of the "free goods" of land, air, and water, which have been so important to human development on earth.

THE EVOLUTIONARY SYNTHESIS

The pattern of human development is therefore seen to be an extension, enlargement, and acceleration of the pattern of biological development, operating through mutation and selection. Selection is ecological interaction constantly creating new niches and destroying old ones; mutation takes the form of invention, discovery, expansions of the noosphere and the human noogenetic structure. Niches open up, and sometimes are filled, sometimes not, depending on the capacity of the system for mutation; each successful mutation opens some niches and closes others. The pattern jogs along in an immensely complex interaction of things, organizations, and people, with biological, meteorological, and geological environments, structures, and populations.

Though the evolutionary model does provide important insights about the future, it does not lead into easy and secure prediction, and its essential indeterminacy makes exact prediction impossible. There is in fact a very simple nonexistence theorem about prediction in evolutionary and especially in social systems. These are essentially based on some form of knowledge or know-how; we cannot predict what we are going to know or what know-how we are going to have in the future, or we would have it now. Social systems in particular, therefore, are characterized by irreducible uncertainty and inherently unpredictable change in parameters. This does not mean that the future is wholly unknown; there are some things that we can say about the future with fairly high degrees of probability. We are all very sure, for instance, that we are going to die some time within a reasonable lifespan. Exact prediction, however, is impossible except in systems whose evolution has ceased, like the solar system.

I have to confess, and it would be false modesty to fail to do so, that I think I have achieved an important synthesis in this volume. I hope it is at least an approximation of a general system of the universe based on a synthesis of the contributions of many different sciences. I am sure that there are serious errors in it that others will detect and remedy. These are days in which no person can hope to achieve more than a small fraction of the knowledge that is available to the whole human race. Even in the absence of detailed knowledge, however, one can have a vision. I believe I have been fortunate enough to have enjoyed a vision of a great pattern of an unfolding universe. In this drama, the human race is playing a very distinct part, which only our ignorance persuades us is unique, but which our knowledge convinces us is beyond anything else that we know about.

COMPETITORS TO THE EVOLUTIONARY VISION

Every vision, of course, conflicts with other visions, and it would perhaps be well to conclude this introduction with a brief account of contrasting visions. Each vision must be understood in terms of what it is *not* as well as in terms of what it is. It is only courteous, therefore, to issue some warnings about those positions that are uncongenial to the "evolutionary" vision of the present volume.

The evolutionary vision is unfriendly to romantic nature worship, the view that the human race and its artifacts are not part of nature and that nature without the human race is somehow wise and good. This is a fallacy into which many people of good will fall. The human race has been produced by the evolutionary process and so have its artifacts. The automobile is just as "natural" as the horse. It is just as much a species, just as much a part of the total ecological system, and the idea that there is something called "ecology" in the absence of the human race and human artifacts at this stage of the development of the planet is romantic illusion. The human race, of course, needs to be aware of its impact on the total system, but the concept of the "environment" as removed from human endeavor is largely illusory. When we talk about the environment, we mean the evaluation of the total state of the planet according to human values, which are the only values we know very much about. If "nature," whatever that is, has values, they are unknown to us. Certainly nature is no respecter of species, and all species are endangered. Nature cares no more about the whooping crane or the blue whale than she did about the dinosaur. Indeed, personification of nature is a romantic substitute for religion without the intellectual substance of a practical argument for faith in the divine as an act of will and commitment.

The evolutionary vision is unfriendly to any monistic view of human history that seeks to explain it by a single factor, whether this is a materialistic interpretation, as in the case of Marxism, a simple theistic interpretation, as in biblical Judaism, an eschatalogical interpretation in terms of some simple denouement, or a revolutionary interpretation in terms of dialectics and class struggle. The evolutionary vision sees human history as a vast interacting network of species and relationships of many different kinds, and there is really no "leading factor" always in the forefront. At times, changes in material technology are the major mutational developments and create niches for social changes of various kinds. At other times, however, intellectual or spiritual movements take the lead and create niches for new material artifacts and technologies; sometimes climatic changes dominate the scene; or sometimes biological mutations, dominate, such as the disease bacteria that caused the great plagues.

The evolutionary vision is unfriendly to any simple reductionism or materialism. It sees the essence of the evolutionary process in the field of information, know-how, programmed instructions, and so on, leading in the human race to consciousness and a great expansion of know-how through the development of "know-what"—that is, conscious knowledge. Over time, systems of increasing complexity have been developed, and the more complex ones cannot be described simply in terms of the less complex. Any attempt to reduce the complex properties of biological organisms or of nervous systems or of human brains to simple physical and chemical systems is foolish.

The evolutionary vision is agnostic in regard to systems in the universe of greater complexity than those of which human beings have clear knowledge. It recognizes aesthetic, moral, and religious ideas and experiences as a species, in this case of mental structures or of images, which clearly interacts with other species in the world's great ecosystem. "Spiritual species," if we may name them so, have strong nonrandom elements in them; they exhibit pattern and order of their own. In respect to mental images, as in respect to our images of the physical world, it seems reasonable to suppose that there is a selective process at work in the interaction of these images with their total environment, a process which is asymmetrical in the sense that there is a continual testing process to segregate and eliminate error. All images in the human mind are mixtures of truth and error, truth being what corresponds to some external reality and error what does not. But we can never directly compare an image with an external reality. The feedback from failures of prediction does tend to eliminate error, so that the truth-error mixture becomes richer in truth. Processes of this kind seem to go on not only in our images of the physical world but also in our images of value, with "better" values having survival value over "worse" values. The same principle applies to apprehensions of spiritual reality. This is, however, a very large universe, and we have experienced very little of it, so that all our images of the ultimate and absolute must be of a highly tentative nature.

SOCIOBIOLOGY AND THE EVOLUTIONARY VISION

The relation of the evolutionary vision of this volume to the new discipline of sociobiology deserves some attention.[1] Sociobiology is a product primarily of the biological sciences and extends the Neo-Darwinian theory of evolution to the evolution of animal behavior. Its major concept is that of "inclusive fitness," which studies the role of the behavior of animals in leading to the survival of the corresponding patterns in genetic structure, which is its foundation and from which it is ultimately derived. It deals with such problems as altruism and sexual behavior, and it has made important contributions to our understanding of the evolutionary process. Its principal weakness, however, is that it concentrates almost exclusively on what I have called "biogenetics" and the way in which behavior is directly determined by the genetic programs coded in DNA and the genes, and it is somewhat neglectful of "noogenetics," the transmission of learned behavior coded in nervous systems toward which the biogenetic structure contributes only potential. Because of this neglect, its applications to societal evolution are apt to be rather naive, for it tends not to recognize the overwhelming importance of the noogenetic factor in this area. Nevertheless, the impact of biogenetics on noogenetics is a legitimate, though difficult, problem, and it is to be hoped that sociobiology will move strongly in this direction. The accusations that have been raised against it by Marxists and other left-wing groups, that it is "racist," seem to me quite unjustified, though there is some possibility that it might be misused in this direction by nonscientists. That there are biogenetic factors in learning capacity and potential can hardly be denied, for it was, after all, biogenetics that made our brains, with their enormous unspecified potential which obviously must have biological limits. Biogenetically imposed limits to human learning, however, seem to be much more remote—except in clear cases of mental deficiency—than are the limitations imposed by the noogenetic structure. We learn not to learn much more than we are limited by biogenetically induced barriers in the brain.

EVOLUTION, DIALECTICS, AND NORMATIVE SCIENCE

Nevertheless, the Marxists and other dialecticians, and revolutionaries, nationalists, and militarists, do have some cause for anxiety, for the evolutionary perspective, which is at least partially expressed in sociobiology, is somewhat threatening to dialectical views of the universe in terms of "struggle" and winning fights. Darwin's unfortunate metaphor of the "struggle for existence" is a very poor description of the immense complexity of ecological interaction and the enormous number of strategies for survival in an evolutionary process. Hegelian contradiction and the thesis-antithesis-synthesis pattern is again a poor metaphor to describe the complexity of evolutionary systems. The simple rhetoric of class struggle and revolution, therefore, must be regarded as an essentially minor element in the ongoing process of human development and societal evolution, although it is sometimes important as a special case under particular circumstances. The evolutionary vision, however, must be seen quite clearly as an alternative to Marxism as a general theory. The general idea of an overall theory of social and historical dynamic processes owes a great deal to Marx, but his particular theories were quite inadequate to describe the complexities of reality and must be relegated to the position of a rather unusual special case. Oddly enough, the Marxian vision is a good deal more applicable to the relative simplicities of pre-capitalist society than it is to the enormous complexity of developed capitalism.

This brings us finally to the implications of the evolutionary vision for what might be called "normative science," which is the study of human values and evaluations and of how in terms of human values things go from bad to better rather than from bad to worse. Without human beings to evaluate it, the evolutionary process is neutral in regard to human values. It has no values in itself, although it does have a certain direction in the movement toward complexity and toward noogenetics and consciousness. To say that this is "good," however, is a human value. Human evaluations, however, as we have suggested, have strong nonrandom elements in them in which orderly patterns can be perceived. Once human evaluations appear on the evolutionary scene, a wholly new selective process appears in the world and the evolutionary process is markedly changed by it. They have produced, for instance, cornfields instead of prairie; cities instead of fields; the space shuttle and the artificial satellites. They may produce, for instance, large-scale extinction of biological species like the dodo or the passenger pigeon. They produce very substantial rearrangements of existing genetic material to produce, say, the toy poodle on the one hand and the St. Bernard on the other. And they may now be on the edge of direct intervention in the process of biogenetic change, controlling biological mutation as well as selection. It may well be that biological evolution is approaching its end and that it will be succeeded by an evolutionary process wholly dominated by noogenetic processes directed by human values.

THE COORDINATION OF HUMAN VALUES

There is not, of course, a single set of human values and each human being has his or her own set. There are, however, processes in the ecological interaction of society by which these differing values, though not reduced to a single set, are at least coordinated in an ongoing evolutionary process. There are three major mechanisms for this coordination in human society. I have called these the three Ps: prices, policemen, and preachments. Prices, of course, are a symbol for the market, which does produce a set of relative prices and outputs as a result of the coordination of the evaluations of all the people in it. If half the human race were suddenly converted to Mormonism and gave up tea and coffee, there would be a sharp initial decline in the price of these commodities. As price declines would make their production unprofitable, resources would stream out of these industries into others. The output of both tea and coffee would decline. The price would rise again, probably to something below the original level, as the least suitable land for producing these commodities would be converted to other uses and the real costs of producing these goals would decline. The great advantage of the market is that it coordinates values without agreement, which is a very scarce commodity that needs to be economized.

The second form of coordination, which I symbolized by policemen, is the political structure—that is, the structure of legitimated threat, as expressed·in legislation and judicial decisions. It is this which provides us with public goods or the elimination or reduction of public bads like pollution. The actual structures that emerge are a result of a great variety and complexity of political processes ranging from tyranny, in which the values of the tyrant are imposed on the whole society, to representative democracy, in which there is a very complicated system of political exchange through logrolling, political tradeoffs, and so on. As a result of these processes, legislation does emerge, decisions are made, and the system is changed. A change in a sufficient number of individual values will change the political species; the temperance movement produced prohibition; the environmental movement has produced the Environmental Protection Agency.

The third form of coordination is through preachment; that is, through ethical communication. This ranges from the raised eyebrow at the social gaffe to ponderous denunciation by prophets and charismatic politicians. All subcultures tend to move toward a reasonably common ethos—that is, a set of individual evaluations that are very similar. Individuals in a subculture who diverge from this ethos are either forced out of it or eventually conform. The football player must put a high value on winning games and on team cooperation. A monk must put a high value on poverty, chastity, and obedience or he will soon cease to be a good monk. Within a larger society, there is pressure to coordinate the value systems of different subcultures, some of which are tolerated and some of which are not. The Communist Party has a hard time in the United States; religion has a hard time in China. These ethical processes interact continually with political processes and even with market processes in the ongoing patterns of evolutionary change. There is a reasonable hope in all this for at least a long-run "time's arrow" toward betterment; that is, for a modest but reasonable faith in progress, just as biological evolution seems to lean toward complexity and cognitive evolution toward knowledge. The evolutionary perspective, therefore, is basically optimistic in terms of human values. It emphasizes the dangers and difficulties of all transitions, the great importance of randomness and of events of low probability, and it certainly argues that progress has a better chance if it is illumined by knowledge. It is a very long way from the crude "social Darwinism" of the late nineteenth century, which rested on a profound misunderstanding of the nature of the evolutionary process, with its overemphasis on struggle and on the market as the supreme, sometimes even the only, coordinator of human values, and a failure to recognize the complexity of the interactions that are involved in the societal evolutionary process. On the other hand, the evolutionary vision does not lead into a blind and facile optimism. It recognizes the possible importance of catastrophe, the appalling moral dilemmas involved in unsustainable dynamic processes—such as uncontrolled population expansion, limited only by misery, uncontrolled arms races, leading to nuclear catastrophe, uncontrolled economic growth, leading to resource exhaustion and a reduction of the human niche. It emphasizes the importance of modesty, adaptability, variety, and complexity in the ongoing evolutionary process, and it warns that there are catastrophic dynamic processes that could bring the whole evolutionary experiment in this part of the universe to an end. Nevertheless, we end with hope that there are developmental processes in knowledge and in values by which the human race can mitigate, survive, and even learn from catastrophe and that lead, by however rocky and hilly a road, to ultimate human betterment.

NOTE

1. A classic work in sociobiology is Edward O. Wilson, *Sociobiology: The New Synthesis* (Cambridge, Mass.: Harvard University Press, 1975). An excellent shorter exposition is contained in David P. Barash, *Sociobiology and Behavior* (New York: Elsevier, 1977).

The Universe as a Stereo Movie

THE UNIVERSE AS A PATTERN IN SPACE-TIME

Inventions occasionally have unexpected dividends in creating new metaphors, thereby facilitating communication. The invention of the movie opened up a new world of experience to the human race by stimulating convincingly dynamic processes through time. This illusion is achieved by projecting a succession of still pictures (known as "frames") onto the screen in a rapid enough sequence so that the eye perceives sequences as motion. Ordinary movies are indeed "moving pictures" that are perceived on the screen as having two dimensions, though we interpret this as a structure in three dimensions. In stereo movies the third dimension is actually perceived by the eyes in stereovision.[1]

The universe is a stereo movie in three real dimensions of space and one of time. We often perceive it as a succession of three-dimensional "frames" or "states." Where the time interval between successive states becomes small enough, we get a direct perception of motion and can have mental images of continuous motion in which the time interval between successive states is indefinitely small. If we think of the universe as a movie of successive frames or states, however, we shall not go far wrong. This is a much simpler way of thinking of it than thinking in terms of continuous motion. The time interval between successive states is that time in which nothing significant happens until there is a changed state at the end of the interval. Changes inside the time interval can be neglected; because we can make the time interval as short as we wish, we can always make it short enough to conform to this condition.

The concept of the universe as a stereo movie is essentially the same as that of Einstein's famous space-time continuum in which the universe is seen as a structure in four dimensions, three of space and one of time. We cannot, for reasons which are not entirely clear, create a mental visual image of a four-dimensional structure, though we can visualize a three-dimensional structure changing through time, which is almost the same thing. This is probably because the time dimension is qualitatively different from the three space dimensions. It is certainly different in perception. To think of time as "length" is clearly a metaphor. Our perception of the passage of time has something qualitatively different about it from our perception of travelling along a line from one point to another. The most fundamental aspect of this qualitative difference is the irreversibility of time. In space we can go from A to B and then from B to A; in time we can go from the past to the future, but never from the future to the past. There is almost certainly a nonexistence theorem about time travel and time machines, which could prove logically that time travel is impossible, though I do not know if this demonstration has ever been made. Certainly any form of time travel that would alter the states of the past would have to be ruled out as inadmissible.

THE LOOM OF TIME

Because time is a one-way street, our images of the past and of the future have a very different quality. We are convinced that the past cannot be changed, although our images of it may change. Our image of the future has a different quality of uncertainty. We are convinced that there is not a single future, but a large array of possible futures. Indeed possible futures are not simply an array; they are a branching "tree" of immense complexity. We may have ten possible images of tomorrow and for each one of these there may be ten images of the next day, giving a hundred possible images of the day after tomorrow, a thousand of the day after that and so on, which means that the uncertainty of the future increases rapidly as we move our imaginations into it. This does not rule out the possibility that there may be converging processes that might make the more distant future less uncertain than the near future. A very old metaphor is that of time as a loom. The present is the shuttle that weaves the pattern. We look back into the past with an image of the pattern that has been woven in the cloth; we look forward into the future projecting patterns from the past, and setting the limits of what the pattern could be, because the pattern itself is capable of great variation as each day produces a new segment of it. The loom, furthermore, is set in the thick mists of time. Even as we look back into the past the record fails us and the pattern disappears into the fog of ignorance. As we look forward into the future the mists of uncertainty close around us even sooner. An even older metaphor is that of the Fates, spinning the thread of life, measuring it and cutting it off at the moment of death.

The metaphor of the thread is remarkably accurate. The four dimensions of space-time can be visualized if, like a movie, we reduce three dimensions of space to two and visualize time as the third dimension in space. We can visualize, for instance, a movie of a map of the world as a succession of frames that are transparent and superimposed on each other in the right order in a three-dimensional box-like structure—two dimensions of space and one of time—to create a complex pattern. Any "thing" or "object," a tree, an animal, a person, a house or an automobile, would appear on the frame at the moment of its birth or production, visualized as a dot on this world map. As the object grows or moves, the dot would expand, change shape, and position, and thus look like winding thread in our three-dimensional structure. With death or destruction the thread would end. Therefore an object is seen as simply a three-dimensional cross-section of the four-dimensional space-time "thread," which constitutes its total being from birth to death, or from production to destruction. All dynamics are simply the patterns of these threads as we perceive them in the total space-time framework.

In some cases these patterns are relatively simple. An object that does not change its shape, structure, or position is simply a straight-line thread in our space-time box parallel to the time axis. In a strict sense there are no such things because all things are subject to continuous change. Even a mountain, which appears fixed and permanent, is continually eroding and often continually being pushed up. Every day a few stones fall down the slopes of Mt. Everest, and possibly tectonic forces are pushing it upward as well. The everlastingness of hills is just a human illusion caused by the slow motion of the movie, a perception that depends on the deficiencies of our observations and time scale.

In some objects, like the planets of the solar system, we perceive beautifully regular patterns, such as the revolution around the sun in elliptical orbits. On our space-time map these would look something like slightly stretched springs. Because the pattern is so regular it can be described with great exactness and projected into the future. This explains why celestial mechanics is so successful in predicting the movement of the planets, eclipses, and so on. The patterns of the total astronomical universe are more complex, and we know less about them. Because of their sufficient regularity the movements of the stars within a galaxy can be projected with confidence, for at least a few thousand years. We also have evidence that the total universe is expanding in a regular way. Once we leave astronomy, however, and the brief time span during which the universe has been observed by astronomers on this planet, all patterns become much more complicated and much less predictable. Indeed, the very success of celestial mechanics may have had a bad effect on the other sciences simply because it has led toward a search for regularities that may not be present in the more complex systems.

THE PAST AS RECORDS BIASED BY DURABILITY

Our image of the past is subject to constant changes with improvement in the records, and our methods of interpreting them. It is only from records which have survived to the present, that any image of the past can be constructed. Our image of the past cannot, therefore, be any more accurate than the records and our interpretation of them. Unfortunately, the records are extremely inadequate. Only durable objects survive, such as shells, bones, rocks, buildings, sculptures, writings, inscriptions, folk tales and stories, and memories. No memory is older than the person in whose head it resides, and often memories are mistaken because they are eroded through forgetfulness, or transformed through selective forgetfulness of unpleasant events, or confused with imagined events. Often even our own personal pasts are reconstructed in our memories to better our self images.

In preliterate societies the only supplement to memory is the stories, poems, and songs, which are passed down from generation to generation and enshrined in successive memories. These also erode and are transformed in the transmission, although in certain stereotyped songs, poems or liturgies, the transmission may be remarkably accurate over many generations.

With the introduction of writing the records of the human race improved enormously and became transmitable over longer periods of time. Even before writing, the development of artifacts, such as stone implements and buildings, created another record that has persisted to the present, which constitutes an almost unconscious writing of the life of the people who made and used the artifacts. Archaeology is the science of interpreting this unconscious record. We also have the record of rocks, various strata, and fossils, which make inferences possible about the forms of landscape and life that unconsciously deposited these records over hundreds of millions of years.

Another source of knowledge of the past consists of the perceptions of patterns that are interpreted as having universal validity through all time and space. The patterns of physics and chemistry are usually interpreted in this way, although with a remarkable leap of faith. The sample of the space-time universe that falls within human observation is almost infinitesimally small. All human observations and records occupy a minute dot in space-time, representing less than ten thousand years out of ten billion, or one millionth part of time, and an even smaller fraction of space, which includes the earth, and large distant objects like stars, and galaxies. There are no observations of life and society outside the earth, however, although we may speculate on the possibility of such phenomena. Our image of the total astronomical universe, however, is based mainly on speculation rather than observation.

Interpreting the record of the past is enormously difficult because of the nature of the record itself. The record is totally biased toward durability: only highly durable light waves reach us from distant galaxies; only durable bone structures reach us from living creatures of the past; only durable artifacts reach us from past societies. Yet, no proposition states that the durable records are necessarily the important records. Conceivably, the most significant records about galaxies, stars, geological events, life forms, and past cultures do not leave traces durable enough to read. In our interpretations of the record, therefore, we are constantly working by analogy, from what we know about systems close to us in time where the less durable traces have survived, to those situations remote in time where only the more durable traces have survived. Consequently, we know little about the history of those processes that leave no traces, such as the development of spoken language or of behavior patterns in past life forms.

PHYSICAL, BIOLOGICAL, AND SOCIETAL EVOLUTION

Nevertheless, though the record is miserable and our interpretations of it dubious, we do have strong, vivid images of the past in which we have confidence. Looked at from the perspective of twentieth-century earth, we see three great stages in the dynamic process of the universe. To this whole process, as it spreads out over perhaps ten billion years of time and ten billion light years of space, we give the name *evolution*, and we see three great patterns within it. The first is *physical evolution*. This presumably started with the development of the most elementary particles (whatever they may be); then of neutrons, protons, electrons, and radiations; then of elements from hydrogen to uranium and beyond formed by combining protons and electrons; then of chemical compounds; then finally of increasingly complex molecules from amino acids, and proteins to the great watershed of DNA, the beginning of life.

In our part of the universe physical evolution apparently reached a relative equilibrium three to four billion years ago when the solar system in which we live received approximately its present complement of elements, and the physical structure of the planets (with the possible exception of earth) was probably not very different from what it is now. Curiously enough, in our part of the universe physical evolution, under the impact of human knowledge, has now been resumed at a fairly rapid rate with production of transuranium elements (which, if they ever existed in the universe, disappeared around here a long time ago) and chemical compounds previously unknown, such as nylon and freon. The consequences may be large and unfortunate. The moon seems to have been in relative equilibrium for some three-and-a-half billion years, with occasional minor accessions from meteorites. Perhaps because of our remoteness from them, the actual processes in physical evolution are very obscure to us.

With the development of DNA, which is capable in a proper environment of self-reproduction and of organizing extremely complex processes that produce living organisms, a whole new phase of evolution in a "higher gear" began: *biological evolution*. The processes that led to this beginning are probably irretrievably lost despite much plausible speculation, unless they can be reproduced. The surviving records of rocks clearly indicate that a long process of constant development of innumerable new species, with a trend toward increasing complexity, occurred that resulted in the development of the human race.

With the emergence of Homo (and Mulier!) sapiens, the evolutionary process again went into a higher gear known as *societal evolution.* Homo sapiens has a biological organization capable of much larger and more complex images of the world than any preceding animal. Perhaps the key to societal evolution was that humans were capable of language. Language produces behavior patterns by which complex images can be communicated from person to person and even, through legends, folktales, and writing, from the dead to the living. The great difference between a human being and the cleverest chimpanzee is that the human being can have images of persons, times, and places that have not been personally experienced. No other animal is capable of this remarkable feat. I have an idea of how the South Pole looks without being there. I also have an idea of what Rome looked like and what life was like there two thousand years ago. I have an image of the whole astronomical universe, clumsy and imperfect though it may be; and I have complex images of the future beyond the day of my own death. It is this extraordinary image-forming capacity of the human organism that has created society, societal evolution, and human artifacts, which are the key to societal evolution. They include not only material artifacts from flint knives to computers, but also social organizations and to a very large extent human beings themselves. Our physical bodies are produced mainly by our genetic structure, but our culture, language, behavior patterns, knowledge, and value structures are created largely by inputs from other humans.

The three great evolutionary processes—physical, biological and societal—are not independent of each other. Each has much internal coherence and its own special characteristics; nevertheless, the three processes constantly interact. Physical evolution, indeed, is a prerequisite of biological and biological of societal evolution. Physical evolution had to proceed to the point where complexity of its structures was adequate to produce self-reproducing structures like DNA. Biological evolution had to proceed to the point where some individual species was capable of language and complex images. There is also feedback from later to earlier systems. The early biosphere on earth, for instance, was apparently a very active agent in transforming the atmosphere from one with large quantities of carbon dioxide to one with a fifth part of oxygen. It is an interesting reflection that the oxygen in the atmosphere that sustains us and all higher forms of life was actually produced by a process of pollution. The biosphere also has a very profound impact on the surface of the earth by creating soils, disintegrating rocks, changing water runoffs, moderating the climate, and so on.

Similarly, the "sociosphere," which is the sphere of the total human race and its artifacts, has had profound effects on the biosphere. For example, it has caused the extinction of large numbers of species. It has intervened radically in the process of natural selection to produce domesticated animals, which differ enormously in genetic mix from or what would have been there in the absence of the human race. The human race has also had a profound effect on the earth's physical evolution: it has built dams, diverted rivers, dug mines, bulldozed mountains, eroded soil, and even created earthquakes; it has polluted the atmosphere, rivers, lakes, and oceans; it has cut down forests and substituted agriculture; it has changed climates, at least over small areas, and perhaps over the whole earth; it has even gone to the moon and left its improbable artifacts, which may be investigated by other intelligent beings millions of years after the human race has disappeared into the past. On the other hand, biological and societal evolution have been affected, sometimes profoundly, by physical changes, especially physical catastrophes. The extinction of many species seems to be associated with physical catastrophes of various kinds, such as magnetic reversals, solar flares, and ice ages. Physical changes have also profoundly effected societal evolution. The transition from paleolithic to neolithic might not have happened without the ice age.

THE MYTH OF THE ENVIRONMENT

All this suggests that we must look at the world, and indeed at the universe, as a total system of interacting parts. There is no such thing as an "environment," if by this we mean a surrounding system that is independent of what goes on inside it. Particularly, there is no sense at this stage of evolution on earth in talking about "the environment" as if it were nature without the human race. It makes sense to divide the totality of the universe into parts that have some degree of independent dynamic pattern, but none of these parts are really independent of others; all interact. Everything is the environment of something else. When we talk about the environmental problem, we are talking about the total state of the world and evaluating it from the point of human values. We are not talking about the nonhuman part of the system and evaluating it by its own values, because it does not have any.

In looking at the three evolutionary systems—physical, biological and societal—we see that they have both similarities and differences, and that each has a set of distinctive patterns. Physical evolution follows for the most part a phase principle—that when conditions are right, something new happens. In physical systems there is no sharp distinction between genotype structures and phenotype structures, as found in biological systems. In biological systems, the distinction is extremely sharp between the genetic structure contained in genes and the phenotypes produced by these genetic structures. In social systems, the distinction is significant, but not as sharp. The genetic structure of social systems consists of ideas, images, knowledge, blueprints, and so on; the phenotypes are the houses, artifacts, and organizations resulting from these plans and information structures. Also societal evolution is multisexual whereas biological evolution never produces more than two sexes, with the exception of a few doubtful experiments, such as in the transmission of genetic material by viruses. Societal evolution involves the coming together of social genetic materials from a very large number of different species and sources. The stallion and the mare can produce another horse; an automobile, however, is the result of the interaction of a large number of different social species—designers, engineers, architects, physicists, chemists, executives, accountants, foremen, factory workers, policemen, lawyers, politicians, and so on—each contributing a small fraction of the social information needed to produce the automobile. Societal evolution has much more control over its genetic changes than biological evolution where genetic changes seem to be almost purely random. It is also guided by images of the future, which biological evolution does not seem to be.

EVOLUTION AS A PROCESS IN "KNOW-HOW"–"WHAT EVOLVES"?

Nevertheless, all three processes are similar because they seem to involve movement toward complexity and improbability of structure. It is tempting to say that all three kinds of evolution are a process in the field of "information," but this is not a very good word to express the evolutionary field. It is not the same as the "Bell Telephone" information of information theory. It also implies know-how, especially in biological evolution, and both know-how and know-what in societal evolution. Perhaps it is not stretching the metaphor too far to say that helium "knows more" than hydrogen, because it knows how to have two electrons whereas hydrogen only knows how to have one. Nevertheless, what happens in the evolution of chemical elements from hydrogen to uranium is increasing complexity of structure, which has many parallels to the increase in complexity of the genetic structure in biological evolution or the knowledge structure in societal evolution. It is an even more accurate metaphor to say that carbon "knows how" to hold on to four hydrogen atoms or to two oxygen atoms, that is, is quadrivalent whereas oxygen only knows how to hold onto two hydrogen atoms, and so on. Valency is a fairly close parallel to information. It is both the high valency and the small size of the carbon atom that permits it to be the foundation of the extraordinary complexity of organic molecules and the chemical foundation of life. All complexity involves some kind of bonding and it seems likely that only the carbon atom would be capable of sustaining the enormous complexity of DNA. Boron is only trivalent, and silicon is too big and gets in its own way.

Biological evolution is clearly a process in the field of informational complexity. It exhibits over time an almost constant elaboration of genetic structure. At first the biosphere could only produce viruses. Then it went on to cells, many-celled organisms, vertebrates, mammals, and then the human race. In a quite literal sense no humans could have been produced ten million years ago because the earth's genetic structure did not know how to do it. Genetic structure is know-how rather than know-what. It is a knowledge structure for all that.

When we get to societal evolution the paramount role of human knowledge is very clear. All human artifacts originate in human knowledge. Just as the biosphere could not have produced a human being ten million years ago because it did not have the know-how, the social system could not have produced an automobile a hundred years ago because it did not have the know-how. It is a powerful and accurate metaphor to see the whole evolutionary process from the beginning of the universe as a process in the increase of knowledge or the information structure. My Oxford philosophy tutor, who had the curious habit of crawling under the table while giving his tutorials, commented in a high British voice coming from underneath the table on a paper I had given on evolution, "It is all very well to talk about evolution, Mr. Boulding, but what evolves, what evolves, what evolves?" After forty years I have at least a glimmering of the answer. What evolves is something very much like knowledge.

KNOW-HOW ENCODED IN MATTER AND ENERGY: THE MEANING OF PRODUCTION

Knowledge, however, cannot evolve by itself and without assistance. It must be coded into something, which points up the role of *energy, matter,* and *entropy* in the evolutionary process. In modern physics, matter itself is increasingly reduced to some kind of structure; what it is a structure of nobody really knows. Whether there is an ultimate encodee in which all structure is encoded, is a question that must be left to future physicists; we have certainly not found the answer yet. We do find a constantly expanding pattern of structure. The molecule is a structure of atoms, of elements; the atom is a structure of protons and electrons; the proton is a structure of still largely unknown particles. At each level, however, there is an encodee. We build elements out of protons and electrons; we build molecules out of atoms of elements. We build the code of life out of supermolecules in different combinations; we build the genetic structure of social artifacts out of language, writing, books, drawings, diagrams, blueprints, and so on. The information, however, transcends the code, for the same information can be coded in many different forms. There may be whole universes of anti-matter. There may be intelligences based on codings of which we have no conception.

Nevertheless, matter matters. Without the right encodee, encoding cannot take place. Biological evolution did not take place on the moon, and probably not on any other planet in the solar system, because of the absence of certain encoding materials such as water or carbon compounds. Similarly, energy matters because energy moves matter, transports it, transforms it, and rearranges it into encodeable forms. Energy can also encode information directly. An essential link in the process of evolution is *production,* which takes place in all three systems. Production is a process by which some kind of information or knowledge structure is able to direct energy toward the transportation, transformation, or rearrangement of materials into less probable structures than those existing at the start of the process. When hydrogen burns in oxygen to produce water, the energy that is released activates the hydrogen and oxygen atoms so that they are able to clasp hands and exercise their valencies, with oxygen with its two hands each clasping two of hydrogen's one hand and making something totally different in properties from either of its components. Below a certain threshold of energy and temperature, hydrogen and oxygen will simply sit together without clasping hands. If there is neither hydrogen nor oxygen, we can never get water. Unless hydrogen and oxygen have these valencies or potentials for hitching up with each other, water again could not be produced.

Biological processes of production are much more complex but still involve the same three factors of knowledge, energy, and materials. A fertilized egg is a most improbable structure containing an enormous amount of know-how. It is able to capture energy, mostly chemical, from its immediate environment using this to reproduce its genetic structure and attract atoms such as carbon, hydrogen, oxygen to build up most extraordinary and improbable molecules of RNA, enzymes, cells, combinations of cells, and organs until finally the egg produces what it knew how to produce, such as a chicken or baby. Again, we see knowledge directing energy to the transportation and transformation of materials into these improbable structures.

The production of a house is not very different. It starts as an idea in an architect's mind; this is its "gene." The idea is translated into blueprints, instructions, and diagrams (the enzymes). These in turn are able to mobilize energy to transport and transform materials into the improbable shape of a house. Without these processes of production, knowledge could not be encoded; if it is not encoded, it cannot grow.

NEGATIVE ENTROPY AS POTENTIAL; THE SECOND LAW

There is, however, a spectre at the evolutionary feast. Its name is "entropy." It is a protean monster. The concept originated in thermodynamics. Even there it has a number of different meanings, the simplest of which perhaps is a measure of the system's potential for doing work, that is, transforming other forms of energy into mechanical energy. The concept, unfortunately, is defined negatively, so that it represents the negative of potential. That is, entropy is that which increases as potential diminishes and is used up. The famous second law of thermodynamics, which states in effect that when anything happens, entropy increases, can be restated in a very general form as the law of potential. This states that if anything happens, it is because there was potential for it to happen, and that after it has happened, that potential has been used up. Any process of this kind is irreversible, and so gives directionality to time. It is indeed one of time's arrows.

The metaphor of a movie with which we started illuminates the process. Most people who have made home movies have run them backwards for fun. In some parts of a movie, we may find it hard to tell that we are running it backwards—grass waving in the wind or clouds scurrying across the sky look the same backwards or forwards. In other parts of the movie it is very clear when we run it backwards—a waterfall, somebody running or walking, two people meeting and shaking hands. A baby growing up, or an egg becoming a chicken are all processes where time has an arrow and is irreversible. They represent processes in which in some sense potential is used up. In the case of the waterfall, it is gravitational potential; in the case of the fertilized egg, genetic potential. Similarly, we see the evolutionary process as the result of the generation of evolutionary potential. This is hard to define and impossible to measure, but it represents something very real. At the beginning of the physical universe, there must have been potential for the development of the elements and the molecules. Once physical evolution anywhere in the universe produced DNA, there was potential for biological evolution. Once biological evolution produced the human race or some equivalent, there was potential for societal evolution.

As any process proceeds, however, the potential for it is realized and the potential itself diminishes, unless it is recreated. All thermodynamic processes that we can observe involve the diminution of thermodynamic potential, that is, the increase of entropy, because we know nothing about the creation of thermodynamic potential. That it must have been created in some sense at the beginning of the universe, however, can hardly be denied. Development in one. system may create potential for another. Societal evolution, by developing science, recreated potential for physical evolution in the development, for instance, of the transuranium elements and the human-created compounds. It is quite possible that the human race will create biological potential as it intervenes in genetic structures. We may recreate extinct species like the dinosaurs; we may create species that biological evolution could never have produced. What constitutes evolutionary potential is extremely puzzling, but we cannot deny its reality.

EQUILIBRIUM AS AN ILLUSION OF PERCEPTION

The full realization of potential is equilibrium. Our knowledge of equilibrium itself is more complete than our knowledge of the path toward it. If we start a ball rolling at the top of a bowl, we are reasonably sure that it will quickly come to rest at the bottom. Our backwards movie shows that this is an entropic process. We would be amused to see the ball start off from the bottom, run around the sides and end up at the top, but we will not believe it. The equilibrium concept is of great importance in science. It is seen in the concept of a climactic ecosystem in biology, in the concept of an equilibrium price structure in economics, and in the concept of an equilibrium in a chemical reaction. It is seen in the concept of the ultimate thermodynamic equilibrium, which is the ultimate whimper that is the end of the universe when all things are at the same temperature, equally diffused, and nothing more can happen in the great thin, tepid soup.

Equilibrium can be dynamic as well as static. Thus, the solar system is very close to a dynamic equilibrium. We do not really know how it evolved, that is, how it got the way it is, but it now is realizing its potential so slowly that celestial mechanics is possible. Some traditional societies have also exhibited a state close to equilibrium, at least over a number of generations, but we have never really studied these over long periods of time, so that we probably overestimate their stability. Our own society is not in equilibrium at all and cannot be understood by equilibrium concepts alone. All equilibria, furthermore, are temporary. The universe is a disequilibrium system and has been from the very beginning. Whether it has a final state of equilibrium, we do not know; we will almost certainly not be there to see it and would not like it if we were. Equilibrium, therefore, is a figment of the human imagination. It is a partial pattern perceived in the great four-dimensional complexity. It is a product of our limited perception. We see the world of objects—persons, houses, mountains—only because they are "frames" of a very slow movie. With faster and longer perception, we would see persons growing and aging, mountains rising and eroding—a constant flux of irreversible change.

THE IMPORTANCE OF RANDOMNESS

To return to our image of the loom, we all stand in the shuttle of our spaceship earth, looking out at what we may think is a window on the past, but is really a closed-circuit TV showing the images of the human race, insofar as these penetrate into our own mind. What we see is a four-dimensional carpet of immense complexity, in which we perceive patterns. It is the business of science or any organized human knowledge to help us perceive these patterns more clearly. The perception of stable patterns enables us to formulate laws; however, not all that we perceive is a pattern. There is real randomness, at least from the viewpoint of our own knowledge and image of the universe, and especially there is inescapable randomness and uncertainty in our image of social systems. The random we cannot possibly know except in probabilistic terms. We can only know probabilities, however, because there are patterns in the seemingly random. We cannot predict a single throw of the dice; we can predict with some confidence what will be the result of a thousand throws.

In the evolutionary process, random factors may be of great importance. A mutation with great evolutionary potential, for instance, may initially only have a small probability of survival. When it does not survive, a whole evolutionary chapter fails to be written. Evolutionary history must be full of these invisible forks in the road. We only know about the ones that were actually followed, not the ones that failed. Similarly, in human history the random element is also large. If Herod had succeeded in killing Jesus as a baby, the history of the next two thousand years might have been very different, at least in detail. It is one of the occupational diseases of historians, indeed, that they think history had to happen, whereas the truth is that what happened is the result of a long succession of improbable accidents. Nevertheless, there are patterns to be detected amid the randomness and it is the business of organized human knowledge to detect them. It is to the search for these patterns that this volume is dedicated.

NOTE

1. It is an interesting commentary on the essentially conventional nature of our perceptions of the world that stereo movies have been little more than a novelty and have not displaced the ordinary two-dimensional motion picture in the way, for instance, that "talkies" displaced the old silent movie. The reason presumably is that stereovision adds very little to our mental image of what we are perceiving simply because of our power of interpreting a two-dimensional picture as a three-dimensional image. This is particularly easy in a two-dimensional moving picture, in which there is differential motion by distance and a constant occlusion of distant objects by near ones. It is the image that is important, not the perception. Sound, by contrast, adds a great deal to our image of what is going on.

Chapter 2

Physical Dynamics and Evolution

DYNAMICS, NOT EVOLUTION

The image of the universe presented to us by modern astronomy, physics, chemistry, geology, meteorology and the other physical sciences pictures evolutionary processes of irreversible change in the whole physical world, just as biological and societal evolution involve irreversible change in the biosphere and sociosphere on earth. We must distinguish, therefore, between physical and chemical dynamics and physical and chemical evolution. Newtonian dynamics is essentially the perception of stable patterns in the four-dimensional space-time continuum. This applies also to classical celestial mechanics, which is simply a complex application of fundamental Newtonian principles. To illustrate this we can refer to the concept of a "space-time box" (see chap. 1, p. 27). Figure 2.1 illustrates the space-time pattern for revolution of the earth around the sun in its orbit. Here we reduce the three-dimensionality of space into a flat map such as $T_1 A_1 C_1 B_1$. On this flat map the earth's orbit is represented by ellipse E, with the sun, S_1, at one of the foci. It is not quite a perfect ellipse because of the disturbances of the other planets, but that simply introduces a larger number of variables into the system without changing the fundamental principle. If we measure time along the axis from T_1 to T_2 the "box" then represents two dimensions of space and one of time. Within the box we suppose that the sun's path is a straight line, S_1 to S_2. Successive positions of the earth are represented by the dots on the dotted spiral or spring. This can be thought of as the path generated by the earth as it moves around its orbit as the orbit moves steadily through time from T_1 to T_2. What we have here is simply physical dynamics, that is, a pattern in space-time. Physical evolution would represent change in this pattern and change in the parameters of the equation that describes it.

The equations of physical dynamics may be expressed either in the form of difference equations or differential equations involving time.[1] A difference equation of the first degree is simply a stable relationship between the value

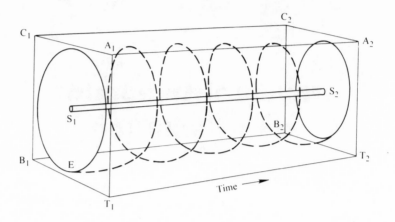

Figure 2.1: Space-time Pattern of the Earth's Orbit

of a variable on two successive intervals of time, such as "days" or "years." A good example of this is the sum in a savings account at compound interest. Suppose, for instance, that we have $100 in a savings account at ten percent per annum interest. Then the value at the end of each year is equal to the value at the beginning of the year multiplied by 1.1. One hundred dollars at the beginning of a year will be $100 x 1.1 or $110 at the beginning of the next year; $110 x 1.1 or $121 at the beginning of the second year, and so on indefinitely into the future.

A car coming toward us at a constant velocity of 20 feet per second that is 100 feet away from us now will be 80 feet from us in one second, 60 feet in two seconds, 40 feet in three seconds, and we had better jump out of the way before five seconds has elapsed. We are constantly solving equations of this kind in daily life—when, for instance, we turn to the left against a stream of traffic and calculate that there will not be an eclipse. All these equations, however, can be expressed as stable patterns in our space-time box.

A difference equation in the second degree implies that there is a stable relation between today, yesterday, and the day before. All falling bodies in a vacuum, and indeed most of celestial mechanics, can be described in terms of such equations involving constant acceleration. The degree of a dynamic process can be found, if the process itself can be represented by a series of numbers, by taking the differences between successive numbers, then the differences between successive differences, and so on, until we reach constant differences. This is illustrated in Table 2.1. The first line shows the position of a falling body from its origin in successive seconds: after one second it will have fallen 16 feet; after two seconds, 48 feet; after three seconds, 96 feet; and so on. The second line shows the first differences, which clearly follow a

TABLE 2.1
The Law of Falling Bodies

Time (seconds)	0		1		2		3		4		5
Distance from start (feet)	0		16		48		96		160		240
1st Difference		16		32		48		64		80	
2nd Difference			16		16		16		16		
3rd Difference				0		0		0			

simple progression: a body falls 16 feet in the first second, 32 feet in the second, 48 in the third, and so on. The third line shows the second differences, which are constant and all equal to 16. The system, therefore, is of the second order. If third differences were a constant, non-zero number it would be a system of the third order, that is, in which acceleration was changing at a constant rate.

The equations of the solar system can mostly be expressed in terms of second order equations. We hardly ever have to go beyond the third order. Simple projections are made by extrapolating systems of this kind. Thus, given the data of Table 2.1, we are confident in predicting that second differences would stay at 16, that the next first difference would be 96, and the distance from the start in six seconds would be 336 feet. This is how the movement of planets, the times of eclipses, and so on are predicted. In a system of constant parameters projection is possible, even though in practice it may be very difficult if the system is highly complicated. The projections, for instance, of Professor Forrester and the Club of Rome reports[2] are systems of this kind. They are not real, only hypothetical predictions; they say what would happen if certain parameters did not change. In both biological and social systems, however, parameters change constantly, and it is this change in parameters that essentially constitutes the evolutionary process. This is why evolution cannot be projected into the future by simple mechanical projection. This does not mean that more subtle forms of projection may not be possible.

THE EINSTEIN-HEISENBERG REVOLUTION IN PHYSICS

The expansion of physics in the 19th century, or what might be called the "Einstein-Heisenberg revolution," has introduced two great new complexities into our image of the dynamics of the physical universe. One, expressed in the famous formula $E = mc^2$, is that matter and energy can be transformed one into the other, which of course led to atomic weapons and the whole nuclear energy industry. Nuclear energy is derived from the transmutation of elements, a process thought impossible by nineteenth century scientists.

The other change is the recognition that physics is not simply a matter of describing something perceived by the physicist, but is the result of a very complex interaction between the physicist and the physical world. This is reflected, for instance, in Einstein's observation that, because the speed of light is not infinite, we can never strictly observe simultaneity. We observe the sun as it was eight minutes ago and the distant galaxies as they were perhaps a billion years ago because it has taken that long for the light to reach us. Insofar as knowledge and communication depend on information input, the constant speed of light could cause a great deal of trouble for the problem of learning and communication over interstellar distances. On earth it does not matter, because for all practical purposes communication can be regarded as instantaneous. Imagine, however, a conversation with another being on Alpha Centaurus, the nearest star, some four light years away. We send out a message: "How are you?" and the message returns eight years later: "Fine."

The problem is compounded by the Heisenberg principle at the micro level, the very small rather than the very large which says in effect that we cannot ask an electron where it is without shifting it. The famous illustration is that of a man who shouts into the door of a hospital room to his sick friend, "How are you?". The friend says "Fine" and the effort kills.him. As we move into the biological and social sciences, the generalized Heisenberg principle—that the attempt to get information out of a system changes it—is increasingly important. Often we cannot investigate living things without killing them. We cannot give a person a questionnaire without changing his opinion. In social systems, a prediction of the future that is believed will change the future itself. Under these circumstances, dynamics becomes much more difficult.

TESTING OUR IMAGES OF THE WHOLE UNIVERSE

Any change in our image of the world is the result of a failure of predictions or expectations. If there is no such failure, there is no need to change our image of the world. Nothing fails like success, because we do not learn anything from it. We only learn from failure, but we do not always learn the right things from failure. If there is a failure of expectations, that is, if the messages that we receive are not the same as those we expected, we can make three possible inferences. We may infer that our image of the world on which we made the expectation was incorrect and hence we have to change it. We may decide that our basic image of the world is right, but we made a false deduction from it and expected the wrong messages, so we changed the deductions. Or we may decide that there is something wrong with the message.[3] It is often very hard to choose among these three possibilities. The revolution in physics in the twentieth century has often made the choice more difficult. The growth of the scientific image of the world on the whole has depended on the assumption that we can protect ourselves against false messages by measurement, instrumentation, careful experiment, and controlled variables. In the simple observation, however, on which we have to rely for most of our knowledge of the astronomical universe, control of messages is impossible. We either do or do not believe them.

A good example is the problem of the "red shift." It is noticed that the more distant the astronomical object which is observed, the longer the wave length of the light from it which reaches us. The velocity of light is assumed to be an absolutely universal constant. This must mean that the universe is expanding so that the further away an object is, the more rapidly it is retreating from us, because in an expanding universe everything is getting farther away from everything else, and the further away things are from each other, the more rapidly is the distance expanding between them. The deduction that the red shift implies expanding distances is derived from the "Doppler Effect," which we have all observed in listening to the whistle of a passing train. Whether the communication is in the form of a succession of waves or particles, if the object producing them is moving away from us, the message will consist of waves or particles that are further apart. If it is moving toward us, they will be scrunched together. Thus, if an object produces messages while moving away from us, the message will reach us with longer intervals between the events than was the case when the message left the emitting object. This is the "red shift" (red light has a longer wave length than blue) of a retreating object, as reflected in the lower pitch of the retreating train whistle.

How do we know, however, that the velocity of light is a universal constant when we have only measured it in our own very small part of the universe? It is certainly constant here, but we have no way of measuring it anywhere else; it is simply an article of faith that it is constant. On this we build our whole physical theory. The plain fact is that direct measurement in the physical sciences is taken from a fantastically small sample of the universe. Believing in the universality of these parameters and constants is a leap of faith no less remarkable than that of Tertullian, who believed in the Incarnation because it was absurd.

INSECURE "HARD" SCIENCES; SECURE "SOFT" SCIENCES

It is a curious paradox that we think of the physical sciences as "hard," the social sciences as "soft," and the biological sciences as somewhere in between. This is interpreted to mean that our knowledge of physical systems is more certain than our knowledge of biological systems, and these in turn are more certain than our knowledge of social systems. In terms of our capacity to sample the relevant universes, however, and the probability that our images of these universes are at least approximately correct, one suspects that a reverse order is more plausible. We are able to sample earth's social systems with some degree of confidence that we have a reasonable sample of the total universe being investigated. Our knowledge of social systems, therefore, while it is in many ways extremely inaccurate, is not likely to be grossly overturned by new discoveries. Even the folk knowledge in social systems on which ordinary daily life is based in earning, spending, learning, adjusting, organizing, marrying, childrearing, politicking, fighting, and so on, is not grossly dissimilar from the more sophisticated images of the social system derived from the social sciences, even though it is built upon the very imperfect samples of personal experience.

By contrast, our image of the astronomical universe, or even of earth's geological history, can easily be subject to revolutionary changes as new data comes in and new theories are formulated. If we define the "security" of our image of various parts of the total system as the probability of their suffering drastic change, then we would reverse the order of hardness and see the social sciences as the most secure, the physical sciences as the least secure, and again the biological sciences as somewhere in between. Our image of the astronomical universe is the least secure of all simply because we observe such a fantastically small sample of it and its record-keeping is miserable as compared with the rich records of social systems, or even the sparse records of biological systems. Records of the astronomical universe, despite the fact that we see distant things as they were long ago, are meager in the extreme.

Even in regard to such a close neighbor as the moon, which we have actually visited, theories about its origin and history are extremely diverse, irreconcilable, and hard to choose among. We know more about the origin of the United States or of any social institution than we do of the origin of the human race, and we know more about the origin of the human race than we do about the origin of the moon. Our knowledge of physical evolution, therefore, is sketchy and highly insecure. Astronomers, for instance, are still debating the "big bang" theory of the origin of the universe. Currently the "big bang" view seems to be dominant over the "steady state" theory of Fred Hoyle, which postulates a very different kind of picture of the evolution of the physical universe; however, this could change overnight.

PHYSICAL EVOLUTION AS INCREASING
COMPLEXITY OF STRUCTURE OF MATTER

Nevertheless, insecure and debatable as it is, we do have some image of physical evolution. Like biological and societal evolution, it seems to consist of a process in time that involves the increase in the number and complexity of individual structures. Even if we accept the "big bang" theory, we still do not know what it was that banged. We do not know what the structure and substance of the universe was "in the beginning." All we can say with any security is that in the beginning was potential. Clearly something happened, and it is almost a matter of formal logic to say that if something happened, it is because there was a potential for its happening. The universe started as an undifferentiated mass of something and since has tended to differentiate into complexity through a great variety of processes. Whether it started with an active creation of a potential out of some previous system of inconceivable complexity, as the religious metaphor suggests, we do not know. Whatever message was emitted from the creation of the universe has not reached us and we speculate in faith.

What does seem clear is that there are processes of complexification in the physical world that are still going on and that we may reasonably speculate went on from the beginning. Evolution of the elements is perhaps as far back as we can go. We know nothing about the evolution of the subatomic particles. We do know, however, that in the extreme conditions of the interior of stars, nuclear reactions occur that produce a succession of elements. The details of this process are still very obscure, but we are confident that it emerges finally with ninety-two reasonably stable elements and a few more that are so unstable they exist only in a most transitory way and have to be created by intelligence. Clearly protons and electrons have potential for producing elements when conditions are right. Once the elements have been produced, they have potential for producing compounds, simply because they have valency and can form configurations that persist over time. The evolutionary history of compounds is also obscure, but we do know that under certain conditions they continue to expand, in size and complexity, culminating in DNA and the beginnings of life. The role of catalysis in all this process is probably significant, though again obscure. There are evolutionary sequences even in the development of elements. Sequences may be even more important in the development of compounds. Certain things have to come together before other things can be produced. The role of radiation and of matter-energy exchanges is extremely important in the formation of the chemical elements. It plays an insignificant role in the formation of molecules and compounds.

THE PHASE PRINCIPLE

The principle that governs this process of formation of elements and compounds might be called the "phase principle." At any one time and place there is always a certain physical environment in terms of temperature, pressure, radiation, and so on. A phase space consists of all the possible combinations of the significant environmental variables. The formation of the elements and the compounds, however, reflects changes in the phase space of different parts of the universe; for example, changes in temperature and pressure that occur because of heating when more radiation is produced than emitted, cooling when more is emitted than produced, increasing pressure when things fall together, or diminishing pressure when they fall apart.

Many kinds of phase changes are familiar in ordinary life, such as the phases of water. If it is cold enough, liquid water turns into ice and, if it is hot enough, it turns into steam. The physicist can construct elaborate phase diagrams showing what will be the equilibrium position of water at all different pressures and temperatures. How much ice of different kinds, liquid water, and steam any given part of the universe will have depends on how much H_2O there was in the first place, which goes back to how much hydrogen and how much oxygen there was, the circumstances under which they combined, and on what the temperature and pressure changes have been.

THE INSTABILITY OF HOMOGENEITY

A very critical question in physical evolution is what are the processes in the universe that produce heterogeneity, such as stars and planets? At the basis of all evolutionary theory there must be some theory of the instability of homogeneity, whether this is like Lösch's theory[4] of the instability of homogeneous economic activity, that is, of evenly spaced economic actors, or a theory of the evolutionary instability of a biosphere containing only a single life form, or a theory of the instability of a universe of uniformly distributed hydrogen atoms.

If a single, universal attraction such as gravity were the only force operating, then presumably everything in the universe would gather into one big ball. The aggregative process as it proceeds, however, is offset by other processes. Things coming together acquire velocity as kinetic energy and when they collide this may be transformed into radiant energy, as into heat. This produces changes in the parameters of the system and it passes over phase boundaries into other systems. Kinetic energy may become centrifugal, as in the solar system, which prevents the planets falling into the sun. As aggregations accumulate in the stars, nuclear reactions are set off and instabilities lead to nova and to supernovae, and so on. All this follows a constantly repeated pattern like the alpha and omega points of Teilhard de Chardin.[5] Some potential for change emerges; as time goes on the potential is realized. In the process of realization, however, new potentials for change are developed. Equilibrium is never reached and evolution continually proceeds. The generation of evolutionary potential of all kinds is a profound mystery, but also a profound reality. Without it, the universe would surely have settled down to an equilibrium of chaos long ago.

Even physical evolution, governed as it is by the relative simplicity of phase boundaries, exhibits patterns in simplified form that are later found in greater complexity in biological and societal evolution. The concept of a population, which will be developed in more detail in the next chapter, is relevant even at the level of physical and chemical objects. The simplest concept of a population is that of a stock of items existing at a moment of time, each of which corresponds to a common definition. Thus, there is a population of hydrogen atoms in the universe or in any defined segment of it, there is a population of galaxies of a given type, there is a population of stars of one type, there is a population of water molecules on the planet earth, just as there are populations of squirrels in North America, humans in Colorado, or gas stations in Denver. All populations in the most general sense of the term follow a very simple principle, which I have for many years called the "bathtub theorem." In any given time the increase in the number of items or elements in the population is equal to the number of items entering it minus the number of items leaving it, i.e., equal to the additions minus the subtractions. The bathtub is a simple example of this principle—if more water is coming in than is going out, the water in the bathtub will grow; if more is going out than coming in, the water will decline. If the population is defined by a geographical boundary, in-migrants constitute additions and out-migrants subtractions.

THE ECOLOGY OF MATTER AND ENERGY

Ecology, as we shall see, is the science of interacting populations. Whether we should consider the physical universe as an ecological system is an interesting point. In the formal sense it can be so considered, but it is doubtful whether this is the most useful model in the case of physical elements. Physical populations, unlike biological and social populations, are incapable of self-generation, that is, of births produced from other members of the population. Nevertheless, when hydrogen and oxygen combine to form water, there is a population of hydrogen molecules and oxygen molecules that diminishes and of water molecules that increases. In a very real sense there is a death of hydrogen and oxygen and a birth of water. Chemical and physical equilibrium systems have something of the characteristic of an ecological equilibrium. The number of water molecules in the atmosphere, for instance, is increased when more are evaporated from the seas, lakes, and rivers than are deposited in rain, dew, or captured by liquid water bodies. Meteorology is the study of a vast complex of interacting populations, mostly of gaseous and liquid molecules. The physical and chemical turbulence of the atmosphere that produces the weather is based on the fact that the earth is a great heat engine, receiving radiation at high densities and potential from the sun, and emitting radiation at lower intensities from the earth's surface. This heat engine not only produces the weather, but it has driven the whole evolutionary process in life and in society.

It is indeed the throughput of energy in the earth that has made evolution possible. Any closed system very soon exhausts the potential within it and reaches an equilibrium, which is then sustained indefinitely. This, of course, is the famous second law of thermodynamics popping up again. The earth, however, is an open system from the point of view of energy, though not very much from the point of view of materials, except as it receives minor accessions from meteorites and loses a few molecules to outer space. It is a little hard to conceive of energy as a population of "ergs," but with a little stretching of the metaphor and the imagination we can, and we then see very clearly that the earth is not just a stationary stock of energy, but is a population of energy with births continually coming in from the sun and deaths radiating out into space.

If there is an equilibrium population of anything where the population neither rises nor falls, but remains stationary, the law of conservation comes into play. This is a generalized version of the first law of thermodynamics, which states that, if there is a fixed quantity of anything, it can only be pushed around, or redistributed among the parts of the system. In the case of thermodynamics, this states that in any closed system with a constant amount of energy, all changes in the form of energy represent equal exchanges. That is, when heat is transformed into mechanical, chemical, or electrical energy, what is given up in one form is exactly what is gained in the other. What this says in effect is that there is no creation or destruction of any particular population, and the only way in which population can change is by in-migration or out-migration. What comes into one population must always equal what goes out from another or, more exactly, from all others.

There is a certain difference here between the way conservation operates in populations that are simply stocks without any additions or subtractions and populations that are in equilibrium in that they remain constant in size because there are equal amounts of additions and subtractions thus creating a throughput. Where there is a throughput, the possibilities of change are larger than where there is simply a static stock. All that can happen to a static stock is a simple rearrangement among the parts; it is a shifting cargo. Where there is a throughput, there can be a dynamic of accumulation at the point of entry, decumulation at the points of exit, and movement from one to the other.

The principle of throughput becomes particularly important when there is a tendency toward decay of structure. We see this, for instance, in the radioactive elements, each of which decays at a constant rate. If there were no creation of radioactive elements, it is clear that their total stock would constantly diminish and that the amount of radioactivity would decline. But there is, of course, creation of radioactive elements, not only on the very small scale in which the human race does it with nuclear reactions, but also in the stars. Whether the rate of creation just offsets the rate of decay within the universe, we do not know.

It is a general principle that any complex structure is subject to decay, simply because random events are more likely to lead from the improbable to the probable and from the structured to the unstructured than vice versa.

This, again, is an expression of the great second law. All complex structures, therefore, must exhibit throughput; if their population is to be sustained, they must have additions to offset the subtractions, which result from decay. Their complexity, in other words, inevitably involves death and, if complexity is to be sustained, it must require births or the formation of new items of complex populations.

INFORMATION IN PHYSICAL EVOLUTION: CATALYSIS

The role of information structures in physical evolution is a tricky problem. One can certainly imagine a system of pure, phase boundary, physical evolution in which new things simply form when the conditions are right, and in which information as such plays a very small role in the process. It can, nevertheless, be argued that any movement toward complexity is a movement in the field of information, just because information is the only thing that can be complex or exhibit improbable structure. There may be, however, a significant role for information, even in physical evolution, in the processes of nucleation and catalysis.

Nucleation is a very general problem also encountered in the other forms of evolution. It goes back to a Zeno-like paradox of how does something ever grow from nothing. It is easy to see how something that already exists, whether it is a crystal, raindrop, chick, or idea, can grow. There is indeed a very fundamental principle of the universe, which I have called "D'Arcy Thompson's Law" after the great Scottish biologist who perceived it so clearly,[6] that states "everything is what it is because it got that way." In other words, any object at a moment of time is what it is because of its previous dynamic history and its laws of growth. This still raises the question, however, of how did anything ever get started, for zero growing at any positive rate is still zero.

The processes by which structures get started or nucleate are often rather different from the processes that enable objects to grow once they have been started and almost always require peculiar kinds of input. We often get what I have called "heterogeneous nucleation;" that is, something nucleates about an object that is foreign to it and different from it. A raindrop nucleates around a speck of dust or a grain of silver iodide on which the liquid droplets deposit themselves. A liquid can be cooled far below its freezing point in a very still and smooth vessel with no discontinuities around which the crystals could form. Glass indeed is an interesting example of a supercooled liquid; it flows so slowly that we mistake it for a solid. It is transparent presumably because it is really a liquid and the crystals that interrupt and infract the light waves passing through it have not formed. Animals nucleate in the form of fertilized eggs. Social species often have heterogeneous nucleation. A church, for instance, spins off a college, which then takes on a life of its own and becomes an independent organization.

In the absence of nucleation, which is really a form of information or some kind of preexisting structure, the new structures that would be created by phase changes often do not take place. We see somewhat the same phenomenon in chemistry in catalysis. Reactions for which the phase is right often do not take place simply because there is no place for them to start. A catalyst is an extraneous substance which has a surface configuration or "template" that in a sense conveys information to the otherwise nonreacting molecules and so brings them together in a reaction. How far catalysts have been important in the physical and chemical evolution of the universe we do not really know, but they may be of considerable importance in determining the sequences or the succession of different physical species, especially of molecules.

MOUNTAIN BUILDING AND PLATE TECTONICS

A system of physical evolution that represents a very minute portion of the universe, but which has been extremely important in setting the stage for both biological and societal evolution, is the geological evolution of the earth. Even though the elements which comprise the material substance of the earth have probably changed very little in four billion years, they have undergone very extensive rearrangements, especially on the earth's surface, producing the diverse landscape of continents, oceans, mountains, valleys, and plains with which we are familiar. Somewhat similar processes have gone on in other planets as the surface of the moon and recent knowledge of the surface of Mars testifies. There has been a revolution of geology in the last generation as a result of the development of the theory of plate tectonics. The continental masses are perceived as floating on the underlying magma, pushing against each other and so pushing up mountain chains, or being drawn down into the interior and then perhaps thrown up again in vulcanism. This view presents an extraordinary picture of irreversible dynamics and constant disequilibrium. If it had not been for these processes, the earth might have been covered by a uniform ocean and an important road of evolution out of the oceans on to land would forever have been denied.

What peculiarity in the history of the earth produced this extraordinary four-billion-year dynamics is unknown. It also seems to have happened to a much smaller extent on the moon and on Mars, although it cannot be ruled out there. The history of biological evolution on earth has been profoundly affected by the geological history. If it had not been for the tectonic restlessness of the planet, the forces of atmospheric erosion would long have produced, if not a uniform ocean, at least flat, swampy continents devoid of the variety of conditions which the mountains give, and hence with far fewer evolutionary niches and much less evolutionary potential. The entropic processes of erosion, which make for flatness and lack of variety, have been offset constantly by processes of orogeny or mountain building. This is a kind of anti-entropic process, which has preserved the extraordinary physical variety of the earth.

We note this variety to some extent on relatively waterless Mars and on the moon. These bodies, however, having little or no atmosphere, suffer very little from erosion; thus, the physiographic variety of the earth must be the result of a very lively tectonic and orogenic process, which offsets the high degree of wind and water erosion. All earth's high mountains are relatively young, geologically speaking. The Alps and the Rockies, for instance, are only about seventy million years old, and the Southern Alps of New Zealand are perhaps only five or ten million years old. The floating away of the Americas, Europe, Antarctica, Australia, and India from the central core of Africa is a great tectonic drama that has not only created the Andes, the Sierras, the Pyrenees, the Alps, the Caucasus, and the Himalayas, but has also provided at times catastrophic geological changes that have profoundly altered the course of evolution. This suggests that without a large moon creating sizeable tides, the course of biological evolution would also have been very different. The intertidal strip provided an extraordinary meeting place for evolutionary change and perhaps was an essential element in the great transition of life from sea to land.

THE "GOLDILOCKS PRINCIPLE"

In the larger sense, the improbable evolution of life and society on this planet can be seen as a result of the fact that it reached some very outlying and outlandish point in the phase space of the universe. The physical limits within which biological evolution can take place are very narrow, and the places that lie within these limits must be correspondingly rare. This I have sometimes called the "Goldilocks principle." In the story of the *Three Bears*, Father Bear's porridge was too hot, Mother Bear's was too cold, and Little Bear's was just right. It is when things are "just right" that evolutionary potential is created and something happens. In our solar system, Venus is certainly too hot, Mars is too cold, and the earth is just right. It is just the right distance from the sun to sustain a temperature that permits liquid water, without which it is hard to conceive evolution having taken place. Liquid water is indeed the water of life. The earth had to be just the right size because, if it had been much bigger, gravity would have been too high, and it would have retained too dense an atmosphere. If it had been much smaller, its gravitational attraction would have been too low and it would have lost its water and atmosphere, as the moon may have done. It had to have about the right combination of elements, for even the absence of some trace elements that exist in quite small quantities might have inhibited the complex chemistry of life. Recent studies suggest that the distribution of elements in living organisms is not very different from that which was probably attained in the primordial seas that gave rise to life in the first place.[7]

What the chances are of this very peculiar combination of physical environments being repeated in other parts of the universe is unknown, though some astronomers think there may be a relatively large number of cases—one suspects, on very skimpy evidence. Whatever may have happened elsewhere, however, we know that it happened here, that physical evolution did in fact produce a setting within which the potential for biological evolution was created.

NOTES

1. If x_{t-1} and x_t are two successive positions of a time series at time $t-1$ and t, then $x_t = f(x_{t-1})$ is a difference equation of the first degree. Knowing this and the value of x_0, we can find x_1; knowing x_1, we could find x_2; and so on indefinitely. If $x_t = f(x_{t-1}, x_{t-2})$, we have a difference equation of the second degree. Then if we know x_0 and x_1, we can derive x_2; knowing x_1 and x_2, we can derive x_3; and so on indefinitely. If $x_t = f(x_{t-1}, x_{t-2}, \ldots, x_{t-n})$, we have a difference equation of the nth degree.

Differential equations are simply difference equations in the limiting case where the time interval between successive values of the variable shrinks toward zero.

2. Jay W. Forrester, *World Dynamics* (Cambridge, Mass.: Wright-Allen Press, 1971).

3. See Kenneth E. Boulding, *The Image* (Ann Arbor: University of Michigan Press, 1956).

4. August Lösch, *The Economics of Location* (New Haven: Yale University Press, 1954).

5. Teilhard de Chardin, *The Phenomenon of Man* (New York: Harper and Row, 1959).

6. D'Arcy W. Thompson, *On Growth and Form* (2nd ed.; New York; Cambridge University Press, 1952).

7. A. Banan and J. Navrot, "Origin of Life: Clues From Relations Between Chemical Compositions of Living Organisms and Natural Environments," *Science,* 189 (Aug. 15, 1975), 550.

Chapter 3

Population Dynamics

THE CONCEPT OF A "SPECIES"

However the universe may have originated, we now perceive it as a very heterogeneous collection of interacting objects—subatomic particles, protons, electrons, atoms, molecules, living species, human beings, and human artifacts—in a great variety of different kinds. In a certain sense each of these billions upon billions of items is unique; each, for instance, has a position in space and time different from that of every other. Nevertheless, we see similarities, so items are grouped into species and classes. All hydrogen atoms in the universe are perceived as being virtually indistinguishable, and for all purposes of chemistry and physics, completely interchangeable. When you visualize one hydrogen atom, you visualize them all.[1]

As we move toward more complex structures, the individuality and uniqueness of each item becomes more important. Even when you have seen one amoeba, you haven't seen them all. A particular amoeba may have peculiarities and "personality" that distinguish it from all other amoebas, quite apart from its position in time and space. When we get to human beings, personality becomes extremely important. When you have seen one human being, you have by no means seen them all. All human beings have certain important features in common derived from common elements in their genetic structure, but each human has peculiarities that are extremely important both to the person and to those with whom there is interaction. Human artifacts exhibit great similarity within each species—one bowl of Wheaties is virtually indistinguishable from another—but it is very easy to invest an automobile with personality, even to the point of giving it a pet name.

Nevertheless, we are forced to classify in order to be able to use language. It is a rare person who has a vocabulary of more than 20,000 words and even in ordinary daily life we encounter far more than 20,000 things. We are forced to classify, therefore, in order to talk about things, and we specify

[53]

particular things by the process of defining subsets in the way we do, for instance, when we write an address. I remember the thrill as a child of writing my address, as innumerable children have done through history—"4 Seymour Street, Liverpool, Lancashire, England, Great Britain, Europe, the world, the solar system, the galaxy, the universe"—and realizing, half subconsciously, that by dividing the universe into parts and dividing each part into parts through very few operations, one could identify the position of any particle within it.

Speciation and classification, however, have their hazards as general semantics has pointed out with great eloquence. Language deludes us into thinking that our linguistic categories are more uniform than in fact they are. The great semantic formula,[2] "this is not that"—this trade union is not that trade union, this Jew is not that Jew, this communist is not that communist, this fascist is not that fascist—is a very important litany which can save us very deep and painful misunderstandings if it is practiced carefully. Nevertheless, dangerous though the practice is, classify we must. We must divide the universe into populations of different species, even though these divisions are in some degree arbitrary and abstract from the individuality of the particular items.

A species is set of items that conform, to a common definition. A population is a way of describing certain properties of this set of items that can be reduced to number or quantity. The dynamics of a population or species can be treated at a number of different levels of complexity. The simplest concept is that of a stock of something that simply stays around and neither increases nor decreases and has neither additions nor subtractions. Even here we may run into problems of measurement. If a stock is a stock of identical items, we can simply count them. If we say that the population of the United States on a given day is 210,385,964, we are implying, first, that the population consists of clearly identifiable objects—a baby just born belongs to it, a baby within minutes of being born does not; a person on the point of death belongs to it, a person who has just died does not; the most vegetable and inanimate live human being belongs to it, the most intelligent chimpanzee does not. Having identified all the items that belong to this stock, population, or set, we assume they can be counted and the number written down. We neglect here the fact that counting takes time and while we are counting the number may change. In an absolutely fixed stock where a number does not change, this does not matter; however, for large numbers counting is impossible and we have to resort to estimation. We cannot possibly count the clouds, and not even the stars; we can only estimate their density in space and multiply this by the total volume they occupy.

COUNTING AND MEASUREMENT

Where we have a stock that consists of a homogeneous mass like the water in oceans, instead of a number of distinct items, we have to measure rather than count. Essentially we assume some quantity to be a unit and count the number of these units. The number arrived at depends on the size of the unit, however. The number that expresses the amount of water in the ocean will be much smaller if we reckon it in cubic miles instead of liters or cubic centimeters. Then the question arises, "What is the significant property that we wish to measure?" We might measure, for instance, the weight of the water in the oceans, or the mass rather than the volume. The units of measurement become important when creating images in our minds of what numbers really mean. They seldom create great logical problems, although there is a very interesting problem as to whether there are nonarbitrary "natural" units of measurement like the velocity of light.[3]

All systems of measurement in actual use are arbitrary, including the metric system, which has no more "scientific" foundation than any other despite some conveniences, and the inconvenience of being less psychologically satisfying than many more traditional measures. It is convenient for us all to use the same arbitrary numbers, which is why the metric system is being adopted. Units of measurement must be clearly visualized by being on a human scale that refers to experiences common to humankind. Thus, the foot is roughly the length of a foot and a yard about the length of an outstretched arm. The meter was clearly designed to be close to a yard or its eighteenth century French equivalent. The inch is roughly the breadth of the thumb. The second is very close to what we think of as an "instant" of time, although it is longer than the shortest time that we can perceive. The furlong is a convenient length of a furrow (furrow-long). An acre is about what a man with an ox could plow in a day. The United States, for instance, seems not to have gone to the metric system originally because it did not have a "foot," which is a highly convenient unit for many purposes. We have a pretty fair idea at any one time what a dollar will buy, despite the impact of inflation.

The whole problem of psychological and epistemological understanding of measurement numbers is neglected. As a result, statistical and scientific work is often much less comprehensible than need be. When there is a clearly defined unit of population, however, it is generally visualized very plainly and these problems do not arise.

A POPULATION AS THE STOCK OF A SPECIES WITH THROUGHPUT

The next level of complexity is that of a stock to which items can be added and from which items can be subtracted. This is the "bathtub theorem," noted in the previous chapter, that the net addition to any stock is equal to the gross additions minus the gross subtractions. If more is being added than subtracted, the stock grows; if more is being subtracted than added, the stock declines. In a given period of time the absolute growth is equal to the absolute additions minus the absolute subtractions. At a moment of time the rate of growth is equal to the rate of addition minus the rate of subtraction, the rate of growth being defined as the absolute growth per unit of time divided by the stock itself; the rate of addition, the absolute additions per unit of time divided by the stock itself; the rate of subtraction, the absolute subtractions per unit of time divided by the stock itself.[4]

A further obvious but important proposition follows that the total stock at any one time is equal to all previous additions minus all previous subtractions. Any stock existing today exists because in the past more has been added than has been subtracted of these particular items since the beginning of time. To understand why anything is here, therefore, we must understand how the stock comes to be added to and how it comes to be subtracted from, and how these additions and subtractions are related to the total environment of the stock.

The properties of an equilibrium stock are different from those of a stationary stock even though in both cases the stock remains constant. In a stationary stock, the individual items do not change; in an equilibrium stock, there is a "throughput" of items with some being added and some being subtracted. Insofar as the items have characteristics different from those constituting the definition of its membership in the stock, the equilibrium stock may change in character even though its quantity remains the same. Thus, the population of a country may be constant, with equal numbers of additions and subtractions to the human population, but the composition of this population will be constantly changing. It may get taller or shorter, healthier or sicker, older or younger, richer or poorer, and so on. All these characteristics are peculiarities not involved in the definition of a human being itself. A tall human being is just as much a member of the human population as a short one, and counts for only one in the total.

This change in the composition of a population is not very important in physics and chemistry, mainly because the items there are very homogeneous. The definition of the hydrogen atom defines virtually all its characteristics. When it comes to living populations and to populations of human artifacts, however, the characteristics become important as well as the size.

POPULATIONS AS "AGING STOCKS"

The next level of complexity is a stock in which individual items have the characteristic of age, which is the time interval between the present and the date it was added to the stock. A sixty-five year old person was added to the stock of human beings sixty-five years ago. The age characteristic is significant for all biological populations and for all populations of human artifacts, such as automobiles or houses, simply because all items in these populations undergo fairly regular changes with age. In other words, the process of aging is fairly similar for all items in the stock. All newborn babies are very much alike; all twenty year old humans are very much alike but very different from newborn babies. The same proposition holds for all living creatures and also for automobiles, houses, and all human artifacts. An automobile ten years old has very different characteristics from one that is new.

It is not surprising, therefore, that population analysis stresses the age composition of a population. Aging is not significant in elements and compounds, though in a certain sense radioactive elements can be said to "age," at least in the mass (though individual atoms of radium do not age, they do die as they are transformed into other elements). Even with phenomena as relatively simple as stars, we find an aging process, that is, a fairly regular pattern of change in the item itself from the moment of its addition to the stock to the moment of its subtraction, so the age distribution of stars is of some interest to astronomers. The term "population" is sometimes for those stocks in which aging is a significant characteristic of the individual items. Because the word is used in several different meanings, perhaps we should use the term "aging stocks" for this level of complexity.

COHORTS OF BIRTHS AND THEIR SURVIVAL HISTORY

The dynamics of aging stocks is governed by the principle that every item in the stock at a given point in time will be t years older in t years if it had not "died," that is, been subtracted. This is one of the few things we know about the future with any certainty. Every person alive today will be either one year older or dead this time next year. This enables us to perform what is called "cohort analysis." A cohort consists of all items added to the stock in a given "year" or other arbitrary period of time. Each cohort then has what might be called a "subtraction history" or "survival history." The bathtub theorem can be applied to each cohort considered by itself as a stock, except that, once it has been generated, there are no further additions, only subtractions. Each year the number in the cohort then equals the number of the previous year, minus the number of subtractions during that year. The number in the cohort diminishes as the years pass until finally the year is reached in which the subtractions equal the number in the cohort, which reduces the number to zero and brings the cohort to an end. A cohort's survival pattern can be represented by a "survival function," or survival "table," which shows what fraction of the original cohort survives to each age following the cohort's birth.

We start with the simplest possible model. Let us divide a population into three age groups: (1) the young; (2) the childbearing age; and (3) the old. Let us suppose, for convenience, that each of these periods is a "year," which can be any arbitrary length of time. In the human population this would be about 20-25 years. There are now two fundamental sets of parameters enabling us

TABLE 3.1
Parameters

Age	1 (Young)	2 (Middle)	3 (Old)	4 (Dead)
Survival Ratio	1	.8	.4	0
Fertility Ratio	0	1.25	0	0

to project the whole future of a population as long as the parameters remain stable. The first set consists of the survival ratios for each age group, which is the ratio of the number in the age group to the total number of births from which they came. Thus, in Table 3.1 we suppose that all the young survive; thus, the survival ratio is 1.0 and the total number of young is the number of births. The survival ratio for the middle or childbearing group is assumed to be .8; that is, out of 1000 births, 800 survive in the next period to be of childbearing age. In the third or old period, the survival ratio is .4, meaning that of 1000 births, 400 will survive to be old. In the next period we suppose everybody is dead leaving no survivors. The second set of parameters is the fertility ratios, which consist of the ratio of the number in any age group to the number to be born in that period. In Table 3.1 we suppose that only the middle age group is fertile with a fertility ratio of 1.25, which means that for every member in this age group there will be 1.25 births. Thus, if there are 800 members, there will be 1000 births. For simplicity we suppose that neither the young nor the old contribute to fertility and have fertility ratios of zero, though this assumption can easily be changed.

THE EQUILIBRIUM POPULATION MODEL

Table 3.2 now shows an equilibrium population with the parameters of Table 3.1. The diagonal arrows show how many survive in each following year from a cohort of births. The 1000 members of age 1 in year 1 become 800 of age 2 in year 2, 400 of age 3 in year 3, and 0 of age 4 in year 4. Dotted arrows show the fertility relationship. The 800 members of age 2 in year 1 produce 1000 of the young. For simplicity, we suppose there are no deaths in this period, so that the number in age 1 is equal to the births of that period. The total population (2200) is constant, the number in each age group is

TABLE 3.2
Stationary Population in Equilibrium

Age Year	1 (Young)	2 (Middle)	3 (Old)	4	Population Total	Growth	Deaths	Birth Rate	Death Rate	Growth Rate
1	1000	800	400	0	2200	0	1000	.4545	.4545	0
2	1000	800	400	0	2200	0	1000	.4545	.4545	0
3	1000	800	400	0	2200	0	1000	.4545	.4545	0
4	1000	800	400	0	2200	0	1000	.4545	.4545	0

TABLE 3.3
Growth as a Result of Rise in Fertility

Age Year	1 (Young)	2 (Middle)	3 (Old)	4	Population Total	Growth	Deaths	Birth Rate	Death Rate	Growth Rate
1	1000	800	400	0	2200	0	1000	.4545	.4545	0
2*	1200	800	400	0	2400	200	1000	.5	.4167	.0833
3	1400	960	400	0	2800	400	1040	.5143	.3714	.1428
4	1728	1152	480	0	3360	560	1168	.5143	.3476	.1667
5	2074	1382	576	0	4032	672	1402	.5144	.3477	.1667

*Rise in fertility ratio in age 2 from 1.25 to 1.5.

constant, and the number of births (1000 each "year") equals the number of deaths (1000 each "year"). The number of deaths can be calculated most simply by subtracting the absolute growth from the number of births, because growth equals the number of births minus deaths. It can also be calculated from the age distribution. Thus, in the year 1, 200 of age 1 die, going from 1000 to 800. Four hundred of year 2 die, going from 800 to 400. Four hundred of year 3 die, going from 400 to zero, which is a total of 1000. The birth rate is the number of births divided by the total population, the death rate is the number of deaths divided by the total population, and the growth rate is the absolute growth divided by the total population. In this case, birth rate and death rate are equal and growth rate is zero. Birth and death rates are often expressed in terms of "per thousand," but there seems no very good reason for this so I am expressing them simply as a decimal.

THE GROWING POPULATION MODELS: FERTILITY VERSUS MORTALITY

Table 3.3 now shows how growth results from a rise in fertility. We suppose the survival ratios remain the same, but the fertility ratio increases from 1.25 to 1.5 in year 2. The total number of births and of young in that year is therefore 1200. The total population rises to 2400, growth is 200, deaths remain at 1000; the crude birth rate has risen, the crude death rate has fallen, the growth rate is .0833, or 8.3 percent per year. Continuing the same procedure into the third year, the 1200 young of age 1 of year 2 become 960 middles of age 2 in year 3. These produce 1440 births, and so on. The birth and death rates and the growth rate stabilize about year 4 and the population is in steady growth.

TABLE 3.4
Growth as a Result of a Fall in "Infant" Mortality

Age Year	1 (Young)	2 (Middle)	3 (Old)	4	Population Total	Growth	Deaths	Birth Rate	Death Rate	Growth Rate
1	1000	800	400	0	2200	0	1000	.4545	.4545	0
2*	1125	900	400	0	2425	225	900	.4639	.3711	.0928
3	1266	1012	400	0	2678	253	1013	.4727	.3783	.0945
4	1424	1139	450	0	3013	335	1089	.4726	.3614	.1112
5	1602	1282	506	0	3390	377	1225	.4726	.3613	.1112

*Rise in survival ratio in 2nd age group from .8 to .9.

TABLE 3.5
Unsustained Growth as a Result of a Fall in "Old Age" Mortality

Age Year	1 (Young)	2 (Middle)	3 (Old)	4	Population Total	Growth	Deaths	Birth Rate	Death Rate	Growth Rate
1	1000	800	400	0	2200	0	1000	.4545	.4545	0
2*	1000	800	600	0	2400	200	800	.4167	.3333	.0833
3	1000	800	600	0	2400	0	1000	.4167	.4167	0
4	1000	800	600	0	2400	0	1000	.4167	.4167	0

*Rise in survival ratio in age 2 from .4 to .6.

In Table 3.4 we see how growth can result from a fall in "infant" mortality, which is the same as a rise in the survival age ratio between year 1 (young) and year 2 (middle). Suppose in year 2 this rises from .8 to .9. There are therefore 900 of the middle age group in year 2 and the fertility ratio is still 1.25; 900 now produce 1125 young. Continuing the process as before, the birth rate, death rate, and growth rate stabilize in about the fourth period, with the growth rate at 11.12 percent per period.

In Table 3.5 we see how growth from a fall in "old age" mortality is not sustained, but simply results in a one-shot increase in population and a one-shot decline in the death rate and birth rate. Again we start with the old equilibrium population and then suppose in year 2 that there is a decline in mortality in the third age group, leading to a survival ratio of .6 rather than .4. This leads to a one-shot increase in the population, which then stabilizes at the new level.

CYCLICAL POPULATION MODELS

These simple models obscure an interesting phenomenon shown in Table 3.6, in which an increase in fertility sets off cycles in growth of about one generation in length. To show this, we must divide the population into five active age groups rather than three. We start with an equilibrium population as before, with survival ratios of .9 for age group 2, .8 for age group 3, .4 for age group 4, 1 for age group 5, and zero for age group 6. We suppose the fertility ratio is zero for all age groups except age group 3, which rises in year 2 from 1.25 to 1.5, and all other parameters remain constant. In year 2 therefore the 800 people in age group 3 produce 1200 in age group 1, instead of 1000. If we project the population, it exhibits a cycle of two "years" corresponding to one generation, because it takes two periods for the in- creased births of one generation to become the increased childbearing group of the next. The birth, death, and growth rates do not stabilize in this case, rather they exhibit a regular cycle.

This problem is important in human populations. In the United States, for instance, there was a substantial bulge in fertility from 1947 to 1961. This generation has now entered the childbearing age and, if the fertility ratio is held constant for various age groups, we would expect another upsurge in the "crude" or average birth rate as a result of this large group of childbearing

TABLE 3.6
Population Growth Cycles as a Result of Increasing Fertility

Age Year	1	2	3	4	5	6	Deaths	Total Population	Growth (Births-Deaths)	Birth Rate	Death Rate	Growth Rate
0	1000	900	800	400	100	0	1000	3200	0	.3125	.3125	0
1	1000	900	800	400	100	0	1000	3200	0	.3125	.3125	0
2*	1200	900	800	400	100	0	1000	3400	200	.3529	.2941	.0588
3	1200	1080	800	400	100	0	1020	3580	180	.3352	.2849	.0503
4	1440	1080	960	400	100	0	1040	3980	400	.3618	.2613	.1005
5	1440	1296	960	480	100	0	1144	4276	296	.3368	.2675	.0692
6	1728	1296	1152	480	120	0	1228	4776	500	.3618	.2571	.1047

*Rise in fertility ratio in 3rd age group from 1.25 to 1.5.

age. Actually, the decline in age specific fertility has been so large that there has been no upsurge in births. If we did not have this large age group of childbearing age, however, the decline in birth rates would be even more spectacular.

THE NET REPRODUCTIVE RATIO

A very important parameter of population dynamics is called the "net reproductive ratio" (R). This may be defined roughly as the total number of children surviving to reproductive (childbearing) age, which each reproductive age group produces. If this ratio is 1.0, each generation of reproductive age produces an equal generation of reproductive age in the next generation. If the ratio is more than 1.0, each generation leaves behind it a larger generation of reproductive age, and the population therefore will continually increase. If the ratio is less than 1.0, each generation of reproductive age will leave behind it a new generation smaller in numbers and hence the population will continually decline.

These principles are illustrated in Tables 3.7A and 3.7B. In both these tables we start with an equilibrium population of 125 in the young age group, 100 in the middle, and 75 in the old. The fertility ratio, F, is 1.25, thus the 100 in the middle group produce 125 in the young each year. Survival ratios are .8 (s_2) from young to middle, and .6 (s_3) from young to old. The reproductive ratio is the product of the fertility ratio and survival ratio for

TABLES 3.7 A and B
Net Reproductive Ratio

Year	Young 1	Middle 2	Old 3	Total Population P	Growth of Population G	Fertility Ratio F	Survival Ratios s_2	s_3	Net Reproductive Ratio $R = Fs_2$	Rate of Growth $g = \frac{G}{P}$	$\frac{R-1}{R}$
A 1	125	100	75	300	0	1.25	.8	.6	1	0	0
2	125	100	75	300	0	1.25	.8	.6	1	0	0
3	150	100	75	325	25	1.5	.8	.6	1.2	.0769	.1666
4	180	120	75	375	50	1.5	.8	.6	1.2	.1333	.1666
5	216	144	90	450	75	1.5	.8	.6	1.2	.1666	.1666
6	259	173	108	540	90	1.5	.8	.6	1.2	.1666	.1666
B 1	125	100	75	300	0	1.25	.8	.6	1	0	0
2	125	100	75	300	0	1.25	.8	.6	1	0	0
3	100	100	75	275	−25	1.00	.8	.6	.8	−.0909	−.25
4	80	80	75	235	−40	1.00	.8	.6	.8	−.1702	−.25
5	64	64	60	188	−47	1.00	.8	.6	.8	−.25	−.25
6	51	51	48	150	−38	1.00	.8	.6	.8	−.25	−.25

the middle group. In the first and second years this equals 1.0, and in the equilibrium population the rate of growth is zero. In the third year we suppose the fertility ratio rises to 1.5 and the reproductive ratio rises to 1.2, which causes a process of population increase. The 100 in the middle group in year 3 produce 150 in the young group, which turns into 120 in the middle group of year 4, which produces 180 in the young group, which turns into 144 by year 5, and so on. The rate of growth soon approximates $\frac{R-1}{R}$; see the appendix for the mathematical proof. In Table 3.7B, we see the same thing, except for a decline in the fertility ratio in year 3 to 1.0, so that the 100 in the middle group in that year only produce 100 in the young group, which turn into 80 in the middle group in the year 4, and so on. Here we have constant population decline with a rate of growth stabilizing at $-.25$, which equals $\frac{R-1}{R}$ again. No matter how the net reproductive ratio falls below -1.0, whether due to a decline in fertility or a decline in the survival ratio of the middle, childbearing group, the population will decline continuously if it is below 1.0; if it is above 1.0, it will increase continuously at a constant rate once the age distributions have worked themselves out.

This principle is of the utmost importance in understanding the interaction of different populations. The net reproductive ratio, which ultimately determines the rate of growth, is itself a function of both of the size of the population of the species in question and also, as we shall see, the size of populations of other species. In a given environment of other species, each population has a net reproductive ratio that ultimately declines with expansion of the population itself. It may be below 1.0 for very low populations, perhaps because fertility is low, the population is very sparse, and the males cannot find the females. If such is the case, the population will decline to extinction. How populations rise above this threshold to the point where the net reproductive ratio is greater than 1.0 is a puzzle. This must take place at a very low population; otherwise the population will never expand. Any mutation therefore must carry a population immediately to a point where the net reproductive ratio is greater than 1.0 if the mutation is going to survive. If the net reproductive ratio is greater than 1.0, however, the population will grow. As it grows, it will find eventually that the net reproductive ratio will fall, either because fertility declines due to crowding, maternal neglect, and so on, or because mortality increases and the survival ratio from the young to the childbearing group declines, which will also bring down the net reproductive ratio. If the net reproductive ratio falls to 1.0, the population will soon stabilize at a zero rate of growth with the birth rate equal to the death rate. This is the equilibrium population for a given environment.

THE EQUILIBRIUM POPULATION AS A "NICHE"

The equilibrium population is the most satisfactory concept of the "niche." Biologists are apt to think of niches in terms of physical environments. Indeed, sometimes the niche is defined by the boundaries of the physical environment, like a coral reef, in the sense that, if the population grows beyond the carrying capacity of the particular physical niche, any expansion of population carries individuals beyond the shelter of this environment into a less favorable environment and hence death rates increase rapidly and the net reproductive ratio of the whole population soon falls to 1.0. The concept, however, is quite independent of the existence of physical niches. It holds for populations, like herring or deer, that do not have a clearly defined physical niche in which increasing population gradually increases the adversity of the condition of the species, causing either falling fertility or falling survival rates until the net reproductive ratio falls to 1.0. As the net reproductive ratio falls, the rate of growth also falls until, by the time the net reproductive ratio is 1.0, the rate of growth is zero. A population starting to expand into a niche, therefore, will have rapid growth at first; there is plenty of room, conditions are favorable, births exceed deaths, the net reproductive ratio is above 1.0. As the population grows, however, its rate of growth will decline and will eventually reach zero, at which time the population will be in equilibrium and constant.

This is illustrated in Table 3.8. Here we postulate that both the birth rate and death rate are functions of the total population. We start with a growing population, a birth rate of 3.5, and a death rate of 2.5 (each time period here would represent about 100 years on a human population scale). The growth rate is 1.0, therefore the absolute growth is the same as the population itself, and the population doubles by the next time period. As the population grows we first see a rise in the birth rate, perhaps because it becomes easier for individuals to mate, and perhaps therefore an initial increase in the rate of growth. As the population grows, however, we get a slow decline in the birth rate due to increasing difficulty in finding nesting places, places to raise offspring, and so on. The death rate might fall at first possibly because the increase in population permits greater cooperation, and so on. Eventually it rises, however, until by the eighth time period in this case it is equal to the

TABLE 3.8
Growth to an Equilibrium Population

Time	1	2	3	4	5	6	7	8	9
P = Population	100	200	480	1104	2208	3754	5255	5780	5780
b = Birth Rate	3.5	3.8	3.8	3.8	3.7	3.6	3.5	3.5	3.5
d = Death Rate	2.5	2.4	2.5	2.8	3.0	3.2	3.4	3.5	3.5
b - d = g = Growth Rate	1.0	1.4	1.3	1.0	.7	.4	.1	0	0
G = Pg = Growth	100	280	624	1104	1546	1501	525	0	0

birth rate. At this point the growth rate is zero and the population is in equilibrium.[5] The actual functions that relate the birth rate, death rate, and growth rate to the population differ greatly with different species. If there is to be an equilibrium population or niche, however, the birth rate must be above the death rate for small or very small populations. But as the population rises, either the birth rate must decline or the death rate must rise, or the death rate must rise faster than the birth rate until the death rate curve intersects the birth rate curve at the point where birth and death rates are equal and the growth rate is zero.

ORIGINS AND SPREAD OF POPULATIONS: TERRITORIALITY

There are tricky problems involved in the origins of populations. In a sexual population it is obvious that there must be at least one member of each sex before the population can start to grow. Furthermore, there is in most populations a level, somewhat above the number two, at which the population is extremely precarious and likely to decline to extinction. That is, the birth rate will fall to zero on the extreme lefthand side of Figure 3.1 before the population is zero and there will be some unstable equilibrium below which the population will not survive, and above which it will grow and survive. The question of how populations get started, therefore, is a very tricky one.

In biological species the most significant population is that of the individual genes. A new gene is "born" when a member of the phenotype population that contains it is born. It dies when such a member dies. A mutation has to take place in the gene that is part of the body of some member of the phenotype population. It may spread through the body of that member by cell division. However, it will soon die with the member if there is no reproduction, that is, if the member does not produce an offspring and containing this particular gene. The spread of a gene through the biosphere depends on the reproductive success of the phenotypes that contain it. If they produce large numbers of offspring and the offspring produce large numbers of offspring, the population of the genes will increase. Genes, like phenotypes, have niches. As their population increases, the gap between their birth rate and death rate or growth rate will decline until it falls to zero, at which time the population of the gene is in equilibrium. In the meantime, of course, the population of the phenotype may have changed somewhat, although there may still be no new phenotypical species. As new species develop and survive, however, the point finally arrives at which a new species appears and the gene pool essentially separates into two populations, the phenotypes of which cannot interbreed, which interact with each other only through the general interaction of the phenotypes.

There are many different possible shapes of the birth and death rate functions of Table 3.8. Some biological species, for instance, exhibit "territoriality," particularly on a pair basis. This means there is a limited number of available nesting sites. A good example is the robin. A robin in possession of a territory will drive off any robins that seek to invade it. A robin that cannot find a territory will not be able to mate and raise offspring, although it may be able to survive in the cracks between territories. In this case, as population rises, both the birth and death rate may remain fairly stable, with the birth rate above the death rate. When the population reaches the limit of the available territory and nesting sites, however, there is a very sharp decline in the birth rate of the total population as the increase of population includes mainly nonreproducing specimens. The birth rate then plunges to intersect the death rate, the equilibrium population.

Sometimes the niche is a physical niche within which there may be an abundance of nesting sites, but beyond which the population becomes much more exposed to predation or to a failure of food supply. Koala bears in a grove of eucalyptus trees, or bats in a cave, would be good examples. Up to a certain point, the birth rate will be above the death rate and the population will grow. At the limits of the physical niche, however, the death rate will take a sudden upward surge and intersect the birth rate, again at the equilibrium population.[6]

BIRTH RATE EQUALS RECIPROCAL OF AVERAGE LENGTH OF LIFE

An important theorem in population dynamics is that in an equilibrium population the birth rate, which is equal to the death rate, is also equal to the reciprocal of the average length of life of individuals in the population. Thus, in a population in which the average length of life is 25 years in equilibrium, the birth rate will be $\frac{1}{25}$, or 4 percent per annum. In a population with an average length of life of 70 years, the birth rate will be about $\frac{1}{70}$, or 1.43 percent. Birth and death rates are frequently expressed in terms of per thousand; thus four percent would be 40 per 1000, and 1.43 percent 14.3 per 1000. There is apparently no particular reason for this custom, but the reader should be aware of it in other literature.

Formal proof of the above proposition must be left to the appendix, but its truth can be perceived in a very simple case if we suppose, for instance, a population in which there are a million births and deaths every year, and in which everybody dies at the same age. If everybody dies at the age of 25, there will be a million people 1 year old, a million 2 years old, and so on, totalling 25 million in all. The birth rate will be $\frac{1 \text{ million}}{25 \text{ million}}$ or $\frac{1}{25}$. If everybody lives to be 50, the total population will be 50 million, a million people at each age, and the birth rate will be $\frac{1 \text{ million}}{50 \text{ million}}$, or $\frac{1}{50}$. This is an important proposition because it suggests that in human populations, for instance, if the birth rates are maintained at 35 per 1000, as they are in many countries today, the death rate will have to rise to 35 per 1000 to sustain an equilibrium population, and then the expectation of life must be $\frac{1000}{35}$, or about 28 1/2 years. If the expectation of life is to be 70 years in an equilibrium population, the birth and death rates cannot be more than about 14.3 per 1000.

r-SELECTION AND K-SELECTION

This close relationship between the average expectation of life of the newly born and the birth and death rates is reflected in a distinction made by biologists between what they call "r-selection" and "K-selection." This represents two extreme strategies of attaining an equilibrium population. Species under r-selection have very high birth rates and very high infant mortality rates; the average expectation of life of new members of the population is very low, simply because only a very few make it to adulthood. This represents the case in which the net reproductive ratio of the equilibrium (niche-filling) population is 1.0 because of a very large F and a very small s_2, that is, very large numbers are born but very few of these survive into childbearing age. The equilibrium population is achieved when the reproductive ratio falls to 1.0. This may happen because of a decline in s_2, that is, increased mortality, as the population increases. We cannot altogether rule out a decline in F, that is, in fertility itself. This would be the case in species like the herring, which produces enormous numbers of offspring though very few of them survive. These "r-selection" species tend to be nonterritorial, limited on the whole by rising death rates or declining survival ratios, to the point where the net reproductive ratio is 1.0.

At the other end of the scale, we have what is called "K-selection." These are the species in which F is low and s_2 is correspondingly high, that is, few offspring are born, but a large proportion of them survive into childbearing age. Those species that are territorial and have strong parental care of offspring tend to fall into this category. Whether, in fact, the fertility ratios and the survival ratios of different species exhibit bimodal distribution, with large numbers of them with large Fs and small s_2s at the other end, I do not know. I have not seen any data on this. In any case, the r-selection and K-selection categories merely represent the extremes of a continuum.

As seen more clearly in the next chapter, the position of the birth and death functions, and therefore the size of the equilibrium population, depends on a large number of variables in the environment, especially the size of other populations. The above analysis is strictly what an economist would call "partial equilibrium." Nevertheless, it is through the birth and death functions that the general ecological equilibrium is mediated. Again we must emphasize that the size of any population of biological elements is the difference between the number of additions and the number of subtractions since the population began. Any biological population is equal in numbers exactly to the difference between the number of births and the number of deaths since the species could first be identified.

POPULATIONS WITH IN- AND OUT-MIGRATION

The next level of complexity is that of a population that has in-migrants and out-migrants as well as births and deaths. Any biological population in a restricted area, whether animal or human, is likely to receive additions from members of the species crossing the boundary of the area inward and subtractions by members crossing the boundary outwards. The bathtub theorem now takes the form that the absolute growth of any population in a given period is equal to the number of births, plus the number of in-migrants, minus the number of deaths, minus the number of out-migrants. In both the biosphere and the sociosphere migration is an important factor in determining the dynamics of the population of any species within a limited area. For the earth as a whole, there is virtually no migration of biological or human species if we discount the minute exports to and imports from outer space from the space program. Dispersion or migration within the earth, however, is an extremely important element in explaining the composition of species in any one area.

The fact that in-migrants and out-migrants can be of any age, whereas births in a biological population at least are obviously at age zero, and deaths are at different ages from out-migrants, complicates the cohort analysis of a population. If, for instance, a country has a large influx of migrants of childbearing age, the proportion of the population of childbearing age will be increased and the crude·birth rate will correspondingly be increased even if there is no change in fertility. Conversely, if out-migration consists of individuals of childbearing age, the population that is losing the migrants will have a smaller proportion of childbearing age and its crude birth rate will decline accordingly. Migrants also differ in many other respects from population members who stay at home. They may be more energetic or active, more subject to mutation, or more discontented and alienated. Migration has played a very important role in both biological evolution and societal evolution. A phenomenon, occasionally important in both cases, is called a "founder effect," where migrants whose gene composition, for instance, is different from that of the rest of the population migrate to found a new population elsewhere. If the difference is large enough, it may increase through mutation and develop a separate species. We see this also in "noogenetic" effects, especially in human populations. English people migrated to America and remained English people for a century and a half, but they were somewhat different in culture from the average of the English people who stayed in England. This difference increased with isolation until eventually they became Americans.

POPULATIONS OF HUMAN ARTIFACTS

The final level of complexity is that of the human artifact. Human artifacts may be "things," such as flint knives, iron axes, loaves of bread, houses, pianos, automobiles, or office buildings, some of which are commodities and enter into exchange. They may also be organizations, such as families, businesses, clubs, church congregations, multinational corporations, associations, or national states. Human beings themselves are in part biogenetic artifacts made by their genes, but insofar as they are trained, educated, and socialized into different roles and occupations, they are also human artifacts, made partly by others and partly by themselves. All such artifacts can be divided into species and each species can be regarded as a population with additions from production and subtractions from consumption. For each such species of artifact we can postulate something like birth and death functions relating, in a given environment, the flow of production and consumption to the total population or the existing stock. These relationships are somewhat different in character and are mediated in ways different from the environment of biological populations, though they are probably of about equal stability. In this case perhaps it is more convenient to think of production (births) and consumption (deaths) flows (units of population per unit of time) rather than of birth and death rates, because there is no particular reason to suppose that the ratio of production to the stock or consumption to the stock, which would be the equivalent of the birth and death rates, has any tendency whatever to be constant.

The birth of human artifacts is not achieved as a result of intercourse between two artifacts of the same species but of different sexes, as in biological species with sexual reproduction. It is a result of intercourse among a large number of artifacts of different kinds. This is what is meant, as noted earlier, by describing social artifacts as multisexual, or more accurately, multiparental. Existing automobiles play a minor role in the production of automobiles. The rate of production flow of automobiles in numbers per annum is not likely to be directly related to the number of automobiles in the total stock, though there is an important indirect relation through demand. It is much more directly related to the number of ore mines, steel mills, automobile factories, assemblies, machines, salesmen, retail outlets, gas stations, and so on. It is not likely to be related to the existing stock of automobiles in the way, for instance, that the number of colts produced per annum is closely related to the number of sexually mature mares. The death rate of human artifacts can be related to the age distribution in much the same way as the death rate of biological species, because artifacts have a life history as do biological individuals. When they reach their particular "allotted span," they are likely to decay to the point where they will be scrapped or "die." The variability of life-history of artifacts may be greater than that of biological individuals because of greater variability in the maintenance function.

An equilibrium population of a human artifact, for example automobiles, is postulated in Table 3.9. The total stock of automobiles in existence at a moment is a population. For each population we postulate levels of production and consumption, and a level of growth in stock equal to production minus consumption. When the stock is zero, we suppose that production will start, assuming we know how to make automobiles. Consumption will be zero so growth in that year will be equal to production. As the stock rises, we suppose production rises as the size of the industry increases. Beyond a certain point, however, we begin to approach the saturation level of the stock of automobiles. With the existing levels of prices, incomes, and so on, production will begin to decline slowly and then after some critical point quite sharply as the stock increases. In Table 3.9 we have postulated that production reaches a maximum at 8 million a year at a stock of 50 and beyond that it declines. Consumption is closely related to the stock itself, neglecting changes in the age distribution, which historically have been important. Consumption will be roughly proportional to the stock if the average age of "death" is constant. On the other hand, particularly in the earlier stages, an increase in automobiles probably means an increase in accidents, so we have postulated a slightly increasing ratio of consumption to stock. At a stock of 70 in the table, the falling production overtakes the rising consumption; therefore, consumption equals production and the stock's growth is zero.[7] From a table such as Table 3.9, incidentally, we could deduce, if we have the intermediate values, the historical course of the automobile population by the same methods used in Table 3.8. It would rise at an eventually diminishing rate to a stationary (equilibrium) level at 70 million. This equilibrium level is the "niche" of the automobile in the ecosystem of the society. Like all niches, it may be constantly expanding and contracting in the light of changes in the total condition of the system.

TABLE 3.9
Equilibrium Population of Automobiles

S = Stock (Population) of Automobiles (Million)	0	10	20	30	40	50	60	70	80
P = Production Per Year (Million)	1	4	6.6	7.2	7.8	8.0	7.8	7.3	3.0
C = Consumption Per Year (Million)	0	1	2.1	3.2	4.3	5.3	6.3	7.3	8.4
G = P - C Growth in Stock (Million)	1	3	4.5	4.0	3.5	3.3	1.3	0	−5.4
$g = \frac{C}{S}$ = Rate of Growth	∞	.300	.225	.133	.087	.066	.022	0	−.067

The intermediate apparatus by which the equilibrium stock is sustained (i.e., by which the stock grows when it is below the equilibrium and diminishes when it is above it) is more complicated than in biological systems. It operates through large numbers of human decisions and through a complex set of parameters in the price system. As shown in Chapter 8, the price of commodities is a function of their stock, other things being equal, and price, especially as it governs the expected future price, is a very important element governing both production and consumption. When the stock is below the equilibrium level, the price will be above the equilibrium price, production will be encouraged, consumption discouraged, and the stock will grow. When the stock is above the equilibrium level, the price will be below the equilibrium price, production will be discouraged, consumption encouraged, and the stock will decline.

IN- AND OUT-MIGRATION IN HUMAN ARTIFACTS

In human artifacts, especially commodities, in-migration and out-migration is represented by import and export. The total gross additions to the stock represent domestic production plus imports; the gross subtractions represent domestic consumption minus exports. Again, the conditions governing the volume of imports and exports are much more complex than in biological systems. The systems are different, and the analogy must not be pushed too far. Nevertheless, the similarities are significant. An economic comparative advantage produces excess production of a commodity, which is then exported, much as a favorable environment may result in a population explosion in a biological species, part of which then migrates to other areas. The membership of a particular church, for instance, may be increased by "births," that is, children who grow up within the shelter of the church and become members almost automatically through confirmation; it loses membership through physical death. It gains membership by "imports," that is, converts from the population of nonmembers; it loses membership by "exports," that is, people who leave to join other—or no—churches. The bathtub theorem applies to church membership just as much as to any other population.

The population of a country also grows because of births and in-migrants, declines because of deaths and out-migrants, and the increase in population in any one period is equal to the number of births and in-migrants minus the number of deaths and out-migrants. All relative population changes in any type of stock are the result of these processes of addition and subtraction. Sometimes a subtraction from one is an addition to another, such as when a church makes a convert or a country gets an immigrant. On the whole, however, these processes of migration are much less significant than the relative change that results from different rates of internal growth.

The same principles apply to the growth of wealth and power. Sometimes there is migration of power, such as when one nation defeats another in war, and migration of wealth, such as when one group exploits another. Over time, however, conquest and exploitation, like other forms of migration, are much less significant than the "natural increase," which is the balance of internal births over internal deaths, internal production over internal consumption, or internal gains of political strength over internal losses of it. Differential development, or differences in the rate of "getting richer" among different countries or regions, is much more important in explaining great regional differences in wealth, that is, why some regions are rich and some poor, than is crude exploitation.

Clearly population dynamics is the key to the rise, decline, and extinction of physical, biological, or societal species of all kinds. The rise, decline, or size of the equilibrium population or niche of any one species, however, is a function of its total environment, which means the total existing populations of all other species with which it is in some kind of contact. This brings us to the theme of ecological interaction, which is pursued in the next chapter.

Appendix to Chapter 3:
THE MATHEMATICS OF POPULATION DYNAMICS

The mathematical treatment of population dynamics and interaction can be quite sophisticated, but what is attempted here is a substantial simplification of these processes, in terms that do not go beyond simple algebra and geometry. What is lost in elegance we may hope is gained in comprehensibility.

Table 3A.1 shows the essential variables involved in population dynamics. In "year" 1 we suppose a number of age groups. The number in the age group between zero and one year old is a_1, the number in the age group between one and two years old is b_1, and so on. The total population, P_1, is the sum of all these age groups, Σa_1. We suppose the number of births is equal to the number in the first age group, which is "net births," neglecting infant mortality before the age of one. Because we are breaking down time discontinuously here, some slightly arbitrary assumptions have to be made. For year 2 we have similar symbols with a subscript of 2. We can now define the total number of deaths in year 2 (D_2) as the births in year 2 (B_2) minus the growth in population between years 1 and 2 ($G_2 = P_2 - P_1$). The birth, death, and growth rates are simply the births, deaths, and growth divided by the total population. The number of deaths must also be equal to the sum of the declines between the size of each age group in the previous year and the next age group in the present year. This is shown in equation (1), which is equivalent to the formula in Table 3A.1.

[72]   ECODYNAMICS

TABLE 3A.1

Population Dynamics

Year	Age Groups 0-1	1-2	2-3	Total Population	Births	Deaths	Growth	Birth Rate	Death Rate	Growth Rate
1	$a_1, b_1, c_1, \ldots, n_1$			$P_1 = \Sigma a_1$	$B_1 = a_1$					
2	$a_2, b_2, c_2, \ldots, n_2$			$P_2 = \Sigma a_2$	$B_2 = a_2$	$D_2 = P_1 - P_2 + a_2$	$P_2 - P_1 = G_2$	$\frac{a_2}{P_2} = Rb_2$	$\frac{D_2}{P_2} = Rd_2$	$\frac{P_2 - P_1}{P_2} = Rg_2$

$$D_2 = (a_1 - b_2) + (b_1 - c_2) + \ldots + n_1 = \Sigma a_1 - \Sigma a_2 + a_2 = P_1 - P_2 + a_2 \qquad (1)$$

The essential parameters enable us to derive the values of year 2 from the values of year 1, given the one-year survival function, $s_a, s_b, \ldots$, in equations (2).

$$s_a = \frac{b_2}{a_1}, \ s_b = \frac{c_2}{b_1}, \ \ldots, s_n = 0 \qquad (2)$$

We can express the same data in terms of cohort survival ratios, S_a, $S_b, \ldots$, to show the proportion in each age group that survives from the original cohorts of births from which each is derived. This is shown in equations (3).

$$S_a = s_a = \frac{b_2}{a_1}, \ S_b = s_a s_b = \frac{b_1}{a_0} \cdot \frac{c_2}{b_1} = \frac{c_2}{a_0}, \text{etc.} \qquad (3)$$

The survivors in year 2 of the (0-1) age group is c_2 in year zero, a_0. We use these cohort survival ratios in the arithmetical examples in the chapter because they are easier to calculate. These may not be stable if the age-group survival fractions are changing.

The fertility parameters are shown in equation (4).

$$a_1 = f_b b_1 + f_c c_1 \ldots + f_n n_1 \qquad (4)$$

The number of births from the age group b_1 is $f_b b_1$, the number of births in the age group c_1 is $f_c c_1$, and so on. The total number of births is the sum of those in all the age groups. These fertility fractions can, of course, be only above zero in age groups of childbearing age. If the parameters of equations (2) and (4) are constant, we can project the population indefinitely into the future. We extend the model by supposing that these parameters are functions of other parameters, for instance, of the total population itself. If the survival and fertility parameters are constant, we will eventually get constant growth in the population when the age distribution works itself out to an equilibrium value. This proposition is illustrated in equations (5).

$$P_0 = a_1 \qquad (5a)$$

$$P_1 = a_1 s_a f_a + a_1 s_a \qquad (5b)$$

$$P_2 = a_1 s_a{}^2 f_a{}^2 + a_1 s_a{}^2 f_a + a_1 s_a s_b \qquad (5c)$$

$$P_3 = a_1 s_a{}^3 f_a{}^3 + a_1 s_a{}^3 f_a{}^2 + a_1 s_a{}^2 s_b f_a$$

$$= s_a f_a (a_1 s_a {}^2 f_a {}^2 + a_1 s_a {}^2 f_a + a_1 s_a s_b)$$ (5d)

$$= s_a f_a P_2$$

Here we suppose a population of three age groups for simplicity; the same process can be applied to any number of age groups. We begin with population P_0 in only the first age group, a_1, in equation (5a). The next year the population is P_1, which is equal to the second age group, $a_1 s_a$, plus a new first age group, $a_1 s_a f_a$. The next year the population P_2 is given by equation (5c). Then we see in the next year (equation 5d) that the population P_3 is $s_a f_a$ times P_2. This relationship will persist with the population growing at a constant rate of $s_a f_a - 1$ as shown in equation (6).

$$R_g = s_a f_a - 1 = R - 1$$ (6)

Please note that the number in each group grows at the same rate. $s_a f_a$ is equal to R, the net reproductive ratio, and the rate of growth in equilibrium is, therefore, R - 1. If R is greater than '1.0, there will be positive growth; equal to 1.0, there will be no growth; less than 1.0, there will be negative growth or decline.

Migration can be handled by cohort analysis, by adding the in-migrants and subtracting the out-migrants from each appropriate age group. We then get net survival coefficients, which translate each age group of one year into the following age group of the next. Suppose we have an age group i_1 in year 1, that d_i died during the year, that there are m_i in-migrants and e_i out-migrants of that age during the year. The number in age group j in the following year would be given by equation (7).

$$j_2 = i_1 - d_i + m_i - e_i$$ (7)

The net annual survival coefficient s_i is given by equation (8).

$$s_i = \frac{j_2}{i_1} = 1 - \frac{d_i}{i_1} + \frac{m_i}{i_1} - \frac{e_i}{i_1}$$ (8)

The next cohort survival coefficient S_i is given by equation (9), where a_0 is the original cohort of births from which the nonmigrant part of the age group is derived. S_i is then a product of all intervening annual survival coefficients.

$$S_i = \frac{i_1}{a_0} = \frac{b_1}{a_0} \cdot \frac{c_2}{b_1} \cdot \frac{d_3}{c_2} \cdot \cdots \cdot \frac{i_1}{h_{i-1}}$$ (9)

Proof that the average expectation of life, which is the average age of death, is equal to the reciprocal of the birth rate or the death rate in an equilibrium population is as follows: Going back to the notation of Table 3.1 and adopting the convention that age groups are defined at the end of the year, the number of deaths in year 2 of people age 1 at the beginning of the year is $a_1 - b_2$; of people age 2 at the beginning of the year, it is $b_1 - c_2$; and so on. The average age at death, X, is given by equation (10).

$$X = \frac{(a_1 - b_2) + 2(b_1 - c_2) + 3(c_1 - d_2) - \dots + nn_1}{D_2} \tag{10}$$

In equilibrium, $a_1 = a_2, b_1 = b_2, \dots, n_1 = n_2$

$$\text{and} \quad D_2 = a_1 \tag{11}$$

$$P_2 = P_1$$

Equation (10) then reduces to equation (12),

$$X = \frac{a_1 + b_1 + c_1 + \dots + n_1}{a_1} = \frac{P_1}{a_1} = \frac{1}{\dfrac{a_2}{P_2}} = \frac{1}{R_b} \tag{12}$$

that is, the expectation of life is the reciprocal of the birth rate and, because the birth rate equals the death rate, it is also the reciprocal of the death rate.

NOTES

1. I have called this "Reagan's Law," after the famous remark, attributed to ex-Governor Reagan of California, that "When you have seen one redwood, you have seen them all."

2. For example, see Wendell Johnson, *People in Quandaries: The Semantics of Personal Adjustment* (New York: Harper, 1946), or Alfred Korzybski, *Science and Sanity* (4th ed.; Lakeville, Conn.: International Non-Aristotelian Library, 1958).

3. David F. Bartlett, "Natural Units: Are They For Everybody?" *American Journal of Physics*, 42 (Feb. 1974), 148–156.

4. If P is the total population or stock, A the additions, and S the subtractions, and P the absolute addition to stock, in any period of time t,

$$\Delta P = \Delta A - \Delta S \tag{a}$$

This is the bathtub theorem. Dividing through by t we have

$$\frac{\Delta P}{\Delta t} = \frac{\Delta A}{\Delta t} - \frac{\Delta S}{\Delta t} \tag{b}$$

There is no well recognized name for these quantities. We could call $\frac{\Delta P}{\Delta t}$ the speed of growth, $\frac{\Delta A}{\Delta t}$ the speed of addition, and $\frac{\Delta S}{\Delta t}$ the speed of subtraction because these concepts are analogous to velocity. Dividing equation (b) through by P we have

$$\frac{\Delta P}{P \Delta t} = \frac{\Delta A}{P \Delta t} - \frac{\Delta S}{P \Delta t} \tag{c}$$

which we can read as the rate of growth is equal to the rate of addition minus the rate of subtraction. Thus, if the addition rate is four percent per annum and the subtraction rate is three percent per annum, the rate of growth will be one percent per annum.

5. Expressed graphically, we see in Figure 3.1 the functional relation between the birth rate, death rate, and growth rate related to the total population assumed in Table 3.7. The point at which the birth rate and death rate curves intersect, where the death rate overtakes the birth rate, is the equilibrium population at which the growth rate is zero. The growth rate is the vertical distance between the birth rate line and the death

rate line. In Figure 3.2 we see the growth of population itself over time. This follows a very familiar curve, which is called the "Ogive curve," with rapid absolute growth at first, trailing off eventually as the growth rate declines to zero. At the point of zero growth rate, of course, the population continues at a stable level (OK).

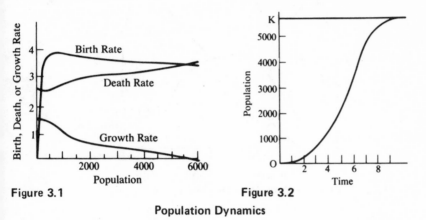

Figure 3.1   **Figure 3.2**

Population Dynamics

6. The first condition is illustrated in Figure 3.3, the second in Figure 3.4. B_1B_2 is the birth rate curve, D_1D_2 the death rate curve. Where they intersect at E gives us the equilibrium population, in each case OF, where the birth and death rates both equal FE.

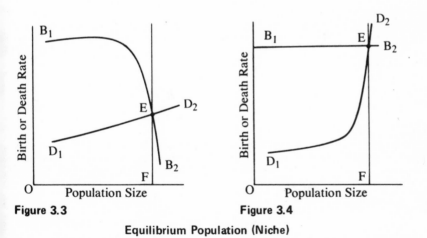

Figure 3.3   **Figure 3.4**

Equilibrium Population (Niche)

7. Figure 3.5 shows the data presented in Table 3.9. The growth per annum is the vertical distance between the production and consumption curves.

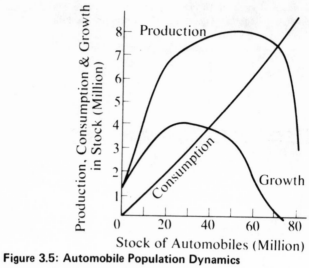

Figure 3.5: Automobile Population Dynamics

Chapter 4

Ecological Dynamics

ECOLOGY AS THE DYNAMICS OF INTERACTING POPULATIONS

Ecology is the study of the interacting populations of different species. The term originated in biology, but the concept is of very general applicability. It is important in social systems, and in some degree, as seen in Chapter 2, even to the interaction of physical systems. Populations interact because each forms part of the environment of all the others with which it is in contact. We will start with a simple model of a closed system in regard to everything except energy, because without a throughput of energy, as we have seen, neither biological nor societal populations will be possible. We will suppose, furthermore, that the populations are relatively uniformly dispersed throughout the field, so that in some degree each interacts with all the others. This might be called the postulate of homogeneous interaction. It is by no means fulfilled in the real world, neither in the biological world with its innumerable subsystems, habitats, and overlapping ecosystems, nor in the geographically structured world of society, but it is a useful simplification as a preliminary model.

Populations interact ecologically in many different ways. All these, however, are mediated through the impact of the size of one population on the birth, death, and growth functions of another; that is, on the relation between births, deaths, or growth of the latter population and its own size. An increase in the wolf population may increase the death rate of rabbits. This will diminish the growth rate of the rabbit population for each value of the rabbit population, and so will lower the equilibrium population of rabbits. The fundamental principle of ecological equilibrium is that there may be some population of rabbits and of wolves at which the interactions are such that the growth rate of each population is zero, each species occupies its full niche, and each is in equilibrium. An ecosystem is in general equilibrium when the population of all the species in it is such that the rate of growth of all populations is zero. At any set of populations that differs from this equilibrium set, some populations will be growing and some will be declining. If the equilibrium is a stable one, those that grow will find that their rate of growth diminishes, so that it falls to zero. Those that decline will find that their rate of decline (or negative rate of growth) diminishes, until it also moves toward zero. When all the rates of growth are zero, we have an equilibrium ecosystem. It is very unlikely that this will ever be reached in nature, but there are places and times in which it is approximated.

TYPES OF ECOLOGICAL INTERACTION

The mechanism of interaction of different populations is extremely complex and we can only outline the simplest cases here. A population A can affect another population B in one of three ways. It may affect it favorably, in which case the relationship is cooperative. That is, a rise in A will increase the equilibrium population of B. Secondly, the relationship may be competitive; that is, an initial rise in A leads to a decline in the equilibrium population of B, a fall in A to a rise in the equilibrium population of B. Thirdly, B may be independent of A; that is, a rise or fall in A may produce no effect on B. Similar relationships can be postulated for the effect that B has on A. In Table 4.1 we put these three possibilities together in a matrix, showing all possible combinations. There are nine cases in all. The case where B affects A favorably but A produces no effect on B seems essentially the same as the case where A affects B favorably and B produces no effect on A. The case where A affects B unfavorably but B does not affect A seems to be

TABLE 4.1
Types of Interaction of Two Species

		A affects B		
		Cooperative (Favorably) $A \uparrow B \uparrow$	Competitive (Unfavorably) $A \uparrow B \downarrow$	Independent (No effect) $A \updownarrow B (0)$
A affects B	Cooperative (Favorably) $B \uparrow A \uparrow$	1	2	(5)
	Competitive (Unfavorably) $B \uparrow A \downarrow$	3	4	(6)
	Independent (No effect) $B \downarrow A(0)$	5	6	7

1 Mutual Cooperation   (A↑ B↑, B↑ A↑)   A helps B, B helps A
2 Parasitism   (A↑ B↓, B↑ A↑)   A hurts B, B helps A
3 Predation   (A↑ B↑, B↑ A↓)   A helps B, B hurts A
4 Mutual Competition   (A↑ B↓, B↑ A↓)   A hurts B, B hurts A
5 Dominant-Cooperative   (A↑ B↑, B↕ A (0))   A helps B, B does not affect A
6 Dominant-Competitive   (A↑ B↓, B↕ A (0))   A hurts B, B does not affect A
7 Mutual Independence   (A↕ B (0), B↕ A (0)) A does not affect B, nor B, A.

the same as the case where B affects A unfavorably but A has no effect on B. We are left, therefore, with seven different cases.

(1) Mutual Cooperation

The first case is that of mutual cooperation, where a rise in population of A expands the niche for B, a rise in the population of B expands the niche for A. There are a very large number of examples of this in nature. Dung beetles and sheep would be a good example: the more sheep, the more droppings, so the more dung beetles; the more dung beetles, the better the droppings are spread, and the more sheep can pasture on a given land. The two life forms (a fungus and an alga) that cooperate to form a lichen is another very good example. Bacteria that help many animals digest their food would be another good example. The great symbiosis between plants and animals in which plants provide both food and oxygen for animals and animals provide carbon dioxide and food (from corpses and droppings) for plants is a celebrated example. We find many examples of this also in social species: the more automobiles, the more gas stations; the more gas stations, the more automobiles.

It might be thought that a situation of this kind would lead to indefinite expansion of each species. This, however, is not necessarily the case, and it is possible (as we see in the appendix to Chapter 4), to have an equilibrium of mutually cooperative species, particularly if the favorable effects that each has on the other tend to diminish with increase in the population of both species. If two species are perfectly cooperative, they act as a single species, and then their population is limited, of course, by the interaction with other species.

(2) Parasitism

The second case is parasitism. This is where A is competitive with B, but B is cooperative with A. Again, there are many examples of this in nature: if A, for instance, causes disease in B through penetrating B's body, or if A lives in B's intestinal tract and eats B's food. This case can give quite a stable equilibrium. A small increase in the ability of the host, for instance, to deal with the parasite will increase both the population of hosts and of parasites, but not by very much.

(3) Predation

The third case is very similar. This is predation, found in innumerable cases in nature, in which A is food for B, in which case the more A the more B, but the more B the fewer A. This is not essentially different from case 2. If we describe it as A eats B, then the more A the less B, the more B the more A, and we are back in case 2. The difference between parasitism and predation is mainly that in parasitism parasite A is smaller than the victim b, whereas under predation the predator A is usually larger than the victim B. The predation-parasitic relationship is surprisingly hard to find in social species. One can find something like it perhaps in civilian-military relationships, whether in terms of population or in terms of product. The more civilians and the richer the civilian sector of the economy, the larger the military tends to be; the larger the military, the less the number of civilians and the more they tend to be impoverished.

(4) Mutual Competition

The fourth situation is that of mutual competition. An increase in A reduces the niche of B, an increase of B reduces the niche of A. This also is very common in the biosphere. Two species, for instance, may share a common food supply, in which case an increase in either one will diminish the niche of the other. Two species may share nesting sites or territories. Wherever indeed two species have some common resource or input there is apt to be mutual competition between them. Biologists have sometimes assumed that mutual competition inevitably leads to the extinction of one species or the other. This is called the "principle of competitive exclusion." It is, however, not strictly true, as we shall prove in the appendix, because there are situations in which competitive species can reach an equilibrium with coexistence. The conditions under which this can happen, however, are rather restricted and any such equilibrium is precarious and is likely to be destroyed if there is change in parameters of the system affecting the relative competitive capacity of the two species. This is a very common situation in social species, where commodities, for instance, almost all compete for the purchases of consumers and factors of production or inputs compete for the purchases of producers. Thus, an increase in population of almost any commodity is likely to decrease the equilibrium population of all the others in greater or lesser degree.

(5) Dominant-Cooperative

The fifth case we call the "dominant-cooperative" case, in which a rise in A raises the niche of B, but in which change in B does not affect A at all. A is then the dominant species. It is not affected by the other, but the size of A now determines the size of the niche of B. The relationship is cooperative, for a rise in A increases B. Examples of this are quite common in nature. A pine forest, for instance, will shelter large numbers of species of birds and insects, perhaps also plants, which would not survive if the pines were not there. On the other hand, these species may not affect the growth, performance, or size of the niche of the pine trees at all. Sometimes there may be a group of dominant species, as, for instance, in the prairie, or the hardwood forest, where there is a variety of trees. Within this group there may be mutually-cooperative and mutually-competitive relationships. For any size and composition of the group, however, there may be many other species for which the dominant group provides a shelter and a habitat, but the size of which does not affect the dominant species. It is not always easy to tell which species is dominant, because we can only detect it when there is substantial variation in the parameters of the system, which does not often take place. The dominant-cooperative relationship has an equilibrium, and can be stable and fairly secure in the sense that changing the parameters of the system will not change it very much.

(6) Dominant-Competitive

The sixth relationship, the dominant-competitive relationship, is where a rise in A will diminish B, but a change in B will not affect A. This situation is probably rare and hard to detect, but it undoubtedly exists. A cactus, for instance, grows under the ponderosa pine forests in the Western mountains, but it declines if the forest gets too thick. However, its decline simply does not affect the trees.

(7) Mutual Independence: The Importance of Isolation

The seventh situation, mutual independence, where neither species affects the other, is not perhaps very interesting, but it should be mentioned for the sake of completeness. It is unlikely to be found in any particular habitat, where everything is likely to affect everything else to some degree. It is found, of course, between isolated habitats. The population of the blue whale, we can be pretty sure, has no affect whatever on the population of mountain goats in Colorado. Mutually independent relationships, however, may have some significance when it comes to examining the effects of isolation upon the course of evolution. If the world were a single ecosystem and everything were in contact with everything else, the possibilities of successful mutation might be much less. When we have isolated ecosystems, the evolutionary processes in them are almost certain to diverge, perhaps because of random factors or perhaps because of differences in the physical environment. There may then be contacts at a later date which would have profound consequences, but which would not be significant if the ecosystems had been in contact in the first place.

This principle is extremely important in social systems, where at least up to the last hundred years very large numbers of human cultures have developed quite independently and hence developed a richness of artifactual species, which almost certainly would not have happened if there had been a single world culture. Indeed one of the dangers of the disappearance of isolation and the development of a single world culture is this destruction of cultural variety, as the stronger species of artifacts simply exterminate weaker ones all over the world. This may have profound consequences for the long-run course of evolution, not only because the diminution of variety and variation diminishes the possible rate of change, but also because it introduces dangers of universal catastrophe rather than local catastrophe. With a number of isolated ecosystems, if irretrievable catastrophe happens to one of them, it does not happen to all, and it is fairly easy for the total system to recover, because the undamaged systems recolonize the damaged ones. Thus, all life was wiped out on Krakatoa when it erupted, but in a few decades the island was completely repopulated, mainly with its original species, though there may of course have been some ecological change, from those surrounding areas which were not damaged. Similarly, in the tenth century the Mayan civilization collapsed without having the slightest effect on either Europe, China, or Japan; they simply knew nothing about it. If, however, we develop a single world civilization and anything goes wrong, everything may go wrong.

ECOLOGICAL EQUILIBRIUM: SHORT RUN

Three kinds of dynamic processes may be distinguished in interacting populations. The first is a process that moves toward some kind of short-run equilibrium. These ecological equilibria are common in nature. Many specific habitats, that is, local ecosystems, exhibit a fair degree of ecological equilibrium. Such may be found in a pond, a swamp, a section of a river, a prairie, a forest, or an estuary. If we take away a certain proportion of one species and let that system alone for a while, and if it has not been disturbed too much, it will tend to return to its original position. Thus, we can often take 20 percent of a given variety of fish out of a pond or we can cut down quite a large proportion of trees in a forest and in a few years the forces of equilibrium will bring back the old populations in much the same quantity they were before. Even human artifacts like cities exhibit ecological equilibrium; Warsaw, destroyed in World War II, has been rebuilt almost exactly like it was before. Underlying mechanisms of interaction may differ from system to system, but where the equations of ecological equilibrium have a solution there is a strong tendency for this solution to be found, and to be reestablished once the system has been disturbed if the disturbance has not been too great. A large disturbance, of course, may push the system over a dynamic watershed and it may never return to its original position. The plowed prairie is probably a good example of this. If left alone, it may return to something approximating its original position, but it will never return to quite the way it was before. A disturbance of equilibrium may change the parameters of the system themselves.

Under certain circumstances the dynamics of the system may lead into a circular path around the equilibrium. Predation cycles of this kind have been noticed in very sparse ecosystems, as in the Arctic in the case, for instance, of the Arctic hare. The more species there are in the ecosystem, however, the less likely do cycles of this kind seem to be. It should be possible to find a mathematical proof of this proposition, but I have to confess I have not yet found it. It is fairly easy to see how such a cycle could happen. If, for instance, the population of wolves were high while the population of rabbits were at the equilibrium level, wolves would decline because of the scarcity of food and the system would pass over into a phase where wolves were still declining, but because of the absence of predators the rabbit population would grow, and as the rabbit population grew the wolf population would grow, then the rabbit population would start to decline while the wolf population was still growing, and we would pass into the first phase where the wolf population was high and declining and the rabbit population was also declining. The more alternative sources of food there are for wolves and for rabbits and the more different kinds of predators there are, the less likely is this cycle to be set up.

These ecological cycles should not be confused with the cyclical equilibria imposed on the earth by the cycle of the solar system, such as the day, the month, and the year. These cycles of sleep, hibernation, tidal response, and so on have been developed in both biological and social systems as a result of successful mutations and adaptations to an essentially external cyclical condition in the solar system. These patterns of equilibrium dynamics then do not constitute evolution, although if they go too far and change the ecological equilibrium, they may be part of a larger evolutionary process.

ECOLOGICAL SUCCESSION

The second type of ecological dynamics is ecological succession in a particular habitat. This is a result of certain irreversible processes in the habitat, which often result from the life cycles of the species themselves, or which may result from irreversible outside or inside inputs or outputs. The filling up of a lake or pond is a good example. A lake, let us say, left by receding glaciers develops its own characteristic ecosystem, which is likely to have a strong geographical structure of species more or less in the form of concentric rings around the shoreline as the lake goes deeper towards the center. The shores will have their own characteristic ecosystems, corresponding to the particular habitat, with reeds, accompanying vegetation, and the accompanying animal life where the shores are shallow or marshy and other forms where they are sandy or rocky. The shallow waters beyond the shoreline may have a fairly distinctive ecosystem and the deeper waters at the center of the lake still another. The habitats may be layered by depth as well as by distance from the shore. In the course of time the lake gradually fills in, partly because of solid matter, sand, gravel, and mud brought in by the stream or streams that feed it, which is in excess of what the outlet carries out (the bathtub theorem again), and partly because the plant life captures carbon from the air and transforms it into organic substances, which fall to the bottom of the lake and accumulate faster than they decay. In the course of time, therefore, the lake becomes shallower and shrinks in size. The successive rings of habitat shrink toward the center. The lake eventually becomes a swamp and the swamp may become solid ground and be covered with forest.

This process of ecological succession proceeds to a habitat and an eco-system that seem reasonably stable, that is, where the potential of ecological succession has been exhausted. We then say it has reached a "climactic" ecosystem, which may persist in almost unchanged equilibrium for quite a long time.

EVOLUTIONARY DISEQUILIBRIUM

Even a climactic ecosystem will be disturbed eventually by the third dynamic—the larger, slower changes of the overall evolutionary process—genetic mutation, which creates new species, climatic change, mountain building, and so on. It is these larger changes that constitute the basic dynamics ·of biological evolution, and there are parallels to this also in the evolution of society. These larger changes, however, operate through ecologi-cal succession by disturbing an old climactic ecosystem and creating poten-tial, therefore, for further ecological succession. Ecological succession in turn operates through the dynamics of ecological equilibrium. This in turn oper-ates in the dynamics by which each population affects the birth and death rates of all others.

Some cyclical or irregular events may profoundly affect the ultimate characteristics of an ecosystem. Forests, for instance, even in the absence of the human race are subject to forest fires set by lightning and these in turn create systems of ecological succession—the fire weeds just after the fire, the bushes which replace this, the young trees which replace them, and finally the climactic or seemingly climactic forest. In the absence of occasional forest fires, however, the climax may be different. As we are beginning to discover from having Smokey the Bear control forest fires all too well, the climactic ecosystem of the forest without fires is different from one that has an occasional fire. Similarly, if we want a pine forest in the southern states, we must cut it down every so often, otherwise the little pines cannot grow in the shadow of the big ones, and when the big ones mature and die only the oaks and hickories that can grow under their shadow will mature and eventually replace the pine forest that sheltered them. On a larger scale, also, there is little doubt that occasional catastrophes have had a profound effect on the general course of evolution.

Another fascinating example of cyclical succession is that of the forest on the edge of the Arctic, where the ability of the trees to flourish depends on the depth of the permafrost. The trees advance across the tundra. Then as they grow, they shade the ground from the sun, the permafrost rises and eventually kills the roots, the trees die, the tundra returns, the permafrost is lowered by the additional absorption of sunshine, and the trees return again.

The larger evolutionary changes (as seen more clearly in the next chapter) consist mainly, though not exclusively, of changes in the "genosphere," that is, the total genetic structure of the biosphere. Ecological interaction is the dominant process in the selection of elements in the genosphere. It probably contributes very little toward mutational changes that introduce new elements and new species into the ecosystem.

THE COMPLEXITY OF HABITATS

The above model is an extremely simplified one and it must never be mistaken for the enormously complex reality of either biological or social ecosystems. The earth is divided into a large number of "habitats," that is, areas within which the distribution of species is moderately uniform and in which the assumption made in the first approximation model—that all populations interact with all others—is not hopelessly inadequate. The boundaries between these ecosystems, however, are not sharp. There is always a fuzzy area between them where species coexist because of mutual migration that might not be able to coexist in the heart of the habitat. This is something we have not included in our simple model, but it is very important in the diffusion of species geographically and in the constant upsetting of old ecological equilibria.

Furthermore, even within what we think of as a single ecosystem, like a pond or pine forest, there are innumerable microsystems such as the microecosystem that lies under a stone, a hole in a tree, or even in a rain puddle. There are whole ecosystems in the bowels and stomachs of animals; in piles of dung there may be an intense interaction among species of minute creatures. The interaction with the larger environment may be largely independent of these intense internal reactions, but the biosphere like the sociosphere is not a system of uniform interaction of populations. It is divided into ecological "nations," "states," "counties," "townships," each of which can be considered to some extent a system of its own interacting with the others. A description of the hierarchy of systems is one of the most difficult problems in all interactional theory and we shall find it cropping up again in, for instance, a discussion of the economy or the international system.

FOOD CHAINS AND RECYCLING

The problem of the hierarchy of systems also crops up in problems such as the "food chains," which represent the hierarchy of inputs and outputs. Every living organism and every social organization has a "throughput" of both energy and materials. In a totally closed system the input of one part, such as an organism, has to be the output of other parts. A developed economy, as we can see, involves a linear movement from fossil fuels and ores to pollution and dumps, but this is something that obviously cannot go on for very long. The biosphere relies on a throughput of energy from the sun to drive it and to move its materials around. It also has a throughput of materials from eroding rocks, soil formation, the formation of deltas, and so on, which are only recycled over very long periods, for instance, through mountain building. For the most part, however, the biosphere recycles its materials through all the organisms that comprise it. The nitrogen cycle is, of course, the most famous of these recycling processes. The nitrogen-fixing bacteria are able to take nitrogen from the great reservoir of the atmosphere and transform it into compounds, which can be utilized by plants, then animals eat the plants, both plants and animals eventually die, and other bacteria decompose them and release nitrogen again into the atmosphere. The carbon dioxide-oxygen cycle is another striking phenomenon. Plants in sunlight absorb carbon dioxide from the atmosphere and turn the carbon into complex organic compounds, which provide the substance of the plant and release oxygen into the atmosphere. Animals take in the oxygen from the atmosphere through breathing, use it to burn carbon in the body, so heating it and providing energy, and release carbon dioxide to the atmosphere through exhaling. Plants and animals are thus highly symbiotic and coexist in a relationship of mutual cooperation.

An important proposition that emerges from the study of these recycling processes is that, if they are to be reasonably secure and not subject to breakdown, there must at some point be substantial reservoirs of whatever it is that is recycled. Thus, the atmosphere is a great reservoir of nitrogen, oxygen, and carbon dioxide, many orders of magnitude larger than the very small amounts of these substances recycled through the biosphere. Without a reservoir of some kind the recycling process would be constantly subject to interruption. A breakdown at any one point would stop the whole cycle. If there are reservoirs along the way, then the cycle can continue from one reservoir to another even though it is interrupted at some point. This principle is important in economic life as well as in the biosphere.

The "food chain" is another aspect of the complex hierarchical relationship of species, which is hard to fit into the simple model of the first part of this chapter. Virtually everything eats smaller species and is eaten in turn by larger species, though sometimes this order is reversed, as in the case of parasites and scavengers. When something is eaten, it dies (if it is not dead already), so that eating is a very important source of death for the eaten. Nevertheless, as we have seen, the predator-prey relationship is often very stable and is symbiotic even if it is not mutually cooperative. The disappearance of a predator can sometimes lead to a population explosion of the prey with subsequent denuding of the prey's foodstuffs, sometimes even to the point of extinction of the prey. In every predator-prey relationship there is a problem of "sustainable yield" of the prey. If a predator increases too much and is too important a source of death, death rates in the prey will rise above the birth rate and the population will shrink. As it shrinks, the predator will find it harder and harder to find the prey, and its yields to the predator will diminish.

We have seen how in simple cases predation can create cycles. These cycles could proceed to the extinction of the prey and the predator. These phenomena are rare, however, because most food chains are not linear, but are enormous branching networks. It is a very rare species that lives on a single food, because this is a precarious condition that can easily lead to extinction. Omnivorousness, unquestionably, has survival value. The extraordinary number, however, of highly specialized food chains and reproductive dependencies suggests that in cracks of the system fairly stable specializations can develop in which organisms become completely dependent on each other, as in the case, for instance, of certain plants and insects; they almost have to be regarded as a single organism and a single population from the point of view of the total ecosystem. It is a real question, indeed, as to whether the biological concept of a species, as defined by a gene pool and the ability to mate, is necessarily the most significant from the point of view of ecological interaction.

On the whole the numbers and the size of the individual in a species are related, although somewhat loosely, to its position in the food chain. Species that "eat" inorganic substances and transform them into organic matter, like the plants and some bacteria, are both numerous and have a very large range of sizes from the microscopic to the redwoods. Herbivores that live on plants are more rare; carnivores that live on herbivores are more rare still. Exactly how the biomass is distributed among bacteria, plants, herbivores, and carnivores, I do not know. Weight, of course, is not necessarily an adequate indicator of biological mass. A mouse has a lot more biological activity than a huge, inert, slow-growing redwood. This problem is of some significance for the human race, which probably has a wider variety of diet than any other living creature and can be herbivorous, carnivorous, or a mixture of the two. Vegetarian societies can unquestionably support a larger population on a given area than meat-eating societies, though whether this is desirable, of course, is quite another matter.

WEAKNESSES OF ECOLOGICAL MODELS

The weakness of purely ecological models is that they treat the individuals of a population as if they were abstract homogeneous units. At one level of abstraction this is entirely legitimate. We must, however, go beyond it if we are to get a clearer picture of the vast dynamic process of evolution. Equilibrium models of any kind are intellectual constructs designed to help our imperfect minds achieve images of complex dynamic systems. Equilibrium in a strict sense is unknown in the real world, which is in constant flux, even though it is only the existence of temporary quasi-equilibria that enable us to perceive objects at all. It is a curious paradox that our perceptions of the world depend on the imperfections of our perceptive apparatus. If our perceptions were acute enough, we would perceive everything disintegrating in a great blur before our eyes—organisms aging, mountains eroding and rising—and we would be hard put to perceive any pattern in it. The equilibrium concept may be part of the pattern we impose on the world, but it is very important to us precisely because in many ways it is necessary for our perception. Nevertheless, we must always realize that it is always an imperfect representation. The world does not consist of homogeneous interacting species. It consists of individuals, all of whom are in some sense different. The dynamic pattern is one in which the nature of the population of the species is constantly changing, that is, those aspects of it that do not constitute a strict definition. Thus, the way in which a change in genetic structure works its way through a population by the competition of individuals within the population is something completely neglected in this chapter. It is of great relevance to the evolutionary process. These are questions, however, that we must take up later.

Appendix to Chapter 4:
THE THEORY OF ECOLOGICAL INTERACTION

The ecological relationships of two populations can be shown very conveniently by graphical analysis. We can start with the predation relationship of, say, rabbits and wolves. In Figure 4A.1 the solid lines show the functions relating population to birth and death rates for, let us say, rabbits. At a given population of wolves, there is an equilibrium at E with a rabbit population of OF. Now let us suppose a given increase, let us say a ten percent increase, in the population of wolves in that particular ecosystem. The death curve is likely to rise from $D_1 D_3$ to $D_1' D_3'$. The net birth curve may fall slightly, if the rabbits are too hard pressed to produce proper litters or if infant mortality rises, say, to $B_1 B_3'$. There is a new equilibrium at the intersection of the two dotted curves at E', with a lower equilibrium population at OF'.

In this particular case in the new equilibrium the birth and death rates are somewhat lower than they were in the old, so that the increase in the number of wolves may actually result in their getting fewer rabbits, but this, of course, all depends on the shape of the curves and the nature of the functions involved. If, for instance, as a result of the increase in wolves, rabbits spend more time in their burrows looking after their young, the birth curve might actually rise, in which case, even though there will still be a reduction in the population of rabbits, the birth and death rates might actually increase. Similarly, we could express the impact of an increase in the rabbit population on the birth and death functions of wolves. This means that, for each value of the rabbit population, there will be an equilibrium population of wolves, all other elements in the environment of course assumed equal. On the whole, the larger the population of rabbits, the larger may we expect the equilibrium population of wolves to be.

In Figure 4A.2 we measure the number of rabbits horizontally and the number of wolves vertically. We can postulate a wolf curve WW', which shows

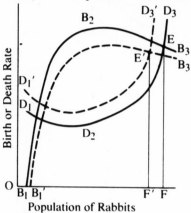

Figure 4A.1: Shift in Equilibrium Population

the equilibrium population of wolves for every actual population of rabbits. Similarly, we can postulate a rabbit curve RR' showing the equilibrium population of rabbits for each actual population of wolves. These curves intersect at E at the general equilibrium of the two species. At a population of rabbits equal to OF, the equilibrium population of wolves will be equal to FE; at a population of wolves equal to FE, the equilibrium population of rabbits will be OF. The rabbit curve RR' shows all those combinations of populations in which the rate of growth of the rabbit population is zero. We could similarly postulate curves R_{-1}, R_{-2}, at which the rate of growth of the rabbit population would be minus 1 percent, minus 2 percent, and the curves R_1, R_2, at which the rate of growth would be plus 1 percent, plus 2 percent.

Similarly, the curve WW' shows all those combinations of the two populations where the rate of growth of the wolf population is zero. Curves above this, W_{-1}, W_{-2}, show positions where there are so few rabbits and so many wolves that the wolf population will decline; W_1, W_2 show combinations where the wolf population will increase. If we start with a point such as A, in the next period of time the wolf population will increase, the rabbit population will diminish, and the next position is point A_1. Successive points are shown by the arrowheads showing the dynamic path of the two populations from the point A. Where this path crosses the wolf line WW', the wolf population is no longer growing and is stationary; the path, therefore, is horizontal, because the population of rabbits is still declining. Beyond the

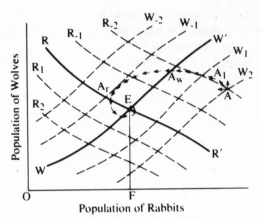

Figure 4A.2: Equilibrium of Predation or Parasitism

point A_w, the wolf population is declining as well as the rabbit population, so the line turns in a southwesterly direction. By the time it crosses the rabbit line at A_r, it is vertical, because the rabbit population is now constant and the wolf population is still declining. In this case, as we can see, the dynamic path may make a spiral approaching the equilibrium at E. It is possible (as seen previously) that under some circumstances this spiral might turn into a circular path around the equilibrium. This is somewhat similar to a phenomenon in price theory known as the "cobweb theorem."[1] For instance, high production of a commodity one year will lead to a low price, this will lead to low production the next year and a high price, which will lead to high production the following year and a low price, and so on.

Suppose now there is some change in the parameters of the system. What happens to the equilibrium population? This is the question of the "security" or "precariousness" of the equilibrium position. This is not the same concept as stability. An equilibrium is stable if a small disturbance sets up a dynamic system, which moves it back to the old equilibrium position. An equilibrium is secure if a change in parameters does not change the equilibrium point very much; it is precarious if a change in parameters shifts the equilibrium position sharply. In Figure 4A.3 the curves WW' and RR' are the same as in Figure 4A.2. Now let us suppose that there is some kind of improvement in the position of the rabbit population. This could take place as a result of a genetic mutation, the introduction of some other species into the system in the form of an improved food supply, a change in the climate, or some other basic change. The definition of an "improvement" is that for each population of wolves, the population of rabbits is larger than before, that is, the rabbit curve RR' moves to the dotted line $R_1 R_1'$. Equilibrium moves from the point E to the point E_1, at which not only are there more rabbits but there are also more wolves. This illustrates nicely a very fundamental principle of ecology, formulated by Garrett Hardin, that you cannot do one thing. A worsening of the rabbit situation would similarly lead to a situation in which there were fewer rabbits and fewer wolves. On the other hand, if the wolf situation improves (again, through genetic mutation, increased food supply, diminished competitors, the disappearance of a disease, or something), then for each population of rabbits the equilibrium population of wolves will be larger, and the wolf line will move to the dotted line W_1W_1'; equilibrium will move to E_2, the rabbit line assumed stationary at RR'. In this case there would be fewer rabbits and more wolves, a conclusion that is not wholly surprising. Suppose, now, there is an improvement in both species. The new lines are the dotted lines W_1W_1' and R_1R_1', the new equilibrium is at E_3, where there are more wolves but the same number of rabbits. This perhaps illustrates the capacity of the analysis of ecological systems to produce at least mild surprises, because without the analysis one would not have expected this result.

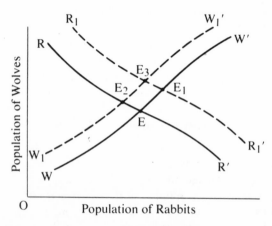

Figure 4A.3: Change in Parameters under Predation

The magnitude of the changes depends on the slopes of the curves. Economists will want to call this elasticity, but there is little point in defining this in the clumsy way that economists do. I prefer to use the term "responsiveness" or, perhaps more accurately, "equilibrium responsiveness." This could be defined as the increase in the equilibrium population of wolves that would result from a unit increase in the rabbit population. If this is low, an increase in rabbit population will not affect the wolf population very much and the curve WW_1 will be flat. An improvement in the condition of rabbits then will increase the rabbit population but will not increase the wolf population very much. If the rabbit population is unresponsive, the curve RR' will be steep; an increase in the wolf population will not change the rabbit population very much. Under these circumstances an improvement in the wolf situation will increase the population of wolves, but will not much affect the population of rabbits. The case which we have been studying applies to parasitism just as well as it does to predation (p. 79).

Figure 4A.4 now shows the case of mutual competition (case 4 of Table 4.1). I use lions and tigers, feeding on the same food supply, as an illustration. In Figure 4A.4 we measure the number of lions along the horizontal axis and the number of tigers along the vertical axis. If there were no lions, we suppose

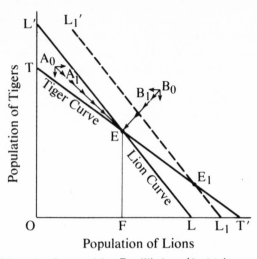

Figure 4A.4: Mutually Competitive Equilibrium (Stable)

that there would be OT tigers; as the number of lions increases, the equilibrium population of tigers diminishes from T to T', at which the number of lions is so large that there are no tigers at all. Similarly, if there are no tigers, there will be OL lions; as the number of tigers increases, the number of lions decreases following the line LL' until when there are OL' tigers, lions become extinct. There is, however, a position of equilibrium in this case at E. In this it is a stable equilibrium. If we follow the dynamic paths starting from the point A_0, we see that lions will increase as the point is below the lion curve, tigers will diminish as the point is above the tiger curve, and there will be a movement from A_0 to A_1 and a subsequent movement into equilibrium at E. Similarly, we can show that from any other part of the diagram, the dynamic process will eventually bring us to E, for instance, from B_0. Circular solutions are extremely unlikely in this case.

Stable equilibrium is clearly possible in this case, but the equilibrium is insecure in the sense that a relatively slight improvement or worsening of the competitive position of one species relative to the other could easily lead to extinction. Suppose in Figure 4A.4 there is an improvement in the competitive position of the lion, meaning that, for each population of tigers, there is a larger equilibrium population of lions than before. A relatively small movement, such as from LL' to the dotted line $L_1 L_1'$ will move the equilibrium a long way down the tiger curve to E_1. If the movement proceeds a little further, E_1 will coincide with T' and tigers will become extinct. The tendency for two mutually competitive species to drive one or the other to extinction could be so strong that it is even postulated as the "principle of competitive exclusion" by biologists. But it is only a tendency, not a universal principle, and many cases of equilibrium of two competitive species are known. If the species are somewhat similar, there is a good reason to suppose that change in the general environment that will benefit one will also benefit the other, which would move the position of equilibrium out with larger populations of each species, but would not tend to destroy the equilibrium if each species benefited from the change in a roughly equal manner.

The precariousness of the mutually competitive equilibrium, however, is illustrated by the fact that, if we switch the lion and tiger curves in Figure 4A.4, the equilibrium becomes unstable, as shown in Figure 4A.5. From a point such as A_0, tigers will increase toward the tiger curve, lions will

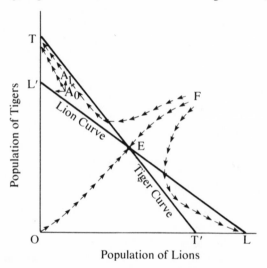

Figure 4A.5: Mutually Competitive Equilibrium (Unstable)

diminish toward the lion curve, and populations will move from A_0 to A_1 and will continue along the line to the point T, where lions become extinct. There is a somewhat precarious boundary OEF along which the populations will either both grow along OE or both decline along FE until the equilibrium at E is reached, but any divergence from this line on the upper side will end up at the point T, and on the lower side will end up at the point L, as shown by the arrows. These kinds of unstable equilibrium systems may be of considerable importance in the evolutionary pattern, as sometimes a quite chance disturbance when close to the line of unstable equilibrium will push the whole system toward one extreme or the other. This is one reason why ecological dynamics, that is, evolution, has a good deal of unpredictability in it.

Mutual cooperation (case 1 of Table 4.1) is illustrated in Figure 4A.6. This, again, is by no means uncommon. Symbiosis, in which two species mutually assist each other, as pointed out first by Kropotkin and later in more detail by Clyde Allee and his followers, is an almost universal aspect of the biosphere, and indeed is very important in giving survival value to the organisms that participate in the symbiotic syndrome.[2] A striking example is

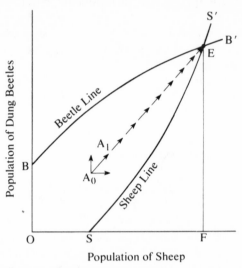

Figure 4A.6: Equilibrium of Mutual Cooperation

the dung beetle and sheep. The dung beetle scatters the manure of ruminants and hence improves the yield of grass. Ruminants, of course, provide the manure for the dung beetle to live on. This is a case of some practical importance, as there were originally no dung beetles in Australia. They were introduced to assist with sheep and cattle raising. If there were no sheep, there might still be some dung beetles, say OB, but as the sheep population increases, the equilibrium population of dung beetles will also increase following the beetle line BB'. If there are no dung beetles, there will still be OS sheep, but after the point S, an increase in the number of dung beetles increases the equilibrium population of sheep following the sheep line SS'. If the two lines intersect at E, there will be an equilibrium with OF sheep and FE beetles. It is easy to see that this is a stable equilibrium. From a point such as A_0, beetles will increase toward the beetle line, sheep will increase toward the sheep line, and there will be movement to A_1, continuing on toward E following the arrows. From any other part of the diagram, likewise, the dynamic path will take us to E. In this case it is extremely unlikely that the position of the lines will be reversed, in which case the

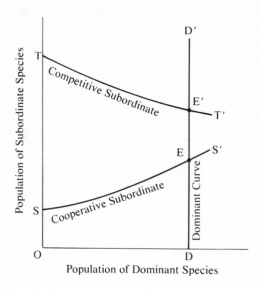

Figure 4A.7: Equilibrium of Dominant Species

equilibrium will become unstable. We are almost certain to start the lines at points like B or S, where there is already an equilibrium population of one even in the absence of the other.

Unless the two lines converge to cross each other, there will not be an equilibrium. If they are parallel, the populations will increase indefinitely. Other factors in the environment, however, are bound to lessen the benefits of cooperation in large populations. It is highly probable that the lines will bend toward each other and eventually intersect. The equilibrium, however, is fairly secure. A worsening of the condition of one of the species, as reflected, for instance, in a shift of the beetle line downwards or the sheep line to the left, will move the position of equilibrium to a somewhat smaller population for both species, but is unlikely to eliminate either. This is in sharp contrast to the insecurity of the equilibrium under mutual competition, where, as we have seen, small changes in the parameters may lead to the extinction of one or the other of the competing species.

Another case is where one of the species is independent of the other, in which case its equilibrium population line will be perpendicular to its own axis (cases 5 and 6 of Table 4.1). In this case the independent species may be said to be "dominant" and the other said to be "subordinate." This is shown in Figure 4A.7. Here we measure the population of the dominant species on the horizontal axis and of the subordinate species on the vertical axis. The equilibrium population line of the dominant species is DD' with a population OD, which is independent of the population of the subordinate species. The subordinate species may be cooperative with the dominant with an equilibrium line such as SS′ (case 5, Table 4.1); the equilibrium position is E and its population is DE. The dominant may even be competitive with the subordinate (case 6, Table 4.1); its equilibrium curve may be something like TT′ and still have an equilibrium at E′. Changes in the parameters of the other species, whether for improvement or worsening in its position, will shift the position of equilibrium up and down the line DD′, but will not change the population of the dominant species.

A forest is often a good example of this phenomenon. A pine forest, for instance, will harbor a large number of species of birds, animals, and insects that depend on it, but upon which it does not depend. The whole ecosystem of a particular area depends very much on the kind of forest that grows on it, the trees being the dominant species and most of the others being subordinate. It is an interesting question as to how far the human race is dominant in the world ecosystem, simply because of its enormous capacity for producing artifacts and for generating a fantastic variety of food supplies. The extinction of many species has followed the expansion of human population, where the human race is competitive with the species. In many cases, as the human population has grown, the population of the competitive species has moved down its equilibrium curve to the point of extinction.

The extraordinary expansion of the human race in the last 10,000 years especially is mainly a result of the fact that human beings are virtually the only species that is cooperative with their own artifacts over a very large range of population. There are a few species that are cooperative with their artifacts, such as ants, termites, and birds with their nests, beavers with their dams, and so on. But most species produce only excrement as an artifact, with which they are mainly competitive. Those nonhuman species that produce artifacts, such as beavers and termites, are only able to modify a very small portion of the environment, such as swampy streams or tropical savanna, although they certainly do modify the environment in their own favor. The human race, however, is able to produce such a fantastic range of artifacts that it can survive in all climates, including at the poles, at the bottom of the oceans, and on the moon. The ecological interaction between the human race and its artifacts, therefore, looks like Figure 4A.8. Here we measure the population of humans horizontally and the population of artifacts (this should be some index of the general stock of human artifacts) vertically. OA is the artifacts curve, showing that the more humans, of course, the more artifacts. If increase in population increases division of labor and produces greater specialization and productivity, this may even be curved upwards over a considerable range, that is, the slope of the artifacts curve will increase, for a while at least, with an increase in human population. An increase in a larger human population produces greater increase in artifacts than an increase in a smaller population.

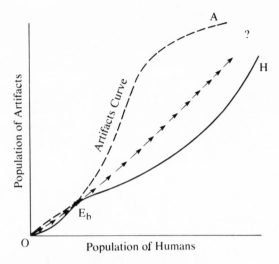

Figure 4A.8: Ecology of Humans and Their Artifacts

I have drawn the curve to make the human curve (OH) bend toward the artifacts curve, representing the diminished efficiency of artifacts in increasing the human population for a while, so touching the artifacts curve at E_b. This illustrates the unstable, one-sided equilibrium of the paleolithic, which does seem to have been a fairly stable population of both humans and artifacts for a considerable period. With the development of agriculture, however, and the coming of the neolithic, the human race breaks out of this equilibrium, following the arrows, with a continued increase of both human population and the stock of human artifacts. At some point the two curves must bend over, converge, and intersect at the ultimate carrying capacity of the earth. If the wild dreamers of Princeton are to be believed,[3] humans and their artifacts may even expand almost indefinitely into outer space. On the earth, however, there must be a limit and at some large enough population the OA curve and the OH curve bend toward each other and intersect. Up to now, however, they do not seem to have done so. There is a grim possibility that they have intersected but we have not noticed, and have simply overshot the equilibrium and will have to return painfully toward it. This is a theme we shall return to later.

We have so far discussed ecological equilibrium and dynamics in terms only of two populations. Virtually all ecosystems involve the interaction of large numbers of species running into hundreds, thousands, even tens of thousands. The general principle, however, remains the same. If the equilibrium population of each species can be written as a function of the actual population of all the others, each species may have an equation in n variables where n is the number of species. There will be n of these equations, and by a famous theorem in algebra a solution is possible, though it is not necessarily possible in terms of real numbers.

If the equations do not have a solution in terms of real numbers for each of the n species, then presumably those species that do not have equilibrium positions will decline until they become extinct. When a species becomes extinct all the equations drop it as a variable and its equation is also dropped and a new equilibrium is sought.

If $x_1, x_2, \ldots, x_n$ are the populations of n species in an ecosystem, and $x_{1e}, x_{2e}, \ldots, x_{ne}$ are the equilibrium values of these populations at which births equal deaths, then we can write:

$$x_{1e} = f_1(x_2, x_3, \ldots, x_n)$$
$$x_{2e} = f_2(x_1, x_3, \ldots, x_n) \tag{1}$$
$$\cdots\cdots\cdots\cdots\cdots\cdots\cdots$$
$$x_{ne} = f_n(x_1, x_2, \ldots, x_{n-1})$$

That is, the equilibrium value of the population of each species is a function of the actual populations of all the others. In general equilibrium,

$$x_{1e} = x_1 \tag{2}$$
$$x_{2e} = x_2$$
$$\cdots\cdots\cdots$$
$$x_{ne} = x_n$$

equations (1) and (2) give us 2n equations to solve 2n unknowns. In the two-species case treated graphically, the algebraic solution is:

$x_{1e} = f_1(x_2)$ (The equilibrium curve of species 1)

$x_{2e} = f_1(x_1)$ (The equilibrium curve of species 2)

$x_{1e} = x_1$

$x_{2e} = x_2$ (The condition of intersection of the curves).

NOTES

1. Kenneth E. Boulding, *Economic Analysis* (4th ed.; New York: Harper and Row, 1966), Vol. I, 229.

2. Peter Kropotkin, *Mutual Aid: A Factor in Evolution* (New York: Doubleday, 1902); and W. Clyde Allee, et al., *Principles of Animal Ecology* (Philadelphia: Saunders, 1949).

3. See Gerard O'Neill, "Testimony," *Co-Evolutionary Quarterly*, No. 7 (Fall 1975), 10-19, for a popular exposition. O'Neill is Professor of Astronomy at Princeton.

Chapter 5

Biological Evolution

THE GENOSPHERE AND THE PHENOSPHERE

Biological evolution is a vast play, performed on the stage of the surface of the earth, in a few inches of soil below the surface, in a few thousand feet of atmosphere above it, and in the water, lakes, rivers, and oceans that cover about two thirds of it. It is a play that has been going on for at least two billion years, with an accelerating tempo. On the time scale of an evening at the theater, the human race has just come onto the stage in the last half second. The great biologist, G. Evelyn Hutchinson, has written a beautiful book called *The Ecological Theater and the Evolutionary Play.*[1] I am not sure the metaphor is wholly a good one. It is this thin skin of the earth that is the theater. Whether there is an audience apart from ourselves, we are not certain. Ecological interaction is part of the subplots. It is a highly multimedia production and there are innumerable subplots going on in different corners of the vast stage.

Ecological interaction also is a play. It implies the working out of some potential, which is implicit in the initial statement of the situation, and it moves toward some kind of realization of this potential. Just as Hamlet moves from the potential of the first act to the dreadful denouement of the finale, ecosystems move from their initial potential toward their final equilibrium. Evolution is the great drama that unites all these subplots in a huge process of increasing complexity, moving toward a denouement hidden from us. We do not even know whether we are the first act or the last. That there is "one far off, divine event towards which the whole creation moves," as Tennyson said in "In Memoriam," or an Omega point of de Chardin (p. 46), we may suspect, but we do not know what it is. What we do have is a garbled record from which we derive a few reasonable and plausible images of the past. We piece together these images from the chaotic ruins of the great library of the rocks, distorted by the fact that the durable is all that survives.

[99]

Nevertheless, some kind of pattern, some kind of sense is created in our minds.

Biological evolution is a pattern in space and time on the earth's skin. It is the whole history over time and space of the biosphere. It consists essentially of the interaction of two processes, or rather immensely complex sets of processes, one involving the change through time of the "genosphere," the other involving the change through time of the "phenosphere." These terms are not perhaps common currency, but they are badly needed.

The genosphere is the sphere of genetic material as it spreads over the earth's skin in the form of eggs, sperm, and the genetic components of cells. It consists essentially of information in the form of know-how. It is coded, as we now know, in extremely complex, spiral molecules of the type of DNA, but these instruction books almost certainly have to be in some kind of structural setting (such as an egg) before the instructions can be carried out. This also is an essential part of the genosphere. The genosphere is realized most perfectly in fertilized eggs in the case of sexually reproduced species, though it is also present in the chromosomes of asexual species. It changes continually as time goes on, and has an irreversible, two billion-year history.

The phenosphere is the sphere of all the actual living organisms on the earth's skin that exist at a moment of time. It is the vast, variegated host of viruses, bacteria, plants, animals, and humans that populate this remarkably productive surface. It too changes continually as time goes on, with populations rising and falling, new species arising, and old species becoming extinct. It too has a two billion-year irreversible history.

EVOLUTION'S 4 Rs AND AN S: REPLICATION, RECOMBINATION, RECONSTITUTION, REALIZATION, AND SELECTION

For the sake of metaphor and rhetorical effect, I have sometimes said that there are four Rs and an S of evolution. Three of these pertain to the dynamics of the genosphere: *replication, recombination, and reconstitution* (mutation). The fourth, which I have called *realization,* more respectably known as epigenesis, is the process that links the genosphere and the phenosphere in the life history of the individual living organism. The S is *selection,* the process by which ecological interaction continually creates and destroys niches.

Replication is the extraordinary process by which a DNA molecule is able to create an exact copy of itself out of the surrounding materials. DNA has been aptly described as the first three-dimensional Xerox machine. It is essentially a linear pattern, an immensely long carbon chain with attached amino acid radicals, rolled into a double spiral, no doubt for convenience, as a long manuscript was once rolled into a scroll. (It is only the human race that seems to have invented the codex or book.) As I visualize the mechanism, each particular structure in the DNA molecule has the power of attracting a similar structure from its material environment. These structures form themselves, as it were, into a mirror image of the original molecule, which then splits off and repeats the process to form an exact copy of the original molecule. The analogy to printing or photocopying is very exact. An improbable structure containing information, for instance a printed page, is imposed as a mirror image on the negative. This in turn imposes its structure on a blank page and reproduces exactly the structure of the original document. This permits the multiplication of information structures of the same kind to an indefinite extent as long as the material environments permit it. How the first DNA molecule ever came to be is, of course, a profound mystery. Once it existed, however, it could be copied indefinitely by processes of replication.

Replication is important not only in the spread of genetic information, but also in the realization process by which a fertilized egg becomes a chicken or whatever phenotype it is, of which it treasures the blueprint. Realization or epigenesis is a process that depends fundamentally on cell division, cell differentiation, and cell rearrangements. In cell division, the whole genetic structure replicates itself so that each cell as it divides normally produces two cells, each containing the whole genetic structure of the organism.

DNA is the foundation of the *gene,* the basic atom of genetic information, the individual word of the instructional language for life. Aggregations of genes form the long chromosomes, which are the sentences, paragraphs, and chapters of these instructions. An aggregation of chromosomes constitutes the genome, which is the total genetic information in the cell or fertilized egg capable of producing the phenotype. The genome is the whole book of instructions.

Recombination is the process by which chromosomes and genomes are continually rearranged out of existing genes or genetic atoms. Just what the gene is, however, or even whether it is really atomic in the sense of operating as a constantly uniform unit, is still a matter of dispute. At any rate, there are building blocks of some kind that build up the larger structures. It is the total book of instructions, that is, the genome, which is significant, however, from the point of view of realization and the growth and life history of the organism.

There are a number of processes by which the sentences, pages, and chapters of this book of instructions may be rearranged and recombined. In bacteria, there can be direct injection of genetic structure from one bacterium to another.[2] It is very doubtful whether this takes place in more complex forms. There are, however, processes by which chromosomes break into pieces and the pieces are rearranged to form different chromosomes even within the cell. The most important source of recombination of genetic material, however, is in sexual reproduction. Reproduction perhaps can be nominated as the fifth R of evolution. It is not the same thing as replication, except perhaps in the case of asexual reproduction when a single-celled amoeba splits into two and each of the two successor organisms is a virtual replica, in genetic structure and as an ultimate genotype after it has grown, of the original cell. In sexual reproduction, however, the offspring of two parents is not a replica of either.

A FIFTH "R": REPRODUCTION

The obvious resemblances of children and parents have produced a folk image of reproduction. Probably as soon as the human race began to think about anything, it conceived of children as in some sense a mixture of the qualities of the parents, though not all societies have thought in this way. In the last hundred years the development of the science of genetics has enormously increased our knowledge of these processes. Our present image is that in the process of fertilization of the female egg by a male sperm, half the chromosomes of the female, selected more or less at random, are combined with half the chromosomes of the male, selected also pretty much at random, to form the complete genome of the new organism, that is, the offspring. The offspring, therefore, is not a mixture of all the qualities of the parents, but only carries half of each parent's genetic structure, selected pretty much at random. This is a very different picture from the folk image of the simple mixture of the "bloods" of the two parents. It means, for instance, that it would be theoretically possible to have two children of the same two parents genetically unrelated if each got a different half of the chromosomes from each parent. This, of course, is very unlikely, but not impossible. It has about the same probability as that of dealing two completely different decks of cards by combining two halves of two well reshuffled packs. The model also implies that outside of the crossing of chromosomes, nobody has more than forty-eight ancestors, one for each chromosome of the human genome.

There are still some pretty tricky problems involved in a model of sexual recombination. The forty-eight chromosomes of each individual human may be compared to a pack of marked cards. In sexual recombination, the father deals twenty-four of his forty-eight cards and the mother deals twenty-four of her forty-eight, and the child picks up what has been dealt. If this is done with cards, it would be extremely unlikely that the child would hold a complete pack, for many cards will have been lost in the transfer and many cards in the child's pack will be duplicated. We know, however, that the child's pack is very similar to that of the parents and is normally able to produce two eyes, nose, hair, heart, lungs, liver, legs and arms, toes and fingers, and all the basic essential characteristics of the human body. It is only rarely that the child's genome produces a defective body with essential parts missing, though this does sometimes happen, as in the famous case of thalidomide. In a certain sense, therefore, the child must get a complete pack with all the essential cards of the parents in it. It is only in the markings of the cards, that is, the minor details, that constitute the differences of, for instance, the relative size of the features, the color of the skin, the quality of the hair, and perhaps some structural characteristics of the brain. It suggests that certain cards or chromosomes, which constitute the essential basic information for constructing the body, always get selected in the final recombination. What machinery does this, I do not know. Perhaps each chromosome is a full pack of the essentials.

MUTATION AS GENETIC CHANGE

Redefinition is not perhaps a very good word for the next R, which is more generally known as mutation. Mutation, of course, is simply a fancy word for change. If the only changes in genetic structure were recombination, evolution would have stopped long ago because recombining the same old words in the same old sentences soon reaches an equilibrium and exhausts its potentialities. The great dynamic of evolution, therefore, has been mutation, that is, change in the instructions contained in the genome, particularly in the direction of constantly increasing the complexity of these instructions.

The actual mechanics of genetic mutation are still far from being perfectly understood. It certainly has something to do with the rearrangement of the amino acid radicals on the DNA molecule. This can happen perhaps because of some failure of replication, due, for instance, to the absence of certain substances in the immediate environment of the DNA molecule, so that we get a kind of printer's error or copying error, which then becomes capable of exact replication and continues as a new population of genes. There are social parallels to this process in the way in which copyist's errors sometimes become enshrined in the sacred scriptures and are recopied indefinitely.

It is well known, also, that changes in genetic structure can take place because of radiation of various kinds. Hitting the DNA structure and changing the order of its amino acid radicals by cosmic rays, X-rays, radiation from radioactive elements, or even ordinary heat or light radiation may make these kinds of changes. Once made, they may continue to have the property of self-reproduction, and so another species of DNA is let loose in the world. There may be changes, also, in the capacity of genes to combine into chromosomes. We do not really know the language of life yet; we only know the letters in which it is written. It is like a script of which we can glimpse the meaning, but which we have not yet really cracked.

The biologists tends to regard mutations as random and to rely on the selective process for an understanding of the actual course of evolution. However, this still leaves a good many questions unanswered. It is clear that mutation is not random in the sense that all mutations are equally probable. Any given genetic structure will have a repertoire of potential mutations, each hypothetically with a probability attached. Small mutations are much more probable than large ones. The succession of mutations that produced the human race may have been extremely improbable, but just happened to come off. There might have been an equally improbable set that would have produced a human intelligence in the dolphin that did not come off. These probabilities of mutation are extremely hard to estimate because we have no universe of experience to draw on. There is perhaps an irreducible mystery here.

WHY IS THERE NO MUTATIONAL EQUILIBRIUM?

By far the larger part of mutations turn out to be adverse. The genetic structures produced by them do not survive because the phenotype, that is, the living organisms that carry these mutations in their genetic structure, do not survive. One of the interesting questions, again to which there is no answer, is whether a mutational equilibrium is possible, that is, a situation in which all possible mutations are adverse and will not survive. There seems to be no reason why such mutational equilibria should not be feasible, and it is an interesting question, therefore, as to why they never seem to have happened. Why, for instance, did evolution not come to an end with the amoeba? Why has it continued to produce organisms of increasing improbability? Whatever the machinery, and however improbable the process may have been, we judge from the records that genetic mutation has continued to occur since the beginnings of life, that the total genosphere has continually changed, and that it has changed on the whole in the direction of increasing complexity.

I know of no model and no theorem that proves the necessity of this increase in complexity. (But see p. 115.) There must surely be environmental circumstances under which the movement of the genosphere is away from complexity, toward simpler and more probable structures rather than less. What these environmental conditions are, however, we do not really know. Our experience of the universe, after all, is very limited. We do know that evolution did not develop on the moon because of the absence of certain essential environmental conditions such as liquid water. Whether in other planets in other parts of the universe devolution toward simpler structures is taking place, and whether it will eventually take place on this planet, again we do not know, but we cannot rule out the possibility.

"REALIZATION"—BIOLOGICAL PRODUCTION, OR EPIGENESIS: GETTING FROM THE GENOTYPE TO THE PHENOTYPE

The last and most important R of biological evolution I have called "realization," more properly called epigenesis, or "production." This is the extraordinary process by which the young amoeba grows until it becomes mature and splits, or even more remarkable, the process by which in sexually reproduced species the fertilized egg becomes a near reproduction of the parents who produced it. This is the problem of the pattern of the life history of a living organism from fertilized egg to death. It involves a fairly regular sequence of changes. In all multicellular living organisms the fertilized egg begins to divide and grow by cell division: one cell becomes two; two, four; four, eight; eight, sixteen; and so on. The cells differentiate, some eventually become liver cells, heart cells, skin cells, brain cells; they develop certain spatial arrangements; they develop connecting cells between them; they grow into organs, eyes, ears, livers, hearts in definite spatial connections. The fertilized egg becomes an embryo or fetus. It breaks the eggshell or it is born out of the womb and emerges as a baby. The baby grows into a child, the child into an adult, and the adult matures and produces egg or sperm. These combine to form new fertilized eggs. The adult ages and finally dies.

Realization is a process with which we are all extremely familiar. We have all watched kittens grow into cats, babies grow into adults, adults age and die. Our very familiarity with these processes dulls us to their extraordinary nature. Embryology and development studies explore this process, but we are still so far from understanding in any detail its enormous complexity that the emotion of wonder is by no means inappropriate. The familiar, commonplace, barnyard processes by which an egg becomes a chicken exceed in complexity the processes by which Napoleon established and lost his empire, the processes by which Carnegie organized a vast corporation, the processes by which the human race has been able to set its footprint on the moon, or the processes by which ideas and images in the minds of the human race are brought together and eventually produce a giant computer.

Epigenesis, the realization of genetic potential, is what we mean by production. To start off with the simplest possible model, we see that it begins within the structure of information, knowledge, or know-how—there is no very good name for this—encoded in a highly improbable arrangement of something. In the case of the fertilized egg, this "something" is presumably the arrangement of chemical atoms and radicals in the DNA, together with arrangements of DNA molecules themselves into larger units. These processes of biological production seem much more mysterious to us than processes of production of our own artifacts because the arrangements of amino acids into DNA molecules in an egg, no matter how we picture it, do not even begin to look like a chicken, whereas the blueprint of a house, which is its genetic material, does look very much like a house in its essential patterns of geographical structure.

Nevertheless, even though we do not really know how the information is encoded, we do know that an egg knows how to make a chicken. It goes about this by being able to capture energy, originally perhaps from chemical processes resembling very slow combustion within the cell. In the case of the chicken, the genetic know-how captures chemical energy from the yolk and the white of the egg. In the case of the mammal, it captures chemical energy from the bloodstream of the mother. With this energy it selects materials, atoms, and radicals from its immediate environment and builds these first into replicas of the genetic structure, then into a structured environment for this genetic structure in the cell, then by cell division and differentiation, into the complex geographical patterns and structures of cells of the embryo.

In a chicken egg, finally the material of the yolk and the white, or whatever has not been burned to provide the energy, is transformed into the extraordinarily complex structure of the chick about to be hatched. Once the chick is hatched, it starts to eat and breathe, it has inputs of reasonably structured organic chemicals—proteins, carbohydrates, and inputs of oxygen through eating and breathing. It "burns" part of its food supply to produce energy. With this energy it runs around and gets more food supply, and also its cells divide, its limbs elongate, and it grows into an adult. Here we see the genetic structure constantly at work capturing energy to move and transform materials, using materials to gain more energy, constantly measuring, estimating, checking, and encouraging growth in a quite extraordinary process of dynamic cybernetics.

I recall once in an interdisciplinary seminar on the general theory of growth an architect asking a biologist, "Was the body a prefab or did it have to have a carpenter?" Buildings that are built from prefabricated units must have units of very high uniformity, standardization, and accuracy. A one percent error in the size of a prefabricated unit would produce a whole foot error in a hundred foot wall. In a house that is built of nonstandardized units, carpenters and bricklayers constantly compare the measurements with the blueprints, cut things off if they are too long, extend them if they are too short, and so on. The biologist was forced to confess that the cell was not a standardized unit, that the body could not be a prefab, and therefore it had to have a carpenter; otherwise, two legs would never be the same length. But how the carpenter, in this case of course the genome, really operated nobody knew. There is clearly know-how in the genome, not only how to make a leg but how to make it the right length and how to stop building it when it is long enough. These are pretty subtle instructions, especially for anything as speechless as DNA, which does not seem to have much capability beyond four-letter words.[3]

SELECTIVE PROCESSES: SIEVES, EXTRUSION, TEMPLATES, SEQUENCES, COORDINATING MESSAGES; THE "CREODE"

In all processes of production, improbable genetic knowledge or know-how structures direct energy toward the transportation and transformation of materials into equally improbable structures of the phenotype or product. These processes always involve selection. The genetic know-how structure selects those materials toward which it directs its energy and selects the direction of the energy which it directs. There is a process here strangely akin to choice and evaluation, by which the knowledge structure of the growing organism takes one atom or radical and not another and puts it in one place and not another. These selective processes, however, can operate at many different levels of complexity. Perhaps one of the simplest selective processes is sifting for size and shape. A sieve will separate fine particles from course particles. An osmotic membrane, which is present even in the cell, has a wall that lets some molecules through and not others and hence acts as a sieve. Even a sieve, therefore, has some kind of know-how. In social life these patterns are common. Inspectors eliminate defective products, personnel managers and deans of admission act as sieves to let some people into employment or some students into college and to exclude others.

A rather similar process is extrusion, which is a kind of continuous sifting. Macaroni is made by squeezing paste through a hole, and the shape of the hole determines the shape of the macaroni. Many plastic articles are made this same way. In biological processes RNA and certain enzymes may be formed by processes which somewhat resemble extrusion through the "holes" of the DNA. Graduates are extruded through the "holes" of degree requirements and their minds patterned accordingly.

Templates and molds are also important instruments of selection, especially of shape. A catalyst is a template for a molecule. The process of replication in DNA involves using an existing molecule of it as a template as we have seen. How far existing cells form templates and molds into which new cells are shaped and molded in the process of embryological growth I do not know, but the process can hardly be ruled out.

All processes of production involve sequences and sequential behavior. For the automobile to be assembled, the parts must previously have been produced and they must be directed toward the assembly line. The growth of the chicken and the egg is very different from that of the automobile on the assembly line, but here too certain prerequisites have to be fulfilled before certain stages can take place. There must be differentiation into, for instance, liver cells before these can replicate themselves and grow into a liver. There is a lot of evidence to suggest that the history of a cell in an embryo depends on its position relative to others rather than its past history, because its position determines the messages that it gets. A cell transplanted from the liver position into the eye position may become an eye cell rather than a liver cell.

In any system what happens in the next minute is the result of the state of affairs at the beginning of it, and the state of affairs at the beginning of it is the result of what has happened previously. There are thus very sharp limits on the patterns of growth. The *coordination* of growth requires messages that change the state of the region they arrive at. There has to be a structure of messengers or at least messages spread out over the body of the growing organism, which directs the growth of each part toward what will fit in with the whole. In the growing organism enzymes seem to be the material-chemical messengers, like postcards, which transmit information from the genetic structure to those parts of the organism where it is needed. Nerves are "energy messengers," rather like a telephone.

If growth is to be orderly and fit into a pattern, there must be some kind of homeostatic mechanism at each point of growth. This is the "carpenter function" referred to earlier. A homeostatic or cybernetic mechanism involves some kind of knowledge structure that is capable of perceiving, presumably through some kind of structural changes in the knowledge structure itself, divergences between some actual state of affairs and some ideal state of affairs, and is capable of selecting and directing energy and matter toward diminishing this divergence. This is "deviation-diminishing feedback." If these processes do not exist, then what we have is a cancer or uncontrolled growth and chaotic cells. The enzymes seem to play an important role in this in the growth of the body, but how they do it I do not know.

The control of growth is a more complex process than the stabilization of a single variable like the thermostat. Waddington[4] has called the normative pattern of growth of the living organism its "creode." The genetic know-how structure, perhaps through the intermediary of the messenger enzymes, has to be able to detect divergences from the creode and to speed growth where it lags behind and check it where it goes too far for any particular kind of cell or structure. It is this that creates the extraordinary uniformity in the world by which kittens always grow into cats and never into hippopotamuses. The genetic information of the growing kitten constantly corrects any deviation from the cat-like direction. It discourages any movement into the hippopotamus creode and only permits those dynamic processes to prosper that lead to the kitten becoming a cat. All our processes of production of human artifacts seem almost childishly simple compared with the vast complexity by which an egg becomes a chicken or a kitten a cat.

BEHAVIOR A FUNCTION OF THE "IMAGE" IN THE BRAIN

Once the living organism emerges from the egg or womb, and in a certain sense even before this, it starts to behave. Behavior is an important part of the evolutionary process, culminating, as we shall see, in social systems in which genetic evolution takes a back seat and behavioral evolution takes over. Even before the complexity of the genosphere rose to the point where it knew how to produce a human being, the behavior of organisms played an important role in the evolutionary process. Behavior follows essentially from the "image"[5] —the knowledge embodied in the organism itself, especially in its brain and other parts of the nervous system. It is this knowledge which enables the organism to get food, to copulate, to take care of its young, to escape from predators, and to play and fool around.

The great complex of know-how and knowledge embodied in living organisms, as it extends through the earth's skin and now of course into outer space, is what Teilhard de Chardin calls the "noosphere."[6] Part of it is unconscious like the genome or the genosphere. It is know-how rather than know-what. Part of it is produced by the genome itself as it builds up the nervous system and creates brains that have specific properties, such as the knowledge in birds of how to build nests or in beavers, beaver dams. This is instinct. It exists in human beings mainly in the form of drives that organize the learning process.

Besides instinct there is learned knowledge, which is derived from the information inputs of the organism over its life. If some experimental psychologists are right, this begins at least as far down as the worms and planaria. If we do not notice it much in fish, perhaps it is just because it is hard to make them swim mazes. It is observable in birds, some species of which have to learn how to sing the right birdsongs, and it is particularly notable in mammals. Kittens have to learn a lot of what is appropriate behavior in cats from their mothers; chimpanzees apparently even have to learn how to copulate—the sex instinct is too vague and they have to learn how to satisfy it. In the human race, by far the larger portion of the knowledge structure of the individual is learned. Our genetic processes provide us with a vast undifferentiated potential in the human brain, which has to be structured by its information input and its internal activity over the whole of life.

Behavior is guided by the knowledge and value structure of the organism just as the growth of the egg and the chicken is guided by the knowledge and value structure of the genome. Psychologists have tried to interpret behavior in the mechanical sense of stimulus-response. There is, however, an "intervening variable" between the stimulus and the response, which is the image, especially images of the future. The economist thinks of behavior primarily in terms of choice or the maximization of utility or value. The choice situation is a behavioral fork—we come to a point where there are two or more paths open to us, each leading into a different future. We evaluate these futures and select that which has the highest value for us. This is the principle of maximization, which simply says that we always do what we think is best at the time. These images of the future, however, are built up out of all past stimuli and inputs. The latest input or stimulus may be just a cue that triggers a set of images derived from the past. Even the dog chasing the rabbit has images of the momentary future and so does the rabbit. Choice indeed is selection. Some patterns of behavior are chosen and not others.

SELECTION AS THE CRITICAL FACTOR IN EVOLUTION: DARWIN'S UNFORTUNATE METAPHORS

We have seen how selection is a critical factor both in the growth of the organism from the egg and in its behavior. In a larger sense it is the critical factor in the whole evolutionary process. Modern evolutionary theory indeed begins with the discovery of the principle of natural selection[7] by Darwin and Wallace.[8] It is an idea breathtaking in its simplicity and scope. As Thomas Huxley[9] said, "How extremely stupid not to have thought of that." Yet it is not easy to formulate in the form of a model. It is extraordinary that neither Darwin nor Wallace knew very much about genetics and were not even familiar with the work of Mendel, which was going on at the time in an obscure monastery in Moravia and which later was to become the foundation of modern genetics. This perhaps illustrates the proposition that selection is far more important in the evolutionary process than mutation. Mutations happen all the time and in enormous quantity and variety. Change is everywhere. It is only those changes that have survival value which survive. The beautiful variety of species and the extraordinary adaption to particular niches and daily, lunar, and annual rhythms, and to each other's peculiarities, which Paley[10] saw as evidences for a divine and infinitely wise creator, Darwin and Wallace saw simply in terms of survival value. Natural selection was a fantastically simple poetic image of the universe, reducing a vast complexity over time to a single principle.

A good deal of misunderstanding of evolution and natural selection has resulted from the fact that Darwin's metaphors were unfortunate and misleading. The phrase "the survival of the fittest," which sums up the doctrine in the popular imagination, was invented by Herbert Spencer,[11] actually before *The Origin of the Species,* and was adopted by Darwin in his fifth edition. The phrase, however, is singularly empty of meaning, because if we ask "What are the fittest fit for?" the answer, of course, is "to survive," so all this tells us is the survival of the surviving, which we knew anyway. A more accurate metaphor would be the survival of the fitting, the fitting being what fits into a niche in an ecosystem. There are innumerable niches, and hence innumerable strategies for survival. The unfortunate chest thumping and dramatic-heroic connotation of the phrase "survival of the fittest" led to extremely false analogies, as we shall see, in Social Darwinism (p. 23). There are niches for the predator and niches for the prey; there are niches for the strong and niches for the weak; there are niches for the selfish and niches for the altruistic. The principle of natural selection in itself tells us nothing about what will survive, or what qualities or properties give survival value.

Another very unfortunate metaphor of Darwin's was "the struggle for existence." Struggle, either in the sense of organized effort to overcome difficulties or in the sense of organized conflict, is very rare in the biosphere. Populations interact, some decline to extinction, and some expand. In an ice age the tundra advances on the forest, but in no sense is there a "struggle" between them. As the temperature gets colder, the forest species decline and the tundra species increase; that is all. There is neither effort nor fight. As we move toward the more complex animals, of course, both effort and fighting become more common, but even in the predator-prey relationship, there is catching and eating rather than fighting. There is some fighting among males for females, and sexual selection may favor aggressiveness in the male as a result, but it also often leads to extinction, as in the case of the Irish elk. It is the lion and the tiger that face extinction today, not the rabbit.

ADAPTABILITY VERSUS ADAPTATION

Even more fundamental in the survival pattern is the relationship between adaptability and adaptation. This is one of the real puzzles in evolution. The environment of any species continually changes, not only because of physical changes—drought, ice ages, and so on—but because of genetic changes in the surrounding species. Niches continually change. They may shrink or they may expand. And if they shrink too much, species that are too well adapted to a particular niche will become extinct as the niche shrinks toward zero. Adaptation to a particular niche, therefore, while it leads to short-run survival, is never adequate for survival in the long run, as the fact that there are far more extinct species than there are extant species demonstrates.

Adaptability is the capacity to expand niches or to find new niches. This may happen simply through accidental genetic mutation. This is indeed an important factor in the whole evolutionary drama. Those species that have the luck to undergo genetic mutations that are niche-expanding either survived or became the ancestors of new species that survived. Species that suffered mutations that were niche-contracting either became extinct or did not become the ancestors of surviving species. In more famous words, it is the meek, that is, the adaptable, who inherit the earth, not the strong, who are well adapted to a particular niche, who are destroyed because they cannot adapt when the niche changes. There is a real dilemma here. If, as seems probable, adaptability and adaptation are somewhat alternative characteristics of a species, how is adaptability selected for? It is adaptation that is selected in the short run. In the short run, perhaps adaptability comes by accident and meekness comes by grace. Mutations that are valuable from the point of view of immediate adaptation also may carry with them accidentally the properties which make for adaptability.

DOES JOINT GENETIC PRODUCTION ACCOUNT FOR THE HUMAN RACE?

The above is an example of a principle of considerable importance in evolutionary processes. We might call it the principle of joint genetic production. The attributes of the phenotype do not bear a one-to-one relationship to the various components of its genetic structure. The genome is a book of instructions with many cross references. We cannot really read it; we have a strong suspicion that even if it is not the whole book, it is at least a certain chapter of it—a combination of genes and chromosomes that produce certain effects. It is not just a particular part of the genome, for instance, which produces the ear, another the eye, and so on, but rather certain combinations of parts. A genetic mutation, therefore, may have multiple effects on the organism it produces. It may, therefore, produce one effect that is adaptive to an existing situation and another effect that lies, as it were, in the background and goes along for the ride, but which results in adaptability, which later turns out to have survival value as the environments change.

It is well known that certain characteristics of the genetic structure are recessive. This, indeed, is one of Mendel's great discoveries. Recessive genes can be carried genetically by organisms in which they have not produced their full effect, but the descendants of these organisms can have properties, which the organisms themselves do not have, but which are carried in their genetic structure. Similarly, we might suppose that the genetic structure can contain deeply recessive elements, which do not appear at all as long as conditions are favorable and niches are large, but which surface, as it were, under conditions of adversity that require adaptability.

The development of the human race, and especially its extraordinary brain, can only be accounted for by invoking some such principle of joint genetic production. The human brain is the result of a succession of mutations, beginning about two million years ago, which enormously increased the size and capacity of the brain in man's ancestors. This is puzzling because the human brain is an extraordinarily redundant organ. We are still a very long way from having fully exploited its learning capacity. The homo sapiens of 50,000 years ago or more certainly had a brain as large and competent as ours, as capable of producing the theory of relativity and Beethoven's Ninth Symphony, but it was largely unused. How then did an organ, which is so redundant, ever confer any survival value on the creatures that had it? The only possible answer is that the mutations that produced the human brain in the genetic structure also produced other things that had short-run survival value. Otherwise, the large-brained creatures would never have survived. What this was we do not know. It may have been manual dexterity or swifter running powers, or something like this. Whatever it was, the brain certainly went along for the ride. The same problem arises many times in evolution, where mutation seems to produce something that has the potential and adaptability for the future but which does not seem to have very much survival value in the present.

THE EVOLUTION OF NICHES: EMERGENT EVOLUTION, ISOLATION, AND CATASTROPHE

Another very interesting, though difficult problem in biological evolution is the evolution of niches themselves. Are there general patterns in ecosystems that are more likely to develop than others, even though the species that occupy these niches may be rather different? Examples of this would be the Oceanic Islands and the great oceanic continent of Australia, which were isolated from the processes that produced the mammals in the great world islands of Eurasia, Africa, and the Americas, which were at times indeed united into a single world island by the land bridge at the Bering Straits. The mammals did not reach the oceanic islands like Mauritius or New Zealand, but the birds could reach them and followed their own line of development in the absence of mammals, occupying many of the mammalian niches. The dodo in Mauritius and the moa in New Zealand were perhaps deer-type birds. There were even rabbit-type birds that burrowed in the ground. The marsupials reached Australia, presumably at the time of the land bridge with Asia, but the mammals did not, and the marsupials occupied a great many mammalian niches. The kangaroo, again, is perhaps a deer-type marsupial (I recall being particularly delighted while driving in Australia at seeing the road sign, which in the United States would have had a picture of a deer on it, and in Australia had a picture of a kangaroo on it). The wombat is a pig-type marsupial; the koala bear a teddy-bear type; the dingo a dog-type; and so on. There does not seem to be any cat marsupial, though I suppose one cannot have everything. The breakdown of isolation with the development of human beings in boats, and the subsequent introduction of mammals into these areas, often led to widespread extinction of earlier species, of which the dodo, of course, is one of the most famous examples.

A somewhat related question is what is called "emergent evolution." It is the question as to whether there are particular characteristics of organisms that have such good survival value that they are likely to pop up under many different conditions and develop perhaps from quite different histories. The eye of the vertebrate on the one hand and of the octopus on the other is a famous example. These apparently have quite different phylogenetic histories, but they perform much the same function of improving the information system of the organism. There is some parallel here to the question in societal evolution of independent invention versus diffusion.

The role of isolation in evolution is another related question. It was the isolation of the finches on the Galápagos Islands that gave Darwin a clue to the theory of natural selection. In a number of isolated ecosystems each will unquestionably follow evolutionary dynamic processes of its own as a result either of random shocks or of environmental differences. This will lead to a very much larger number of different species in totality than would a single, large ecosystem, in which many of the mutations that have survival value in the small system would not have survival value in the large.

On the other hand, large systems have a better chance of producing unlikely mutations. This perhaps is why the mammals evolved only in the great world continents and not in the smaller islands and in Australia, even though there would have been a niche for them and opportunity if they had developed. Isolation, therefore, leads to variety, but it may also lead to evolutionary stagnation. Its total influence is, therefore, hard to evaluate. The whole question of missed opportunities in evolution is difficult, virtually insoluble. We cannot tell what would have happened if some improbable event had come off, particularly in regard to improbable mutations and drastic rearrangements of genetic structure, which turn out to be favorable but are extremely unlikely.

The whole role of improbable events, not only mutations but also catastrophes, in the evolutionary process is of great importance. When we are looking over a period of two billion years, even events that are extremely improbable in any one year are likely to take place at some time during the interval. An event with only a one percent probability of happening in any one year has about a 63.4 percent chance of happening in a hundred years, a 99.996 percent chance of happening in a thousand years, so that over two billion years some extremely improbable things can happen. This makes the application of conventional scientific method to evolutionary problems very difficult, because conventional science on the whole deals with the probable, and laboratory science with the virtually certain. An event that will only happen once in a billion years is extremely unlikely to be investigated in a laboratory. With the records as fantastically imperfect as they are, the details of these improbable events will probably always be unknown to us.

The geological record suggests that the course of evolution has been punctuated by catastrophes, which separate one geological age from the next. These catastrophes have all involved very large-scale extinction, often the development of new phyla, and frequently an increase in complexity. There is still some debate about whether these were real catastrophes or whether they were simply catastrophes in the record. If we are reading a book with most of the pages missing, as we are when we read the record of the rocks, it would not be surprising if we interpret the missing pages as evidence of a real catastrophe, but it may just have been a catastrophe to the book and a defect in the record.

The balance of considered opinion, however, seems to fall on the side of those who think that some of these catastrophes at any rate were real and not just gaps in the record. Certainly the extinction of the dinosaurs, and the vast catastrophe that seems to have followed the pollution of the atmosphere with oxygen by the first anaerobic forms of life—are reasonable inferences from the record. The question as to how far the course of evolution has been affected by these catastrophes is an important one. It may be indeed that without them the earth would have settled down to mutational equilibrium long ago and that evolution might indeed have stopped with the amoeba. Even the development of the human race may be related to the last ice age, which must have had catastrophic consequences for many species, as they were pushed south against mountain or water barriers like the Alps or the Mediterranean in Europe or the Gulf of Mexico in North America. Catastrophe favors adaptability and eliminates the previously well adapted but unadaptable. It may, therefore, be an important element in the pattern of increasing complexity, which is otherwise rather puzzling.

Another possible explanation of the pattern of increasing complexity is the principle that "there is always room at the top." An ecosystem may have an unfilled niche for a species just above the level of complexity of those which constitute it. Hence, mutations toward increased complexity, and especially those toward adaptability, are likely to find new niches even in existing systems that seem rather full, and so survive. Mutations that do not increase complexity, or which diminish it, have to compete with the existing niches in the existing structures with well-established occupants, and have a worse chance of surviving.

I have sometimes accused evolutionary theory of being a great poetic vision of the universe rather than a scientific theory, though this in no way diminishes its power or truth. It is not a model even in the sense in which economic theory is a model. Many of the essential details of the process are unknown to us. We have never yet made a fertilized egg with our own fingers. We have intervened only marginally in the process of the growth of the biological organism. We understand virtually nothing about aging; we certainly do not know how to stop it. We are only on the edge of making conscious genetic mutations with re-combinant DNA, but we have done pretty well with artificial selection in the production of St. Bernards and Chihuahuas, oxen and horses, and we have always been good at selecting from existing genetic materials. We can make very productive hybrids, but we cannot replace the genetic materials that we are losing. We cannot really specify the survival function that would express the probability of survival of any genetic mutation as a function of the other relevant variables. We are not even sure what all the relevant variables are. If there are dynamic equations of evolution, we do not know what they are and we certainly cannot solve them. Nevertheless, it is a great poetic vision, somewhat in conflict, as we shall see later, with other poetic visions, and it does give us in the theory of natural selection an enormously important clue to the dynamics of the universe.

It is important to recognize that our image of evolution is not deterministic in the way in which a system of differential or difference equations is deterministic, but is probabilistic. The dynamic of the system is guided to a considerable extent by the development of "empty niches" in ecosystems in the course of mutation and migration. Mathematically we can define an empty niche as a situation in which the addition of a new species to a total ecosystem will produce an equilibrium in which the new species can survive at a population above the extinction level. Wherever there is an empty niche in an ecosystem there is some probability that a mutation of some kind, whether genetic or migrational, will produce a new species to occupy the niche. This probability depends on the probabilities of mutation from existing structures. The longer the niche remains empty, the greater the probability that some mutation will take place to create a species to fill it. On the other hand, no niche remains empty for an indefinite period because changes are going on in the rest of the ecosystem that may tend to close it. If any empty niche closes before it has been filled, an opportunity has been irrevocably lost and the whole course of evolution is different from what it would otherwise have been. In the evolutionary process, therefore, we are constantly getting to branches in the path where the branch taken depends on the throw of the great dice of the universe.

The concept of an "empty niche" is a hard one for biologists because it is very difficult to study what did not happen and what is not there. In social systems, perhaps because of our more intimate personal knowledge of them, empty niches can be more easily recognized. There is an empty niche, for instance, in the ecosystem of human artifacts for a battery that would store large quantities of electricity cheaply. There have been enormous payoffs for this for nearly one hundred years, yet it has not been invented. Even in the biosphere there is now clearly an empty niche for anything that will eat nylon, a substance that was unknown until the human race started to make it. A mutation in a bacterium, for instance, which will enable it to eat nylon, would have been quite worthless before the development of the chemical industry, thus it is not surprising that there is no organism that eats it. Now, however, such a mutation would immediately create a species to occupy an empty niche.

The relative role of mutation and selection in the evolutionary process is by no means easy to determine. There may have been times in earth's history when, because of magnetic inversions and the consequent destruction of the Van Allen Belt and the penetration of the atmosphere by hard radiation, the rate of genetic mutation may have substantially increased. Whether this would produce an increase in the rate of evolution, however, depends on the extent to which mutation creates a system of empty niches in the world ecosystem, which can then be filled by new mutations. It is by no means obvious, therefore, that an increase in the rate of mutation will in fact accelerate the pace of evolution. It may simply result in more adverse mutations that do not survive.

Appendix to Chapter 5:
THE PATTERNS OF GENETICS

The following diagrams may be helpful to those who, like myself, often think in terms of pictures. They illustrate the four Rs of evolutionary processes as expounded in this chapter. Figure 5A.1 shows replication. The spiral, which spells abracadabra in Figure 5A.1(i), is a highly simplified form (omitting the "c") of the double helix of DNA, with its four "letters" of the amino acids. This exists in an environment containing these letters. Each letter in the word attracts another letter toward it as we see in Figure 5A.1

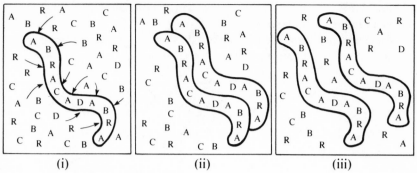

(i)   (ii)   (iii)

Figure 5A.1: Replication of Genes

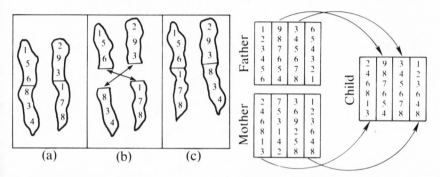

(a)   (b)   (c)

Figure 5A.2(i): Recombination by Crossover in Chromosomes

Figure 5A.2(ii): Recombination by Sexual Reproduction

(ii). We do not bother here about the mirror image problem. Then the two spirals separate and we have two identical abracadabras as in Figure 5A.1(iii).

The genes now combine into long paragraphs of instructions, the chromosomes. In Figure 5A.2 each gene in the chromosome is represented by a number. Recombination can take the form of a crossover of chromosomes, as in Figure 5A.2(i). Each of two chromosomes splits in two and the parts cross over to form two new chromosomes. In sexual reproduction, illustrated in Figure 5A.2(ii), most species have far more than the four chromosomes listed here as illustration. Two chromosomes are selected from the father, two from the mother, and they combine to form the chromosomes of the child. The total pattern of chromosomes is the genome.

In Figure 5A.3 we see redefinition or mutation, first in 5A.3(i) by misreplication, where we see abracadabra has produced arbacadabra by misplacing the "r" and the "b" at the top. Arbacadabra is a different spell and will produce a somewhat different organism. In Figure 5A.3(ii) we see lightning, as radiation of some kind striking at the gene or the DNA, misplacing one letter and putting another in its place, so that instead of abracadabra we now have abrabadabra, which again will produce something different in the phenotype.

These are real abracadabras, rather than the fake ones of magic spells, because they have the capacity, as illustrated in Figure 5A.4, of producing

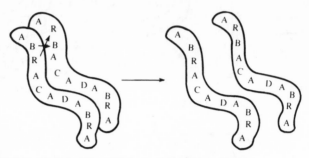

Figure 5A.3(i): Redefinition (Mutation) by Misreplication

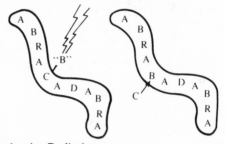

Figure 5A.3(ii): Mutation by Radiation

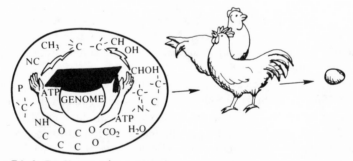

Figure 5A.4: Realization (Epigenesis)

genomes, know-how structures that can take energy from its environment and with this energy move and reorganize atoms and radicals first into the building blocks and then into the architecture of living organisms, thus producing the chicken from the egg and the chicken will of course then produce another egg.

NOTES

1. G. Evelyn Hutchinson, *The Ecological Theater and the Evolutionary Play* (New Haven: Yale University Press, 1965).

2. Human intervention into this process of re-combinant DNA has created quite a furor, and there is legitimate fear that artificial bacteria might get out of the laboratory and decimate the human race. Our adjustment to the world of bacteria is always a little precarious, as witnessed by the great plagues, which biogenetic mutations seem to have produced from time to time.

3. There seem to be only four major radicals (amino acids) that are attached to the central spiral backbone of DNA.

4. C. H. Waddington, *The Ethical Animal* (London: 1960), 82.

5. Kenneth E. Boulding, *The Image* (Ann Arbor: University of Michigan Press, 1956).

6. Pierre Teilhard de Chardin, *The Phenomenon of Man* (New York: Harper and Row, 1959).

7. For an excellent collection of material on this history, see *Darwin*, edited by Philip Appleman (New York: W. W. Norton, 1970).

8. The two famous papers by Charles Darwin and Alfred Russel Wallace were presented at the Linnean Society in London on July 1, 1858.

9. Leonard Huxley, *Life and Letters of T. H. Huxley* (New York: Appleton, 1901), Vol. I, 183.

10. William Paley, *Natural Theology* (1802).

11. Herbert Spencer, "A Theory of Population, Deduced from the General Law of Animal Fertility," *Westminster Review,* LVII (1852), 499-500.

Chapter 6

Societal Evolution
The General Pattern

HUMAN HISTORY AS THE EVOLUTION OF HUMAN ARTIFACTS

When the know-how of the genosphere had risen to the point where it could produce a human being, that is, Adam and Eve, or whatever their names were, evolution on this planet went into a new gear. Two billion years or so earlier, the introduction of life had set the dynamics of earth into a new gear; the bare, stony, sandy earth and the empty oceans entered into a process that eventually made them team with bacteria, insects, fish, and animals of enormous variety. Similarly, the advent of the human race started a process that turned the empty woods into busy fields, dotted the surface of the earth with houses, farms and cities, roads and railroads, sent ships sailing over the oceans, airplanes flying through the air, and now space vehicles exploring the solar system. This is societal evolution.

Social dynamics can be thought of primarily as the evolution of human artifacts. Before the human race there were some living organisms that produced artifacts—nests, beaver dams—but these were very small and localized. It is the peculiar characteristic of the human race that it set in process a vast evolutionary dynamic of production of its own artifacts, with species more numerous than the insects, ranging in size from the microscopic transistor circuit to thousands of miles of thruways and skyscrapers a third of a mile high. We make things far bigger than the whale and smaller than an amoeba, though we still have not gotten miniaturization down to the miraculous microstructure in the human brain.

Human artifacts not only include material structures and objects, such as buildings, machines, and automobiles, but they also include organizations, organizational structures like extended families (no other animal knows what it is to have a grandfather), tribes, nations, corporations, churches, political parties, governments, and so on. Some of these may grow unconsciously, but they all originate and are sustained by the images in the human mind.

[121]

Even human beings themselves are in considerable part human artifacts, shaped by the cultures in which they grow. I am writing in English mainly because my mother and father spoke it, and I grew up in an English-speaking society. Had I grown up in France, I would almost certainly be writing this in French. I am able to write this book because I have been through a life-long process of education by inputs from parents, friends, peers, teachers, letters, books, art galleries, radio, television, and so on. These things, coupled with a good deal of internal activity of reflection, thinking, and meditation, make the content of my mind what it is. I started my university career in chemistry, then switched to the social sciences. If I had stayed in chemistry, I would certainly not be writing this book. I am what innumerable people, sights, sounds, information inputs of all kinds, and my own internal activity have made me. I am as much a human artifact as the chair I sit in and the house that shelters me. When I sit in a room, virtually everything I see is a human artifact. I have to look out the window to see the trees and grasses, which are biological artifacts, and the rocks, which are geological artifacts.

Human artifacts are species just as much as biological artifacts. The automobile is just as much a species as the horse. Human artifacts enter into ecological relationships with each other and with biological artifacts. The automobile is competitive with the horse and has reduced its numbers; it is cooperative with gas stations and has increased their numbers; it is cooperative with the species of "human beings able to drive an automobile" and has increased the number of drivers. It is a predator with regard to oil supplies because it is diminishing their quantity to the point where in a few decades both species face extinction.

Virtually all the processes that we have described in the last chapter in biological dynamics are also found in the dynamics of human artifacts. The distinction between the genotype and the phenotype is perhaps not quite as clear in social systems as it is in biological systems, because the genotypes themselves are very often human artifacts and not simply made by other genotypes, but the distinction is nevertheless important. Just as there is the genosphere or genetic know-how in the biosphere, so there is a noosphere of human knowledge and know-how in the sociosphere. The noosphere is the totality of the cognitive content, including values, of all human nervous systems, plus the prosthetic devices by which this system is extended and integrated in the form of libraries, computers, telephones, post offices, and so on.

BIOGENETICS AND NOOGENETICS

It is important to recognize that there are two different genetic processes at work in the world. The first of these may be called "biogenetics." It is the process whereby the know-how by which biological organisms are made is encoded in the DNA and the genes. Change in the biogenetic structure takes place through mutation in its own patterns in the genes. These are not produced by any learning process of the organism, as Lamarck [1] thought, though the total biogenetic structure (the genosphere) is changed continually by the selective process that goes on in the populations of phenotypes which it produces. No matter how many generations of mice have their tails cut off, mice will continue to grow tails because this is contained in the genetic instructions, and cutting off the tails does not affect these instructions. If, on the other hand, there were a niche for tailless mice in some ecosystem, a genetic change that eliminated the instructions for making a tail in the genetic structure would produce tailless mice which then would survive and occupy the niche.

Besides the biogenetic structure, however, there is also what might be called the "noogenetic structure" within the nervous systems of organisms, which is transmitted to offspring by a learning process. We find traces of this even in pre-human organisms, even perhaps in worms, and especially in the higher mammals and birds. Presumably thè learned knowledge is represented by some kind of acquired brain structure, which is not produced by the biogenetic structure, though the biogenetic structure does produce the potential for it. A bird's genes produce a brain in the bird, which has a potential for learning the bird's song, but if it does not hear other birds, this potential will not be realized and the brain will remain unstructured. Here we do have something like a Lamarckian genetic process. It is a different kind of process, however, from pure biogenetics, which is clearly not Lamarckian.

Once we get to the human race noogenetics dominates biogenetics to a remarkable extent. We know very little about the relation between the human genetic structure and the human phenotype apart from a few abnormalities. We know a little about genetic defects in the human being and practically nothing about genetic excellence, particularly in the brain. Indeed, in the present state of human knowledge eugenics, the theory that better human beings can be bred by careful selection of mates, is an illusion except perhaps at the level of obvious defects such as hemophilia. The processes by which each generation of human beings learns from the last are far more important than the process by which biological genes are inherited.

The genetic structure of an individual human can certainly produce certain limitations in the learning process. For instance, a person who is genetically tone deaf, if there is such a thing, would certainly not be a great musician. For the most part, however, these genetic learning obstacles are probably not large and could be overcome by improvements in human learning techniques. It seems clear that for the most part genetic limits on learning are quite rarely reached. It is the learning patterns themselves that are self-limiting. The human mind is a vast ballroom. Most of us can paint ourselves into a tiny corner of it because we learn not to learn. It is very rare that we press against the genetically imposed walls.

THE PRODUCTION OF HUMAN ARTIFACTS

The production of human artifacts is a process essentially similar to the production of biological artifacts, that is, of living organisms. As we saw in the last chapter, living organisms originate with a fertilized egg or its asexual equivalent. This contains an enormous amount of information or know-how, which is capable of selecting and directing energy toward the selection, transportation, and transformation of materials into the improbable shapes and conformations that make up the architecture of the body of the living organism. A horse begins as the extraordinary structure of know-how in the fertilized egg of a mare; an automobile begins in an image in the mind of the human being, or perhaps in a set of related images in the minds of a group of human beings. These images are translated into drawings, blueprints, and instructions, which are the genotypes of the production of human artifacts. These produce messengers (social enzymes) in the form of instructions that can direct energy toward the selection, transportation, and transformation of materials in various shapes, conformations, transformations, and so on, until finally an automobile emerges off the assembly line from the womb of the factory. All human artifacts originate as an image in somebody's mind, even though this image may be below the level of consciousness at times.

Just as in the case of biological organisms, production may be limited by the absence or scarcity of any one of the three factors—knowledge, energy, and materials. Just as the earth could not have produced a human being two million years ago because the genetic know-how was not there, so the human race could not have produced an automobile a hundred years ago because the social knowledge was not there. Also we probably could not have produced automobiles if we had not tapped fossil fuels for energy and mines for iron, steel, and other metals. If the geological history of the earth had been such that there had not been any oil and gas, the artifacts of the last hundred years would have been very different. Nevertheless, it is the knowledge process that dominates. It provides the adaptability that expands the niches and that finds substitute forms of energy and materials when an existing form becomes scarce. Energy and materials are very flexible limitations, because they can both be pushed out by the growth of knowledge, though sometimes this fails to happen. It is the knowledge limitation that tends to be dominant.

THE FOUR Rs AND THE S IN SOCIETAL EVOLUTION

The processes in biological evolution, which I call the four Rs and an S (p. 100), are also found in the evolution of human artifacts. Replication is of great importance in the development of the noosphere, as it is in the development of the genosphere. Even before the advent of writing, spoken language was capable of a great deal of replication. A speaker can say a sentence in a room full of people and each of them may be able to repeat it the next day. Gossip is essentially a replicator, although there are often considerable errors in replication. After the invention of writing, the replication of linguistic knowledge structures became much easier, much less liable to error. Now with printing, xeroxing, phonograph records, and tapes, the record of past knowledge is improved all the time and the replication of knowledge has increased enormously. This power of replication gives an enormous resilience and stability to the system, as in biological systems. If an epidemic killed all the sparrows in the world except a little cluster in Australia and the epidemic then disappeared, the world would be full of sparrows again in a hundred years because of their powers of genetic replication and expansion into empty niches. If all human beings and their artifacts were mysteriously destroyed over night in every country of the world except Australia and the destructive force disappeared, in three or four hundred years the world would be full of Australians and all the cities would be rebuilt and the world of human artifacts reestablished.

Recombination is a very important element in the noosphere. The "philosophers" of Adam Smith are able to bring together and combine elements from many diverse sources.[2] The processes of recombination in the noosphere are far more varied and much larger in scope than they are in the genosphere. I have called human artifacts "multisexual" (p. 68). The biosphere never got much past two sexes, with the exception perhaps of one or two rather odd experiments in plants or viruses. A horse is produced by a stallion and a mare by selecting and combining their chromosomes in the fertilized egg, which is then developed in the womb of a mare. An automobile is produced by the coming together of a large number of social species and artifacts—material artifacts like factories, machines, assembly lines, steel mills, blast furnaces, bulldozers, mining equipment, and so on; by a large number of human occupational species—managers, stockholders, bankers, executives, foremen, assembly line workers, lawyers, and so on; and by a large number of organizational species—corporations, trade unions, law courts, and the like, all of which bring certain "social chromosomes," that is, certain items of knowledge, to the process. These are all combined and organized in the factory, and out of this multisexual orgy the automobile emerges. If the sexual metaphor breaks down in human imagination, we can regard it, if we like, as an enormously complicated process of crossing over of social chromosomes.

Redefinition or mutation is also an extremely important part of the evolution of human artifacts. This corresponds to invention and discovery. It goes on all the time. It very often comes to nothing because it does not find a niche. Many times, however, a niche is available and a new social species is born. Mutation has been rampant in the social system ever since the first stone or wood implement. Sometimes there is clearly (with hindsight at least) a niche available that is not filled because the invention or mutation is not made. The Romans, for instance, had horses, but never invented either the horse collar or the stirrup. When these did reach Europe from China about the eighth or ninth century, they were rapidly and widely adopted. In biological systems, likewise, there are occasionally empty niches that are sometimes filled by migrations without much disturbance of the existing ecosystem, even to the benefit of existing species.

On the other hand, there are times when invention is extremely fertile and novelties are rapidly spread by imitation. When a new niche arises, inventions and innovations to fill it are often made almost simultaneously by different people in different parts of the world. The question of independent invention versus diffusion is a difficult one, particularly where records are defective. We do not really know, for instance, how many times agriculture, or various arts of metallurgy were invented in different parts of the world. The answer may depend very much on the rate of mutation. When this is rapid, independent inventions are much more likely, whether biological mutations or social innovations.

The processes of realization and production are, as we have seen (pp. 33-34), very similar in biological and social systems. Just as the genome in the fertilized egg soon develops "messengers" (in the form of RNA and then enzymes and so on) to transmit to different parts of the growing system of the embryo instructions to develop in certain ways, so in producing the automobile or anything else, there has to be an elaborate system of communication from the central organizing office to the various parts of the process. The telephone represented an improved enzyme for social organization and for the production of human artifacts. There are probably analogs to this in biological evolution, but these tend not to appear in the records and are lost.

THE HUMAN BRAIN MAKES THE MAIN DIFFERENCE BETWEEN BIOLOGICAL AND SOCIETAL EVOLUTION

Up to this point we have been considering mainly the similarities between biological and social dynamics, which are very important. There are some patterns that are spread over wide fields of the structures of the universe and some that are confined to narrow areas. Therefore, it is also important to identify the differences among the narrow areas, and for this particular discussion, to note the differences between biological and social dynamic processes. In the absence of any clear measure of complexity, it is hard to say whether social processes are more complex than biological ones, but they are different. The differences arise primarily because social processes are the result of the intervention of an extraordinary organ, the human brain, and its associated nervous system into its environment.

We still know very little about the human brain in spite of a great deal of inquiry into its structure and functioning, simply because it is an apparatus of literally inconceivable complexity. It has some ten billion neurons. If we suppose that the capacity of an organization is the number of different states it can assume, and even if we suppose the neuron only has two states—on or off—this means the ultimate capacity of the human brain is measured by the number $2^{1,000,000,000}$. This is a very large number indeed. It would take us 90 years to write it down at the rate of one digit per second. The number of significant states of the brain is probably considerably less than that, but it is probably still a very large number indeed, far larger than any merely astronomical number. It is not surprising, therefore, that the brain contains not only a moral law within, as Kant said, but also the starry universe within as well as without. It is capable of images of the universe outside it that at least represent approximate models of the vastness and complexity of the totality without.

It is this extraordinary capacity of the human brain for making images not only of the world outside it, which it sees as reality, but also, in fantasy, of innumerable worlds of the imagination, which distinguishes it from even the highest brains of nonhuman animals. The sheer size of the brain has something to do with it. This is a case perhaps where, in the words of Engels,[3] a sufficient change in quantity produces a change in quality. But there is probably more to it than that. The dolphin has a brain as large as ours in volume, but it seems to lack something in complexity in the pattern of its neuronal networks. Just what it is that gives the human brain its extraordinary imaging capacity, however, we do not really know.

We do not even really know whether the "engram," that is, the unit of memory, is electrical or molecular. Furthermore, the brain, especially in its higher facilities, is a remarkably unspecialized system. There is a famous story of the brain surgeon who said to his nervous assistant as he plowed his way through his first brain operation, "You don't have to worry about what you're doing here. This is just the thinking part of the brain." There are specialized parts, of course, that deal with perception and what might be called "physiological emotion," the release of adrenalin and other chemical messengers. But when it comes to the "thinking part" of the brain, we begin dealing with something that looks much more like an economy, capable of enormous regeneration and having extremely complex properties, which are properties of the system as a whole rather than any part of it. This is something that so far we have been quite unable to simulate. Our computers have some resemblance to the lower parts of the brain, but they are still a very long way from simulating the extraordinary capacity of the thinking part. It is because of this extraordinary capacity for complex images that the human brain exercises its genetic funtion in the form of human artifacts, and it is, as we saw earlier, a striking parallel to the genome in biology, which produces "biological artifacts," that is, living organisms.

LANGUAGE AS A DISTINCTIVE HUMAN ARTIFACT

Apart from a few primitive tools, the first major artifact of the human brain was undoubtedly language. We can define language as consisting of communication among organisms that have some kind of image of the world within them, such that the image within one organism can be changed by communication from another in the direction of the image within that other. In this sense language is something that begins quite early in biological evolution, because there is no doubt that even quite primitive animals communicated with each other. The language of nonhumans, however, with the possible exceptions of the educated chimpanzee and the honey bee, is entirely confined to signs, that is, to communications either by sound, by visual motion, by smell, or even by touch or by some forms of taste, which have some kind of one-to-one relationship with the image that they are intended to convey. The cry of warning, the innumerable symbols of love that are preludes to mating, the gaping of the little bird in the nest, and the bright colors of the flower are all signs conveying a one-to-one message of danger, sex, hunger, or pollen.

Signs exist also in human languages. We too have cries of warning, cues of love, and hints of reward. Human language, however, goes far beyond the communications of signs into symbols. This seems to be unique to the human brain and is perhaps the key to all of social evolution. The human mind can form images of large, complex, and integrated systems of which it has no personal experience through the magic of human language and other forms of human communication, such as pictures, music, and so on. I now have a rough image in my mind of what the back side of the moon looks like although I have never been there and almost certainly never will. Language would have no power to create images, however, if there were no capacity, first within the one who puts out a communication, and then within the one who receives it, to form complex images and to develop enough different symbols to describe them in ways that can recreate an image that already exists in one mind in another.

Language also gives the extraordinary power of communicating into the future. When I see Macbeth performed, Shakespeare is projecting something that happened in his mind into my mind over an interval of 400 years. When I hear a Mozart piano concerto played on a record, I participate in an experience that took place within Mozart 200 years ago and 5,000 miles away. When I read the New Testament, I participate, however imperfectly, in the experience of a few people in Palestine 2,000 years ago. Therefore, language, especially recorded language, including writing, sculpture, painting, photography and recordings, binds the whole human race, or at least large portions of it, together as if it were in a single mind, insofar as one mind participates in the experience of other minds through the intermediary of communication.

THE EVOLUTION OF LANGUAGE

The evolution of language itself is a highly specialized study to which we cannot afford to give much space in this volume. Once human language, that is, the power of communication of complex images, is achieved, the details of how it was achieved are of minor importance in evolution, interesting as they are in themselves. It does not matter very much whether we communicate in English or Chinese, provided we communicate the same things. Languages differ, of course, in their power of communication mainly, however, because of differences in the things that have to be communicated. A primitive tribe does not have to communicate about game theory or the theory of relativity; it will not have words for the communications of modern science because it does not have to talk about these things. All languages, however, seem to be capable of ready expansion as the field of discourse increases. We have many examples of languages that have expanded rapidly in their vocabulary, usually without much change in structure, to take account of the new things that have to be talked and written about.

The actual origins of language are very obscure, mainly because language originated as spoken language, with some assistance from gestures and visual signs, and the record of the origins of spoken language is irretrievably lost. We have no records of past language until writing begins, a mere 5,000 years ago, by which time complete languages had been in existence for a very long time. A complete language is a language the structure of which enables the communicators to communicate anything they want, and which can easily be expanded to meet new needs for communication. In this sense no human beings have ever been found who did not have already a complete language. We have no way of finding out how these complete languages and all the stages in their evolution evolved because the record of it consists of only gestures and sound waves, which are irretrievably lost.

The evolution of language from the time we can follow it in writing or recordings does follow certain rather regular principles, which have the form of an evolutionary system. A word actually spoken or written can be thought of as an individual of a species, of which the total existing number of such words is a population. Its genome is the knowledge of the word in human minds; it is born when it is used either in speech or in writing. In spoken language it dies when it reaches the recipient's ear and is registered in the recipient's mind; in written language the word lives for a very long time until the writing or the message is lost. Even in spoken language words become extinct; they are forgotten and their genomes in human minds disappear. Other words are invented by a process of linguistic mutation. Some invented words do not survive the inventor. However, if there is a niche for them, they pass into the language and become a living word-species.

Sentences are ecological communities of words. The ranges of these communities are confined within the limitations of grammar rather in the way that biological communities are confined by their physical surroundings. Grammar is a structure of niches to which only certain species of words are admitted. As each word occupies a niche, it creates a niche for others. When one word has been uttered, this limits the number of words that can follow it. Starting a sentence with "I" implies that the next word cannot be "banana." It almost has to be a verb or a conjunction. Linguists are divided about whether these grammatical rules, which are extremely subtle, are limited by some innate physiological structure of the human nervous system, as Chomsky[4] seems to think, or whether they are entirely learned from the language we hear in childhood and even more from what we do not hear, which enables us to select those sentences that are acceptable. The combination of sentences into paragraphs, chapters, and books is subject to a certain stylistic grammar of its own, again of great subtlety, which need not concern us now.

THE "WHORFIAN HYPOTHESIS" AND THE RELATIVE RELATIVE IRRELEVANCE OF LANGUAGE FORM

It has been suggested, especially by Benjamin Whorf,[5] that the structure of the language that we use affects in some degree the messages that we communicate with it. Thus, it is argued that because virtually all Indo-Aryan languages use a subject-verb-predicate structure, we are forced into absurd expressions like "It is raining" when what we are communicating is "raining" and the "It" is a purely nonexistent invention of language. But it is also argued that such a language forces us into "reifications," that is, we tend to turn processes or our images of processes into an image of things. Thus, we talk about "values," which almost certainly do not exist except in some unknown structures of the neurons, as a noun, whereas the reality experienced that we wish to communicate is a process of valuation. Similarly, we reify a vast and complex set of political processes into a nonexistent noun called "the United States" and think of it as a thing rather than as a complex of processes.

The "Whorfian hypothesis" cannot be brushed aside totally, though on the whole one suspects that it is a secondary phenomenon, a mild disease as it were of the communicative process rather than a deadly trauma. One notices it particularly, oddly enough, in mathematics, which is a good example of an incomplete language. It is a language in which we can talk about some but not all things. Mathematics is extraordinarily deficient in verbs beyond "equals," "greater than," or "less than," and this limits it to the study of rather simple kinds of processes. It is very hard to put "I love you" into mathematics. It is a very real question, therefore, as to whether the use of mathematics in the social sciences has not introduced a kind of Whorfian, linguistic bias that has prevented the study of complex relationships. Biologists, perhaps fortunately, have never been very much impressed with mathematics, though they use it a little, and their language is replete with delicious complexities. Mathematical language, of course, gains in accuracy, but at the cost of abstraction from complexity, and it is sometimes better to be inaccurate about something than accurate about not very much.

The long process of evolution of whole languages, for instance, the great phylum of the Indo-Aryan as it moves into Sanskrit, Pali, Hindi, Urdu, and Bengali on the one hand and into Greek, Latin, and almost all the European languages outside of Hungarian and Finnish on the other hand, is a fascinating problem for the specialist. It is, however, not of great significance for the general processes of societal evolution. Conquerors sometimes impose their own languages. Turkish supplanted Greek in Asia Minor; English supplanted the Indian languages in North America, and tends to supplant the language of immigrants. There are no doubt subtle differences in languages, which produce effects on the societies that speak them. Perhaps the great sonorities of the King James Bible helped to produce Protestantism in England, which the domestic intimacies of the French Bible were unable to produce in France. I had the firm conviction as a schoolboy that nobody could have ever chatted in Latin, and this no doubt was an illusion. Some languages lean more to the lyric and some to the epic. It is hard to imagine Haiku in Greek or Homer in Japanese. I take these propositions as amusing speculations, however, rather than solid theory and I suspect that, no matter what the language for the most part, what has to be communicated will be communicated, and that what is talked about or written about is much more important than the way in which it is said or written.

Difference of language does reinforce cultural isolation, and isolation has importance in societal evolution just as it has in biological evolution. All differences in language are presumably the result of isolation. In the early days of the human race it existed in the form of a large number of isolated communities, each of which developed its own language. A common language can only result from a great deal of common communication. Each hunting and gathering band in the paleolithic period would be likely to produce a language of its own. The different languages would then reinforce the isolation and often lead to hostility. Barbarians, after all, are people who say "Bar, Bar" incomprehensibly, and the incomprehensibility of neighboring groups would certainly add to hostility and reinforce the isolation of all. As communication extends, however, through conquest and trade, intermediaries develop between different languages, the payoffs for learning other languages and for translating become quite great among certain groups, and the world develops a communicational unity even though it does not have linguistic unity.

The large number of different languages in the world today represents a relatively small obstacle to communication. Because of the extraordinary replicative characteristic of language, a single translator can break down a linguistic barrier for centuries to come. If the whole world spoke a single language—as indeed may be the case in a thousand years—very little would be changed. Cultural obstacles to communication would still exist, hostilities would still exist, and there would be a loss of variety that one could only deplore. Even in the present world, the difference between monolingual and multilingual societies is not really very great, and people with common languages are just as prone to go to war with each other as people with different languages.

HUMANS FORM IMAGES OF THE
FUTURE, DECISIONS, AND PURPOSE

Another capacity of the human mind, which is of great importance in the genesis of human artifacts, is the capacity for forming complex images of the future, as a product perhaps of the larger capacity of forming images of space and time. The capacity for forming images of the future is a necessary prerequisite for behavior directed toward fulfilling them. Stimulus-response behavior can, of course, be built into an organization without involving much in the way of an image of the future. An amoeba that selects a piece of food and rejects a stone unquestionably has values, or rather a process of valuation, but these can be attributed to its genetic constitution. We do not have to assume that it says to itself, "If I absorb this piece of food, I will enjoy it and, if I absorb this stone, it will make me sick." As we move toward the higher animals, however, images of the future become apparent in their behavior. A dog chasing a rabbit again may redirect his attention to where he thinks the rabbit is going to be in the next few seconds. The investigation of images of the future has not occupied much of the attention of animal psychologists, obsessed as they have been with the stimulus-response models, but there is surely a wide field of experimentation open here. In the human race there is no doubt at all about the importance of images of the future. The making of the first tool could not have taken place out of response to stimulus; it must have involved an image of the future of the use of the tool.

A decision is essentially a choice among competing images of the future, as we have seen, and with the development of complex images of the future decisions become an increasingly important element in the dynamics of the individual human being and his society. This introduces what might properly be called a teleological, purposeful element in the process of social dynamics. The human race is not merely pushed by past events or present circumstances, but it is also pulled by its own images of the future into a future, which may not be the same—and in fact is not likely to be the same—as its images of it, but which is nevertheless powerfully affected by those images. The image of the future is of course some projection of the image of the past. We have no experience of the future and only an imperfect record of the past.

Out of this record, however, as we have seen, we build up patterns and project them in complex ways to become images of the future.

In the early stages of human development these images of the future involve only the individual person and perhaps a few people, such as a family or band. With increasing communication, however, images of the future have become wider in scope, more widely shared, and a very important part of religious and ideological movements, which in turn have profound effects in shaping the future, though not necessarily according to their own images of it. Early Christianity had a strong image of the future, which consisted of a catastrophic end of the world or a judgment at some unspecified time, and of a future of eternal bliss or eternal damnation for the individual depending on his faith and works. This image is still very much alive in the world, organizing strong subcultures, such as Seventh Day Adventists and Jehovah's Witnesses, in ways that lead to earthly futures different from what they might otherwise have been. Marxism also developed a strong image of the future, what has been described as a secular eschatology, which also involved a kind of last judgment in revolution and an earthly kingdom of bliss, at least for the descendants of those who saw the light. This, again, has produced substantial consequences quite different from the image itself.

HUMAN LEARNING

What is even more important than the capacity for forming images is the capacity for changing them in the light of further information inputs. This is in essence the learning capacity of the human organism and it exceeds by orders of magnitude that of any other animal. Learning is a process, as Pringle has pointed out,[6] parallel in many ways to the mutation-selection pattern of evolution. Mutations in the image are a result of the enormous imaging capacity of the human system and its constant activity in creating images. Selection comes through a process of "disappointment." We start with an image of the future and the lapse of time turns this into an image of the past. I start to bite an apple expecting a pleasant sensation of eye and taste. In the next second I find a worm in it; the expectation has been disappointed. I build a machine expecting it to work and it does not; I make a proposal expecting it to be accepted and it is not. Disappointment forces a learning process of some kind upon us; success does not.

The learning process may not be accurate in the sense that we may learn the wrong things from our disappointment. If we do, we are pretty sure to be disappointed again. The capacity of the human race to fall into very stable superstitions is not to be underestimated, superstition being a perception of order where there really is none. Pigeons apparently can fall into the same trap in experimental situations, so at least we are not alone in this capacity. Superstitions, however, do have a certain tendency to be found out eventually. The truth has the remarkable capacity that it cannot be found out. It is this asymmetry between truth and lies and between truth and error that makes for the ultimate growth of human knowledge as an image of the universe, which increasingly conforms to the realities.

THE EVOLUTION OF HUMAN
KNOWLEDGE—FOLK, LITERARY, AND SCIENTIFIC

We can trace perhaps three stages in the evolution of human knowledge. The first is the state of folk knowledge, by which we gain images of ordinary life and the ordinary world in our immediate environment. This knowledge is usually quite accurate. We have images of our own house, of our possessions, of the town where we live, of our activities and work and play, all of which are reasonably accurate simply because they are subject to very rapid disappointment when they are wrong. If I have an image of the house of a friend and go to visit him and find he has moved, I very soon find that out and my image is correspondingly changed. I do not go to the old address again. Paleolithic man, likewise, had a set of folk images of his cave, the surrounding woods, the people in his own and other bands, where there were animals to hunt, and where there were vegetable foods to gather. This too was quite accurate, again because of very rapid feedback. Folk knowledge is just as much alive and just as accurate today as it was in the earlier states of the human race.

The next stage might be called the "literary-philosophical" or "speculative," and again it undoubtedly began very early. Because of the extraordinary fertility of the human imagination, we make analogies, perceive similarities and differences, and evoke fantasies of worlds and experiences that we do not experience. We can imagine ourselves flying like a bird or growing and shrinking in size like Alice in Wonderland; we can imagine animals talking, creatures with one eye in the middle of their foreheads, and all the vast fantasy world of fairy tales, gods, and epics. In modern times we write novels of plausible stories about imaginary human beings who belong to a world that might have happened.

The individual is conscious of himself or herself as conscious beings. We observe other people like ourselves around us and conclude that they too are conscious beings by inference mainly from the communications they emit. We find that communications emitted by ourselves can affect the behavior of others: a proffered handshake is accepted, a warning shout is heeded, an invitation to sit down is taken, and a question is answered. It is not surprising that behavior, which is so successful in regard to fellow human beings, should also be tried out on the nonhuman world. When rain is needed, for example, we devise rain dances to ask for it; we populate the trees and the rocks and the landscapes that arouse us to emotion with spirits we feel are communicating with us. Neither is it surprising that we attribute to animals emotions similar to our own. Children observe that animals do not talk to them; they often observe also that some human beings do not talk to them, and the conclusion is not absurd that, if animals do not talk, it is because they are reticent, not because they do not have anything to say.

The great spectacle of the heavens likewise arouses deep emotion and attempts at explanation that go beyond the folk experience. Quite early in human history indeed the perception of the regular cycles of the solar system appears, if we are to interpret the marks on some extremely early artifacts as calendars. The capacity for imagining the future soon enabled us to perceive the daily rhythms and the monthly rhythms of the moon and the annual rhythms of the sun. The perception that the sun that has just set is the same sun that will rise tomorrow may have come quite early in the human experience and it was a great step forward. Beyond the realm of personal experience, however, images are very hard to test, and this leads into a mutation without selection, a large proliferation of fantasies and images of the universe beyond our immediate environment. Insofar as these images cannot be tested, they do very little harm; they do not very much affect behavior. Some superstition has a strong pathological side. If we really guide our behavior by the omens, we may get into serious trouble. Nevertheless, as is often the case, the auguries may be merely a way of making random decisions feel more comfortable. There is a little toy for executives, a top that can be spun and will yield at random either "Yes" or "No." The oracle bones of Shang China, the entrails of the Romans, the horoscopes of the astrologers, and even the models of the economists are not very much different. When, however, we make essentially random decisions in situations where nonrandomness can be known, we are doing worse than we might do.

THE EVOLUTION OF SCIENCE

Science, the third process of acquiring human knowledge, is a subculture that has developed in full splendor only in the last 500 years, though it had forerunners in earlier periods among the Greeks, Persians, Chinese, and Mayans. It is essentially a system of organized learning from disappointments and a device for testing images beyond the range of folk knowledge. It has been strongly influenced and indeed made possible by the development of artifacts that expand perception and permit measurement. The telescope, microscope, spectroscope, thermometer, barometer, photograph, and so on in vast variety have all expanded our powers of perception not only of immediate experience but also of our records and perceptions of the past. Without the telescope, it is doubtful whether the Copernican system, which originated essentially in a speculation, would have been successful. If Galileo, Kepler, and Newton had had computers, they might have been able to do the more complicated arithmetic of the Ptolemaic system, which might then have survived, though the aesthetic taste for simplicity in itself would probably have caused the Copernican system to triumph. Without the microscope, and now of course the electron microscope, modern biology would be inconceivable.

Experimental science is a culture that produces artificial images of the future and then compares them carefully with the images of the past produced with the passage of time. Experimental science has fairly narrow limits. It can only investigate very short processes and events of high probability, but these do cover an important field of human knowledge. Observational science is concerned with the records of the past and with improving the records in the present so that, when they become records of the past, they will be better and we will then have a better chance of perceiving the patterns and regularities in them. The improvement of the record of the past, indeed, whether through astronomical observations, archeological and paleontological discoveries, carbon dating, national income statistics, or social indicators, is one of the major and most important activities of the scientific community and it has a cumulative effect, because the better our records of the past are, the more accurate our images of it will be, and the better our chance will be of perceiving regularities and projecting them into the future.

HUMANS AS NICHE-EXPANDERS: FOLK KNOWLEDGE IN THE PALEOLITHIC AND NEOLITHIC

The great difference between biological and societal evolution is that, whereas prehuman organisms occupy niches and expand to fill them, the human organism is a niche-expander creating the niches into which it will expand. Richard G. Wilkinson has brought this out very delightfully in his book, *Poverty and Progress*.[7] Three great epochs of niche expansion of the human race may be noted corresponding roughly to our three forms of knowledge formation. The first, of course, is the advent of Homo sapiens himself, 50,000 to 100,000 years ago, as a language-forming, image-making, artifact-making, art-creating, organization-making being. The ancestors of Homo sapiens, such as Homo erectus and Neanderthal man, had essentially local niches. They did not expand to the whole planet, though we do not really know whether in the absence of competitors one or other of them might have done so. There is no doubt about Homo sapiens, however. Even though he exercised very little of the capacity of his nervous system, he was still able to expand his niche to the whole planet, except the South polar region, adapting to a great variety of environments—prairies, forests, mountains, plains, tropical, temperate and subarctic climates—wherever there were animals to hunt or plants to gather.

Because of isolation, Homo sapiens developed subspecies or races differing in minor characteristics like skin color, height, facial features, and so on. All of these were varieties of the one biological species. Even in the early days of relatively isolated bands there was either enough passage of individuals between them and interbreeding to prevent the isolation developing into new biological species, or else the mutational potential of this particular phylum had become somewhat exhausted and mutation had slowed down. There has been very little biological change in the human race in the last 50,000 or 100,000 years, compared with the very rapid biological changes that seem to have taken place in the previous 2,000,000 years among the human ancestors.

To judge by the records of their artifacts, the culture of paleolithic man also was subject to very little change over many hundreds of generations. This is puzzling. One wonders how a creature biologically identical with us and possessed by the same restlessness and extraordinary potential for noogenetic mutation could have managed to remain in a relative cultural equilibrium for so long. One possible explanation, which is not however very convincing, is that it took this long for the human race to learn how to talk, that is, to develop the complete language which is in the potential of the human nervous system. Another possible explanation is the precariousness of the cumulative learning process in a very small group. The cave paintings of Cro-Magnon humans suggest that there must have been periods of rapid development of ideas and artistic skills. In bands of at most a few dozen people, however, the transmission of knowledge from one generation to the next is precarious. A catastrophe such as an epidemic or a fight could kill off all the people in the band who knew anything very much, the band then would revert to the immature knowledge of the young, and the accumulation of the previous generations could easily be lost.

In part, of course, much of our image of paleolithic stability may be created by the appalling lack of records. There may have been all sorts of artifacts and continuously all sorts of artistic creation on highly perishable materials. It is only the accident, for instance, that the cave paintings are unusually durable, which gives us a clue as to what may have been going on. Still, if the surviving paleolithic peoples can be projected into the past, it still suggests a very long period of cultural stability. Paleolithic man probably occupied his niche pretty fully by 20,000 B.C., when he had certainly expanded into North America and all over the Old World from the tropical forests to the edge of the northern tundra. North America seems to have been invaded anew about 11,000 B.C. by late paleolithic people who proceeded to exterminate most of the large animals and may, who knows, have been forced into an independent discovery of agriculture as a result.

There is still a great debate about diffusion versus independent invention of agriculture. There is no doubt that it represents a very major niche expansion of the human race. With the coming of neolithic agriculture not only did the expectation of life increase, perhaps from 30 to nearly 40, but the population also increased many times because a given area could support a much larger population with agriculture and domesticated animals than with hunting and gathering. About 10,000 B.C. is the date for the first beginnings; by 5,000 B.C. we have a great belt of agricultural peoples from

China, through India, the Middle East, to Europe, and perhaps a little later in meso-America. The hunting and gathering peoples were pushed to the edges of this large agricultural population.

CIVILIZATION AND LITERARY KNOWLEDGE

Out of agriculture comes a food surplus of storable foods. Hunting and gathering societies sometimes had surpluses, but fish and meat are not very storable, and grains and roots are hard to find and it is hard to get a surplus of them beyond daily use. With agriculture, however, surpluses of storable grains became common and out of this came civilization: irrigation, the "oriental despotism" of Karl A. Wittfogel,[8] cities consuming the agricultural surplus, empires, armies and wars, temples and palaces, kings and conquerors. The development of civilization probably expanded the niche of the human race from what it had been under neolithic agriculture, though perhaps not by very much. Rulers have usually forced the agriculturalist to work harder and increase the food surplus, which was then eaten by the people in the cities—kings, priests, artisans, and soldiers.

The age of civilization, which we may put at about 3,000 B.C. to 2,000 A.D., has seen the gradual spread of cities and agriculture over the world, reaching some parts such as Central Africa only in the twentieth century. It is characterized by literary and philosophical knowledge among the educated and the elite, and almost continual expansion of folk knowledge—what might almost be called "folk science"—among farmers and craftsmen, the people who actually made the artifacts. Only at certain times and places, such as the Roman Empire after Augustus, were civilized societies technologically stagnant. For the most part there was constant invention and diffusion of improved artifacts during this period, leading to a slow expansion of the human niche and a slow, but fairly steady expansion of the human population, interrupted occasionally by plagues, wars, and social collapse.

SCIENCE AND POST-CIVILIZATION

With the development of science, a new niche expansion began into something that might be called "post-civilization," particularly after the beginning of the application of scientific knowledge to the production of human artifacts, which can be dated roughly about the mid-nineteenth century. Thus, the chemical industry began in the 1860s. Beginning about 1860 also, new applications of science came to metallurgy. The electrical industry started in the 1880s. Since 1930, the application of science to agriculture has enormously increased agricultural productivity, per man more than per acre, although there has been a noticeable increase also in yields per acre. It is the yield per acre that determines the size of the human niche. The yield per man is important in determining the distribution of human activity between agriculture and other pursuits. The limit of the total human population is determined by the average number of people an acre can feed and the number of acres. The number of people in agriculture depends on the yield per person, that is, on the number each person in agriculture can feed. If one family in agriculture can feed 25 others, then we need only 4 percent of the population in agriculture; 96 percent can be devoted to producing other things.

SOCIAL ORGANIZATIONS AS HUMAN ARTIFACTS: THE "SOCIAL ORGANIZERS"–THREATS, EXCHANGE, AND "LOVE"

A final set of characteristics of social dynamics that differentiates it from biological dynamics is the existence of what might be called "social organizers," involving types of relationships between individual human beings that create organizations. Organizations are a major category of human artifact. Relationships between individuals of other living species are rarely continuous enough to develop organizations. There are some exceptions to this—in the slave-holding ants who capture aphids and milk them or other ants and make them work for them. Outside of this there is very little social organization in the nonhuman animal world. There is of course the family, patterns of which vary considerably from species to species, but there is never even an extended family. There are something like "tribes," for instance, of baboons and groups of rats, but these never extend beyond a few individuals. Biologists frequently describe an ecosystem as a "community," but this is usually a false metaphor. Each species goes its own way. It interacts with others, but it does not have a community with them; it does not form organizations. The individual living organism is an organization built by the information of its genome, but as between living organisms, organization is rare.

In social systems, however, organization is of great importance. We talk, indeed, about the "body politic" and the metaphor of the organism is often used to describe organizations. The metaphor, however, has to be used very warily. Organizations are not organisms, though in some ways they are like them; they are something different. One human being is capable of changing the behavior, the role images, even the identity of another. This is very rare in the animal kingdom. The wolf catches the rabbit and eats it; it does not threaten the rabbit and make it work for him. A tree may shelter a bird, but it does not exchange with it. Two species may be symbiotic, but they do not love each other.

Organizations come into being through activities that can be described as "social organizers." These have no close parallels in biological dynamics. The closest thing to them is perhaps the enzymes, the chemical messengers that organize the growth of different parts of the body, but the analogy is not at all close. The social organizers are relationships among two or more individuals that change role structures, which thereby create organizations, and which create great networks of hierarchy, dependency, and mutuality.

There are three major classes of social organizers: the threat relationship, the exchange relationship, and the integrative relationship ("love"). Each is discussed in the following three chapters. Each of them creates a great network in the social fabric of space and time, which we may call the threat system, the exchange system, and the integrative system. One is almost tempted to call these the polity, the economy, and the integry.

Another peculiarity of the social system is the extent to which it is characterized by dialectical processes involving struggle and conflict of organized groups. These processes are rare in the biological world. The struggle for existence, as we saw earlier, was a completely misleading metaphor. War or revolution is a phenomenon almost entirely confined to the human race, with the possible exception of the ants.

Clearly social dynamics are extremely complex and there are many things about them we do not understand and perhaps never will. The dynamics of symbolic systems, for instance, are very puzzling. Why do certain symbols have great power over human minds in one period and not in another? The outbursts of energy and expansion that seem to take place in social systems from time to time and from place to place are also very puzzling. A realistic image of social dynamics, however, is of great importance for human behavior. False images in the past have led to such catastrophic results and such an enormous amount of human misery that, for anyone concerned with human improvement, the increase in the realism of our image of the dynamic processes of society should be the first priority.

NOTES

1. H. Bentley Glass, O. Temkin and W. L. Strauss, eds. *Forerunners of Darwin*, 1745-1859 (Baltimore: Johns Hopkins Press, 1959).

2. "Many improvements have been made by the ingenuity of the makers of the machines; . . . and some by that of those who are called philosophers or men of speculation, whose trade it is not to do anything, but to observe every thing; and who, upon that account, are often capable of combining together the powers of the most distant and dissimilar objects." Adam Smith, *The Wealth of Nations* (New York: Modern Library Edition), 10.

3. Friedrich Engles, *The Dialectics of Nature*, trans. by Clemens Duff (Moscow: Progress Publishers, 1966).

4. Noam Chomsky, *Syntactic Structures* (New York: Humanities Press, 1957).

5. B. L. Whorf, *Language, Thought and Reality* (Boston: Technology Press, 1956).

6. J.W.S. Pringle, "On the Parallel Between Learning and Evolution," *Behavior*, Vol. 3 (1951).

7. Richard G. Wilkinson, *Poverty and Progress* (New York: Praeger, 1973).

8. Karl A. Wittfogel, *Oriental Despotism* (New Haven: Yale University Press, 1957).

Chapter 7

The Threat System

THE MEANING OF "THREAT" AND REACTIONS TO IT

The word "threat" has at least two meanings in English, which may cause some confusion. It may mean simply a condition in which there is an uncertain expectation of something bad happening—the skies look "threatening" when there a threat of a storm. This first meaning, however, is derived by a somewhat false animistic analogy from the second meaning, which is the one used in this chapter, which is that of a threat as a statement, explicit or implicit, made by one person to another to the effect that "You do something that I want or I will do something that you do not want." That is, "You do something that I will perceive as improving my condition or I will do something that you perceive as worsening yours." When we talk about the threat of a storm, we personify the weather.

The idea of a threat implies there is a relationship between at least two people. It implies that these people are capable of images of the future and that they are capable of evaluating these images, that is, of ordering them in some sense as either better or worse. Threats are carried out when the threatener actually does something that is perceived, probably by both parties but certainly by the threatened party, as making the condition of the threatened party worse according to that party's own value orderings. An action of this kind is one of the meanings of the word "aggression," though this again is an unfortunate word that has a number of different meanings. It may simply mean active and expansive as opposed to inert or contractive—a movement toward higher values as perceived by the aggressive organism without much regard as to whether other organisms are moved to lower values. On the other hand, we are quite within the regular meanings of the word to regard the carrying out of a threat as an act of aggression.

A threat creates a field of choice on the part of the threatened party. Four types of reaction or alternative futures may be open: submission, defiance, counterthreat, or flight. The future course of the system depends very much, of course, on which of these is selected. One of these, of course, may be perceived as so overwhelmingly superior to the others that there is no sense of choice. The potential field of choice, however, must always be kept in mind.

Submission

In submission, the threatened party does what the threatener demands and the threatener does not carry out the threats. This may create a temporary organization, as when, for instance, a bandit says "Your money or your life," the victim gives the bandit his money, and the bandit goes off with it, leaving the victim with his life. This looks a bit like an exchange but, as we shall see later, as an exchange it is a fraud. On the other hand, a threat-submission system may create a more or less permanent relationship and a permanent organization, as in the case of the master and slave. The master says to the slave in effect: "Work for me or I will kill you." This threat is continued throughout the relationship, and the slave continues to work for the master under the constant, at least implied, shadow of the threat. All legal systems involve threat-submission relationships of this kind. We obey speed limits and pay our taxes because of some quite explicit threats, which are made by the political structure of society in the shape of the law and its enforcement apparatus in traffic police and courts, Internal Revenue agents, law courts, judges, prisons, and so on. We obey the law mainly because we decide that, if we do not, we have a sufficient probability of getting into more trouble than it is worth.

If the threat-submission system is to persist over a substantial period of time and so form the basis of organization, it must in some sense be legitimated, that is, it must be accepted by both parties. Legitimation is part of the integrative system and we will discuss it in more detail later. For the moment it is sufficient to note that threats that are perceived as in some sense legitimate are much more powerful in organizing than those which are not. The political system or "polity," which involves the whole apparatus of legislative, executive, and judicial branches of state or local governments and organizations such as elections that put people in the roles appropriate to these functions, is all part of a legitimated threat system based on legitimated submission. Just why such systems arise and why they are necessary will be discussed later.

Defiance: Challenges, Feints, Bluffs, and Boasts

Defiance is a second possible response to a threat. The threatener conveys a message to the threatened: "You do A, which I want, or I will do B, which you do not want"; and the threatened party replies: "Go jump in a lake." That is, "I will not do A." This then throws the initiative back to the threatener who then has to make a choice between carrying out the threat or not carrying it out.

The defiance response raises problems of considerable subtlety. In the first place, we have to make a distinction between capability and credibility. Capability is the question of whether the threatener is capable of carrying out the threats? Credibility is the question of whether the threatener and the threatened party believe that the threatener is capable of carrying out the threat and will in fact carry it out if the threat is defied. For each party the threat may be credible or noncredible, and this gives us a matrix of four possible situations as we see in Table 7.1. If both the threatener and the threatened believe the threat will be carried out if his conditions are not met, we have what might be called a "challenge," in which both parties believe. The threat is perceived by both parties as real. If the threatener does not believe he will carry out the threat, but the threatened party does believe it, then the threatener is telling a lie. If the threatened party does not know this, however, this is a bluff. As long as this situation persists, however, it will presumably have the same effect on the behavior of the threatened party as a challenge. If the threatener believes the threat will be carried out, but the threatened party does not believe it, this is a feint—the threatened party believes the threat is feigned, but the threatener does not perceive it in this way. If neither party believes the threat will be carried out, what we have is a boast. This may be part of the conventions of social intercourse. It may have effects in changing the image each party has of the other, but it will not produce much immediate effect.

The conditions of defiance are different in these different cases, dependent particularly on the perceptions of the threatened party. If the threatened party believes in the threat, that is, under the conditions of challenge and bluff, defiance will only take place if the cost of submission or of the other alternatives of flight and counterthreat are regarded as higher than the costs

TABLE 7.1
Patterns of Threat

		Threatener	
		(Credible)	(Non-Credible)
		Believes Threat Will Be Carried Out	*Does Not Believe*
Threatened Party	(Credible) Believes	Challenge	Bluff
	(Non-Credible) Does Not Believe	Feint	Boast

of defiance. If the threat is perceived as a small one, whereas the costs of submission, flight, or counterthreat are perceived as high, then the threatened party may simply, "Carry out the threat and see if I care." This is not altogether an infrequent pattern, although probably much more rare than submission. One spouse says to the other, "You do so and so or I will divorce you," and the other says, "All right, go ahead and divorce me." A says to B, "Do such and such or I will sue you," and B says, "All right, go ahead and sue."

Defiance is much more likely, however, under the conditions of feint and boast where the threatened party does not believe the threatener will carry out the threat. The feint is a situation in which the threat is most likely to be carried out, often to the detriment of both parties.

The situation is even more complicated than we have represented it to be in Table 7.1 because the dynamics of the situation depend not only on what each party thinks about his own future and his own behavior, but also on what each party thinks the other thinks. Thus, each of the four boxes of Table 7.1 can be expanded into four other boxes. In Table 7.2, we expand the pattern of challenge to where both the threatener (A) and the threatened (B) believe the threat will be carried out if there is defiance. The threatener, however, may think either that the threatened believes it or that the threatened does not believe it; the threatened may think either that the threatener believes it or that the threatener does not believe it.

This again leads to a matrix of four possible situations. If each party believes that the other believes, we have what might be called "real challenge," where each party's perceptions of the other are realistic. If the threatened party thinks the threatener believes it, but the threatener thinks the threatened party does not believe it, we have what might be called the "false bluff," that is, the threatener perceives his own position as a challenge, but thinks the threatened party perceives it as a bluff. Similarly, if the threatener thinks the threatened party believes it, but the threatened party thinks the threatener does not believe it, we have a "false feint." If each thinks the other does not believe it, we have a "false boast." In each of the three "false" cases, there is misperception on the part of at least one party of the beliefs of the other. Each of the four boxes of Table 7.1 could similarly

TABLE 7.2

Patterns of Challenge

Threatened (B) Believes		Threatener (A) (Believes)	
		Thinks B Believes	Thinks B Does Not Believe
Thinks A Believes		Real Challenge	False Bluff
Thinks A Does Not Believe		False Feint	False Boast

be expanded, giving us sixteen cases in all, but at this point I am afraid ordinary language simply breaks down.

RELATIONAL SEQUENCES

What we are struggling with here is the problem of relational sequences. We have two parties, A and B, in some sort of contact. A does something, so B does something, which makes A do something else, then B does something else, A then does something else, and so on in the relational sequence. To describe these, we must have some kind of theory of behavior. The most elementary form of this is what economists call the theory of maximizing behavior, which states that everybody does what he thinks is best at the time. That means, however, that behavior is directed by perception, not by realities. We choose what we think is most highly valued of our perceived images of the future. In relational sequences, however, these images are changed in the course of the sequence. Any particular act of behavior or decision is made in the light of the existing images, that is, the subjective view of the world of the behaving or deciding party. As other parties make decisions, this produces messages that may change the images of the first party and so change subsequent decisions.

Why does the threatener then make an initial threat? Presumably because he has an image of the world in which he visualizes the threatened party as responding in a way that will move the threatener to a preferred view of the world. Now suppose he is disappointed because, for instance, he expects submission and gets defiance. Then there is a learning process. He has to change his image of the world in some way. In the light of this changed image, he has to decide between carrying out and not carrying out the threat. If he carries it out, this will be costly to him as well as to the other party; if he does not carry it out, this may damage his credibility. The threatened party may cease to believe in the threat, thinking that the threatener's bluff has been called, or may equally well argue that a second act of defiance is all the more likely to produce the threatened response. In the light of these uncertainties, the carrying out of a threat is often more an attempt to restore the threatener's belief in his own credibility after an act of defiance than it is designed to create conformity on the part of the defier. Defiance, indeed, always moves close to counterthreat in the sense that it involves a threat to the credibility of the threatener.

The perceptions of the cost of carrying out a threat are an extremely important element in the dynamics of the threat system. Threats are costly to the threatener as well as to the threatened if credibility is to be sustained, that is, if the threatener is to continue to believe that the threatened believes in his threats, thus sustaining the pattern of "real challenge." There almost has to be investment in capability if credibility is to be sustained.

CAPABILITY AND CREDIBILITY

The long history and evolution of weapons is very closely connected with this phenomenon, and the obvious possession of a weapon is in the first instance a message about capability, intended to produce credibility. The gun in the hand of the bandit is in the first instance a message intended to produce credibility in the victim. If the victim believes it is a toy gun and defies the bandit and is killed, both parties are presumably worse off than if the victim had believed and handed over his money. The acquisition of the gun, however, is part of the cost to the bandit, not to the victim.

The high cost of both creating credibility and carrying out threats to the threatener as well as to the threatened is one reason why many of the most successful threats have been very strong bluffs. Slavery is a possible example. The master in effect says to the slave, "Work for me or I will kill you." If the slave defies him and the master kills him, the master does not have a slave and is clearly worse off. The submission of the slave, therefore, rests more frequently on the false belief that the master will kill him although, of course, punishments have played an important role in creating the credibility of the master and the submission of the slave. As we shall see later, however, when the integrative system develops to a certain point, slavery simply falls apart because the bluff that lies at its core is revealed.

Organized religions, insofar as they have been based on threats, are an even more striking example of the extraordinary persistence of bluff. The situation is perhaps better called "invalid challenge," because both parties may believe that the threatener is capable of carrying out the threat. That is, we have a situation of real challenge in terms of Table 7.2, but both parties may be mistaken. Thus, both the Aztec priests and the people probably believed they had to have human sacrifices in order to make corn grow, despite the fact that this is an invalid proposition. Similarly, in the medieval church probably many popes believed they could sent people to Hell and the people believed it too. This again was a situation of real challenge, but the capability has never been demonstrated. The weapons of bell, book, and candle remain extremely effective symbols capable of inspiring credibility without ever having to demonstrate capability.

Counterthreat and Deterrence as an Unstable System

Defiance passes very easily over into counterthreat. The threat-counter-threat system is deterrence. A says to B, "You do something that I want or I will do something that you do not want." B replies to A, "If you do something that I do not want, I will do something that *you* do not want." If A threatens to move the state of the world to a position where B is worse off, B responds by threatening to move the state of the world to where A is worse off if A attempts to carry out his threat. There is a certain difference perhaps in the time relationship between the initial threatener and the responder. Once the responder has made the response, however, the situation becomes highly symmetrical and each party says to the other in effect, "If you do something I do not like, I will do something you do not like." Or, "If you make things worse for me, I will make things worse for you."

The effect of deterrence is to stabilize the situation, at least in the short run. A refrains from doing what B does not like and B refrains from doing what A does not like. There is, however, an important theorem about deterrence which states that it can be stable in the short run, but it cannot be stable in the long run. This theorem can be proved in a sentence by saying that, if deterrence were stable, it would cease to deter because the threats would lose their credibility. There must be a positive probability of the threats being carried out because, if this probability were zero, they would obviously cease to be credible. If, however, there is a positive probability of anything happening and we wait long enough, it will happen—a theorem of great importance to evolutionary dynamics.

This proposition, although it is essentially a logical deduction from the he time relationship between the initial threatener and the responder. Once the responder has made the response, however, the situation becomes highly symmetrical and each party says to the other in effect, "If you do something I do not like, I will do something you do not like." Or, "If you make things worse for me, I will make things worse for you."

The effect of deterrence is to stabilize the situation, at least in the short run. A refrains from doing what B does not like and B refrains from doing what A does not like. There is, however, an important theorem about deterrence which states that it can be stable in the short run, but it cannot be stable in the long run. This theorem can be proved in a sentence by saying that, if deterrence were stable, it would cease to deter because the threats would lose their credibility. There must be a positive probability of the threats being carried out because, if this probability were zero, 'they would obviously cease to be credible. If, however, there is a positive probability of anything happening and we wait long enough, it will happen—a theorem of great importance to evolutionary dynamics.

This proposition, although it is essentially a logical deduction from the nature of the system, is abundantly confirmed in human history, where systems of deterrence have constantly broken down into war. Not all wars are wars of deterrence, but a considerable number of them are. They take place for two reasons. One is that random events may provoke belief that the threats will be carried out, so one party often carries out threat in the belief that the other party is about to carry out its threat. A second reason is that the credibility of threats tends to depreciate over time like almost everything else. When the credibility of one party's threat falls below a certaint point in the mind of the other, the deterrence system may lapse into challenge and one party may say to the other in effect, "I do not believe in your counterthreat. You do what I want, or I will carry out my threat." This in turn, as we have seen, often leads to defiance and to the carrying out of the threat.

The present uneasy situation of nuclear deterrence, for instance, between the United States and the Soviet Union is a depressingly good case in point. It certainly achieves temporary stability. Neither the United States nor the Soviet Union has dropped nuclear weapons on each other for the 30 years or so that they have had them. Nevertheless, there is clearly a positive probability that they will go off—an accident, a mad bomber, or a tense situation in which one party or the other decides to make a demonstration could all trigger a catastrophic interchange that perhaps would be fatally destructive for both parties.

The duel is another historical example of the same phenomenon. As long as the duel was sanctioned in a culture, it probably acted as a certain deterrent to quarrelsome behavior, though it may also have incited certain conventions of quarrelsomeness. There were many occasions, however, on which this deterrence broke down and even in which both parties were killed. As we shall see later, deterrence can be transformed into something else and indeed, if it is not so transformed, it will inevitably result in eventual disaster. Another example of the pathological results of the deterrence system is the feud, which has existed in many societies. There is, for instance, the famous Hatfield and McCoy feud in Kentucky. The phenomenon is still not extinct in the underworld of organized crime. Again, we have a situation perceived by both parties as deterrence, but which continually breaks down into murders.

THE ARMS RACE

A system of deterrence tends to become increasingly costly to the participants through the phenomenon of the arms race. In order to maintain the credibility of its threats, each party has to have an organization for carrying out threats. This indeed is one of the principal functions of the armed forces of national states. They are designed to produce "bads" on call. A "bad" is a "negative good," a diminution of values in terms of life and commodities in the mind of a potential enemy. Armed forces are designed to change the state of the world in such a way as to make a potential enemy worse off. During peace, which actually is most of the time, armed forces are a mere potential of activity. That is, they are not doing what they are designed to do, which is to produce bads. They are simply standing ready to produce bads if they are called upon. This makes the whole organizational psychology of armed forces very different from that of a productive enterprise, such as a manufacturing firm designed to produce goods in which actually producing them is a test of success. A test of success of a system of deterrence is not producing the bad that is threatened. This is why armed forces tend to deteriorate in peace time and why there is constant erosion of the threats they represent. The arms race may be interpreted partly as a device to overcome this erosion, but also as a phenomenon arising out of the mutual responsive behavior of two opposing military organizations. It has a strong tendency to take pathological forms.

The mathematical theory of arms races is outlined in the appendix to this chapter. It involves, first, some definition of the size of the armed forces of each nation. Ideally, this should consist of the absolute amount of gross national product devoted to the military budget multiplied by some measure of efficiency. However, because efficiency is extremely hard to judge in these matters, usually the total military budget in terms of real dollars is accepted as a substitute. Then the question arises, what does this amount depend on? In the simplest model it is assumed that the size of the armed forces of nation A depends only on the size of the armed forces of nation B, and conversely, the size of the armed forces of nation B depends only on the size of the armed forces of nation A. These relationships are generally assumed to be positive; that is, a rise in the armed forces of B will produce a rise in the armed forces of A, and a rise in the armed forces of A will produce a rise in the armed forces of B. This is very similar to the interaction of mutually cooperative species discussed in Chapter 4. It may seem like a paradox, but in fact the armed forces of different nations are mutually cooperative with each other and competitive with the domestic-civilian activity of each nation. That is, a rise in the armed forces of one nation will produce a rise in the armed forces of the other and a diminution in the civilian product of each nation.

Under circumstances that can be specified mathematically, there may be a position of equilibrium under this situation, in which the armed forces of each nation are compatible with that of the other. It is shown in the appendix that the position of this equilibrium depends on two major parameters of the system. The first is called "initial hostility," that is, the size of the armed forces of each nation in the absence of the armed forces of the other. The second parameter is the "reactivity" of each nation, that is, the degree to which it will expand its armed forces in response to an increase in the armed forces of the other. If an increase of one dollar in the armed forces of B produces an increase of one dollar in A, the reactivity is 1.0. If it produces less than a one dollar increase in A, the reactivity is less than 1.0. It can be shown that the product of reactivities of two nations must be less than 1.0 if there is to be an equilibrium, and that the size of the armed forces of each nation will be larger the larger the initial hostility of either and the larger the reactivity of either. The way to get low levels of armaments is to have low initial hostilities and low reactivities. It can be shown mathematically that the more nations are in contact in the arms race, the lower the reactivities have to be in order to get an equilibrium at all.

If there is no equilibrium position of the arms race, armaments will continue to increase until some kind of a boundary is reached that is imposed by other factors. This may be a boundary of war. Historically there is a strong tendency for vigorous arms races to end in war, because the arms race itself becomes intolerable to one of the parties. Apart from war the only solution of an arms race seems to be some kind of agreement, such as the Rush-Bagot Agreement of 1817, which achieved partial disarmament of the American-

Canadian frontier and turned out to be a great success. The size of the armed forces of a nation depends, of course, on many other things besides the armed forces of competing nations. The theory of arms races is by no means a complete theory for the determination of the size of armed forces. It is however a very important beginning.

Flight as a Response to Threat

The fourth possible response to threat or to an initial challenge is flight or escape. Historically, this has been very important and has almost certainly been one of the main forces making for diffusion of the human population over the planet. It is a response that is not unique to threat situations. It may be a response to any situation perceived as less favorable than the "haven," the place toward which the flight is made. History is full of the record of more-or-less successful flights. The less successful ones tend not to be recorded unless they are of a particularly dramatic character. Notable examples are: the exodus of the children of Israel from Egypt to get away from the threat system of the Pharaohs, the flight of the holy family into Egypt to get away from the threat system of Herod, the flight of the Pilgrim Fathers to the New World, the flight of the Jews into Israel, the flight of the Mennonites into and out of Russia, the long march of the Chinese communists, the great trek of the Boers, the long flight of the Mormons to Utah—the list goes on and on.

Flight in general is simply a movement from what is perceived as a worse place to what is perceived as a better place, whether it is a divorce out of a marriage that has turned into an unfavorable exchange, or a search for opportunity and wealth in a new and more empty land. Flight from threat, however, arises out of a peculiarity of the threat relationship, which is that the capacity to inflict injury usually diminishes with distance. There is a cost of transport of bads just as there is of goods. As an army gets further and further from its own base, it becomes harder to provision and supply and less and less capable of inflicting injury. The relationship is not even linear because the suppliers have to be supplied, and the suppliers of the suppliers have to be supplied. In any kind of operation, one gets to a certain distance where further action is impossible.

This is the principle I have called "the further, the weaker." It is a perfectly general principle of action, intercourse, or communication. It appears in economics in the cost of transportation of commodities, in communications as a loss of information through distance. Flight from threat is possible, therefore, because the further we go from the origin of the threat, the weaker it becomes. At some point as we move away from it, the threat can be defied with impunity, or at least it is severely mitigated in its effects. The American colonists could defy the might of the British threat system and get away with it, but the Irish could not, at least until much later, mainly because the Americans were so much further away than the Irish.

Those who run away from threat have a strong tendency to set up a threat system of their own, as indeed the American colonists did when they founded the United States. Or, of course, people who have not run away, but who simply happen to live at a distance from an existing threat system, are also able to set up one of their own. If two sources of threat are far enough away from each other, neither can really threaten the other. It is this principle that gives rise to the multiplicity of political states and empires over the course of human history. Political states and political cities tend to rise, as we have seen, when there is a surplus of food from the food producer and a "ruler" is able to create an organized and at least partially legitimated internal threat system, which is able to extract a portion of the food surplus from the food producer. With the food thus extracted, the ruler is able to feed artisans, builders, tax collectors, soldiers, lawyers, judges, and executioners, which are the main occupational types of "civilized" cities.

The first threat systems often seem to have been spiritual threats imposed by the persuasive powers of the priesthood. Farmers seem to be simple, gullible souls and the clever symbol maker seems to be able to persuade them that, if they do not relinquish their "tithes" to the priesthood, the proper ceremonies will not be performed and the crops will not grow. In any system dependent on an environment with fairly strong random elements in it like the weather, superstitions are easier to form as we perceive temporary but invalid regularities. Once formed, superstitions have a strong tendency to persist, as we selectively perceive only those random events that support them, and reject the perception of events that seem to contradict them. There is a tendency in history, however, for the king to supplant the priest, and for the physical threat system to supplant the spiritual one, as recorded in the Bible in the story of Saul and Samuel.[1]

Even for the king, however, the principle of "the further, the weaker" applies, and at some distance from the palace he will no longer be obeyed. What this distance is determines the boundary of the threat organization. It depends on what I have called the "loss of strength gradient," that is, the amount by which the effectiveness or the credibility of threats diminishes per mile as we go away from the source. If this is high, the kingdom will be small; if it is low, the kingdom will be large. This is undoubtedly why the first empires were along the cheap water transportation of the great navigable rivers of the Nile, the Euphrates, the Tigris, the Indus, and the Hwang-Ho. The development of swift horses in·well organized relays permitted the growth of the great nomadic empires of central Asia. It was the combination of the cheapness of sea transport in the Mediterranean and the Roman roads that created the Roman Empire, and it was sea transport likewise that created the British and French Empires of the late nineteenth and twentieth centuries, and the Spanish Empire of the sixteenth, seventeenth, and eighteenth centuries.

The Aztecs and Incas are a bit of a puzzle because they did not use water transportation to any extent and they did not have the wheel for transportation, though they did have swift runners on highway paths. It may have been the sheer magnitude of the threat and the total disregard for human life that permitted these empires to spread further than they otherwise might have done. The Russian Empire is also something of a puzzle as it spread across Siberia in the eighteenth and nineteenth centuries over enormous distances. Its spread was due in part to the absence of any resistance, and in part perhaps to the greater ease of transportation by sled in the winter snows. Snow is really a great road builder. A graphic treatment of this problem is presented in the appendix to this chapter. It shows that there is a distinction between offensive armament, initiated, say, by A, which increases the threat of A to B at any particular point of space, and defensive argument, initiated, say by B, which diminishes A's threat to B at any particular point of space. Offensive armament involves increasing the range of deadly missiles; defensive armament involves such things as building walls like castle fortifications, city walls, or even the Great Wall of China as devices for the detection and deflection of missiles before they reach their objective and so on. Unfortunately, the distinction between offensive and defensive armament is often not at all clear because one instrument often performs both functions. Defensive armaments, however, tend to increase the stability of existing systems, whereas offensive armaments tend to upset it. The instability of threat systems in general perhaps arise partly because offensive armament often has defensive functions, whereas specifically defensive armament does not usually have offensive functions. In biological evolution it is clear that both strategies have created niches—the turtle is a fine example of almost defensive armament, the teeth of the carnivore offensive armament, and the porcupine perhaps somewhere in between.

Between any two threat centers there tends to be a "boundary of equal strength" at which neither can dominate the other. The stability of a threat system depends a good deal on the values to the parties of the field immediately around this boundary. If it is not valuable to either, the boundary tends to be stable and there may be an equilibrium of mutual threat. If the field of the boundary is important to one party, but not to the other, the boundary may be adjusted by exchange. If the field around the boundary is important to both, however, each may try to move the boundary and we will have threat escalation.

An improvement in offensive weapons may eliminate the effectiveness of defensive structures. They may be used, for instance, to knock walls down. The military use of gunpowder was particularly important in this regard, because it destroyed a great deal of the value of defensive armaments. One sees this in a very interesting way in Europe, especially in the Loire Valley, by looking at the great medieval castles, such as the Chinon, with huge walls that could easily keep out the spears and arrows of the older attacking forces. The castles built after the invention of gunpowder changed. They first tried building very wide moats to keep the guns away from the walls, but this did not work. One sees that Chambord, the great castle built by François I, has all the form of the medieval castle but none of its substance. One could practically break into it with a burglar's jimmy. In the eighteenth century one gets completely undefended houses with great windows opening onto broad lawns, reflecting the consolidation of royal power and the disappearance of feudal fighting.

Before the development of aerial warfare, armies provided a kind of living wall, which under some circumstances could keep invaders away from the center of the society in the capitol city, as seen in the trench warfare in World War I. In World War II, however, offensive weapons again had outrun the defenses, but even then, as Hitler advanced into Russia, his armies eventually reached a temporary "position of equal strength." Because as they advanced, their own supply lines became longer and were running through hostile territory while the Russian supply lines became shorter, until by the time the Germans were at Leningrad, Moscow, and Stalingrad, the position stabilized and for a considerable time neither party could advance on the other. The Japanese similarly reached a temporary boundary of equal strength in the Pacific and in Burma. Equilibria of threat systems, however, are as precarious as all equilibria. The effort to sustain the threat system beyond the capacity of the society in Germany eventually led to a total collapse of the system. The boundary of equal strength moved inexorably toward Berlin until the Western allies and the Russians finally met there and Hitler's Germany at least was extinguished.

The conquest of North America by the European immigrants is an example of a situation where the disorganized and fragmented threat system of the Indians was quite unable to cope with the constantly expanding and well organized threat system of the European colonists. The Indians tried flight by retreating out of the range of the colonists, only to find the expanding system of European and later American culture and government catch up with them until they finally all lapsed into the state of colonials on Indian reservations, not even being permitted the luxury of satellite states.

With the diminution of loss of strength gradients, the size of the unconditionally viable state has been increasing, until now it virtually encompasses the whole world. A key factor in this development is the increase in the range of the deadly missile as one of the principal implements of the carrying out of threats. A city-state with a wall could be unconditionally viable against roving bands of bandits armed only with stones, arrows, or spears. Even before the advent of gunpowder, walls were not much use against a really well organized besieging army armed with movable towers and catapults (the first guided missile!). The most developed catapult (the trebuchet) indeed was probably more deadly and had a longer range than the first cannon, though the cannon had a bigger potential for development. Aerial warfare and now of course the guided missile and the nuclear weapon have completely destroyed the concept of defensive armaments, except in the form of silos for missiles or vast underground shelters such as the Chinese are building, which are, however, fundamentally not worth living in. It really looks as if the end of a very long process of expanding political organizations is in sight and that within the next hundred years either mankind will destroy itself in large-scale nuclear war or the beginnings of a viable world political organization capable of policing disarmament will be just around the corner. We shall return to these problems later.

THREAT SYSTEMS IN THE BIOSPHERE

We have discussed threat systems almost wholly in terms of social dynamics, because it is in social systems that they reach their full development. They do exist, however, in the prehuman, biological systems, though on a relatively small scale. Certainly if one mark of threat is weaponry, the animal kingdom can claim a fair amount of it in tusks, horns, claws, and teeth. Nature perhaps has a somewhat undeserved reputation for being red in tooth and claw. Certainly all species eat other species, until we get down to the very bottom of the food chain where plants and bacteria may live off air, rocks, and soil. Predation, however, is not the same thing as threat. The ruminant does not use threats to grow grass; it just uses its teeth to eat it. Eating grass is not all that different from eating rabbits. Animals do occasionally, although rarely, fight among themselves, in pairs, and within species rather than between species. Political organization, however, which is based on the modification of the behavior of others by threat, is pretty rare in the animal kingdom, and certainly unknown in the vegetable kingdom. The closest we get to political organization is territorial behavior. Dogs, birds, baboons, and some herding animals do seem to stake out territory and fight off other individuals,. especially of the same species, who invade it. Animals also employ symbols of threat in their relationships—they growl, beat their chests, show their teeth, and so on—which are pretty clearly threat messages: "If you come any closer, I will bite you." They very rarely use these messages, however, to make another animal do anything else that they want it to do; with the possible exception of the ants, there is no slavery, organized war, and practically no political organizations among the animals. There are thieves—hyenas and vultures—but only very rarely do we find a real bandit, that is, the lowest and most temporary political organization possible.

What might be called the "original sin" school of sociobiologists—Lorenz, Ardrey, Tiger and Fox, and so on[2]—placed a good deal of stress on the genetic origins of aggressiveness, fighting, and the use of threats in the human race. On the whole this seems very ill founded. Genetically, we are probably just as much related to the gentle democratic gibbon as to the baboon with its snarling machismo. Territoriality is only one among many strategies for survival. It is very doubtful whether the human race has an instinct for territoriality like the robin. Even in the animals, territoriality is probably partly learned from observing the behavior of parents or, if instinctual, it is likely to be a highly flexible trait, easily transformed into something else in the way of behavior when that turns out to have survival value.

The extraordinary variability of the behavior of the woodchuck or the gopher, for instance, under different conditions of environmental hardship or food scarcity, from the snarling territorial individualist of Pennsylvania to the gentle communitarians of the West, testify to the malleability of behavior patterns, even in the same species of animal. Human behavior is far more malleable than that of the gopher. Threat systems develop in human society because of a specifically social dynamic, not because of any strong genetic urge toward them. In the use of threat, there may be subtle sexual differences that have their origins in some genetically induced structure of the nervous system, though I doubt this. The muscular strength of males may predispose them to weaponry, while the childbearing and lactating roles of females may move them toward more verbal forms of threat, but one doubts whether the difference between the sexes in this regard is all that great, and genetically the difference between the sexes is far more significant than the difference among the races or among the classes.

One does detect a certain tendency among biologists to overestimate the significance of genetic factors in human behavior. Darlington,[3] for instance, lays far too much stress on the possession of a common gene pool in the different social classes, whereas what is probably by far more significant is the possession of a common culture pool. The whole problem indeed of the relative significance of heredity and environment, nature and nurture, is an old chestnut that nobody has quite pulled out of the fire simply because we understand so little about the structural limitations of the human nervous system as compared, say, with the learned incapacities to learn as a result of early childhood experiences. I must confess that on the whole I am on the side of those like Ashley Montague,[4] who laid great stress on the learning experience of the human individual rather than on the genetic structure of the brain. Nevertheless, the experiments with identical twins raised under different conditions, whose life patterns sometimes indicate astonishing similarity, suggest that the genetic structure is not insignificant; just how significant it is, however, is something we still do not really know.

THREATS AS A SOURCE OF DOMINANCE AND INTERNAL DISCIPLINE

The use of threat in maintaining a "discipline" within organizations, that is, a relation of dominance and subordination—a dominant person giving orders or instructions and a subordinate person following them—is an aspect of the threat system that we must notice even though we cannot explore it fully. From the very beginning of the human race and even earlier, threats have been important in the maintenance of dominance-submission relationships: in the family, commonly to ensure dominance of the husband, less commonly to ensure dominance of the wife, and in certain family roles almost universally to ensure dominance of parents over children. Threats and punishments are an almost universal element in childrearing, although the amount of threat and punishment used varies from culture to culture and from time to time. There are cultures in which children are almost continually threatened and beaten at all levels of society from the most primitive to the most advanced. There are other cultures in which at all levels threats and punishments are used infrequently and children are raised permissively.

There are processes of the relation of parents to children, not unlike those of the arms race outlined above in this chapter, where threats and punishments on the part of the parents produce sullenness and resentment on the part of the children, which lead to behavior that produces a higher level of threats and punishments, more resentment to that behavior, and so on until some kind of equilibrium is reached, which may be at a high level in the extreme indeed such as in child abuse and even child murder. These family cultures tend to perpetuate themselves. If all a child has known in the family has been threats, punishments, beatings, and humiliations, he or she is likely to become like the parents and to exact revenge on the next generation of children for the punishments received as a child. On the other hand, a child reared in a loving and supportive environment is likely to become loving and supportive to his or her children in return. Sometimes there are dramatic reversals; the child revolts so much against the parents that he or she changes the family culture of the next generation, but these occasions seem to be rare.

Armed forces, because they are designed to threaten others, also use threat a great deal internally in maintaining discipline. Insubordinate soldiers are punished and occasionally executed. This tradition also tends to perpetuate itself. Historically in schools and educational establishments the use of punishment also has been very important in maintaining discipline and subordination of the pupil to the teacher. The physical threat of caning has now tended to give way to the "spiritual" threat of humiliation, low grades, or social punishments. The ability on the part of the teacher to impose threats of punishment of the student has been, and to a lesser extent still is, very important in the educational system. In business organizations industrial discipline is maintained by threat also, if not by physical punishment, at least by fine, dismissal, or withdrawal of privileges.

THE PATHOLOGY OF THREAT

A very important question, to which I think we do not yet know the answer, is the extent to which this ancient and almost universal use of threat in the human learning process, whether on the child in the home, the pupil in the school, the soldier in the armed forces, or the worker in the factory, aids or cripples the learning process itself. One of the most striking phenomena of the human learning process is the extent to which it seems to be self-limiting. Far beyond the physiological capacity of the human nervous system, we learn not to learn. We paint ourselves into a tiny corner of the vast ballroom of the human nervous system. The role of threat and fear in this process is extremely important to evaluate. One suspects that in small doses threat is not very harmful, but that there is some kind of a threshold beyond which it becomes increasingly damaging. Unfortunately, the dynamics of the threat system in all its forms tend to follow the pattern of the arms race and hence constantly to expand far beyond the optimum into highly pathological states, whether this is in the international system or in the human learning process.

Fortunately, threat is not the only human relationship; fear is not the only motivator. Even in political organizations—the family, the school, the business, or for that matter the church—the threat system has a low horizon of development. Threats may have produced classical civilizations, societies in whose greatest achievements in architecture, literature, and philosophy are only an iridescent reflection in the great pool of human misery. If we are to achieve something better than classical civilization—and this is now an urgent priority for the human race or the patterns of classical civilization will certainly destroy it—we must go beyond the threat system into the other organizers—exchange and love—which we will explore in the next two chapters.

Appendix to Chapter 7:
THE THEORY OF ARMS RACES AND VIABILITY

The theory of arms races was worked out first by Lewis B. Richardson.[5] The processes are sometimes called "Richardson Processes." The theory can be expressed in a somewhat simplified form in the graphical analysis of Figure 7A.1. In this very simple model we measure the size of the armed forces of one country, A, horizontally, and the armed forces of another country, B, vertically. We postulate an A-line, F_aF_a', which shows for each size of the armed forces of B, the equilibrium size of the armed forces of A at which it will neither increase nor decrease. Similarly, the curve F_bF_b' is the B-line showing what armed forces B will be satisfied with for each level of the armed forces of A. In each case we suppose that there is some initial level OF_a in A and OF_b in B, which the countries would have even in the absence of any armed forces in the other perhaps for dealing with other countries, for purposes of internal control, or for sheer prestige and display. As the size of

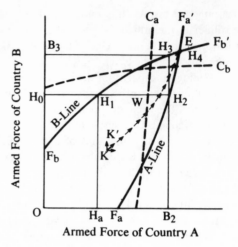

Figure 7A.1: The Arms Race

the armed forces of each country rises, we suppose the size of the armed forces of the other correspondingly rises, perhaps at a somewhat diminishing rate.

The measurement of the size of the armed forces presents some problems, which we will neglect here. For most purposes the total military expenditure, weighted for inflation or deflation, is a reasonable indicator. In Figure 7A.1 we have drawn the two curves to intersect at E, which is a point of stable equilibrium. If we start at a point such as H_a, the armed forces of A is OH_a and B will increase its armed forces to H_0H_1, this being the meaning of the B-line. A will then increase its armed forces to a point H_2, that is, to OB_2. B will then increase its armed forces to OB_3 at H_3, A to H_4, and so on, converging toward E. If we started above E, there would be a disarmament race with each party successively reducing its armed forces until the point E is again reached. We do not need to assume these discontinuous movements. We could very well suppose that at any point K, A will move toward the A-line and B toward the B-line, and there will be a resultant at K'. These dynamic paths will all converge on E.

The similarity to Figure 4A.6 (p. 94) is no accident. The armed forces of two competing countries are indeed populations in mutual cooperation or symbiosis, in the sense that an increase in one leads to an increase in the partial equilibrium position of the other. It is the armed forces of the Soviet Union that create the armed forces of the United States; the armed forces of the United States that create the forces of the Soviet Union. Both are in competition with the wealth and welfare of their own people.

The situation is complicated in practice, of course, by the fact that it is never realities which determine behavior, but only perceptions of them. Constantly we have to introduce into our more realistic model A's perceptions of B's armed forces, B's perceptions of A's armed forces, A's perceptions of B's perceptions of A's and B's armed forces, and so on. There are frequently quite strong biases in perception that accentuate the arms race. Each partly frequently overestimates the threat that the other armed force poses to itself, and underestimates its perception of the degree to which its own armed forces are perceived as a threat by the other. This tends to make the A-line and the B-line in Figure 7A.1 steeper and push the point of equilibrium further out. If the two lines are parallel, of course, there is no equilibrium at all; the arms race proceeds indefinitely until there is some kind of system breakdown, usually into war.

Breakdown into war may come at any point when one party perceives that a continuation of the arms race would simply be too burdensome to it. Hence, it precipitates a war rather than continuing the arms race. Suppose, for instance, that each party has a breakdown line represented by the dotted lines C_a and C_b in Figure 7A.1. The line C_a represents the boundary within which the arms race is tolerable to country A. If it goes beyond this line, country A will declare war. The same is true for the line C_b and country B. If the equilibrium of the arms race at E is beyond the boundary of these lines, as in the figure, an arms race will proceed not to equilibrium but to war. Thus, if the line of arrows from K, representing the various adjustments of the two countries, proceeds to where it hits the boundary of tolerance at W, there will be war.

Which party is the aggressor and initiates the war depends of course on which tolerance boundary the dynamic process hits first. This explains why it has been so difficult to define the aggressor in war and why, for instance, the Wilsonian notion of collective security, which depended on the quick and easy identification of the aggressor on the part of all parties, has been such a total failure. If we suppose that the reaction curves (the A-line and the B-line in Figure 7a.1) are linear, they can be represented by equations (1a) and (1b). If M_a and M_b are the sizes of the armed forces of country A and country B, then the equations of the partial equilibrium lines (assumed linear) are

$$M_a = H_a + r_a M_b \tag{1a}$$

$$M_b = H_b + r_b M_a \tag{1b}$$

Solving these equations we have in equilibrium

$$M_a = \frac{H_a + r_a H_b}{1 - r_a r_b} \tag{2a}$$

$$M_b = \frac{H_b + r_b H_a}{1 - r_a r_b} \tag{2b}$$

If there is to be an equilibrium at positive and finite levels of M_a and M_b, then we must have

$$r_a r_b < 1 \tag{3}$$

Otherwise the lines will diverge indefinitely above the origin.

$H_a H_b$ may be called the "initial hostilities" of the two countries, which correspond to the lines OF_a and OF_b in Figure 7A.1. This is the size of the armed forces even in the absence of any armed forces of the other nation. The parameters r_a, r_b may be called the "coefficients of reactivity." They show how much each country reacts to a unit increase in the armed forces of the other. If r_a, for instance, is .7, this means an increase in the armed forces of B by one unit will increase the armed forces of A by .7 of a unit. Equation (3) says that the product of two reactivity coefficients must be less than 1.0 if a finite equilibrium is to be obtained. This is a slightly depressing conclusion, because the natural assumption is for the reactivity coefficients to be 1.0 or greater. If the Soviet Union increases its military expenditure by one dollar, we would certainly not be surprised if the United States increased its expenditure by one dollar rather than by less than one dollar. This is particularly likely to be the situation if, as is so often the case, the military threat from the potential enemy is exaggerated, so that there is a perception of a greater increase of military expenditure than in fact took place.

From the point of view of the best uses of resources and even of human survival we want to get military expenditures, M_a, M_b, as low as possible. We can do this either by lowering the initial hostility levels or by diminishing the reactivity coefficients. If the reactivity coefficients are zero, there will be an equilibrium at the initial hostility levels. That is, M_a will equal H_a and M_b will equal H_b. For general and complete disarmament to be stable there must be no initial armaments. That is, H_a and H_b must be zero and $r_a r_b$ must be less than 1.0.

If there are more than two parties involved, each of which is a potential enemy to every other, the probability of an equilibrium in the arms race is even less, as the reactivity coefficients would have to be well below 1.0.[6]

The spatial interaction of two threat systems is illustrated in Figure 7A.2. Here we measure distance along the horizontal axis, assuming for the moment a simple linear world. Suppose there are two centers of power or threat at A and B. Vertically we measure the strength of threats that each can exercise. AA' is the "home strength" of A at its central location. The line $L_a A' M_a$ shows how the strength threat of A diminishes as we go away from A. By the

time we get to M_a, A's threat strength is zero. Similarly, $L_b B' M_b$ shows the
threat strength of B. The point where these two lines intersect, F, is the point
of equal strength. Thus the point E, that is, distance AE from A and BE from
B, is the boundary of equal strength, where the threat strength of each party
is equal to EF. At any point to the left of E, A is stronger; at any point to the
right of E, B is stronger.

If what lies around E is not very important to either party, there may be a
fairly stable equilibrium. Suppose, however, B wants something to the right
of E and raises his home strength to say BB'', moving his threat strength line
to the dotted line $L_b' B'' M_b'$; the point of equal strength moves to E', where
the curves intersect at F'. B has captured from A all that lies between E and
E'. If A is not satisfied with this, he may raise his home strength to A'', raise
his threat strength line to $L_a' A'' M_a'$ and move the equilibrium back to E

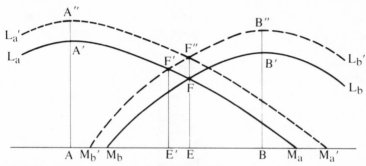

Figure 7A.2: The Boundary of Equal Strength

again, the two lines intersecting at F''. This is an arms race and it will go on,
as suggested in Figure 7A.1, until either it breaks down in war or an
equilibrium is reached at the point where neither party feels it is worthwhile
trying to shift the point of equal strength. If now A is able to increase
superiority over B to the point where the point of equal strength, E, moves to
B or beyond, then A is able to dominate B on B's home territory and B
becomes what I have called "conditionally viable" and can only exist at the
will of A. A may absorb B into its empire, in which case B disappears as an
independent system, or A may decide that the costs of doing this exceed the
benefits and B survives as a satellite state. Conditionally viable states often
survive between two larger powers as buffer states, which neither power
wishes the other to have.

Defensive armament consists of structures that over a range increase the
loss of strength gradient of the potential enemy. Suppose now in Figure 7A.3
that B builds a wall at E; A' loss of strength curve, instead of going from A to
M_a (as in Figure 7a.2), will now follow the dotted course $A' F A_w M_w$.
Defensive armaments, therefore, may increase B's viability and capacity for
survival, because it may now be impossible for A to increase his home

strength enough to dominate B through B's walls. The innumerable city walls that form tourist attractions all over the old world are testimony to this

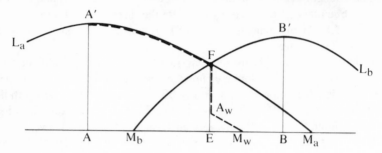

Figure 7A.3: Defensive Armament

principle. A buffer state between two powers may act as a joint "wall," diminishing the strength of both powers at the boundary, and thus increasing the stability of the system.

The analysis of Figure 7A.2 can also be extended easily to any number of threat power centers on a plane rather than on a straight line. We could surround each point representing a power center on the plane with a set of contours, each representing points of equal threat strength. At each point on the plane there will be one center which is dominant, that is, which has the highest threat strength, or there will be two equally powerful centers. There will be a set of lines on the plane that represents boundaries of equal strength. All the other points can be allocated to one center or the other, so that this set of lines will divide the plane into a series of cells or boundaries around each power center within which it is dominant. As any one power center increases its own strength, it pushes the boundary away from it toward the others. If it pushes the boundary far enough, some of the others may be overwhelmed by it and their area of dominance will shrink to zero and they will become only conditionally viable.

NOTES

1. I Samuel, Ch. 8

2. Konrad Lorenz, *On Aggression* (New York: Harcourt, Brace and World, 1966); Robert Ardrey, *The Territorial Imperative* (New York: Atheneum, 1966); L. Tiger and R. Fox, *The Imperial Animal* (New York: Dell, 1972).

3. C. D. Darlington, *The Evolution of Genetic Systems* (2nd ed.; New York: Basic Books, 1958).

4. Ashley Montague, ed., *Man and Aggression* (New York: Oxford, 1968).

5. Lewis B. Richardson, *Arms and Insecurity* (Pittsburgh: Boxwood Press, 1960). See also Kenneth E. Boulding, *Conflict and Defense* (New York: Harper & Brothers, 1962).

6. See Kenneth E. Boulding, "The Parameter of Politics," *University of Illinois Bulletin*, 63, 139 (July 15, 1966), 1-21. Reprinted in *Kenneth Boulding/Collected Papers*, Larry Singell, ed. (Boulder: Colorado Associated University Press, 1975. Vol. V, 95).

Chapter 8

Exchange as a
Social Organizer

EXCHANGE ORIGINATES IN AN INVITATION

An exchange relationship between two parties in its more general form begins with an invitation rather than a challenge. The invitation is in the form, "You do something that I want and I will do something that you want." The invitation is a conditional undertaking to deliver "goods" for the other person if the other person will deliver goods in return. A commodity exchange is one in which A gives B something that B values and B gives A something that A values, whether this is barter in which both things exchanged are goods or services or monetary exchange in which one of the things transferred is money. A commodity exchange is a subset of the larger concept of social exchange, which includes such things as marriage, in which each party does something for the other; political exchanges of votes or support for favors; conversation, which is the exchange of good communications—which may degenerate into a debate that edges toward threat and the exchange of bads; and the innumerable courtesies of human intercourse by which we convey an exchange of respect, status, and so on. On the other side from threat, exchange edges into reciprocity, which is something a little different, as we shall see in the next chapter. The exchange of smiles and greetings is an interesting example. I do not say "I will smile if you will smile at me." I smile at you because I like you and you smile at me because you like me. On the other hand, if I smile at you and I get a growl in return, my smile is likely to vanish and the underlying exchange element in the transaction becomes apparent.

EXCHANGE RATIOS AND VALUATION COEFFICIENTS

Why then do people exchange? The initial invitation to exchange is obviously made because the party making it thinks it will bring benefits, and that what is received in the exchange will be of more value to the party than what is given. The invitation is accepted if the other party also thinks that what is received is of more value to them than what is given. There is an apparent puzzle here, in that, by a useful convention of accounting, exchange is regarded as the exchange of equal values. The failure to solve this puzzle, which is the source of a major fallacy at the basis of Marxist thought, has caused an enormous amount of unnecessary human suffering. If five tons of wheat are exchanged for a ton of iron, there is an "exchange ratio" between them of equal exchange value. That is, we say that a ton of iron is "worth" five tons of wheat or a ton of wheat is "worth" a fifth of a ton of iron—"worth" meaning "equivalent in exchange to." This, however, is a useful accounting convention and no more. At any one moment there is a whole set of relative prices or ratios of exchange in actual transactions that are taking place. This is an important characteristic of the social system and an important body of information. It enables us to value all the heterogeneous commodities that are being exchanged in terms of one of them, usually money, and this enables us to reduce heterogeneous stocks or flows of commodities to a single measure of quantity of, say, dollars. Suppose I have five pounds of bread and two pounds of butter and you have four pounds of bread and three pounds of butter. Who has the larger amount of goods? We cannot answer this question unless we know how many pounds of butter are equivalent to one pound of bread, or what is the same thing or its reciprocal, how many pounds of bread are equivalent to one pound of butter. If, for instance, one pound of butter is equivalent to three pounds of bread, my two pounds of butter is equivalent to six pounds of bread; this plus my five pounds of bread gives me a total of eleven pounds; your three pounds of butter is equivalent to nine pounds of bread and with your four pounds of bread this gives you thirteen pounds, and you have the larger amount. If one pound of butter were equivalent to one pound of bread, we would each have seven pounds; if it were less than that, I would have the larger amount. All this, however, is accounting convention. It is by applying the relative prices or valuation coefficients that we calculate things like net worth, profit, GNP, and so on, but the reality behind these calculations is a vast complexity of stocks of different kinds of commodities and the changes in these stocks. The problem is a little bit like what we would face in biology if we had to say whether one ecosystem or large number of living species was bigger or smaller than another. The only way we do this in biology is by calculating the total mass of living matter, which is not necessarily a very significant figure. If we want to know whether one system is better than another, we have to calculate the total value by adding up the values for each of the components.

These could only be obtained by multiplying the mass or other measure by some valuation coefficient, protein, say, being "worth more" than wood.

WHY EXCHANGE TAKES PLACE

To return now to exchange itself, the exchange ratio, that is, the ratio of the quantities of things exchanged, is an important characteristic of an exchange, but it does not explain why the exchange takes place. For this we have to develop the concept of the subjective terms of trade, which is the ratio for each party of the subjective value of what he gives up to what he gets in return. Subjective value is what economists have called "utility." Unless the subjective terms of trade of the invitor to exchange are greater than unity, the invitation will not be made. Unless the subjective terms of trade of the other party, the acceptor, are greater than unity, the invitation will not be accepted and the exchange will not be consummated. Therefore, exchange is a positive sum game; it makes both parties feel better off at the time.

If we ask how this can happen in the presence of an "objective" ratio of exchange, the answer is that the subjective value of the last unit we give up ("marginal utility") depends on how much of the commodity we have. The more of anything we have, the less likely we are to want more of it and the less sacrifice there is in giving it up (the law of diminishing marginal utility). If I have a lot of wheat and you have a lot of iron, I may say "I will give you two tons of wheat if you will give me one ton of iron," because giving up two tons of wheat is not much sacrifice and getting a ton of iron is a substantial gain. You may accept the offer because giving up a ton of iron is a small sacrifice and getting two tons of wheat is a substantial gain. This process will go on until one of us says "Stop!" In a free exchange, either party has a veto. There is no law about who says stop, but when one party gets to the point where he estimates that what he is going to get in the next transaction is just worth only what he is going to give up, the exchange stops. Beyond that point it is not a positive-sum game because both parties do not feel that they benefit.

The principles are illustrated in Figure 8.1. Here we take the more familiar situation in which a commodity of some sort, let us say wheat, is exchanged for money. The ratio of exchange is now the price. Thus, if the price of wheat is three dollars a bushel, this means that for every bushel the seller gives up he gets three dollars in return, and for every bushel the buyer buys he has to give up three dollars. In Figure 8.1a we measure the price horizontally. There will be some price, B, above which the buyer will not buy because the value of the dollars he would give up would in his estimation be more than the value of the wheat he would receive. At any price below B he will buy, so there is a buyer's range as indicated in the figure. Similarly, there is some price, S,

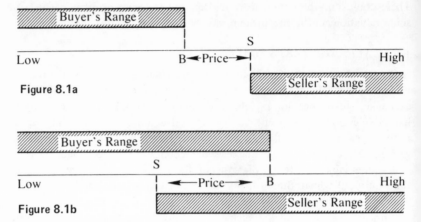

Figure 8.1a

Figure 8.1b

Figure 8: Bilateral Exchange

below which the seller will not sell because the dollars he receives will be of less value in his estimation than the wheat he gives up. At any price above S is the seller's range. If the buyer's range and the seller's range do not overlap, there is no price at which exchange will take place. As time goes on, however, the buyer's range is likely to expand and indeed move toward higher prices as the buyer perhaps uses up his wheat and perhaps acquires money from other sources, so that wheat becomes more valuable to him and money less. Similarly, the seller's range may shift downward as his money stock diminishes by being spent for other things and money becomes more valuable to him. This may lead to the situation of Figure 8.1b, in which there is an overlap between the buyer's range and the seller's range. At any price within the overlap between S and B exchange is beneficial to both parties and, if one party makes an invitation to exchange, the other will accept it.

There is a curious paradox of exchange. Free exchange will not take place unless both parties think they will benefit at the time. It is, therefore, a cooperative act. On the other hand, if there is an overlap between the buyer's range and the seller's range, as in Figure 8.1b, there may be conflict about the terms of the exchange. While anywhere between S and B both parties will benefit, at S the buyer will benefit a good deal and the seller hardly at all, at B the seller will benefit a good deal and the buyer hardly at all. Within the range the higher the price the better it is for the seller, and the worse it is for the buyer; the lower the price the better it is for the buyer, and the worse it is for the seller. The actual bargaining process may take place within the range of mutual benefit. The use of bluff, strikes, boycotts, and other devices in the threat system may be brought into play in order to settle the terms of the exchanges that take place. Once the terms have been settled, however, the exchange is purely cooperative. But a change in price or ratios of exchange, or more generally a change in the relative price structure, always produces a distributional impact. In a sense it makes some people better off, other people worse off, and may leave some people unaffected. We shall return to this concept later.

EXCHANGE AS A SOCIAL ORGANIZER

How then does exchange operate as a social organizer? At 'first glance it might be thought that it is not an organizer, and that it does not create organizations and role structures in the way, for instance, threats do. In an exchange two parties remain separate. They have a temporary relationship as, for instance, when we go into a store and buy a shirt from the storekeeper. In no sense do the customer and storekeeper form anything more than a highly temporary organization, even more temporary than that of a bandit and victim. This conclusion, however, would be a serious mistake because it neglects the role of exchange in fostering the division of labor and in providing a social matrix of inputs and outputs within which exchange-oriented organizations can grow and develop.

It was Adam Smith who first emphasized the role of exchange in creating the division of labor,[1] that is, specialization in occupations and in the production of commodities. It may be indeed as Sir John Hicks[2] suggests that the division of labor first began in the courts of kings and the temples of priests as a by-product of the threat system. Taxes or tributes were collected ultimately in the shape of food from the farmer by threat and were then distributed to artisans, craftsmen, builders, weavers, jewellers, and so on, who were then able to develop special crafts or skills in the temples and palaces. International trade certainly began when kings started sending their surpluses of goods as gifts to other kings, who then reciprocated. The stewards who carried the gifts caught on to the process and developed into merchants.

Exchange on a local level began early in tribal exchanges and in a kind of informal division of labor in the family and in the village. Much of this was in the form of reciprocity rather than bargaining and contractual exchange. The market, as a place to which people came to buy and sell, is certainly almost as old as the first cities and may even have predated the cities. Certainly at the time of the rise of civilization exchange systems and threat systems grew up side by side. In primitive markets people came with food from the country and others came with trinkets, furniture, clothing, etc. from the city work-shops, and they haggled and bargained until a price or exchange ratio was agreed on.

MONEY AS A FACILITATOR OF EXCHANGE

Money as a medium or intermediary in exchange originates in the form of some commodity which is so widely acceptable that it begins to circulate. That is, people take it in exchange for what they have to sell, not because they want it themselves, but because they can exchange it with somebody else for something they do want. A large number of commodities have acted as money in different times and places: cattle, from which the word pecuniary comes, tripods (whatever they were) in Greece, iron, knives, shells, and in a lot of prisoner-of-war camps, cigarettes. Quite early, however, metals acted as money because a small amount had a high value, they did not deteriorate, and they were easy to subdivide and so were convenient to carry around. The precious metals, which had an exceptionally high value per unit because of their scarcity, especially gold and silver, finally were moved into the niche of the money commodity and maintained that role for two or three thousand years, until paper money and bank money eventually replaced them. Coinage began about 700 B.C. in Europe, and much earlier in China. It was simply the king's stamp on a piece of metal, originally certifying its weight and fineness. The coin, however, soon became accepted as a unit of account and coins simply became "paper money" printed on metal instead of paper.

Today money is almost universally an abstract claim that is widely accepted as information that it can be exchanged for other things. A private banknote tells the holder and the world that the holder can exchange this for its face value in other things at their market prices, even though it legally may simply state that it can be exchanged at the bank for legal tender. Legal tender is a piece of paper that states the owner can legally pay all debts with it including debts to the government and taxes. A bank deposit is simply a record believed by everybody that the bank owes the depositor the amount of the deposit payable in legal tender whenever the depositor wishes. Hence it is usually transferable to almost anybody else in payment of debt.

With the invention of money, exchange began to expand very rapidly. Barter exchange is difficult because each party has to find another party who will want what he has and will have what he wants. With money as an intermediary we do not have to worry about this. We can sell what we have for money and then with the money find somebody else who will take it for what we want. As exchange became widespread it encouraged specialization in both products and tasks. When exchanges were confined to a single village there might perhaps have been a weaver, blacksmith, or individual craftsmen, but there would certainly not have been a factory for making pins. As markets widened through the development of inter-village, inter-city, and international trade, it became possible to specialize in producing something that perhaps only one person out of a thousand might want. It also became possible to organize factories or workshops within which there was a division of task or operation, with each worker performing a specialized function in the process of production. The then much larger total product could be exchanged in the wider market than could be exchanged in a smaller market.

HOW EXCHANGE FACILITATES PRODUCTIVITY

In Adam Smith's famous example of the pin factory,[3] he pointed out how by subdividing the operation of making pins into 18 or so different activities, a group of workers could produce thousands more pins in a day than a single worker could working alone. Here, therefore, we have the widening of the market increasing productivity and providing an environment in which exchange-oriented organizations could grow. An exchange-oriented organization or a "business" is one that is able to survive because it can go into the market and purchase raw materials, equipment, and labor and transform these into some sort of product that can be sold for at least enough money to pay for all the things which have to be bought. This is a sharp contrast with political organizations, organized through the threat system, which derive input of food materials and so on from producers and to whom they give nothing in return but threats of loss and damage, and which use these inputs solely for the purposes of the organization itself, such as for fine palaces and temples. With an output only in the form of the organized threat system itself, it then is able to collect the input. The threat-based organizations are at least a zero-sum game; what the king gets the farmer loses. It is more likely indeed to be a negative-sum game; those who provide the inputs lose more than those who receive them gain, unless the king provides order within which exchange can survive. The exchange organization or business, on the other hand, is a positive-sum organization. Insofar as its inputs are purchased by exchange of money derived from the proceeds of the sale of its outputs, its inputs and its outputs benefit the people who make the inputs, the people who receive the outputs, and the organization itself.

Furthermore, the extension of the market creates specialization in transportation, in the organization of markets, and so on, which further facilitates the extension· of the market. We get, therefore, an extraordinary process of positive feedback and expansion in which the development of a market increases the division of labor, which increases productivity, which expands the market, which increases the division of labor further, which expands productivity further, which expands the market further, and so on. This process has carried us from the family reciprocity and the meager products of paleolithic hunting and gathering bands to the vast network of world trade we have today that produces an immense variety of commodities, houses, clothing, automobiles, airplanes, completely transforming the environment of large masses of people. As Adam Smith again said, "The accomodation of a European prince does not always so much exceed that of an industrious and frugal peasant, as the accomodation of the latter exceeds that of many an African king. . . ."[4] The ordinary working man in eighteenth-century England enjoyed riches, which in some, though not all respects might be the envy of an African king. The American worker today with his boat, his car, his hi-fi, has a material environment that in richness of personal input exceeds that of oriental monarchs with their drafty and uncomfortable palaces, retinues of inefficient servants and strumming musicians, and the grim atmosphere of fear that pervaded every minute of their day.

I am, of course, overdoing it. Exchange has its pathologies no less than threat. It produces alienation of personality as Adam Smith himself saw in his less well known attack on the division of labor.[5] There are also pathologies of the exchange system in terms of deflation and unemployment, inflation and maldistribution, as again we shall see. Nevertheless, we are often unconscious of the benefits of exchange because we take them for granted. Exchange is almost like the air we breathe. We take it for granted that we can go down to the store and buy food, clothing, furniture, and gadgets in a great variety to suit our taste without inquiring about what organization produces this miracle.

EXCHANGE IN THE EVOLUTION OF COMMODITIES AS SPECIES

Let us then look at the exchange system as it spreads out over time and the space of the surface of the earth from its first beginnings in primitive barter. The process has many resemblances to the evolution of the biosphere. Each commodity is a species. Shirts, loaves of bread, automobiles, and radios are as much a species in the sociosphere as lichen, mushrooms, horses, and parrots are in the biosphere. At any one moment in time there is a stock or population of each commodity like a stock or population of a biological species. This stock is added to by production ("births") and diminished by consumption[6] ("deaths"). The bathtub theorem applies. Stocks are increased in any one period by the excess of production over consumption; they are diminished by the excess of consumption over production. Mutations take place when new commodities are invented. Extinction takes place when old commodities become obsolete and disappear.

The ecological interaction of populations of all different exchangeables is mediated through the structure of relative prices and profits in the market economy. This is something for which there is no close parallel in biological interaction. Exchanges that take place during a short period of time, say a day, rearrange the ownership of the stock of exchangeables among owners. In the stock of exchangeables we include commodities like wheat, buildings, equipment, money, and all financial instruments, and indeed anything that participates in exchange. These exchanges take place at a set of market prices, that is, the actual prices in actual exchanges, which measure how much of one exchangeable is exchanged for one unit of another. The extent of the rearrangements of stocks of exchangeables among owners will, of course, depend on the prices for which they are exchanged. If A sells 200 bushels of wheat to B at $2 a bushel, A gives up and B gains 200 bushels of wheat, B gives up and A gains $400 of money. If the price is $3 a bushel, B gives up and A gains $600 in money in return for the 200 bushels of wheat that A gives up and B gains.

Now we ask ourselves, why should relative prices be different the next day? Prices may be quoted as an offer to sell by potential sellers or an offer to buy by potential buyers. If the offer of a potential seller is accepted by a buyer, the exchange goes through; if it is not, it does not. If the offer of a potential buyer is not accepted by the seller, the exchange again does not go through. Prices can also be set by bargaining, but this is a complication we will neglect at the moment. Why then should anybody quote different prices from the ones that prevailed the day before? A seller whose offer has not been accepted may lower the price at which he is offering to sell; a buyer whose offer has not been accepted may raise the price at which he is offering to buy. If there is a general excess supply on a given day, that is, if a lot of potential sellers are finding they canot get buyers, there will be a strong tendency for the market price to fall the next day. Similarly, if there is an excess demand, a lot of buyers who cannot find sellers, there will be a strong tendency for the price to rise. The market price is said to be in equilibrium when there is neither excess demand nor excess supply. It is a situation in which all buyers can find sellers and all sellers can find buyers at the prices they are quoting. This is what is known as "clearing the market."

The market is cleared when people on the whole feel that they are holding about the right amount of all the commodities in their possession. A person who feels he is holding too little of something will go out and buy it; if he feels he is holding too much of something, he will go out and sell it. The equilibrium set of market prices is that in which these desires just offset each other, so that on the whole people in the market are willing to hold those stocks of all kinds of commodities that are there to be held. The equilibrium set of market prices, therefore, is determined by two major factors: the actual stocks that are there to be held and the aggregate preferences of people in the market about holding these stocks of exchangeables. If there is an increase in the stock of a particular commodity, say wheat, with no change in preferences or in other stocks, the price of wheat will tend to fall in order to persuade people to hold these increased stocks. If there is an increase in the preference for wheat, even if there is no change in stocks, the price of wheat will tend to rise as people are willing to pay more to hold the existing stock.

Preferences depend in part on expectations about the future relative price structure. If people in general tend to think that the relative price of wheat is going to rise, there will be an increased preference for it; if people think it is going to fall, a decreased preference for it. This introduces a considerable element of short-run instability in the structure of market prices. Preferences tend to be fairly volatile. Over a long period, however, average preferences are much more stable and the market price will fluctuate around a moving equilibrium level, which is called the structure of "normal" prices, or in Adam Smith's terms, "natural" prices.

The structure of normal prices is closely related to the fact that the profitability of different occupations and the production of different commodities depends on the relative structure of market prices over time. There will be some average level of the market price of wheat over time at which wheat production is "normally" profitable relative to other alternative productive activities in the sense that producers are neither attracted in to expand production nor attracted out to diminish it. This level of average market price at which production is normally profitable, therefore, would be the "normal" price of wheat. If the market price is persistently above this, wheat production will be perceived as abnormally profitable, people will go into it, and it will expand; if the market price is below this persistently, wheat production will be perceived as abnormally unprofitable and its production will contract.

The consumption of commodities is likewise related to the relative price structure. If the market price of wheat is persistently high, consumers will turn away from it to substitutes; if it is persistently low, they will turn toward it and expand their consumption.

The increase in the stock of any commodity in a given period is the excess of production over consumption. An excess of consumption over production, of course, represents a diminution of the stock. There is some level of average market price over a period at which production and consumption are equal and in which there is no change in the stock. If the average market price is higher than this, production will be encouraged, consumption discouraged, and the stock will persistently increase. As it increases, however as we have seen, in the absence of a change in preferences, the market price will tend to fall. As the price falls, production is discouraged, and consumption is encouraged, until we get to the point where stocks are no longer increasing. Similarly, if the market price is persistently low, that is, below the normal price, production will be discouraged, consumption will be encouraged, consumption will exceed production, and stocks will diminish. As they diminish, however, the price will rise.

CONSUMPTION AND WELFARE

We must now look more closely at how commodities are consumed and used. The word "consumption" in economics unfortunately often has a narrow and rather unsuitable meaning to signify simple household purchases, that is, those commodities which are purchased by households and then apparently are presumed (quite absurdly) to disappear from the economy. We use the word consumption in its literal sense to mean the disappearance or "death" of a commodity. This can happen in a number of ways. It can happen through "using up," as when we eat food and it thus disappears from the scene. Commodities can also "wear out," that is, they depreciate in quality as time goes on, a process very similar to that of aging in the animal, until they are no longer useful and are scrapped. A third form of consumption is "waste," which yields no utilities. This is the consumption of grain by rats and vermin, the building of "follies" and buildings that are never used, and so on.

The question of how consumption is related to welfare is tricky and there is much disagreement about it. From Adam Smith on, economists have always regarded the household as the supreme objective of economic life and the notion of consumption as household purchases probably stems from this. Consumption, as Adam Smith says, is the chief end of production.[7] On the other hand, I have argued that the major source of welfare of the individual is his "state" or condition, for instance, of being in good health and well fed, surrounded by comfortable houses, furniture and clothing, automobiles, books and records. The consumption of these things is for the most part independent of their use, and it is their use, what Irving Fisher called "psychic income,"[8] which is really significant from the point of view of welfare. If our clothing, houses, and automobiles were more durable, we would consume less, but we would be better off.

The truth probably lies somewhere between these two positions. If we postulate a welfare function, all the things that welfare depends on, the capital stock around us and the state of our bodies are surely the most important variables in the argument, but we do also value the throughput that is involved in literal consumption. We like eating and drinking as well as being well fed, although even here the efficiency of eating and drinking, that is, the extent to which it contributes to our being well fed and in good health, is by no means an inconsiderable factor. Roughly speaking, those things that are used up involve consumption or income; those things that wear out are better measured by the stock or capital rather than by throughput of consumption and production. The question of what constitutes welfare, however, is very tricky and we shall return to it again.

THE "FACTORS OF PRODUCTION"

Production is necessary in order to replace consumption and increase the stock. In conventional economics it is assumed that there are three factors of production—land, labor, and capital—and that all products or commodities are produced as a result of some interaction among these three. There is a possible fourth factor in the shape of entrepreneurship or organization. This, however, is a very inadequate account of the productive process. As we have seen, commodities are produced in ways that are not essentially different from the ways in which living organisms are produced—by the operation of some kind of *knowledge* structure or know-how or plan, which has the ability to direct *energy* toward the selection, transportation, and transformation of *materials* into the appropriate forms, whether this is a chicken or an automobile. Land, labor, and capital—the conventional trinity—are each highly heterogeneous aggregates of the three real factors—knowledge, energy, and materials. Labor is such a mixture. It involves knowledge and know-how in the brain of the laborer derived partly from personal skill, partly from instructions he may receive from the organization to which he belongs. It involves the energy of the strong right arm, burning fuel in the body in the form of food stuffs, moving the materials of the human body such as the hands into the appropriate places, which then grasp other materials that are moved into appropriate places in digging, hammering, machine tending, and so on. It involves the materials of the human body that code the know-how and channel the energy.

Capital is an even more heterogeneous collection of things. It might be defined as the stocks or populations of all economically significant objects. Defined in this broad way, of course, it would include what is called "human capital," that is, the bodies and minds of the human population insofar as they are economically relevant, though this has enough peculiarities to make it at least a sub-category. It also includes all the stocks of commodities, buildings, houses, warehouses, streets, railroads, ships, machines, and so on. Capital is surrounded by a penumbra of potentially relevant objects—the fish in the sea, the ores and mines still to be discovered, and perhaps the knowledge lying in wait for us. Capital also then consists partly of energy and potential energy—stocks of wood for burning, stocks of oil and coal, and so on. It consists also of materials—ore in the mines, pig iron, aluminum, grains, chemicals, and so on—in various stages of production, that is, at various points on the path that energy is moving them, guided by knowledge, into the forms and shapes that constitute commodities. Capital also has a knowledge element, especially if we consider human brains to be capital, as in a broad sense we should. Even on a narrow definition the knowledge protheses—libraries, plans, programs, blueprints, computers, and so on—which store and enlarge human knowledge, are clearly capital.

Land for the most part is just a subset of capital, particularly insofar as it consists of soil, which again consists of materials, with a certain amount of genetic know-how in the bacteria and the worms and perhaps a little energy stored from the warm sun. Land in its aspect of spatial extension is something different, so different indeed that perhaps we ought to add this as a fourth factor to our knowledge, energy, and materials. Production cannot take place unless it has some empty space, which can be appropriated for the process, for both the inputs and the products of production, which always occupy space. Under some circumstances this may be just as much a limiting factor as the other three. Indeed, the total biomass is much more sharply limited by the total surface of the earth than it is by any deficiencies of energy and materials. The total mass of human artifacts, likewise, is limited in some sense by the spacial limitations of the planet, unless of course we shoot things off into space. The sheer area of arable land is an important limit on total crop production. Land area also limits the size of cities. There are size limitations imposed by the need for transportation—some area has to be taken up in roads or railroads. This is a very important factor governing urban ecology. There is also a sheer spatial-volumetric limit to human density, which New York is probably approaching.

The division of factors in economics into land, labor, and capital has its origins not so much in the theory of production, where these fit very awkwardly as heterogeneous and almost meaningless aggregates, but rather in the exchange economy, because these are aggregates that conveniently form units of exchange. We hardly ever buy knowledge, energy, and materials separately, although sometimes we do. For instance, when an organization employs a consultant, it is buying knowledge, though the quantity—and price—are hard to measure. When it buys electricity it is buying energy at a price of so many dollars per kilowatt hour. When it buys steel rods it is buying materials. Ordinarily, however, we buy knowledge, energy, and materials, and even space in packages and pay for them by the package.

THE LABOR MARKET

Labor is such a package, and wages are its·price. Hiring somebody at five dollars an hour is just as much an exchange as buying wheat at three dollars a bushel. It is, however, a peculiar kind of exchange and the peculiarities have profound sociological and political ramifications. In the wheat market there is little sociological difference between the buyers and sellers; they are all the same people—the man who is a seller one day may be a buyer the next. In the labor market, there is a much sharper differentiation between the buyer of labor (the employer) and the seller (the worker), though even here there are situations in which a carpenter, for instance, can hire himself out to someone one week and the next week play the employer role and hire somebody to do some work for him. This, however, is rare. For the most part, especially in developed industrial societies, there are sharp differences between the culture of the employer and the culture of the employed, and the crossing of the lines is fairly rare.

Furthermore, the exchange looks very different from the points of view of the two parties. Both parties must benefit to some extent in all exchanges, as we have seen, or they would not take place at all. But in a sale of wheat for money, the wheat that is bought is pretty much the same as the wheat that is sold, and the money that is paid out is pretty much the same as the money that is received. In the labor exchange this is not so. What the laborer gives up is the alternative use of his time, which might have been spent doing something more agreeable. What he sacrifices is the difference between the utility of the alternative use and the utility of the time spent in labor. This may be "toil and trouble," a negative evaluation of the utility of the time spent in performing the labor itself. Even if the work is pleasant, however, the alternative leisure is perceived as more pleasant still. Labor is something you would not do unless you were paid to do it. What the employer gets—the product of the work—is quite different from what the worker gives up. The worker brings a certain amount of knowledge and know-how and energy applies this to some kind of transformation of materials, which gives them a higher value first in the mind and ultimately presumably in the pocketbook of the employer.

As we shall see later, there are strong integrative elements as well as exchange elements in the labor relationship. Nevertheless, the wage or price of labor is a very important element in the price system. If we think of carpenters as a population, then the wage of carpenters relative to other wages and to other prices is an important element in determining the additions to and the subtractions from the stock of carpenters, and whether this stock will rise or fall. If the wage is perceived as high relative to alternative occupations, it is likely to attract people into the population of carpenters, which will rise; as it rises, it will be harder to get employment at the old wage. There are three possible responses to this situation. First, the wage may fall if there are no obstacles to making bargains at lower wages, such as may exist if the industry is heavily unionized. Second, unemployment may persist and there may be a circulation of carpenters between unemployed carpenters and employed carpenters. Third, carpenters will leave the occupation and become plumbers or something else, thus there will be a diminishing number of carpenters. Depending on the circumstances, therefore, there will be some wage, or perhaps a range of wages, above which the number of carpenters will grow, below which it will decline, and both the growth and the decline will tend to bring wages back to the equilibrium range.

CAPITAL AND FINANCIAL MARKETS: THE SEPARATION OF OWNERSHIP FROM CONTROL

Capital is an even trickier problem with regard to its relation to the exchange system. Items of physical capital—buildings, machines, land, and so on—can be bought and sold, assuming the legal institutions of the society permit this and permit private property in capital. Even in communist societies, "trusts," which are the equivalent of firms in capitalist societies, buy and sell goods of all kinds among each other and to households. We can postulate a model of equilibrium price structure, just like our discussion of the market price of wheat, which will persuade everybody to hold what stocks of all physical goods are there to be held.

This, however, is not the whole story. We not only have capital goods, but in most societies we also have securities and large populations of financial instruments—stocks, bonds, bank loans, bank deposits, government securities, and so on. A security by and large is a promise to deliver something in the future. A bond or promissory note is a promise to pay specified sums of money on specified dates. A stock certificate is a promise to pay uncertain sums of money on certain dates, the sums depending on what is happening to the complexes of real capital to which the stock certificate gives ownership rights. A futures contract, which is a kind of commodity bond, is a promise to deliver specified quantities of a commodity at specified dates. There are also contracts that promise to deliver specified quantities of specified securities on certain dates. From the point of view of the issuer these contracts are promises; from the point of view of the holder or owner they are expectations of some degree of uncertainty that the promise will be fulfilled. These contracts or instruments are traded in the financial markets just as wheat is traded in the commodity market, and their prices are also determined at the level at which the market is cleared and people are willing to hold on to the existing quantities.

The main reason for all this apparatus and why there is a niche in many societies for these types of artifacts is to overcome what would otherwise be a serious defect in the system of private property and private ownership of capital. All private property is ultimately owned by persons. All persons eventually die and somebody else inherits their property. There is a strong tendency for property to fall into the hands of elderly widows, simply because women generally outlive men, they tend to be younger than the men they marry, and older people have more property than the young. The basic purpose of the financial system is to separate the ownership of physical capital from its control. If there were no financial system, the elderly widows who own so much of the physical capital would have to administer it, which would be bad for both them and the rest of us. The financial system, therefore, enables those who own capital, but do not wish to control it, to own stocks and bonds, mortgages, and so on, which pay them interest or dividends, while those who are good at administering capital are able to get together, by selling stocks and bonds, aggregations of capital far larger than they personally own, which they are then able to administer.

The corporation has been a particularly useful device in this regard, as it has developed a specialized occupation of managers and executives who administer the capital, the factories and machines, the land, the railroads, and so on, which constitute the physical capital aggregates of the corporations, even though they may own very little of it. In socialist states the capital is supposedly owned by the people or by the state on behalf of the people, but again it is managed by a class of managers under somewhat different guidelines, it is true, but with very much the same problems as those faced by capitalist managers. A business in a market society is an organization essentially in an exchange environment. Not only does it buy its commodity inputs and outputs and its labor and sell its products, but it also acquires capital by selling financial instruments such as stocks and bonds of various kinds in the capital market.

The capital market, like the wheat market, is a group of traders and facilitators of traders such as stock brokers, who own financial instruments of various kinds, including various kinds of money, and who exchange these instruments mainly for money or sometimes for other instruments, much as wheat is exchanged for money in the wheat market. The price of stocks like the price of wheat follows principles of "clearing the market." An increase in preference for any particular stock will raise its price; an increase in preference for stocks in general will raise the general level of stock prices; an increase in the quantity of stocks tends to lower their price; an increase in the quantity of money tends to raise them. The price of any particular stock tends to be that at which people are willing to hold the total quantity of the stock that is there to be held. If most people feel they are holding too much of a stock, they will try to unload it and the price will fall; if they feel they are not holding enough of it, they will try to buy it and the price will rise.

Securities markets like the commodity markets are subject to speculative fluctuations, a little bit like the predator-predatee cycle. When the price is perceived as low, people expect it will rise. Because they expect it will rise, their preference for holding it will increase, which will raise the price and confirm their expectations. This may induce expectations of a further rise just on the principle of projection of trends, so the rise will go on until the price is perceived as high. Then increasing numbers of people expect it will fall, increasing numbers of people will try to sell, and the price will fall. As it falls expectations are confirmed, many people think it will go on falling, it does go on falling, but as it falls it eventually becomes low, which is where we came in, and the whole process starts again.

THE THEORY OF PROFIT

A corporation could not pay interest on its bonds or dividends on its stock if it did not make profits by the manipulation of its physical capital. How profits arise in the course of the exchange system is a major source of controversy in economics. Every institution potentially can construct a balance sheet. This contains a list of all real capital owned by the institution on one side, to which are added money stocks and securities and debts (receivables). These are the *assets* owned. On the other side are the debts payable and bonds issued, the liabilities, which are simply negative assets. All these things are valued in terms of dollars and the difference between the value of all positive assets and the value of negative assets is the net worth. The excess of net worth over the nominal value of stock issues is called surplus.

Profit is made when net worth increases in the course of business. Every event in the life of a business has some impact on its balance sheet, which is its summary of its state or condition, a frame, as it were, of the great movie constituting its life and history. By accounting convention a purchase diminishes the money stock and increases the item of whatever is bought by the same amount. The purchase of labor diminishes the money stock and increases the value of stocks of materials and finished goods by the same amount. Production diminishes the things used up in the production and increases the things produced. If valued at cost, the increase in value of the product equals the decrease in the value of what is used up. When a miller grinds wheat into flour, the stock of wheat diminishes and the flour increases; the money stock diminishes as laborers are employed in grinding, and there may be depreciation of his fixed capital. If these items are costed correctly, the increase in the book value of the flour will exactly counterbalance the decrease in the book value of the stock of money, wheat, and fixed capital.

If all the exchanges in the balance sheet are of equal value, how then does profit ever arise? This is a conundrum that has caused a lot of trouble. The immediate answer is through the revaluing of assets, especially at the point of sale. Finished goods are carried on the books at a cost of $100 and are sold for $120; the net worth then goes up by $20. The Marxist regards this as exploitation, believing that only labor creates value. Mainline economists generally do not hold this view and I myself think it is mostly fallacious. The revaluation is a result of the operation of the enterprise, which buys things that people are willing to sell freely for a total cost of say $100, and which then transforms these things through the power of its organization into something for which somebody is willing to pay freely $120. There is no simple parallel for this phenomenon in the biological world, though there is a concept of "biological advantage." Man is the only animal that keeps accounts. Profit is a phenomenon that emerges out of the accounting system and the system of relative prices.

Just what determines the amount of profit and, for instance, the proportion of profit in national income is another very much disputed question. I have my own answer to this question, however, which nobody else seems to believe, so the reader follows it at his peril.[9] The real key to the problem is precisely the question: "How can there be a gross increase in the net worth of businesses?" This is really what constitutes profit. The net increase in net worth is what is left after dividends and interest have been paid, which is something else again. That represents "business saving." If there is business saving, that is, a net increase in net worth, there must be a net increase in all the other items, that is, real capital, and the debts and financial instruments, that is, in the value of all other assets positive and negative. This we see from the balance sheet identity itself. Furthermore, the total business savings of a closed society in any one period is the increase in the sum of all these other items, that is, the increase in total real capital evaluated in dollar terms, in the total money stock, and in the net increase in debts of businesses to nonbusinesses (households and governments). When we add up and consolidate *all* the balance sheets of businesses, inter-business debts cancel out. Every financial instrument is an asset in somebody's balance sheet and a liability in somebody else's. If business A owes business B $100, that is a $100 liability to A and a $100 asset to B. When we add up both balance sheets these cancel out.

Business savings, therefore, are identically equal to the increase in the value of real capital held by businesses, plus the increase in the business money stock,[10] plus the increase in the net financial obligations of businesses to nonbusinesses. Here we get an extraordinary result, which is a paradox we shall meet in another form, that business savings are not determined mainly by the decisions of business to save, but by the decisions of business to invest, that is, to increase their real capital. They are affected also by any increased nominal dollar value of capital due to inflation of prices, which is not much in the control of businesses, and also by any increase in business obligations to households and governments in accounts payable or in new stocks and bonds, which partly enter the decision-making power of businesses.

Profits, then, in aggregate are equal to business savings plus business distributions in interest and dividends. We thus get the astonishing conclusion that, if the decisions in regard to investment in these other things remain constant, a decision to increase dividends will actually increase the profits out of which the dividends are to be made. This is what J. M. Keynes called the "widow's cruse," after the story of Elijah,[11] for the more profits are paid out, the more they return to be paid out. This means that the equilibrium of the relative price system does not determine the distribution of national income (or whatever aggregate is most suitable) between profit or more generally nonlabor income and labor income. The price system really has one too few equations to determine it and we must have an apparatus for determining this distribution between nonlabor income and labor income before the price system itself is determined.[12]

UNEMPLOYMENT AS A PATHOLOGY OF EXCHANGE

The profit paradox, if we may call it that, is quite closely connected with the problem of unemployment, which is another peculiarity of the exchange system. This is the situation in which there are more people looking for jobs than there are jobs available for them. The opposite situation is a labor shortage in which there are more jobs than there are people to fill them. Different industries, of course, may have labor shortages and surpluses in the course of the dynamic approach to an equilibrium of the price structure, but general unemployment, in terms of an overall operation of the economy in some sense at undercapacity with less of its resources utilized than is desirable, is a phenomenon peculiarly characteristic of exchange systems. Price theory would suggest that all we have to do is lower money wages and the labor surplus would be absorbed, just as when there is a wheat surplus all we have to do is lower the price of wheat so that consumption will increase and production decline. The situation, however, is not as simple as this. Wages are a very large element in costs and, if for the moment we assume profits are stable, because of the process outlined above, a fall in money wages will simply result in a fall in commodity prices and real wages may be unchanged. It is only by decline in real wages that we can increase employment in the face of a given demand for labor.

We must seek other sources for unemployment, therefore, and we find one in the inability of the economy to absorb all the products that it would produce at full employment. A fundamental identity of the exchange system (again really another example of the bathtub theorem) is that any commodities produced in a given period must be consumed or they will still be around adding to the total stock, that is, overall production minus overall consumption is equal to the addition to the total stock. The total stock is largely in the hands of businesses, though household stocks are by no means insignificant and play some role in this process. Suppose now that stocks are increasing at a rate that is faster than people are willing to hold them. First of all, holders may try to dispose of them by selling them, but this does not dispose of them, it merely rearranges their ownership. Exchange is not consumption. A general desire to diminish holdings will result in a general fall in prices—a deflation.

Falling prices, as we have seen, tend to reduce profits by lowering the dollar value of existing stocks of capital. We see in another way how deflation leads to a decline in profits. We make profits by buying something at one price and selling it later at a higher price. If in the interval all prices have fallen, it will be much harder to find a higher price at which to sell any particular thing. If prices are inflexible, as in many industries they are, especially in the short run the only other reaction to unwanted accumulations is to cut back production. I remember once asking a manufacturer of washing machines what constituted a "crisis" in his firm. He said immediately, "Three days' accumulation of washing machines." These are so bulky that they are very hard to store. Then I said, with I am afraid a feigned innocence, "Then I suppose you would lower the price and have a sale and sell off the excess stock." "Oh, no," he said, "price policy is determined a year in advance. We can't do that. We have to cut back output at the factory and fire some of our workers."

Unwanted accumulations, therefore, will lead to reduction of output and consequent involuntary unemployment and the whole economy will operate below capacity. This also may not work, however, because with lower incomes there will be smaller household purchases and the sales of businesses may decline as much as their output declines, so they are still facing unwanted accumulations, which may lead to further cutbacks and further reductions in consumption, until we get down to a point of unemployment equilibrium where output is so low that consumption cannot fall much further and stocks begin to be reduced. This is essentially the core of the Keynesian analysis of unemployment and it is a very important discovery.[13]

The most obvious remedy is to lower taxes and run a cash deficit in the government budget, which increases the money supply,[14] and all of which should hopefully increase consumption. This is "fiscal policy." There are also various devices—tax concessions, lowering interest rates, and what is called monetary policy—which may have the effect of encouraging investment, that is, making people more willing to hold increased stocks of commodities and capital. In the last 30 years these devices have been moderately successful, though we have run into a severe problem of how to achieve full employment without inflation. We will return to these problems later.

It is clear that the exchange system in social dynamics exhibits complexities not found in biological systems. With regard to the production and consumption of commodities and human artifacts the similarities are very great. Production is an essentially similar process in both systems. Any population or stock will expand into a niche at which it is in approximate equilibrium. The biological niche is determined by all the populations in the environment. In the world of commodities the niche is created mainly by demand. A commodity that can be produced profitably at a price that will attract resources into its production and will still persuade consumers to buy it has a niche, and it will tend to expand until it fills the niche. The phenomena of profit and of unemployment and undercapacity operation, however, have no simple parallels in the biosphere. Profit has a certain parallel to survival value, but it is a much more explicit and specialized phenomenon.

Threats and exchange systems by no means exhaust the social organizers. We will go on in the next chapter to consider the third group of organizers, which are harder to pin down but are of vital importance, which we may call the integrative system.

Appendix 1 to Chapter 8:
INTERRELATIONS AMONG PRODUCTION,
CONSUMPTION, PRICES AND STOCKS OF COMMODITIES

The relation among the production, consumption, prices and stocks of commodities can be analyzed as follows:

The rates of production and consumption of commodities are a function of many other things. As a first approximation, however, we can suppose that, as in the case of biological species, they are a function of the stock of the commodity in existence. In Figure 8A.1 in the first quadrant we measure the stock, that is, the population of wheat, horizontally and the production or consumption vertically. Production consists of "births" into the stock of wheat as additions to it, and consumption represents "deaths," that is, subtractions from the stock of wheat. We can postulate birth and death functions as we did in Figure 3.3 (p. 72), though they are likely to have a somewhat different form from what they have in biological populations and many of the intermediary mechanisms are different. We postulate a birth function, B_1B_2, sloping downward indicating that the higher the stock of wheat, the lower will be the incentives to produce it, and the production of wheat will decline. We also have a consumption or death function, C_1C_2. We suppose that this rises with increases in the stock. The larger the stock in hand the greater the incentive to consume it.

The intermediary mechanism here is the price of wheat and we suppose in the fourth quadrant of the figure that we have a function, the line P_1P_2, relating the stock of wheat to its price. We have drawn it so that the higher the stock the lower the price. This function rests on the assumption of "clearing the market," and its position depends on the preferences of buyers and sellers for stocks of different exchangeables. To take wheat as an example, let W bushels be the quantity of wheat in the possession of the wheat traders and M dollars the quantity of money. Let a_w be that proportion of the dollar *value* of wheat to the total assets of the traders at which they are on balance content to hold the stocks they have. It may be called the "wheat preference." a_m is similarly the "money preference," often called "liquidity preference." It is the preferred rates of money stocks to total assets. Then, if the price of wheat is p_w dollars per bushel, the dollar value of the wheat stock is Wp_w. If T is the total value of the traders' assets.

$$a_w = \frac{Wp_w}{T}, \ a_m = \frac{M}{T},$$

Whence $\quad T = \dfrac{Wp_w}{a_w} = \dfrac{M}{a_m}$

or $\quad p_w = \dfrac{Ma_w}{Wa_m}$

This useful identity shows that the price of wheat in the market will rise:

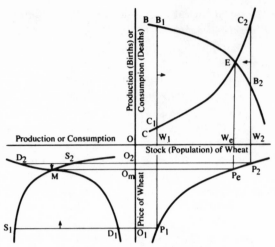

Figure 8A.1: Population, Stocks, Births, and Deaths; Related to Demand and Supply

(1) if M, the stock of money, rises;
(2) if W, the stock of wheat, falls;
(3) if a_w, the preference for wheat, rises;
(4) if a_m, the preference for money, falls:

and the other variables are held constant.

We have drawn these functions to be nonlinear, because there is not the slightest reason to suppose they would be linear. At high stocks we have made the birth and death functions a little steeper, for as stocks get beyond a certain point they become very burdensome because storage facilities are inadequate and incentives to either cut off production or increase consumption increase. By the stock of wheat here we mean not the growing field but the stock of harvested wheat in warehouses and granaries. Exactly the same principle would hold for stocks of pig iron, automobiles, houses, or any other commodities.

From these three functions we can derive the ordinary, long-run (Marshallian) demand and supply curves familiar to economists in the third quadrant. From any point W_1, where OW_1 is a given stock of wheat, we draw a vertical line to meet the consumption curve at C_1, the production curve at B_1, and the stock-price curve at P_1. The price at which the stock OW_1 will be sold is then W_1P_1. If now we draw a horizontal line from P_1 to cut the vertical axis at O_1, we measure O_1D_1 equal to W_1C_1, which is the consumption at that price, and measure O_1S_1 equal to W_1B_1, which is the production at that price. We can repeat this for all points on the curve and will trace the demand curve, D_1D_2, and the supply curve, S_1S_2 ($W_2B_2 = O_2S_2$, $W_2C_2 = O_2D_2$). As we have drawn the functions there will be a point of equilibrium E in the first quadrant and a stock of wheat equal to OW_e, with production and consumption equal, and both being equal to W_eE and the price of wheat being W_eP_e.

This is also shown at the intersection of the demand and supply curves $D_1 D_2$ and $S_1 S_2$ at M, where $O_m M$ is equal to $W_e E$. If the page is turned through 180 degrees, the economist will recognize the familiar demand and supply diagram.

This is a stable equilibrium. If the stock of wheat is below the equilibrium level say at W_1 or the price of wheat is above the equilibrium level at $W_1 P_1$, consumption ($W_1 C_1$ or $O_1 D_1$) will be less than production ($W_1 B_1$ or $O_1 S_1$) and the stock will grow, and as it grows the price will decline. Consumption will increase and production will diminish, until we get to the point E where production and consumption are equal. Similarly, if we started at OW_2, the stock of wheat above the equilibrium, consumption would exceed production, the stock would decline, and the price would rise until the equilibrium was reached again. Where there are lags in response to price changes, as there may be, we may get a cyclical movement around the equilibrium, as we do in rather similar cases in biological populations.[15] The expansion of the stock, for instance, in response to high prices and low consumption and high production may gather momentum until it overshoots the equilibrium, the stock becomes too large, and the price falls below the equilibrium level. This, of course, will eventually reverse the process. Stocks will begin to decline again and then may again overshoot the equilibrium, repeating the cycle. The equilibrium stock is in a very real sense a niche and part of the dynamics of the exchange system consists of the movement of stocks and commodities toward occupying their niche when they are below it, or withdrawing from it when they are above it. As in biological systems, however, the niches also change all the time and the sources of these changes are important to investigate.

Appendix 2 to Chapter 8:
INTERRELATIONS OF EXCHANGES AND THREATS

The exact relationships between exchanges and threats are quite complex, and the systems outlined in the two previous chapters cover only part, though probably the most important part, of the possible field of relationships of these kinds. The pattern of these relationships is suggested in the following table, Table 8A.1.

Either exchange or threat is initiated by a conditional statement of some kind, of the form, "I will do x if you will do y." In Table 8A.1 there are four possible versions of x: (1) I will give you a good if, (2) I will withhold a good if, (3) I will give you a bad if, and (4) I will withold a bad if. These are combined with four versions of y: (1) You give me a good, (2) You withhold a good, (3) You give me a bad, and (4) You withhold a bad. A good is something that has a positive utility to the person who receives and wants it. A bad is something that has a negative utility for the person who receives it but does not want it. These four clauses combine to give 16 possible initial conditional statements, promises, or challenges.

The combination X_1Y_1, I will give you a good if you give me a good, is the invitation to simple exchange. It implies X_2Y_2, I will withhold a good if you withhold a good. If the invitation is accepted, as we have seen, the exchange takes place; if it is rejected, there is no exchange. X_1Y_2, I will give you a good if you withold a good, is an invitation from a grantor to a grantee and falls within the study of the grants economy. X_2Y_1, I will withhold a good if you give me a good, is somewhat similar. It is an invitation by a grantee to a grantor that the grantee will accept a grant. These four cases in general constitute what is usually thought of as the field of economics.

X_1Y_3, I will give you a good if you give me a bad, might be described as sainthood. This is Gandhi blessing his murderers. The opposite, X_3Y_1, I will give you a bad if you give me a good, might be called deviltry. These might be called standing invitations or character patterns, which indicate potential responses rather than invitations or challenges as such.

The rest of the table represents varieties of threat situations. X_3Y_2, I will give you a bad if you withhold a good, is the classic threat challenge of the bandit, tax collector, or teacher threatening bad grades. It implies X_4Y_1, I will withhold a bad if you give me a good. If the challenge is accepted, we get of course a threat-submission pattern. X_3Y_3, I will give you a bad if you give me a bad, is the deterrence response and it implies X_4Y_4, I will withhold a bad if you withhold a bad. X_1Y_4, I will give you a good if you withhold a bad, is the case of bribery, and it implies X_2Y_3, I will withhold a good if you give me a bad. Around these rather standard cases we get some other rather odd ones. X_4Y_2, I will withhold a bad if you withhold a good, and X_2Y_4, I

TABLE 8A.1
Threat and Exchange Patterns

		X_1	X_2	X_3	X_4
		I will give a good if	I will withhold a good if	I will give a bad if	I will withhold a bad if
Y_1	You give a good	Economic Exchange	Grantee	Deviltry	Threat (Bandit) & Submission (Tribute)
Y_2	You withhold a good	Grantor	Economic Exchange	Threat (Bandit) & Submission (Tribute)	Tolerance or Indifference
Y_3	You give a bad	Sainthood	Bribery	Deterrence	Forebearance
Y_4	You withhold a bad	Bribery	Tolerance or Indifference	Spite	Deterrence

will withhold a good if you withhold a bad, represent nothing very positive, but they do suggest a situation of mutual indifference or tolerance. X_4Y_3, I will withhold a bad if you give me a bad, might be described as forebearance or patience, while X_3Y_4, I will give you a bad if you withhold a bad, could be described as spite. Each of these 16 initial conditional statements can be met with a variety of responses. Nevertheless, we do see that there is a clustering of the exchange patterns and of the threat patterns, so that the distinction between threat systems and exchange systems made in these two chapters is a fair approximation of reality, even though it does not cover all the potential complexities of human relationships.

NOTES

1. Adam Smith, *The Wealth of Nations* (New York: Modern Library Edition), Book 1, Chapter 1.

2. Sir John Hicks, *A Theory of Economic History* (London: Oxford University Press, 1969).

3. Adam Smith, *The Wealth of Nations*, Book 1, Chapter 1, 4.

4. ――― *The Wealth of Nations,* Book 1, Chapter 1, 12.

5. ――― *The Wealth of Nations,* Book V, Chapter 1, Article 2d, 734.

6. "Consumption" is here used in its literal meaning of "destruction."

7. Adam Smith, *The Wealth of Nations*, Book IV, Chapter 8, 625.

8. Irving Fisher, *The Theory of Interest* (New York: Macmillan, 1930), 453.

9. See Kenneth E. Boulding, *A Reconstruction of Economics* (New York: Wiley, 1950), Chapter 14.

10. This can happen either because of a general increase in the total money stock or because of a shift in the money "cargo" out of households and governments into businesses.

11. I Kings 17: 13-16.

12. For a more technical discussion of this problem, see again Kenneth E. Boulding, *A Reconstruction of Economics.*

13. Let P be the total full-capacity real output of an economy, in a "year,"

C the amount taken by households,
G the amount taken by government,
A the actual amount accumulated by businesses.

Then

$A = P - C - G$, or $P = A + C + G$.

Suppose C is a linear function of $P - G$ (this is roughly equal to household income).

$C = C' + K(P - G)$

Suppose A_0 is "willing investment," so that any accumulation beyond this will result in cutbacks in output and employment.

P_0 is the amount actually produced in undercapacity equilibrium,
C_0 the amount then taken by households, and
G_0 the amount then taken by government.

$$C_o = C' + K(P_o - G_o)$$

$$P_o = A_o + C_o + G_o = A_o + C' + K(P_o - G_o) + G_o$$

$$P_o = \frac{1}{1-K} (A_o + C') + G_o$$

$$P = \frac{1}{1-K} (A + C') + G$$

$$P - P_o = \frac{1}{1-K} (A - A_o) + (G - G_o)$$

If there is to be no unemployment,

$$P-P_o = 0, \text{ and } \frac{A-A_o}{1-K} = G_o-G$$

That is, an *increase* in government take (G_o-G) somewhat less than a decline in willing investment $(A-A_o)$ will suffice to maintain full employment.

14. If a government takes in \$100 and pays out \$110, the money supply in the hands of nongovernment sectors is increased by \$10.

15. In economics this is called the "cobweb theorem." See Appendix to Chapter 4, p. 90.

Chapter 9

The Integrative System

THE "INTEGRY"

The patterns of the evolution of social structures, social organizations, and social artifacts are by no means exhausted by organization through threat and the fear of consequences or through exchange and economic reward. There are many other relationships that hold us together or make us fall apart as humans. There are relationships of love and hate, pity and envy, sociability and misanthropy, assent and dissent, legitimacy and illegitimacy, dominance and subordination, equality and inequality, identity and alienation—all their vast subtlety and variety. These relationships are perhaps too diverse and scattered to be called the "integrative system." Nevertheless, there is a good deal of pattern to them, and while the integrative system is less orderly than the threat system or the exchange system and it is harder to find good models in it, it nevertheless has a perceivable unity of its own.

We must recognize, of course, that all actual relationships involve some combination of all three systems. It is hard to find any organization or any human interaction that does not have certain elements of threat, exchange, and integration. It still makes some sense, however, to divide the patterns of the social system as it spreads out through time and space into the *polity* in which the threat system is predominant, the *economy* in which the exchange system is predominant, and the *integry* in which the integrative system is predominant. Social institutions and organizations can be allocated roughly to one of these three phyla. Governments, armed forces, war and peace, and police and law fall to the polity; firms, corporations, banks, and insurance companies fall to the economy; churches, lodges, families, dinner parties, and friendships to the integry. Some organizations like labor unions may straddle all three, but that does not destroy the usefulness of the taxonomy.

THE IMAGE OF IDENTITY AS A CENTRAL
ORGANIZER OF THE INTEGRATIVE SYSTEM

The integrative system is so diverse that it is not easy to find a central concept like the concepts of the threat or exchange relationships in the other systems. Perhaps the central concept is that of an individual's image of his personal identity and of the identity of others. The core of the integrative relationship then becomes a statement such as "I will do something or I will ask you to do something because of what I am and because of what you are." What I am is what I think I am. What you are in the above statements is what I think you are. It may not be the same as what you think you are, but it is still the image of identity to which the appeal is made.

Our image of our own identity is a complex structure consisting partly of our image of our own body and our own knowledge, memories, skills, and potentialities. It is what we see when we look into the mirror of our mind, but it is also an image of a complex structure of roles, a role being the part we play or the pattern of behavior we adopt in some group or organization. I visualize myself as a husband, father, grandfather, resident of Boulder, citizen of both Colorado and the United States, economist, professor, member of the university faculty, Quaker, recorder player, author, lecturer, and so on, and so on. In each of these roles I relate to a different group, social structure, or organization and behave somewhat differently in each role. I behave in one way toward my wife, in a slightly different way toward our children, and still differently toward our grandchildren. As a resident of Boulder I pay taxes and vote in elections. Similarly, I pay taxes and vote in elections as a citizen of Colorado or the United States. I occasionally write to my congressman, or the governor, or the president when issues excite me. As a professor, I teach classes, direct theses, sit on committees, and answer an enormous volume of correspondence. As an author I write books, as a lecturer I give lectures, and so on. I see myself at the intersection of a large number of intersecting sets, the largest of which is the whole human race. Identity consists in large measure of the group one identifies with. If you ask somebody, "What are you?" he may reply, "I am a garage mechanic," or "I am a Baptist," or "I'm a McCoy," depending on whether the occupational identity, the religious identity, or the family identity is uppermost.

When two persons identify with the same group an integrative relationship of some kind, however tenuous, is established between them. A husband and wife in a successful marriage have a strong mutual integrative relationship and each identifies with the "couple" of which they are a member. The family is still the strongest integrative unit, as we shall see later, by the evidence of the "grants economy." Americans identify with other Americans, Germans with Germans, Japanese with Japanese as fellow members of a national state. The church is a collection of people each of whom identifies with the church and therefore with the other members. There may, of course, be disintegration as well as integration. When one member of a couple no longer finds a satisfactory identity in that role, the marriage is likely to end in divorce. People leave churches and transfer their citizenship to another nation.

There are negative identities as well as positive identities. I may be highly conscious of a group or organization with which I do *not* want to associate myself. A negative identity is what I am not rather than what I am. There are people indeed whose identities are built out of negative identities, who are much more conscious of what they are not than what they are. In Northern Ireland, for instance, people seem to be not so much Catholics and Protestants as they are not-Catholics and not-Protestants. Negative identities are likely to lead into disintegration and ill-managed conflict. On the other hand, negative components sometimes help to organize the total identity. A common enemy is sometimes a powerful bond and even the strong sense of being against something may organize behavior more successfully than being for something, if only because it is usually easier to know what you are against than what you are for. The radical identity is very frequently of this type.

BENEVOLENCE AND MALEVOLENCE

The structure of perceived identities often leads into corresponding patterns of benevolence and malevolence. A person is benevolent toward another if his perception of an increase in the other's welfare increases his own welfare, that is, his perception of the other's welfare is in the argument of his own welfare or utility function. This is a phenomenon known to economists as "interdependence of utility functions." Similarly, a person is malevolent if a perception of a decrease in the other's welfare increases his own. Selfishness is simply the zero point on the scale of benevolence and malevolence. It is a situation in which a person's perception of a change in the welfare of another makes no change in his own welfare. This is actually very rare. Most people are either mildly benevolent or mildly malevolent toward others, simply because the people around us in a very real sense form part of our own identity. They are in a certain sense extensions of ourselves, as indeed are the automobiles we drive, the clothes we wear, and the houses we live in.

When we have benevolence or malevolence we have to take account of the distributional impact of our decisions, that is, how our decisions will affect the welfare of other people, or at least our perception of this. The distributional impact of any decision or event describes who is favorably affected, who is unfavorably affected, and who is unaffected by this decision or event—and strictly, of course, we ought to add by how much. In a decision whether to issue a threat, a challenge, or an invitation to exchange, the distributional impact on other people has to be taken into account as affecting our own welfare. Every decision, as we have seen, involves an agenda of possible futures. We evaluate each item on the agenda and choose the "best," that is, the most highly valued. The evaluation of any particular item depends on its distributional impact as we perceive it. If we perceive those toward whom we are benevolent to be benefited, or if we perceive those toward whom we are malevolent to be injured, we are more likely to raise the value of that agenda item, and therefore probably choose it.

If we have high levels of benevolence, we are much more likely to initiate an exchange than to initiate a threat. Initiating a threat will result in a worsening of the welfare of the threatened party. If we are benevolent toward him, this will be perceived as a worsening of our own welfare; if we are malevolent toward him, of course, the very worsening of his welfare will improve ours. In exchange, as we have seen, both parties benefit, so that for the benevolent the benefit of the other party is perceived as an increase in their own welfare, and exchange is a much more likely relationship than threat. We see, therefore, how these integrative relationships modify the threat and the exchange relationships.

Pity and envy are aspects of benevolence and malevolence. Pity is a decline in our own welfare, which results from our contemplating the misfortunes or the low welfare of others. It is related to benevolence somewhat as a stock to a flow. In pity it is the condition of another rather than the worsening of that condition which produces a decline in our own welfare. Envy similarly relates to malevolence. It is the decline in our welfare, which results from our contemplating the good fortune of another. Pity and envy perhaps can be regarded as sources of malevolence and benevolence, though by no means the only sources.

POSITIVE AND NEGATIVE GRANTS (ONE-WAY TRANSFERS) AS INDICATORS OF AN INTEGRATIVE SYSTEM

Benevolence tends to produce grants, that is, one-way transfers of economic goods from the benevolent person to the person whose welfare he cherishes. Grants in the form of uncoerced gifts that are not expected to be reciprocated are the purest expression of benevolence. They are given presumably because the transfer increases the net welfare of both the giver and the recipient. There is a direct effect in diminishing the welfare of the giver because he is poorer in economic goods, and in increasing the welfare of the recipient because he is richer in economic goods. This effect is presumably offset by an indirect increase in the welfare of the giver as he contemplates the increased welfare of the recipient. There may be complex secondary reactions on the part of the recipient also. If he is benevolent toward the giver, he may regret the economic loss to the giver. There may be psychic costs to the recipient also in terms of the necessity for gratitude and a sense of being under an obligation or of having a lower status. One of the very real problems of grants is that they almost inevitably imply a higher status for the giver and a lower status for the recipient. This may add to the welfare of the giver and lower the welfare of the recipient.

The structure of positive grants is an important indicator of the extent and structure of the integrative system. We do have to distinguish, however, between gifts, which are made out of benevolence, and tribute, which is paid out of fear and is a byproduct of the threat system. These are often hard to distinguish in practice. Many grants are motivated by a mixture of the two. A rough distinction is possible however, between the voluntary gift and the involuntary tribute, for instance to the tax collector or bandit.

Just as benevolence produces positive grants, malevolence may produce negative grants in the way of theft, expropriation, and damage to life, health, and property. War is the most striking example of the production of negative grants to the enemy with the use of weapons. A weapon, indeed, can almost be defined as an instrument for producing a negative grant. There is a certain asymmetry here because negative grants are also costly to the donor, as we have seen (p. 146).

Theft is a form of forced grant from the victim to the thief. Burglary may not involve threat, but armed robbery does. Theft is most likely to take place, however, under conditions of selfishness. The thief or mugger may feel no malevolence toward his victim, but merely wish to transfer economic goods from the victim to himself; the loss to the victim neither increases nor diminishes his welfare. It is only his own gain that concerns him. Under conditions of malevolence, as for instance in war or revolution, a malevolent person may actually choose to injure himself if his enemy can be injured more by this action. One of the real puzzles in social dynamics is why malevolence is so popular when it is so clearly a losing, negative-sum game. Under mutual benevolence we all get better off; under mutual malevolence we all get worse off, each beating down the other and each giving negative grants to the other. Benevolence has been preached by all religions; "Love thy neighbor as thyself." Christianity even preached the love of enemies, that is, those who are perceived as malevolent toward one. Nevertheless, something like six or eight percent of the world product is devoted to armaments and to armed forces, which represents an organization, as it were, for producing negative grants, and it could hardly exist without malevolence. One of the puzzles we shall examine later is how social dynamics so often operates to make us all worse off instead of better off. This indeed might be called the "paradox of decision": when all decisions are for the best, how is it we so often move from better to worse rather than worse to better? We shall return to these problems when we look at the total dynamics of the structure. We still have some way to go, however, in exploring the structure itself.

STATUS, HIERARCHY, AND CLASS

One of the important aspects of integrative structure is status. Though it is hard to identify and virtually impossible to measure, it represents an aspect of society with which we are all familiar. When pollsters go out and ask people to rate a number of occupations in terms of status, for instance, people usually answer the question and the answers are not hopelessly far apart. Supreme Court justices at least always seem to come out at the top of the list. One of the marks of status is deference, which may be expressed in certain symbols—bowing, scraping, kneeling, hat-raising, and so on—or which may simply be expressed in the lower status person doing more listening and the upper status person doing more talking. Subordination is another aspect of status. The lower status person is expected to obey the orders that the upper status person gives.

Status is expressed both organizationally and linguistically in hierarchy or rank, which is an ordering of status positions from top to bottom, such as pope, cardinal, archbishop, bishop, priest in the church; or commander-in-chief, general, major general, major, colonel, lieutenant, sergeant, private in the army; or president, provost, dean, chairman of the department, professor, associate professor, instructor, student in the university. Sometimes these status names become honorific symbols without much actual content, such as the titles of nobility—king, duke, earl, baron, knight—or even degrees—summa cum laude, magna cum laude, cum laude, and ordinary degrees. In organizations, however, the hierarchy and its names are very significant because they show who gives orders to whom. There is often an important difference between the nominal hierarchy of names and the real hierarchy of power. The secretary or advisor to a commander-in-chief with a very lowly rank or no title at all may have more actual power than those with handsome titles in the hierarchy.

The development of hierarchy is closely related to the development of class in society. A class is a group that is characterized by all the members having roughly common status. Societies are often perceived to stratify into a lower class, a middle class, and an upper class. Each of these perhaps we can identify with upper, middle, and lower divisions, giving us nine classes in all. These classifications, however, are very loose. They never correspond to any organizations, although there are many organizations that concentrate their membership at one or more levels of the class stratification. There is a loose correlation between class and income that is hard to measure because it is very hard to measure or identify class. It is not surprising, however, to find that the lower the class the lower the income, though this is by no means universal. In some societies monks and clergy have very low incomes but a high status and are fairly high in the class structure. The nouveau riche are often lower in the class structure than their incomes would lead one to expect.

Class awareness is widespread. Most people, if asked, will place themselves somewhere on the class scale presented to them, although a very large majority of people in the United States identify themselves as belonging to the middle class. Class consciousness in the sense of finding a significant identity in class is pretty rare. The workers of the world do not unite. As two world wars certainly have shown, national identity is much stronger both in creating organization and in demanding sacrifice than class identity. Compared to the number of people who have died for their countries, practically nobody has died for his class. Those who try to arouse class consciousness are frequently upper or middle class radicals who visualize themselves as leaders, that is, as belonging to an upper class, leading the working class to victory.

INTEREST CLASSES AND CLASS CONFLICT

Part of the weakness of class as an integrative structure and a source of organization is the fact that interest classes very rarely coincide with social classes, status groups, or self-conscious classes. An interest class is a set of people whose welfare is affected in the same way by something. Every event, every change in the system, every new piece of legislation, every new organization, or every decision hypothetically creates three interest classes: those who are favorably affected, those who are unfavorably affected, and those who are unaffected. We may divide these into smaller classes if we wish, such as those who are very favorably affected, moderately favorably affected, and so on. The interest classes are often very hard to identify. Even legislation designed to affect some groups favorably and others unfavorably often does not succeed in its intention, and its results produce interest classes completely different from the intentions or expectations of its promoters. I have sometimes called this the "law of political irony"—that a great deal of what we do to help people actually hurts them, and a great deal of what we do to hurt people actually helps them. There are many exceptions to this law, but its operation is frequent enough to be a serious cause for concern. It is the sheer complexity of the real interrelations of the social system, as compared with the very much over simplified models of the system, with which most decisionmakers operate in either politics or other fields of life, which creates this law of political irony. We very rarely know what the effects of our actions will be. Again, the great principle of the ecologists—that you cannot do one thing—applies. When we try to do one thing, we succeed in doing half-a-dozen other things that we had no intention of doing and probably did not want done. We will consider examples of this in a later chapter.

This means, however, that class conflicts are extremely diffuse; it is very hard to do anything that will benefit all the members of one social class at the expense of all the members of another. Even communist revolutions, which are supposed to be an example of class conflict, usually consist of an internal conflict within the upper class, or at least the lower upper class, for control of the society's resources, and distribution of the losses and benefits among the other classes may turn out to be pretty random. One possible exception to this is when a revolution occurs in a society in which a few rich landowners dominate a large class of landless cultivators. Under these circumstances class war takes on some significance because the social and income classes may correspond to the interest classes, and the landowners may be deposed and extinguished as a class. The previously lower class probably has to pay less in rent than it did before, though it may end up paying a good deal to the middle-class organizers of the revolution.

LEGITIMACY, INTERNAL AND EXTERNAL, AS A DOMINANT SYSTEM

Another very important aspect of the integrative system is legitimacy. This is hard to measure, and not even easy to define or identify, but it is nevertheless something of enormous importance. Legitimacy has two aspects. The first might be called internal legitimacy, in which it is an aspect of a person's identity and is almost equivalent to morale. Legitimacy is "OKness." A person who feels that his body, mind, skills, and roles are OK is likely to operate with conviction and style in such a way indeed as frequently to reinforce these images. A person who perceives himself as weak, ugly, stupid, incompetent, and who is occupying roles that he despises is not likely to function very well. The second aspect, external legitimacy, is the belief on the part of others that a person, organization, or institution is OK. External legitimacy arises out of a grant of acceptance from those who are part of the environment of the person or organization concerned. External and internal legitimacy often reinforce each other. The person who is convinced he is OK acts in such a way as to invoke a corresponding result from others. There are, however, exceptions to this rule. The person who is insensitive to the subtle feedbacks involved in legitimacy may be overconfident of his own legitimacy and act in a way that will cause others to reject him and hence deny him legitimacy.

We ascribe legitimacy to roles, to organizations, and to institutions, as well as to persons. A teacher in front of a class, a president addressing Congress or the nation, and a king in his court are all exercising the legitimacy of the role. Legitimacy of the role indeed is often so strong that a weak and incompetent person who occupies the role nevertheless receives the legitimacy that the role has created. If enough incompetents occupy the role, this legitimacy may be withdrawn, as a good many kings and even presidents have discovered. This granting of legitimacy is a very important element in the establishment of hierarchy. Authority, as Chester Barnard said,[1] is always granted from below, even though it may be exercised from above. Once the legitimacy is withdrawn, whether by the students from the teacher, the enlisted men from the officers, or the priests from the pope, the organization collapses. No continuing organization is possible indeed without substantial grants of legitimacy from the lower to the upper roles in the hierarchy.

It can be argued indeed with considerable evidence from history that the dynamics of legitimacy ultimately dominate all other elements of social systems. Once legitimacy decays either in the minds of the upper members of a hierarchy in the form of internal legitimacy, or is withdrawn by the lower members, the whole structure collapses. The legitimacy of the institution of monarchy, for instance, was eroded in the seventeenth and eighteenth centuries in Europe perhaps by the increase in the complexity of the state and governmental task and a succession of weak or exploitative monarchs. Once people ceased to believe in the absolute monarchy it was not long before it ceased to exist, and the reigning incumbent either had his head cut off or was exiled. It is significant indeed that the only surviving monarchs in Europe are those who abandoned their power and became symbols of legitimacy, like the British, Dutch, and Scandinavian monarchs. One sees a similar phenomenon in empire. The legitimacy of the European empires was severely eroded in the early part of the twentieth century, and it took only a generation after the loss of that legitimacy before they were disbanded.

SYMBOLS IN THE STATE, CHURCH, AND ART

The messengers—the enzymes as it were—of the integrative system are *symbols*. As we have seen (p. 128), one of the things that distinguishes the human race from the other animals is its capacity to use symbols as well as signs in the development of language, so that complex images, which transcend personal experience, can be transferred from one mind to another. Along with this capacity goes the power of abstraction, the ability to develop abstract symbols and concepts such as number, causation, and geometric patterns such as circles, squares, and lines, symbols for elements, models of atoms and electrons, and the whole great gamut of mathematics, all of which is an abstraction from the immediacy of personal experience, although it is all abstracted from personal experience. Without personal experience the abstraction would be impossible, because the mind would be empty and there would be nothing for it to abstract.

The integrative system is particularly dominated by emotive symbols, which symbolize a whole complex ingroup or an outgroup such as a nation and its enemies, the family and the non-kin, a religion and the non-believers. The flag, the cross, the crescent, and the coat of arms become in the eyes of those who raise them "a standard to which all shall repair." It is hard to imagine a nation without a flag. The extent of the display of the flag indeed is perhaps a good social indicator of the strength of national sentiment, though very strong and secure sentiment may require less of a symbol rather than more. The flag probably originated in the medieval standards by which the followers of a particular knight were able to find him on the battlefield.

Without the symbol, it is hard to say how much national sentiment would be generated; without the sentiment, it is hard to say how much the symbol would be used. One can be pretty sure the symbol and the sentiment reinforce each other.

Religion is particularly influenced by symbols. Even the theology of a religion and its doctrines are a symbol of something larger and more complex than itself. It is a model of the universe, which is usually impossible to test by simple sense observation, but which attracts adherents because of its poetic quality and appeal to the deep fears and desires of the human being. Theology itself becomes clothed in symbols that sometimes become even more important than the theology. So we get crosses and icons, altars and vestments, liturgies and rituals, candles and incense, the whole paraphernalia in which the more ritualistic churches like Orthodox and Roman Christianity or Shingon Buddhism and certain forms of Hinduism develop a vast richness and complexity. Sometimes symbolism goes too far and we get a reaction of iconoclasm—the breaking of idols and images and a desire for symbols of purity and austerity. The iconoclasts of Byzantium may very well have been influential in laying the ground for Islam and the simplicity of the mosque. Within Christianity protestantism also represents an iconoclastic movement—smashing the images of the saints, the reredoses, and even the stained glass windows of the churches, abolishing the burden of purely symbolic pious works like pilgrimages or symbolic remissions of sin and indulgences, and leading finally to the almost mosquelike chapel and the austerities of the Quaker meetinghouse, which is devoid even of crosses and altars.

Another realm of symbol is that of art, which often begins as the servant of a church or a state providing symbols of pomp and power in the shape of impressive buildings, stained glass windows, clothing, music, all combined in rich complexes to capture the loyalties and imagination so that people grant the legitimacy necessary to sustain the state and church.[2] The robes of kings, the wigs of judges, carriages, processions, pomp, martial music, palaces, and dignified courts all reinforce the legitimacy of the state. Cathedrals, stained glass, paintings, tapestries, carvings, statues, crosses and altars, vestments, and music all reinforce the legitimacy of the church. Eventually, however, art breaks away from its masters and becomes independent and develops a symbolism of its own. Realistic art, for instance, in painting and statuary symbolizes the world of the senses; abstract art symbolizes the world of the emotions, often pretty abstract emotions.

DYNAMICS OF THE INTEGRATIVE SYSTEM

We have still not exhausted the richness of the "species" of the integrative system. We need not pile any more instances on instances to show that it exists. It is indeed all around us in daily experience and in the deepest reflections of theologians and philosophers, and in the most inspired symbols of artists. What is puzzling is the dynamics of the system. What are its patterns of change, if any? It is what it is today because of what it had become in the past. Can we look at the whole history of the system, as it spreads from the first human beings over time and space to the present day, and ask ourselves what patterns can be perceived in it? This is a particularly difficult problem because the integrative system for the most part consists of species that inhabit the structural forms of the human nervous system. Material artifacts can be observed and they leave traces and records. Organizational artifacts also can be observed, though less easily, and they also leave very extensive traces and records. Love and hate, dominance and subordination, assent and dedication, legitimacy and illegitimacy, and the whole vast world of symbols that makes up the complex image of human identity is a subterranean ecosystem hidden beneath the hard surface of skulls, apparent only when it results in communications and records of communications, that interacts only through communications. No person has ever been inside another skull. It is not surprising that this is a world of cloudy obscurity, unlike the sharp, clear ecosystems of plants and animals or even of knives and forks, corporations, churches, and states.

Yet the "integry" is an essential part of the genetic structure of society. It is part of the noosphere. The products of society in terms of material artifacts or social organizations cannot be understood without it. As part of the noosphere, it is parallel in social systems to what the genosphere is in biological systems. Because of the enormous power of communication, however, it is far more complex than the genosphere. The genosphere consists of information shut up in sperm cells and egg cells, mixing occasionally in sexual reproduction, that changes very slowly through mutation or through the crossing over of chromosomes. The noosphere, by contrast, of which the integrative system is a vitally important part, is not shut up in the four billion individual skulls that constitute, as it were, the cells of the system, or even in the 70 or so billion human skulls that have ever been made. It is the great network of interaction and communications among these individual minds that largely determines the content of each. Human minds, therefore, constitute almost a single social genome extending over the whole surface of the earth and back into time as far as the records permit.

My 48 chromosomes, apart from a certain amount of crossing over, presumably came from only 48 ancestors, and from their ancestors back through time to the significant mutations that produced them. The intellectual, affectional, moral, and symbolic "chromosomes" that inhabit my mind must be traced back to millions of intellectual, affectional, moral, and symbolic ancestors who have contributed to this complexity. The language stored somewhere inside my skull goes back to the millions of English speakers and writers who formed it. Every word of my vocabulary could strictly be traced back to the person who first started it as a mutation, and to its ancestors out of which it mutated. The complexities of syntax, grammar, and style could also theoretically be traced back to their originators, and from mind to mind by communication over 20 generations back to Shakespeare, 30 or 40 to William the Conqueror, and perhaps 200 to the original Indo-Aryan sources. The intellectual content of my mind goes back to my teachers, the 500 or 1000 books I must have read, the lectures I have listened to, the gossip I have heard, the thousands of authors, many of whom are quite unknown to me, who influenced somebody, who influenced somebody, who influenced somebody, who in turn influenced me. My mind likewise is full of symbols, memories, quotations, affections and disaffections, likes and dislikes, all of which come out of the interactions between the constant informational or symbolic input over 68 years and the constant production of internal inputs by the mind itself—new thoughts, new questions, new symbols, new structures of poetry or theory.

It is not surprising that the symbolic ecosystem, which combines so much complexity with so much obscurity, is hard to follow and that much of what happens in the integrative structure of the world is a puzzle. What is it that gives an idea, an affection, an association, or a symbol survival value in competition or cooperation with others? As we look at the development of the human noosphere as it spreads over the earth from our first parents, whatever they called themselves, we see this as an evolutionary structure, developing large numbers of interacting species of ideas, images, valuations, affections, and symbols, often hard to define sharply and distinguish from others but nevertheless forming a differentiated structure. We find mutation—new words, new ideas, new emotions, new affections, new symbols. Most of these perhaps do not survive, but some of them do, introducing new equations into the ecosystem, diminishing some older species, and reinforcing others.

SYMBOLIC HABITATS AND REVOLUTIONS

The patterns are not uniform. There are subsystems within subsystems—islands of the noosphere cut off from communication or the effects of communication by schizophrenia, isolation, or ignorance. There are habitats as different as the polar ice and the tropical jungles. There are the lush forests of Orthodox Christianity and Shingon Buddhism, the bare high plains of Unitarianism and Zen, the mechanized agriculture of hardheaded rationalism, the snowy peaks of the hermit and the mystic, and the boiling ant hill of the sports fan. Species that survive in one habitat could not possibly survive in another, yet what differentiates the habitats, why do they expand and contract? In the biological world it is climates, topography, soils, wind distribution, temperature, and so on that define habitats. What the corresponding things in the strange habitats of the noosphere are we really do not know.

Sometimes there are ecological revolutions in the noosphere, as happened in the middle of the nineteenth century in Europe, when the topics of conversation at Oxford shifted suddenly from Low Church versus High Church to broad-gauge versus narrow-gauge railroads. Dun Scotus, according to Gerard Manley Hopkins,[3] "fired France for Mary without spot," which would be much more difficult to do today. The physical and technological environment, of course, does make a difference. It is not wholly surprising that Islam goes along with the desert and Christianity with the cathedral-like shape of the forest. But then, of course, we do have Moslems in Indonesia and Catholics in Kansas. It is not surprising that in Europe Protestantism is northern and Catholicism is southern, but in the United States this is largely reversed. The habitats of the noosphere take on a life of their own and propagate themselves because they become conscious, integrative systems to which people give loyalty and affection and from which people derive their identity. In the integrative system we sometimes do find a tropical forest at the North Pole protected, of course, by greenhouses.

HUMAN LEARNING AS THE KEY TO INTEGRATIVE DYNAMICS; ACCULTURATION

The structures of the integrative system in the human mind, like all its structures, are almost entirely learned, subject to certain physiological limitations imposed partly by the genetic structure and partly by the accidents of growth. These limitations are often so far off, however, that they are not very significant, which is the great fallacy behind a simplistic eugenics. If, to revert to a previous metaphor, we all paint ourselves into a corner of the vast ballroom of the potential of our nervous systems, it does not matter very much whether the far walls are a little closer to us or a little further away. To vary the metaphor, the newborn baby is a bit like a settler going forward into an almost empty territory—he has to fill it with the roads, farms, and cities of the mature mind. There will, however, be certain differences in the physiological terrain—different river valleys and passes for each individual in his physiological patterns. For some there are real hardships and deficiences. To the defective child, learning may be more like trying to settle Nevada than trying to settle Oklahoma. It is fairly easy to identify deficiencies, but extremely hard to identify genetic or physiological excellences. Distinguished families like the Churchills or Roosevelts are much more likely to be the result of cultural and even economic inheritance than they are of genetic inheritance.

The key to the evolution of the integrative system, therefore, is first the process by which a human being learns throughout the whole of life; and second the process by which the culture and knowledge structure of the society are transmitted to the growing child, which anthropologists tend to call "acculturation" and sociologists "socialization." This is the process that turns the Swedish child into a Swede and the Italian child into an Italian, an upper class child into an upper class adult, a lower class child usually into a lower class adult.

Acculturation begins in the family for the most part. It takes a lot of time and attention on the part of parents. Studies of children raised in orphanages from an early age, for instance, suggest that they are liable to cultural, and what might be called integrative, deficiencies mainly because they have not had enough adult attention. The culture of the family is all that most children know. It is tremendously important in establishing the basic integrative structure not only in terms of language but also in terms of values and symbols. Other influences may come in later years, such as schools, mass media, peer groups, and so on, which can sometimes cause "revolutions" in the acculturation process, so that a child growing up in a Catholic family may become an anti-religious rationalist, a child growing up in an English family, like myself, may become an American, a child growing up in a liberal family may become a fascist, and so on. We do not really know how often this happens. One suspects it is moderately rare. Cultural mutation, of course, is the failure of acculturation, just as it is very often a failure of replication in the case of the gene. Without these failures, indeed, every generation would grow up to be exactly like its parents, as is often the case in highly traditional cultures, such as the Amish or Hutterites even though they are embedded in a nontraditional and very rapidly changing society.

It is the transmission of valuation systems that is perhaps most important here. Because the child receives love and care from the parents, he values the parents and hence values their values. The learning of values—and almost all human valuation structure is learned—takes place partly through this kind of imitative process and occasionally, of course, by way of revolt from it. There are many puzzles here, however. Parents often produce children very different from themselves. How we really do not know.

In conclusion, we may go through some of the elements of the integrative structure we have outlined to see if any peculiar dynamic processes are found in them. The dynamics of benevolence and malevolence are quite puzzling. These are often engendered in processes something like arms races involving reciprocal deviation-amplifying positive feedback. Lewis Richardson (p. 162) indeed pointed out that falling in love was a process essentially similar to that of the arms race—"Lay down your arms and surrender to mine," went the old popular song. Thus, A perceives that B is benevolent toward A, so A increases his benevolence toward B; when B perceives that, B increases benevolence toward A, A increases it toward B, and so on in a "benevolence race." The reactivities, that is, how much A's benevolence increases with the perception of an increase in B may diminish as benevolence increases and some equilibrium is reached. A similar process takes place with malevolence: A perceives that B is malevolent toward A, so A increases the malevolence toward B, B increases malevolence toward A, and so we go on in a "malevolence race." This again may exhaust itself; the reactivities will decline and an equilibrium of malevolence may be reached. For most relationships these equilibria are reached at fairly low levels of either malevolence or benevolence. I feel very mildly benevolent toward ordinary people with whom I come in contact and mildly malevolent toward political enemies and people of whom I disapprove, but it takes fairly close interaction to produce high levels of either benevolence or malevolence.

A very difficult but important question of social policy is how far benevolence can be relied to organize society. There are unfortunately "limits to love" as there are "limits to growth," and the question of how to expand these limits is very important in any social system. At the other end of the scale there is the question of how social systems defend themselves against reactively increasing malevolence, which can be enormously destructive to both parties, as we see for instance in relations of the Israelis and the Arabs, the Turks and the Greeks on Cyprus, or the Protestants and Catholics in Northern Ireland.

An encouraging feature of the model, however, is that a relatively small movement of the reaction function of either party toward benevolence, which involves the giving of a little more than each gets, can shift the whole system toward much higher levels of benevolence. The process of falling in love clearly falls into this pattern, and a very small difference in the initial state can make a large difference in the final state. We cannot rely on the falling-in-love pattern, however, to raise general levels of benevolence. For this we have to rely on a movement of childhood training practices to develop a generalized sense of obligation, or the development of symbolic systems like "the love of God," which again create a sense of obligation toward generalized benevolence.

THE "PRISONER'S DILEMMA"

The higher payoffs for benevolence suggest that, even though the dynamics of the system often move it toward malevolence, the long-run evolutionary process will cause a spread of benevolence and a diminution of malevolence. We have a rather similar problem in the famous game theory problem of the prisoner's dilemma, which has been so extensively researched by Anatol Rapoport.[4] In Figure 9.1, we suppose two parties A and B. We suppose each can be either good or bad, which can stand for all sorts of things. If both parties are good, both are better off in the good-good box. If B is good, however, it pays A to be bad. If A is good, it pays B to be bad, following the arrows. If A is bad, it pays B to be bad; if B is bad, it pays A to be bad, following the arrows, so that we end up in the bad-bad box, where everybody is worse off than they are in the good-good box. The only answer

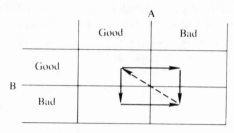

Figure 9.1: The Prisoner's Dilemma

to this situation is the development of long-sighted, cooperative behavior, suggested by the dotted arrow, which enables people to climb into the unstable but superior good-good box.

A large series of experiments have shown that there is a very common pattern. The experiment may begin with what may be called "naive trust" in the good-good box. One of the parties betrays this and becomes "bad," whereupon the other party immediately follows suit and both get trapped in the bad-bad box. After a while, however, it begins to dawn on the players that this is a mug's game and they climb back, often rather painfully, into the good-good box again, perhaps with a number of tentative retreats, finally achieving what might be called "mature trust" and a sense of community. This suggests that the long-term payoffs are for being good, that is, benevolent, trusting, and so on. There is a very long-run evolutionary process in this direction that is precarious, however, in the sense that it is constantly being interrupted by lapses.

DOMINANCE VERSUS EGALITARIANISM

The dynamics of dominance, subordination, assent, dedication, and the whole complex of attitudes that creates and legitimates hierarchy is complex in the extreme and it is hard to formulate any very simple principles about it. Charismatic leadership produces dedication, as we see in innumerable religious and political movements from the Reverend Moon, to Moral Rearmament, to the communists. A threat-submission system is often legitimated by those who submit in terms of granting legitimacy and respect to the threatener, thereby perhaps taking some of the sting out of submission. It is not surprising, therefore, that there is a constant tendency for social patterns to move into hierarchy and into dominance and subordination. We see persistent patterns of subordination; for instance, of women in the family, subjects in the state, parishioners in the church, workers in the factory, soldiers in the army, students in the university, pupils in the school, players on the team, and so on.

On the other hand, there is also a countervailing tendency, an age-long, subterranean demand for equality, which seems continually to grow in force as time goes on, and which produces offsetting institutions to hierarchy such as elections, welfare states, the priesthood of all believers in the "believers' church," the revolt against empire, and movements for national independence, movements for federalism and local autonomy, liberation movements on the part of the subordinated such as women, blacks, chicanos, gays, and even the development of staff in organizations who undermine the strict hierarchical structure.

The underlying dynamics of these two opposing tendencies are complex in the extreme and no simple model of them can be made. Part of it arises because hierarchy itself increases human productivity only up to a certain point. Beyond this point it develops pathologies in the shape of corruption of information, which produce worse and worse decisions on the part of upper members of the hierarchy and also a corruption of the sense of community on which an organization ultimately may rest. On the other side, there is the growth of benevolence, which eats away at the foundations of the threat system and produces a demand for equality and a sense of community and a dissatisfaction with alienation. How all these things interact, however, is beyond the reach of any simple model.

THE DYNAMICS OF LEGITIMACY

Finally, we can say something about the dynamics of legitimacy, a process that, as we have suggested, tends to dominate all other social dynamic systems. Neither threats nor exchange can organize large-scale systems unless the institutions that embody them have legitimacy. A great deal of work on this problem still needs to be done. Nevertheless, one can suggest some plausible hypotheses.

First, legitimacy does come from positive payoffs in the sense of institutions or individuals that create satisfactions. It is perhaps seen most clearly when institutions, which previously paid off, no longer do, and they then often tend to lose legitimacy even though the inertia of the system may keep them going for quite a while. The institution of monarchy, which was an excellent "salient solution" of conflict between competing barons in the early middle ages, gradually lost its payoffs as the functions of government became more complex and as the heredity principle produced more and more incompetents in the positions of power. Once a monarch is deposed or executed, the divinity that doth hedge a king suddenly collapses.

The loss of legitimacy in empire, which we also noted earlier, is closely connected with the fact that empire simply did not pay off for the imperial power, at least in the nineteenth and twentieth centuries; or perhaps it would be more accurate to say that the very small group for whom it did pay off lost power internally in the imperial countries and it was not long before the whole legitimacy of empire collapsed. The empires were disbanded a generation later. I remember singing as a boy in England

Wider, still and wider may thy bounds be set,
God who made thee mighty,
Make thee mightier yet.[5]

This could hardly be sung without embarrassment today, but it was sung with a perfectly straight face in the 1920s. The decline in the legitimacy of war is a very striking phenomenon in the twentieth century, again partly as a result of the enormously increased costs and diminished benefits of the institution. This is reflected, for instance, in the decline of war songs, which were numerous and enthusiastic in World War I, virtually absent in World War II, and appeared mainly as anti-war songs in the Vietnam war.

The problem is enormously complicated, however, by the fact that it is not only mere positive payoffs that create legitimacy but also negative payoffs. This is a phenomenon I have called the "sacrifice trap."[6] If people can be persuaded to make sacrifices for something, their identity becomes deeply involved with it and they find it extremely hard to admit to themselves that their sacrifices have been in vain. Consequently it is easy to persuade them to make more sacrifices. This is why the blood of the martyrs is the seed of the church, the blood of the soldiers is the seed of the militant state, the tears of the children perhaps the seed of the family, the agonies of the student the seed of the alumni association. On the other hand, the process cannot go too far or it will collapse—suddenly conscription is resisted, Protestantism with its much milder demands shakes itself loose from the Catholic Church, a long suffering spouse files for divorce, alumni stop contributing, the overdemanding king gets his head cut off, the bloody religion of the Aztecs collapses overnight in the face of a handful of Spaniards and missionaries, and so on, on innumerable occasions in human history. This is why the dynamics of legitimacy is very hard to predict. Institutions that seem absolutely unshakable today may be in ruins next year when the system goes over an unforeseen precipice.

Positive and negative payoffs are the main sources of legitimacy, but there are a good many minor ones. Age is one—young things and new things tend to be legitimate simply because they are young and new; middle-age things become old fashioned and illegitimate. If they survive this, they become antiques and legitimate again. Anything that survives for a very long time like the Catholic Church or even the United States, the eleventh oldest among the nations, acquires a legitimacy of sheer age, which is hard to overthrow It is perhaps only the legitimacy of habit, but habit is very powerful. It is reinforced by continual use, though again if it leads to being unadaptable, it may be shattered overnight. This kind of legitimacy is a little bit akin to the sort of quasi-equilibria we find in various geological ages, like that of the dinosaurs, which lead to a lack of adaptability and perhaps ultimately to catastrophe. The senator may have enormous legitimacy, but he is close to death for all that.

Other sources of legitimacy that we have noted earlier are the persuasive uses of the arts, speech, music, architecture, literature, painting, and so on, such as Versailles, Chartres, ancient Rome, and modern Washington. All say very clearly, "I am important, I am, and you had better believe it." Again, for a long time this may be very successful, but if it is not supported by real payoffs, it will eventually be found out. The Emperor's clothes become really invisible. Magnificent clothing and palaces no longer protect the king. The cathedrals, vestments, music, and ritual no longer attract a congregation. Academic processions become smaller and more ragged.

One aspect of the creation of legitimacy is mystification. We find this often in religion. We find it also in politics and especially in the mysteries of foreign policy and the military. A holy of holies, which the common man may not approach whether in the temple, in the Pentagon, or in the Politburo, creates an aura of legitimacy as part of the aura of mystery. This too erodes, however, and can be found out. The sacred places are invaded and found to be empty. The mysteries of the church, of medicine, even perhaps of economics may lose the power to sway.

The loss of an old legitimacy, however, is often a very dangerous time. There is an enormous demand for legitimacy and worse ones can easily arise to take the place of those that have collapsed. The Kaiser gives place to Hitler, the Czar to Stalin. The building up of a legitimacy that is "true" is a long, painful learning process, the rules for which are most imperfectly understood. It is not surprising that we seem to make one mistake after another in this regard.

What we have here is pretty far from a coherent, general theory of integrative systems. Perhaps we will never have one; however, I am convinced the integrative system ultimately dominates the others. The better we can understand it, the better chance we have of moving into a more desirable future. This, however, is the problem of the next chapter.

Appendix to Chapter 9:
THE THEORY OF BENEVOLENCE AND MALEVOLENCE

The interaction process between benevolence and malevolence is illustrated in Figure 9A.1, which resembles Figure 7A.1 (see p. 160). Here we suppose two parties, A and B, interacting. We measure A's benevolence or malevolence toward B horizontally, B's toward A vertically. The zero we suppose represents selfishness, that is, indifference. As we move to the right of the zero point, A increases his benevolence; as we move to the left, he increases his malevolence. As we move upward from the zero point, B increases his benevolence; as we move downward, B increases his malevolence.

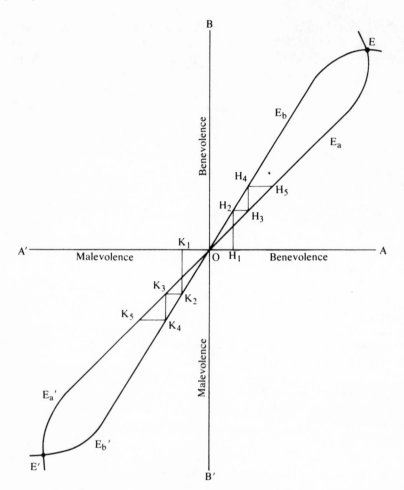

Figure 9A.1: Malevolence-Benevolence Dynamics

If we suppose that the benevolence or malevolence of each is a function of that of the other, neglecting for the moment the difference between perception and reality, we can draw a line $E_a E_a'$ showing what level of benevolence A will generate toward B for each level of benevolence of B toward A. Similarly, the line $E_b E_b'$ shows the level of benevolence that B will develop for each level of A's benevolence. As drawn in Figure 9A.1, these lines go through the origin, which suggests that selfishness simply generates selfishness. The origin is then a position of unstable equilibrium. If some chance disturbance makes A benevolent, moving the position, say, to H_1, B will move to H_2, A to H_3, B to H_4, A to H_5, and so on. Unless the lines move together and intersect, this will proceed indefinitely. Eventually, of course, they will converge and intersect. There will be some position of mutual equilibrium of benevolence at E. On the other hand, if the first move is toward malevolence, say to K_1, B will move to K_2, A to K_3, B to K_4, A to K_5, and so on, with levels of increasing malevolence. Still this ends up in an equilibrium at E'. If now we reverse the positions of the two partial equilibrium lines, so that $E_a E_a'$ becomes $E_b E_b'$, and $E_b E_b'$ becomes $E_a E_a'$, there will be a stable equilibrium at selfishness, and any impulse toward either benevolence or malevolence will be offset by a return to selfishness. It could

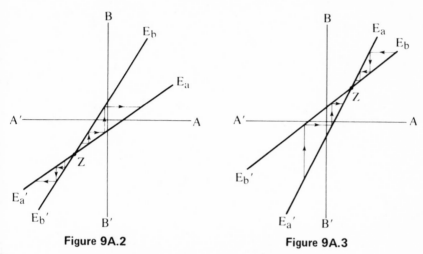

Figure 9A.2

Figure 9A.3

Malevolence-Benevolence Dynamics

be, of course, that selfishness on the part of one would produce malevolence on the part of the other, in which case the point of intersection of the two lines would be in the third quadrant and down and to the left of the origin, at point Z in Figure 9A.2. In this case, also, there might be either an unstable or a stable equilibrium at this point of intersection. Quite similarly, we often see a stable equilibrium position of mild benevolence, such as point Z in Figure 9A.3.

NOTES

1. Chester I. Barnard, *The Functions of the Executive* (Cambridge, Mass.: Harvard University Press, 1938).

2. This is what Charles E. Merriam (*Political Power*. New York: Collier Books, 1964; first published 1934) calls "miranda."

3. Gerard Manley Hopkins, *Poems of Gerard Manley Hopkins* (2nd ed.; London and New York: Oxford University Press 1930), 40.

4. Anatol Rapoport and Albert Chammah, *The Prisoner's Dilemma, A Study in Conflict and Cooperation* (Ann Arbor: University of Michigan Press, 1965).

5. Edward Elgar, "Pomp and Circumstance."

6. See Kenneth E. Boulding, *The Economy of Love and Fear: A Preface to Grants Economics* (Belmont, Calif.: Wadsworth, 1973), 27-28, 98-99.

Chapter 10

An Evolutionary
Interpretation of History

THE SEARCH FOR PATTERN IN HISTORY

Almost ever since there has been any history there have been attempts to interpret it. In the Bible we find the history of the Jews interpreted in terms of the disastrous consequences of breaking the covenant with Jehovah. The Greeks are supposed to have seen history as a cycle of ages—gold, silver, bronze, iron, and hopefully back to gold again. Marx saw history dominated by materialist dialectic; Max Weber by religious movements and trends toward bureaucracy. Spengler like the Greeks thought always in terms of cycles of rise and fall, growth and decay; Toynbee saw it in terms of challenge and response; the Club of Rome in terms of exhaustion and pollution. We will examine some of these interpretations in greater detail in Chapter 12. What is emerging in this volume, however, is an evolutionary interpretation of human history as a continuation, though in a more complex pattern, of the long history of biological and even prebiological evolution. It is seen in terms of ecological interaction, population dynamics, and the production of phenotypes from genotypes. It is not monistic, as many earlier interpretations were, looking to a single dynamic process such as, for instance, material technology or dialectics for one true dynamic on which everything else depends. The watchword of evolution is interaction, not causation. It is therefore a pluralistic interpretation to the core, even though we recognize that some processes frequently dominate others.

THINGS, ORGANIZATIONS, PEOPLE: THE "TOP" SAGA

What has emerged from the previous chapters, curiously enough, is a trinity of trinities. We see, first, all human history involving three great interacting phyla of families of species: Things, Organizations, and People. One is tempted to call this the "TOP" saga because each of these phyla develops in innumerable subplots, all interacting on the others. Things or material artifacts form a vast phylum of species beginning with the simplest stone tools and wooden sticks, going to fires, which we must count as human artifacts, skins, shelters, and bone implements, developing in an almost endless variety of forms of increasing complexity to the spacelab and the latest computer.

The phylum of material artifacts can perhaps be subdivided into raw materials on the one hand and finished or part-finished products on the other. Each interacts on the other. The materials go from stone and wood, animal skins, and bones to fruits, nuts, grains, and meats, and to clay, gold, silver, copper, bronze, iron, steel, through to aluminum, plastics, and the latest chemicals. Improvement in final products is often dependent on and also promotes improvement in materials. The change from stone and wood to metals led to a great improvement in the finished products, which led eventually to the rise of the chemical industry with its fantastic cornucopia of new and sometimes dangerous materials.

Along with the development of material artifacts goes the development of organizations. The organization of the nuclear family long predates the human race. It is, however, the human capacity for complex organization far beyond the family that has permitted the great expansion of material artifacts and of the human population itself. The history written in the history books, indeed, is written often unconsciously about the ecological succession of organizations. An organization can be defined as a structure of roles linked by lines of communication. The role rather than the person is the essential unit of the organization. Persons occupy roles and behave accordingly, but the same role may be occupied by different persons in succession or indeed occasionally by artifacts such as a machine. A role is only part of a person, as we have seen (p. 190). If roles become too fragmented, the person may also become fragmented and alienated. Nevertheless, a distinction between the person and the role is the key to the whole vast expansion of organization, which has gone on in the history of the human race.

The first organization is undoubtedly the family. Occasionally in a pre-human species we see the family as a role structure where, for instance, with the death of the father another male will take his place, but this is pretty rare. The expansion of the human race must have begun when an uncle or some other male took over the role of the dead father or an aunt, grandmother, or other female took over the role of the dead mother. Even so, the family itself is a precarious and temporary organization actually bound much more to persons than to roles. Perhaps we should count as the first real organization the hunting-gathering band, because there is a clear division of labor and specification of roles. These bands often may have been without much in the way of hierarchy, which is the next mutation, in which the chief appears not as a person, but as a role with the function of organizing the subordinate roles and saying to one person, "Do this," and to another, "Do that." It seems likely that hierarchy develops out of some situation of stress in which the voluntary acceptance of roles by individuals is no longer adequate to meet the role structure of the society or group. This may happen, for instance, in fighting. One of the earliest organizations was undoubtedly a raiding party, which is pretty hard to organize without a chief. Stress may also have been created by migration, by a worsening environment, or by an epidemic. Other examples of stress situations that might produce hierarchy would be the trading caravan, which had to have some kind of leader, and the ship, which is hard to imagine without a captain. All this of course is speculation.

With the development of agriculture there is a large increase in the size and variety of organizations. The village itself is an organization and almost has to have at least a loose hierarchical structure. Political and legal organizations begin to emerge in dispute settlement. Cooperation is necessary to down trees, carry wood, build houses. It was Chester Barnard (see p. 207) I think who observed that organization began when two men had to carry a log. The workshop, in which there is a division of labor in the form of different work roles, may go back as far as the mesolithic flint factories. It certainly developed with metallurgy and the making of metal tools and weapons. The workshop also requires hierarchy; somebody has to organize it and tell the others what to do.

The age and sex structure of the human race is part of the environment of organizations and explains something of their form. The uneasy dominance of the male over the female, which has plagued human history for a very long time, has something to do with role structures imposed by biological functions, such as childbearing and lactation on the part of the women and the consequent greater capacity for long-distance travel on the part of the male. This leads to an almost universal division of labor in hunting-gathering societies where the men do the hunting and the women do the gathering. Nevertheless, these societies seem to have enjoyed a good deal of equality of status between the sexes in the past because, in most of them, gathering was really more efficient in food producing than hunting, so women had a key role. The men are really more dependent on the women for food than the women are on the men. With the agricultural revolution this changes; the men are in the village all the time and tend to have less to do than the women and hence fall into political and religious roles, which enhance their dominance.

The existence of children likewise creates hierarchy. The young are almost universally in a subordinate position to the old. Age indeed is assumed very often to be the major criterion for dominance, at least until senility sets in. It is the apprentices and youngsters who are told what to do and the old people who tell them. If by some quirk of nature human beings had been born fully grown out of an egg, it would have been much more difficult to establish organization and hierarchical structure.

Allometry (Diseconomies of Scale) Limits Size of Structure

A very fundamental principle limiting the growth of organizations is what biologists call allometry.[1] This is the principle that every particular kind of structure tends to have an optimum size below which it is too small to function well and above which it is too big. We see this in the biological world—insects cannot be much larger than the praying mantis, and the optimum size seems to be between the ant and the bee. One-celled organisms cannot be much bigger than the paramecium. Mammals have a range between the shrew and the whale and the human race seems to be about the optimum size. The optimum size of the bird seems to be somewhere between the sparrow and the crow.

What determines the optimum size is a subtle set of relationships involving the relations among length, area, and volume. If we take a one-inch cube and double its linear dimensions, making it a two-inch cube, we have quadrupled its area because each side is now four square inches instead of one square inch, and we have octupled its volume from one cubic inch to eight cubic inches. In any particular structure of organization some properties, such as communications, tend to depend on the linear dimensions; other properties, such as strength of bones or muscles, relate more to the area of a cross section; while other properties such as weight are related closely to volume. If we were to double the linear dimensions of any particular organism, therefore, we would increase its weight eight times, its strength perhaps only four times, and its communications only two times. As we increase the size of an organism, therefore, gravity (which depends on weight and volume) becomes more important. As we diminish its size, surface tension (which depends on surface areas) becomes more important. Gravity is extremely unimportant to a fly, but if it ever got wet, it would carry many times its own weight in water and would be completely incapacitated.

Similar principles apply to social organization. In a nonhierarchical organization everybody has to communicate with everybody else. This is not too difficult among six or eight people, though even with six people there are 30 possible message relations and 15 possible pairs. With 100 people there are 9,900 possible message relations and it is impossible for everybody to talk to everybody else. Hierarchy is a method of economizing communication. There is a famous principle of the "span of control," which states that one person can only communicate effectively, at least in giving orders and seeing them carried out, with about ten other people. An organization with 100 people, therefore, tends to have two layers of hierarchy: the chief, who communicates with ten subchiefs, and the subchiefs, each of whom communicates with ten ordinary members. The span of control may, of course, vary with the nature of the organization. The less control that has to be exercised, the larger the span can be. It is much larger, for instance, in a church than in an army or factory, but the general principle always applies.

Organizational Inventions

The urban revolution and the rise of civilization may have been produced more by social invention in the field of organization than by the often accompanying material inventions. The major social invention was the development of hierarchies with three, four, or five layers, which gave rise for the first time to large-scale organization. How this was actually done is still something of a puzzle. The fact that the first cities seem to have been theocracies ruled by priests rather than by kings may be related to the fact that religious organizations, whose functions are mainly ceremonial and ritualistic, can have a large span of control and hence get along with a smaller number of layers in the hierarchy. A good preacher may be able to dominate the thought of a congregation of several hundred. The early religious organizations seldom seemed to go much beyond priests and high priests. The first empires undoubtedly depended on the growth of military organization with several ranks of hierarchy, which permitted the organization of thousands of people. We tend to take this for granted, but actually this represents a very large mutation in social organization. We do not really know how it was originated. Once somebody, presumably Sargon, had done it, the idea of course got around and could be imitated, but the first full-fledged imperial army was a very remarkable invention. One may wish it had not been invented but, having been invented, it was very difficult to get rid of.

Interaction of Things and Organizations

There is constant interaction even in this early period among materials, material artifacts, and social organizations. It is often very hard to say which is the leader in the movement. We certainly cannot take the simplistic view that it is always material artifacts which create the social organizations or that it is always the social organizations which create the material artifacts. Each reacts on the other in a constant process of positive feedback. Did agriculture produce the village or did the village produce agriculture? We do not really know. A hunting-gathering band may have developed an unusually large size due to a breakdown of population control and then, perhaps through a charismatic leader, acquired some skills in organization, which enabled it to increase its temporary stay at some location for longer and longer periods, until finally it became a settled village with agriculture. Somewhere along the way the women probably noticed that in the more settled places the seeds of last year's gatherings produced a crop, especially the new mutant natural wheat hybrids, but this knowledge would go unused if the social organization did not permit settling down.

The role of metallurgy in producing empires is likewise almost certainly significant although obscure. Metallurgy improved weaponry and the shape of daggers and swords, although it is not altogether clear why swords gave an advantage to large groups that stone weapons did not. It is more likely that large-scale organization permitted trade with the metallurgists and therefore specialized armories developed within the royal household, which gave rise to large-scale armies. The horse, wheel, supply wagon, and chariot also played a part. Alexander's empire undoubtedly rested on the social invention of the highly mobile army much more than on any technical improvement in weaponry. Gunpowder, as we saw in Chapter 7, produced very striking changes at least in Europe in both architecture and political organization, although it apparently did not affect China to anywhere near the same extent. The stirrup undoubtedly helped to produce chivalry in the European Middle Ages, but was the absence of the stirrup among the Romans a result of ignorance or was it a rejection of the idea because it was inappropriate to their social organization? Lynn White[2] has suggested that the invention of the chimney and fireplace in the early Middle Ages in Europe had a profound effect on social structure. Whereas previously everybody including servants sat together around the open fire in the middle of the Great Hall, with the development of the chimney the lord retired to his apartment, increasing social distance between the lord and his subordinates. On the other hand, it may have been subtle changes in the social organization of the manor that permitted the rise of a chimney technology.

There is undoubtedly something in the thesis of Max Weber that the varying religions and religious organizations affect change. In particular, Protestants, having broken with the past religiously, could more easily break with it technically and were likely to have a greater range of technical and organizational innovation than Catholics, although the evidence for this has been somewhat disputed. One certainly cannot credit Protestantism with the energetic development of northern Italy or Japan! Here perhaps it is the Puritan rather than the Protestant ethic that is significant. If we look at the agricultural and industrial revolutions in England in the eighteenth century and the relative technical stagnation of France in the same period, it is certainly plausible to attribute this to the different types of social organizations; the fact that England tolerated nonconformists, such as Methodists and Quakers who practiced a religion of convincement and conversion rather than of confirmation, enhanced its ability to generate and to tolerate innovations in technology and economic life.[3] In France, on the other hand, the revocation of the Edict of Nantes deprived the society of its energetic Protestant minority, achieving uniformity at the cost of progress. Here again the interaction among technical, material, and social development is enormously complex and can proceed with any one of the three in the lead.

The Development of "People"; Human Capital and the Rise of Knowledge

The development of "people," the third great phylum of societal evolution, adds still another complication to the interaction. Sheer gross population growth or decline itself may have a profound effect on the development of both material artifacts and social organizations. We have already. noted the "Wilkinson thesis," (p. 140) that a breakdown of population control and subsequent population pressure often creates the technical and organizational changes that lead to niche expansion. Population pressure is of course by no means the only source of mutation in either material artifacts or social organization. The role of idle curiosity and playfulness is something that should never be overlooked. Nevertheless, it is hard to deny that population movements have played an important role in creating stresses which lead into change in things and organizations. On the other hand, it is equally true that changes in things and organizations have had profound effects on population. The development of agriculture undoubtedly led to a population explosion, and in our own day the catastrophic population explosion in the tropics has been the result of the spread of technology, for instance DDT and malaria control, which arose essentially out of a mixture of idle scientific curiosity and economic incentive in a totally unrelated system. Demographic catastrophes like the Irish famine of 1846 may also produce marked social changes, sometimes for the better as in Ireland and sometimes for the worse as in the collapse of the Mayan civilization in the tenth century.

The aggregate population is of course only one aspect and by no means the most important aspect of the development of the evolutionary phylum of people. What is most significant here is the overall learning process by which the knowledge and the total noosphere maintains itself, grows, or declines. Over most of human history the knowledge structure has grown, though very slowly at first. All other changes ultimately are limited by this. Growth of the total knowledge stock is the result of a society's being able to devote more resources to its "knowledge industry" than is necessary merely to maintain the existing knowledge stock.

As we suggested on page 137, probably the reason that paleolithic culture was so stable over such long periods of time was that the "knowledge industry," that is, the amount of human time and energy devoted to passing on the knowledge stock, was so small, simply because of the sheer poverty of the society, that the elders were barely able to transmit the existing stock of knowledge to the next generation and had no time or energy left over for increasing that stock. The low expectation of life also had an important impact here. The neolithic revolution and agriculture not only expanded the expectation of life so that people had more time in their life to learn more, but also by making life easier and increasing real income, permitted expansion of the knowledge industry to the point where people could add to it as well as simply replace the existing stock of knowledge in each generation. This led to a cumulative increase in knowledge, which is the ultimate source of all societal evolution since that date.

The rising stock of knowledge is what changes the materials and the artifacts and the social organization, which in turn feeds back on the increasing stock of knowledge. All these things together feed back on differentiating the human population into different occupational groups, status groups, and so on, producing development of the phylum of subpopulations such as farmers, soldiers, miners, metal workers, weavers, seamen, scribes, and so on. Their specialization leads to greater productivity, which leads to more intercourse. Moral or political control of private threat systems (bandits), which permits distant trade, leads to more specialization, greater productivity, and more intercourse, and so we go on (p. 142). This is an example of the most profound disequilibrium process, called "deviation-amplifying positive feedback,"[4] that is, more of A leads to more of B, which leads to more of A, which leads to more of B, and so on until something stops the process.

"Great Men" Theory of History

It is interesting that one of the most unresolvable problems of human history is that of the role of unusual individuals. The "great men" theories of history, like that of Thomas Carlyle[5] (p. 236) (which usually are singularly silent about great women), lay great stress on unusual individuals, insisting that history would have been very different without them. The evolutionary interpretation leads somewhat toward minimizing the role of the exceptional individual by stressing the long, slow growth of knowledge, technology, and organization as the dominating dynamic. Yet there is nothing in evolutionary theory which says that exceptional individuals cannot have very profound consequences. They often operate, however, through changing the parameters of the ecological interaction of all the other social species rather than through the direct consequences of their own acts. The significance of Alexander, for instance, is not that he created a great empire, which fell apart on his death without making much impact on the world, but that he opened up western Asia and northern Africa to Greek ideas that changed the social ecological environment of these societies. Whether these ideas would have spread anyway is a question that is very hard to answer. India certainly did not have to conquer the rest of the world in order to spread the idea of a zero. Nevertheless, the fact that Greek ideas did not penetrate China did have a profound effect on the societal and technical evolution of that part of the world, so perhaps if Alexander had had the technology to conquer China the subsequent history of the world would have been different. Cortez and Pizarro had a profound impact on the history of what is now Latin America; without them it might not have been Latin. On the other hand, the puzzling explosion of Spain and Portugal all over the world in the fifteenth and sixteenth centuries cannot be associated with any single individual.

It is perhaps at the mysterious level of symbolic systems, as noted in Chapter 9, that the impact of the exceptional person is most felt. Perhaps it is the religious and ideological leaders like Confucius, Jesus, Mohammed, and Karl Marx, who have been the most influential individual persons in history and who have most changed its course, because of the symbols they either deliberately or unconsciously created. I have a little litany that runs "Who would have thought at the time,"—that Buddha or Jesus, Mohammed or Marx, or even Joseph Smith would have had such evolutionary potential. The evolutionary potential created by these individuals was something quite real. Conquerors come and go and leave little but ruins. The great scientific discoveries would almost certainly have been made by somebody else if they had not been made by the men by whose name they are known. The great symbols, however, may be quite peculiar to the people who made them, though that is something of which we can never be sure.

THE TRANSMISSION OF KNOWLEDGE

The major difference between biological and societal evolution, as we have seen, lies in the mode of transmission of the genetic structure, the knowledge or know-how, which is the real field within which evolution takes place. In biological evolution, genetic structure is transmitted and propagated by simple replication modified occasionally by mutation. In the social system the noosphere, the stock of knowledge and values that is the genetic structure of all social construction, is transmitted by extremely complex processes that involve the phenotypes or artifacts as well as the knowledge structure itself. Transmission of the knowledge structure from one generation to the next is still fundamentally a process of replication, that is, the knowledge among older people is transmitted as images to the minds of younger ones through communications of all kinds. Nevertheless, the process is much more complex than the mere replication of the DNA molecule. A younger mind is not a simple tabula rasa waiting to receive the imprint of knowledge from older minds. Minds are very active in the evolutionary processes, constantly creating internal images and subjecting them to selection. Furthermore, both material artifacts and organizations can either assist or hinder this process. Books, pictures, movies, schoolrooms, desks, pens, and paper are all material artifacts that play an important part in the transmission of knowledge from one mind to another and from one generation to the next.

The development of organizations of formal education—schools, universities, churches, and secret societies—also had an important influence in permitting larger knowledge structures to be transmitted. As long as the only organization for transmitting knowledge was the family, the amount of knowledge that could be transmitted was very limited, simply because the transmission was mainly one of parent to child on a one-to-one basis. The social invention of the school, in which one teacher can transmit knowledge to a whole room full of students, was of enormous importance in permitting the growth of the knowledge structure, simply because it permitted a smaller portion of human resources to be devoted to this transmission. In knowledge transmission indeed the school was the equivalent of agriculture. It represented a large increase in transmission productivity and hence permitted the release of resources for other purposes, particularly in this case for the increase of knowledge.

We can visualize this very clearly if we suppose that all institutions of formal education are suddenly abolished. The transmission of knowledge would again be reduced to the family. Language of course would survive, but very few people would know more than one language. Advanced mathematics might be transmitted for a few generations from parent to child, but it would soon disappear or exist only as an esoteric cult in the possession of a very few. Science would likewise suffer the same fate and the human race would soon return to its condition of say 5,000 years ago. The potential speed at which knowledge can be lost is indeed frightening; it only takes one generation of failure of transmission and all previously accumulated knowledge is gone. This is presumably what happened to the Mayans; advanced knowledge was contained in the minds of a very few people, then a revolution killed them all and that was the end of it—there was nobody left to transmit the knowledge to the next generation.

KNOWLEDGE, ENERGY, MATERIALS: THE "KEM" SAGA—PRODUCTION

Common to both biological and societal evolution, as we have seen, is the process of production by which the phenotypes, of living species on the one hand and material artifacts, organizations and different types and qualities of persons on the other, actually come into being. In each case the process is one by which *knowledge* or know-how structure, that is, the genetic structure, selects and captures *energy* for the selection, transportation, transformation, and rearrangement of *materials* into the improbable form of the phenotype, whether this is a chicken, human being, flint ax, automobile, or computer. I am tempted to call this the "KEM"saga because it is a saga—a great story with the same fundamental plot repeated in innumerable variations over billions upon billions of cases.

It is easy to see this process in the case of material artifacts, but less easy to see it in the case of social organizations, and still less easy to see it in the case of persons. Nevertheless, the same principles apply, even though in the case of organizations and persons the knowledge element dominates the scene so much that we are apt to forget the energy and materials. Any social organization, however, involves at least bringing persons together, which takes energy. The unaided human being using energy acquired only from burning his food intake cannot travel more than 20 or at most 30 miles a day. All social organizations involve communications among the people who occupy the roles. Before the development of long-distance communication through the mails, telegraph, phones, and so forth, communication could only be on a person-to-person basis, with a few exceptions like Indian smoke signals, which again, however, communicate over a very small distance. No social organization under these circumstances could cover a geographical area larger than that which would permit people to walk to some center to meet. The counties in the United States have survived from this primitive time and are designed to be of a size that would permit people to walk to the county courthouse. They are absurd anomalies in the world of the automobile, but there seems to be no way of getting rid of them. The materials of organizations consist mainly of human bodies arranged in positions where they can communicate, but it is precisely because human bodies are materials and need energy to move that the energy supplies limit the formation of organizations.

Most organizations also require material artifacts—ritual objects, places in which to meet, furniture, personal symbols such as clothing or appropriate vestments, and so on. Military organizations require weapons,· means of communication, chariots, carts, kitchen equipment, tents, all the physical apparatus of armies and navies and now, of course, air forces, which would hardly exist without airplanes. These artifacts also require knowledge, energy, and materials. A steel company is an organization that likewise requires large amounts of artifacts before it can function.

It is only a slightly farfetched metaphor, indeed, to think of human artifacts as "secretions" of social organizations, much as oysters secrete shells. Material artifacts come into being only because there is a demand for them and the demand is usually from an organization. Thus, one thinks of a cathedral as a kind of oyster shell secreted by the church, originating in know-how structures and plans realized through the directed use of energy on materials. Most of the paleontological and archeological records indeed consist precisely of these secretions. In the case of dead biological organisms the surviving records are the durable, material constructions (bones, shells) arising from the production of a living organism from a genetic structure. Archeological remains likewise are bones and shells left by social organisms, which have since died, that were secreted by them as part of the total organization.

The evolution of persons—the movement from unspecialized paleolithic hunters and gatherers toward farmers, metal workers, soldiers, officials, scientists, and computer programmers—is likewise profoundly influenced by parallel development of material artifacts and social organizations. Persons are what they have learned to be. This learning may take place in the social organizations of formal education, or in the organization of apprenticeship, or simply in the casual learning of how to occupy the innumerable roles involved in social relationships. Even friendship and love have to be learned. These learning processes are affected by material artifacts like libraries, the arrangements of streets and homes, which can either promote or discourage neighborliness or crime, the presence or absence of privacy, and the existence of large numbers of social organizations all clamoring for persons to fill roles. The individual human being as he or she grows up is constantly molded not only by the internal environment of an immensely active nervous system, but also by the external environments—houses, streets, families, friends, missionaries, teachers, personnel directors. Out of all this vast clamor the individual moves one way or another to become either a leader or a follower, an honest citizen or a criminal, a church member or a skeptic, a family man or a philanderer, in the great ballet of life in which we move toward what we think is best at the time, guided partly by the internal and partly by the external environment.

THREATS, INTEGRATION, EXCHANGE: THE "TIE" SAGA–THE SOCIAL ORGANIZERS; BONDING

The third trinity is that of the social organizers: threats, integration, and exchange. I am tempted to call this the "TIE" saga because, again, it is a great evolutionary subplot, repeating itself billions of times in innumerable different forms, but always with something of the same pattern. The acronym, accidental as it is, is a good one, because the social organizers are precisely the relationships that tie people together, and hence establish role structures, communications, and social organizations. Even a threat is a bond, though perhaps an unwilling one. An exchange is a loose and temporary bond. The integrative relationship is nothing but a bond.

Although we have made a sharp distinction in principle among these three forms of bonding, almost without exception all actual bonds and relationships consist of all three in varying proportions. Even in the case of what looks like pure threat, like the bandit's "Your money or your life," there are elements of exchange. The bandit after all might kill first and then take the money, and if he does not do so, it would presumably be because of a very tenuous integrative relationship that makes him see even the victim as a person. In what looks like the pure exchanges of the stock market, there are strong integrative components in the shape of trust and personal knowledge. It is hard for exchange to take place between two people who do not trust each other and who do not know each other at all. Even in a retail transaction there is usually some attempt at establishing a slight integrative bond through smiles, courtesy, passing the time of day, and so on. The message is "I am your friend and I want to buy from you." Even in what looks like the purest integrative relationship of the young couple in love, there are strong elements of exchange. If the internal terms of trade are not right, that is, if either party feels they are giving more than they are getting, the relationship will break up.

Threat relationships likewise lie in the background of even exchange and integrative relationships. The stock market is undergirded by the threat system of the law, so that anybody who breaks a contract will find himself in trouble. Even the relationship of a loving couple has an undercurrent of implicit threat and can easily degenerate into a lover's quarrel with each threatening the other. Even the most utopian community always has undergirding in the threat of expulsion of the intolerable dissident.

What is even more important, most bonding relationships are not simple mixtures of the three basic forms, but are, as it were, compounds. That is, the different relations are not merely additive, but may either reinforce or counteract each other. In each situation, indeed, there seems to be some optimum mix of the three, in which the overall bond is strongest, and as we alter the mix it may weaken, sometimes quite sharply. Thus, I pay my taxes primarily because of the threat system of the government. If there were no sanctions, I would certainly not pay what I do now. On the other hand, unless there are some elements of exchange in the tax relationship, that is, unless I feel I get something for taxes, the legitimacy of the tax will erode in my mind. In extreme cases, I may become a tax refuser and take the consequences, or I may become active politically to change the government or public authority that imposed the tax. Similarly, if there were no integrative component and for instance I had to pay taxes to an authority I utterly despised and thought was evil, again the tax system might be ineffective and unstable.

In some taxes the exchange element is very clear, as when a person who has children pays school taxes and may indeed get much more in return than he pays. On the other hand, school taxes are often voted down by the elderly, who feel they get nothing out of them and, if the exchange relationship breaks down, the threat relationship is likely to break down too. The alliance of church and state, which is a very common phenomenon in human history, is an alliance of the threat system and the integrative system and is often quite successful in terms of survival. The carrying out of threats may destroy the legitimacy of the church through weakening its integrative structure, however, and if this happens, the church itself may be destroyed. Threats, and especially the carrying out of threats, may be very costly to the threatener and may destroy his integrative power, as we have seen.

Threats and integrative and exchange relationships take place constantly in an environment of material artifacts, organizations, and persons. Threat capability depends on the possession of certain artifacts, such as a gun, the capacity to control energy, such as gunpowder, and the ability to rearrange materials to the threatened party's disadvantage. The knowledge-energy-materials saga applies to the production of bads (negative goods) just as it does to the production of goods. A bad is usually encoded in a rearrangement of materials such as may be involved in injuring or killing someone or blowing up his house, which is perceived as a detriment, just as a good is a rearrangement of materials, which is perceived as a benefit. Exchange, of course, cannot take place unless there is something to exchange, which is mainly material artifacts. Social organizations can be created by threat, particularly in the threat-submission relationship, by exchange, with the acceptance of an invitation to exchange, or by an integrative relationship, for instance a leader creating a "following" in the field of identity. Usually, indeed, they are created by some optimum combination of all three. It is these bonding relationships that establish differential role structures, permit communications among them, and so create organizations. Bonding indeed is always initiated by some form of communication.

EVERYTHING DEPENDS ON EVERYTHING ELSE – BUT HOW?: THE MULTIPLIERS

The social dynamics of human history, even more than that of biological evolution, illustrate the fundamental principle of ecological evolution–that everything depends on everything else. The nine elements that we have described in societal evolution of the three families of phenotypes–the phyla of *things, organizations* and *people,* the genetic bases in *knowledge* operating through *energy* and *materials* to produce phenotypes, and the three bonding relations of *threat, integration* and *exchange*–all interact on each other. Nevertheless, it is not a wholly unreasonable response to the proposition that everything depends on everything else to say "So what?" It is not enough to say that everything depends on everything else. We need to know in more detail what depends on what and we also need to know what things are more important and what things are less important. What are the changes or events that have large "multipliers"? To answer these questions fully requires the complete study of human history, which is far beyond the intent of this volume. Nevertheless, we can point to certain priorities, changes that are likely to have more effect than others, and that may guide the historian in his attempts to disentangle the "tangled bank," as Darwin called it, of inter-relationships.

Knowledge or Know-how as That Which Evolves

The first element in the system is undoubtedly knowledge, by which we include know-how and know-whom as well as know-what. This, as we have seen, is the field within which evolution takes place. It is the only thing that can really change, the only thing that is not conserved. Changes in knowledge are the basic source of all other changes, even though changes in knowledge themselves depend on other changes. In biological evolution it is the genetic structure that evolves. The phenotypes are encoded carriers of it. It may be a little insulting to a chicken to describe it as an egg's idea for producing eggs, but there is a real element of truth in the quip. Similarly, it may insult the dignity of the human person and the dignity of the majestic states, churches, libraries, universities, and art galleries that we have created to suggest that all these things are encoders of the knowledge structure. A human being is not only a gene's idea for producing genes, but it is also the noosphere's idea for transmitting and extending the noosphere. Now, of course, the metaphor, as all metaphors tend to do, has run away with us. Knowledge does not know anything; only persons know anything. Knowledge is not merely encoded, it is realized in persons in a way perhaps that the genome itself of the egg is not realized, but only further encoded in the chicken. This constitutes an important difference between biological and societal evolution. Nevertheless, in the evolutionary process itself knowledge is primal, because this is "what evolves."

The realization of knowledge into things, organizations, and persons, of course, will be limited by the absence of energy or materials. Energy and materials, however, are limiting factors rather than creative factors. The increase in knowledge furthermore pushes back these limits continually as new energy sources and new materials are discovered, although there may be an ultimate limit to this process. In interpreting history, therefore, one looks for the points at which knowledge rises to the point where new energy sources and new materials are captured for the productive process. The domestication of both crops and animals was one such occasion of change, which increased the efficiency of the capture of solar energy for human purposes. The development of the steam engine was a similar step forward, even when it only burned wood, because it made energy much more available for work, that is, precisely for the transportation and transformation of materials. The discovery of oil in 1859 was another such step, even if it is only temporary.

It is significant that we name the early stages of development of the human race by the materials which they used—stone, bronze, and iron. Maybe these ages were preceded by an age of wood and bone, the artifacts of which have not come down to us, being too perishable. The use of metals involves the use of energy—fire. Metals increase the efficiency of the production of both goods and bads. They give rise to a great extension of the system of exchange, and also the threat system and the formation of military states and empires.

Communication as a "Multiplier"

Changes in communication and transportation also have important "multipliers." The wheeled carriage facilitated the transportation materials and goods as well as the transportation of threats through the chariot. The invention of the sea-going vessel, dating at least from the neolithic in some primitive form, had a great impact in opening up trade and communications with distant parts of the earth. The constant improvement in communications has turned the human race from a set of isolated and independent bands and tribes into a single world community. Changes in transportation and communication have constantly had an impact in increasing the size of the social organization. The earliest empires were all based on river communication; the somewhat later ones on roads and sea transportation, or like China, on canals. Cheaper communication and transportation extends the area over which both threats and trade can operate.

Improvements in food production also have a large multiplier. Civilization can almost be defined as agriculture plus organized threat. As we have seen on page 137, it is the increase in food product per acre that increases the human population and the increase in food product per worker that creates the cities.

Symbols and Sacredness

The role of symbolic systems in all these developments is of great importance, but as we have seen in Chapter 9, it is very hard to assess. An important part of the integrative system is persuasion, by which one person through communications changes the image and the value of another in directions that are presumably favorable to the persuader. Symbolic systems are part of the techniques of persuasion and improvement in these techniques may have the same kind of effect as improvements in communication and transportation in expanding social organizations. Legitimacy is an important product of these symbolic systems. An image of the world which makes somebody important and valued and which makes other people feel important and valued is likely to create legitimacy and to have survival value. The long survival of the institution of war, for instance, despite its pathological destructiveness often to both participating parties, may be as much a result of the place of war as a powerful symbol in the ecology of symbolic systems as it is an exercise of threat. People are willing to die for their country or their emperor or the revolution because it is a symbol that gives them a sense of larger identity. On the other side of the coin, these symbols often legitimate evil acts from which otherwise people would recoil. A man who would never throw a child on a fire is often willing to drop a firebomb on a city.

In this connection one should not underestimate the importance of ceremonials. Ceremonies reinforce legitimacy and it is legitimacy that holds organizations together. The whole question of the role of "sacredness" in human society has been inadequately explored. Sacredness is part of the integrative structure and its erosion may easily destroy those integrative structures that hold societies and organizations together. A good deal of human history indeed is written in terms of the substitution of one system of sacredness for another. The sacredness of the Roman emperors was supplanted by that of the Christian altars, which in turn were supplanted in part by the sacredness of the national state or the sacredness of revolutionary symbols, as in China. But exactly what the dynamic processes are that create or destroy sacredness in a puzzling question. We live in an age of great desacralization—of sex, of war, of religion, of royalty, of the state. Both the causes and consequences of this movement are obscure.

Redistributions Through Inflation and Deflation

Changes that lead to redistributions of power and wealth may also be of great significance. In this connection the "monetary" theory of history, as expounded for instance by J. M. Keynes in his *Treatise on Money*,[6] while it is only a small part of the total process, is nevertheless a significant part of the total picture.[7] Inflation and deflation had profound effects on the distribution of wealth and power and also on subsequent changes in production where, for instance, wealth and power are redistributed to those who are more productive and away from those who are less. Keynes was undoubtedly right in pointing out that the long inflation in Europe after 1500, which was a result of the introduction of large new gold stocks from the Spanish Empire in the Americas, had profound effects in redistributing wealth away from the old feudal landowners, who by this time had largely commuted their rents into money payments that then proceeded to lose value much faster than they could be adjusted. The loss to the landlords was the gain of the new bourgeoisie, the profit-makers who always, as we have seen (p. 181), gain in inflation. We can trace the impact of the gold inflation as it hits one country after another, and while it is perhaps too much to attribute Shakespeare to the period when inflation hit England and hence created a demand for the theater among the newly rich bourgeoisie, at least there is an element of truth even in that proposition.

Even in the brief history of the United States the impact of inflation and deflation has been profound. The deflations following 1815, 1865, and 1929 were periods of relative stagnation and slow growth, as deflation redistributed income and wealth away from the energetic and active profit-maker toward the passive bondholder living on interest. The inflations following the various gold discoveries after 1849, and again after the 1890s, seem to have had a stimulating effect, though how far this was simply the fruition of innovations generated under the stress of the previous deflations is hard to estimate. The long inflationary period following 1932 has been one of spectacular economic development, even though again the cleaning out of dead wood in the Great Depression of 1929-1932 may have laid the foundations for it.

All we have really done so far is to lay out the skeleton of the basic processes of evolution, whether biological or societal. In reality the flesh and blood is in the lives of all living organisms who have ever lived and, particularly, the reality of human history is in the 70 billion or so human beings who have ever lived and their innumerable thoughts and emotions, loves and hates, pleasures and pains, creations and destructions, joys and sufferings. We shall put a little flesh on the bones in subsequent chapters, but we must never forget that all this is an abstraction from the almost infinite richness of the reality and must never be mistaken for the reality itself.

Appendix to Chapter 10:
DIAGRAMMATIC REPRESENTATIONS

The following diagram, Figure 10A.1, illustrates the critical question of dynamics, which is how do we get from one period to the next? We suppose that in Period 1 we have six characteristics of the system: knowledge, energy, materials, things, organizations, and people. Knowledge captures energy to select, transport, and transform materials into things following the heavy line. These things may be either in Period 1 or in Period 2. This is the "KEM" saga. Knowledge in Period 1, especially knowledge of how to increase knowledge, increases knowledge in Period 2, and it may also increase energy in Period 2 and materials in Period 2. Things may also increase in Period 2, mediating through energy and materials. Knowledge also may create new organizations in Period 2 and change the condition and role of people. Energy in Period 1 may produce more energy in Period 2 and more materials in Period 2, which likewise may produce energy, materials, and things in Period 2. Things help to produce things, organizations, and a change of people. Organization creates things, new organizations, and changes people. People increase knowledge and help to make things, organizations, and change people. Relations between organizations and people (marked TIE) are the bondings, which may be various mixes of threats, integrative relationships, and exchange. These may all be mediated through things.

Figure 10A.1 by no means exhausts the complexity of the system, but it at least gives some image of what this complexity is like. It is a sharp contrast from monistic interpretations of history, represented in Figure 10A.2. Here the only connection between Period 1 and Period 2 goes through "the explanation," whatever this is, whether this is technology, economic interest, class dialectics or religion, or anything else which has been so used. The rest of the system simply hangs from this and is carried along by it, represented by the empty circles.

Combinations of threats, integrative relations, and exchange can be represented in a triangular diagram as in Figure 10A.3. TIE is an equilateral triangle: the point T presents 100 percent threat; I, 100 percent integration;

Period 1   Period 2

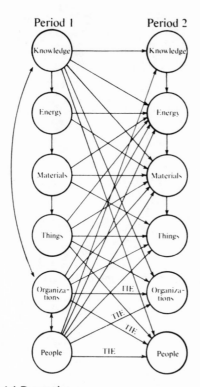

Figure 10A.1: Social Dynamics

and E, 100 percent exchange. A line such as I_1I_2 shows all the points with a 60 percent (TI_2 or EI_1) integrative component. Line T_1T_2 similarly shows all the points with a 10 percent threat component. Line E_1E_2 shows all points having a 30 percent exchange component. The point P, therefore, represents a combination of 60 percent integration, 10 percent threat, and 30 percent exchange. Any point on the diagram similarly represents a combination of these proportions. The closer the point P is to I, the more integrative relation there is; the closer it is to T, the more threat is in it; the closer it is to E, the more exchange is in it. It is an interesting exercise to try to identify particular organizations with regions in this figure. One possible identification is shown if Figure 10A.4. This, it must be emphasized, is purely illustrative and is not based on any kind of quantitative research.[8]

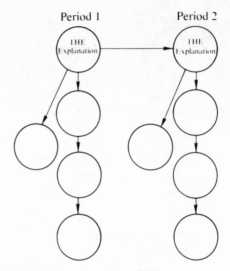

Figure 10A.2: Monistic Interpretation of History

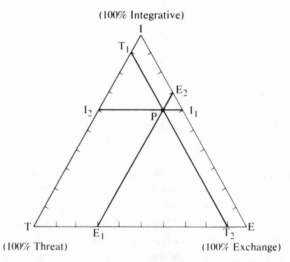

Figure 10A.3: Combinations of Threat, Integrative, and Exchange Systems

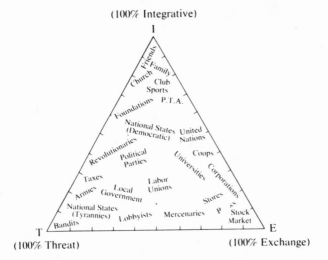

(100% Integrative)

(100% Threat)   (100% Exchange)

Figure 10A.4: Combinations of Threat, Integrative, and Exchange Systems

NOTES

1. Ludwig von Bertalanffy, *Problems of Life* (New York: Harper. 1960).

2. Lynn White, Jr., "Technology Assessment from the Stance of a Medieval Historian," *The American Historical Review*, 79 (Feb. 1974), 1-13. See page 9.

3. Arthur Raistrick, *Quakers in Science and Industry* (New York: Kelley, 1968).

4. See Magoroh Maruyama, "The Second Cybernetics: Deviation Amplifying Mutual Causal Processes," *American Scientist*, 51 (1963), 164-179.

5. Thomas Carlyle, *On Heroes, Hero-Worship, and The Heroic in History (1841)*.

6. John Maynard Keynes, *A Treatise on Money* (London: Harcourt, Brace, 1931).

7. It was reading Keynes' *Treatise on Money*, Chapter 30, when I was an undergraduate, that first gave me the idea history might make sense.

8. Further exercises in the use of this diagram are found in Kenneth E. Boulding, *The Economy of Love and Fear: A Preface to Grants Economics* (Belmont, Calif.: Wadsworth, 1973), 106-109; and in Keneeth E. Boulding, *A Primer on Social Dynamics* (New York: Free Press, 1970), 24-31.

Chapter 11

Power in Society

DECISION IMPLIES POWER AND FREEDOM

One of the fundamental differences between biological dynamics and social dynamics is the much greater importance of decision in the social system by comparison with the biosphere. This is not to say by any means that the phenomenon of decision is unknown below the level of the human race. Animals, even down to the lowly amoeba, undoubtedly possess some kind of image of at least an immediate future and choose the better future rather than the worse. It is very difficult to say where the image of the future really begins in the long process of evolution. There is no doubt that the higher animals possess it in some small degree and that they have some kind of primitive value system enabling them to make choices. The behavior of predators and of predatees is not simple, immediate stimulus and response, as perhaps the behavior of the amoeba is. It is based to some extent on expectations, particularly when we come to dogs, coyotes, raccoons, and the higher apes. There are quite active learning processes at work and many examples of cooperative behavior, which have the form of very primitive organization.

With the coming of the human nervous system, the development of societal evolution, and the vast proliferation of human artifacts, however, complex images of the future and decisions emerge, involving choice among images of the future according to some patterns of valuation, which, as we have seen, is what an economist means by "maximizing behavior." It is being conscious of an "agenda," that is, a range of possible futures, and it involves being able to order these on some scale of values and choosing the "best" from this scale.

It is only with the coming of decision as a major element in dynamics that the question of power becomes important. Unfortunately the word "power," like so many others, has a considerable range of meanings. It conjures up images of wrestling, weight lifting, bulldozing, and rocket launching, which do not necessarily gather the essence of the concept; even in physics there are anthropomorphic overtones of the concepts of force and work. All we can observe is system change. We can never observe directly the force, whatever it is, that changes it, except as far as we have internal reflections on our subjective experience of will, that is, deciding to move something, and then acting in such a way that it is moved.

As a first approximation we might define power as the change in the future state of the universe brought about by a decision. If I get into an elevator, press the button for the fourth floor, and the elevator rises to it, then by a decision to press the button, I have changed the state of the universe, though not by very much. If I had not pressed the button, the elevator would have remained on the ground floor. If the elevator had been out of order and I had pressed the button, it would still have remained on the ground floor and I would have had no power over it at all. If I had pressed the button and destroyed the whole earth, obviously I would have a great deal of power. The power of an individual decision maker, therefore, is the amount of change in the state of the universe he can accomplish by choosing one future rather than another. If we can suppose that one choice is always to do nothing, which may not of course always be true, but is useful as a simplifying assumption, then power is the difference in the state of the universe between doing something and doing nothing.

The measurement of power is a tricky business. In the first place, a change in the state of the universe is going to be highly multidimensional in many cases. If we change A, B, C, D, and E, we can only measure the total change by some process of putting value weights on the changes in these various components. That is, we always have a problem of indexing, and with different value weights the answer might come out differently (p. 164). Another even more fundamental difficulty is that all we can ever observe is what happened; we can never observe what did not happen and, if power is the difference between what did happen and what did not happen, we always have to make some kind of evaluation or estimate of what real difference the decision made. In the case of pushing the elevator button and going to the fourth floor, this is fairly easy; when it comes to things like making a law, a presidential veto, a declaration of war, or an assassination, the difference between what would have happened if the event had not taken place and what actually happened is often extremely difficult to evaluate. In this sense, power is always based on some kind of subjective estimates, rather than objective "fact," in the sense that it is not wholly subject to observation.

A concept closely related to that of power is freedom. This, again, is a concept of many meanings and many dimensions. One meaning is that of the range of choice, that is, the size of the agenda of decision. If I have no alternative, that is, if only one possible future is available for me, I am clearly not free to choose. Freedom of choice always implies alternatives. Up to a point, perhaps, the more alternatives there are, the more freedom we feel. The rich man in this sense is much more free than a poor one; the poor man cannot afford to go outside his own village, the rich man can go anywhere he likes in the world.

Another dimension of freedom is that of the absence of restrictions imposed by others. If I am conscious of a potential range of alternatives, but some of these are denied me because of the decisions of others, I feel unfree in the sense that I am dependent on the decisions of others. The power of one person may or may not limit the freedom of another, depending on the circumstances. Thus, when there are only a few cars on the road, the power that the possession of a car gives a person does not limit the freedom of others to drive, though if I get a car, it may limit your freedom to get one. If everybody has a car and roads get congested, however, then one person trying to exercise his power to drive may limit the power of others, and hence the freedom of others.[1]

POWER AS CAPACITY TO CHANGE THE FUTURE

We can think of the total power of the human race as measured by the degree to which it can change the future. King Canute had no power over the tides. The mightiest empire has no power over the sun and the moon; even our space exploration does not change the length of the month perceptibly. Up to now we have had very little power over natural disasters—earthquakes, hurricanes, tornadoes and floods—though we do have some power in mitigating their effects and preparing for them. We have some power over the course of biological evolution. The human race has caused an appreciable number of species to become extinct before they otherwise would have. By artificial selection we have created domesticated plants and animals, corn and hogs, and so on. We have affected the gene pool of the earth somewhat, but only by selection. So far we have not been able to intervene much in genetic mutations, although this is not far off.

Our intervention in climate is still minimal. Nobody can pretend that the human race caused the last ice age, and it is clear that the earth is in the grip of very large systems, in the face of which human activity is still relatively peripheral. We do change the climate of cities a little, we do a little cloud seeding; however, we really do not know what will be the effects of our burning fossil fuels, creating contrails, or releasing freon into the atmosphere. It is a little distressing indeed that the meteorologists do not seem able to decide whether the activities of the human race are warming the earth up or cooling it down. A few years ago they were all worried about a "greenhouse effect." The rising level of carbon dioxide in the atmosphere as a result of burning fossil fuels acts as a greenhouse, letting the high-intensity radiation from the sun in, but preventing the low-intensity radiation from the surface of the earth from getting out. This of course would warm up the earth, causing the fear that the polar ice caps might melt and flood most of the land area where the human race now lives, thereby altering the patterns of world climate very profoundly. Now, however, the fear seems to be of a new ice age. The earth is cooling off very rapidly, with an almost unprecedented decline in temperature in the last 20 years, but nobody I think really knows why. We may have been suffering from slight delusions of grandeur in respect to our impact on the earth.

THE UNCERTAINTY AND ILLUSIONS OF POWER

When it comes to social dynamics, the extent of human power becomes a very tricky question and is not capable of easy resolution. We know certainly that some persons are more powerful than others. We will return later to the problem of the distribution of power. The decisions of most people affect themselves, their immediate families, perhaps their employers or employees, their circle of friends, and so on, but the effects do not extend much beyond this. For most people, if every decision they made in their lives had been different, their own lives would have been different, but the life of mankind would not have been changed very much. On the other hand, there are people of whom this is perhaps not true: the "great," the rulers and conquerors, political leaders, founders of religions, makers of great discoveries, and so on. The difficulty here is that we never really know what would have happened if a decision had gone the other way. In a great many decisions, even by powerful people, the major alternatives may be quite small. The powerful are hedged in by their own circumstances, their own organizations, the information which reaches them, the staff with which they are surrounded, and so on, so that their agendas are smaller than is often thought. In many cases, even if other persons had occupied their roles, the decisions would not have been very different, because it is the role rather than the person that determines the decision. This is an old and rather unresolvable argument in the interpretation of history.

On the one side, there is the "great men" theory of history, as represented for instance by Thomas Carlyle (see p. 218). This attributes great importance to the influence of powerful people, and states that history would have been very different if certain decisions had gone the other way. At the other extreme, we have a kind of mechanistic determinism to which Marxism comes very close, in which the great forces of social dynamics are regarded as virtually independent of the decisions even of powerful people, and independent pretty much of whoever occupies the roles. We could hold this position whether we believed in dialectics or in evolution, provided we hold the view that it is only larger dynamic forces that matter, so that particular human decisions can only cause ripples on the surface of the great on-going river of history. This is a question that is very difficult, perhaps impossible, to resolve because of the principle that we can only know what happened (as far as the, imperfect record permits) and never "what would have happened if." Even if we believe there are strong random elements in human history, a proposition for which a very strong case can be made, we cannot quite dismiss decisions as part of the random structure. Decisions may have random elements in them, as in a dilemma where we decide between two equally attractive alternatives by tossing a mental coin, but they also have strong nonrandom elements. Furthermore, random decisions may or may not cumulate, that is, they may either be offset by the nonrandom forces or they may cumulate into a pattern very different from what would have been the case if the random factors had gone the other way.

History is at least in part a Monte Carlo simulation with somebody throwing the dice every so often and putting in the numbers that turn up. Then how far do these random perturbations cancel each other out according to the famous law of large numbers? And how far do they cumulate to carry us over watersheds into different dynamic systems than we would have had if random shocks had not accumulated in the way that they did? Unfortunately, there is no really secure way of answering these questions. The most we can do perhaps is to suggest those parts of the total system within which neither the whims of the powerful nor the random shocks of nature make very much difference in the long run, and those parts in which we may suspect that these things do make a difference.

The "Outability of Truth": Reality Imposes Itself on Knowledge

One suspects, for instance, that the cumulative growth of knowledge, that is, the whole development of the noosphere and the genetic structure of human artifacts, follows an unfolding pattern, which may be speeded up or slowed down by random events or by the decisions of the powerful, but which cannot fundamentally be changed in its course in the long run simply because of what I have sometimes called the "outability of truth." Also, if we think of the growth of knowledge as the growth of structures within the human organism that correspond in some way in their patterns to structures outside it, then the structures outside it ultimately dominate the growth of the structures inside it. Just as there is a profound asymmetry between truth and lies, in the sense that lies can be found out whereas truth cannot, there is similarly an asymmetry between truth and error in the sense that erroneous images are much more likely to change in the direction of truth rather than true images in the direction of error, even though this may occasionally happen. We may indulge in occasional philosophical doubt about the existence of a real world but, if our image of the world is that we can fly by flapping our arms when we jump off the Empire State Building, the real world will break into our illusions with considerable rapidity. Superstition may be long lived, but truth is immortal and will outlive it. A small sect may cherish the belief that the earth is flat, but if any of its members becomes an astronaut or even an airline pilot, that belief will certainly have to be abandoned in practice.

There are difficulties, of course, in social systems in that beliefs about the system and images of it are an important part of the system itself. Hence, there is sometimes no objective truth to ride herd on the cavorting legions of error. In social systems, some beliefs are self-justified, at least in the short run. If everybody believes the price of stocks is going to rise, rise they will. If everybody believes there is going to be a gasoline shortage next week, they will fill up their tanks and create it. The belief that two countries are on the road to war propels them along that road and it often makes the war inevitable, even though it might not have happened otherwise. Nevertheless, the entire social system is not a product of the fevered human imagination. There are certain stabilities in its dynamic, and self-justified beliefs and expectations tend to be short run. We return to the old image of the loom: one sees these disturbances as a kind of temporary gathering of the warp, producing perhaps a hole or a blotch in the fabric, but as time goes on the fundamental patterns reassert themselves and the end result is as if the disturbance had never happened at all.

Determinism versus Randomness in History

Thus, it is quite legitimate to ask whether the overall history of the human race, at least in its broad outlines, would have been very different if decisive battles of history had gone the other way. One suspects the answer is "not very much." We might have had one empire rather than another, or we might be speaking one language rather than another, but the long process of the growth of human knowledge, invention, discovery, and the development of artifacts and organizations might not have been very much affected. The common phenomenon, for instance, of simultaneous invention and discovery of the same thing by different people in different places at about the same time suggests that, when the time is ripe, the fruit will be picked no matter who picks it. Certainly if Columbus had not discovered the American shores, some other European would have. Once the Europeans had the rudder and could set a course, and once they improved navigation to the point where they could travel 3,000 miles in a straight line, as somebody once said, "How could Columbus miss it?" It is hard to see how we could have avoided inventing the automobile about the time we did; and if Henry Ford had died in infancy, surely there would have been another person to invent the assembly line, because there were at least 200 firms already making automobiles.

Niches Dominate Mutations, and Power Changes Names More Than Patterns

In evolutionary terms it is rarely mutation that imposes limits on evolution; it is the development of niches in the course of selection. Once a niche has been created in the slow, grinding ecological interaction of populations, it is extremely probable that some mutations will take place to fill it, simply because mutation is something of which there is very little scarcity either in biological systems or in social systems. It goes on all the time. Most mutations, of course, do not survive; they are adverse in the present structure of niches. Decisions, conflicts, fights, discoveries, inventions are all part of the mutational structure of society. Hence, paradoxically, they are not very important when it comes to the pattern of the long-run movements, although they may be important in the short run in creating disturbances. Discoveries, inventions, organizations, battles and wars, conquests and all that may determine exactly what is going to fill the niche, but they do not create the niches. Given the knowledge technology of the day, if the Carthaginians had won the Punic Wars, there would have been a Mediterranean Carthaginian Empire rather than a Roman Empire and St. Peter's might later have been built in Tunis instead of Rome, but there still would have been a Mediterranean empire facilitating the spread of Christianity, which would later collapse under the impact of migrations from Asia and so on. Power changes names, but it does not change patterns.

Power Important at Thresholds

On the other hand, one has to admit that there may be exceptions to this rule, particularly in the early days of an evolutionary phylum. Evolutionary potential may not be realized because of some random accident or because of some power structure and the decisions emerging from it. We cannot quite rule out the possibility that there have been times and places in which the cast of the die, the fate of the particular occupant of a powerful role, or the way in which a decision was made either failed to create evolutionary potential that might have been created, or destroyed the possibility of some potential becoming actual. We see this in the case of the individual life, particularly the exceptional person. The fertilized egg that became Shakespeare certainly had a rather unusual genetic structure, no doubt a result of a chance aggregation of chromosomes. Genius does not have to be hereditary in the strict sense. It may be the result of an unusual combination of quite common genetic structures created by the constant rearrangement of genetic structures that takes place in sexual reproduction. If Shakespeare had been aborted or had died in infancy (and there must have been a quite noticeable probability that this could have happened in light of the infant mortality of the day), the history of the English language or even of English-speaking peoples might have been somewhat different. On the other hand, there may have been many mute, inglorious Miltons and Cromwells guiltless of their countries' blood in innumerable Stoke Poges.[2]

There are "threshold phenomena," which can be perceived when they do happen, but we never know how close they came to happening when they do not happen. If Hitler had died in infancy, the history of Europe in the twentieth century might have been substantially different, simply because the rise of the Nazis to power was one of these threshold phenomena that just made it over the top. If it had not been for the peculiarly charismatic nature of Hitler, there would undoubtedly have been something like a Nazi movement, but it might never have made it over the threshold to power. A very similar phenomenon is that of the critical mass, which is particularly important at the beginning of both organizations and social movements. Historians are not very much help to us here, simply because they are quite obsessed with what did happen (from their own point of view, of course, quite rightly), and their main concern is with maintaining and improving the record, and it is only what did happen that is recorded. From the point of view of understanding the record, however, it is what did *not* happen that is important, and studies of this are very rare and also very difficult.

The question as to whether power is important in human history, therefore, is something that within a wide range we must leave somewhat undecided. My personal view is that it is much less important than most historians, philosophers, social scientists, and certainly most ideologists have thought. Power is dramatic and visible and great decisions are interesting, while the aspects of the great pattern of society through space and time that are independent of power are drab, hard to perceive, undramatic, and fail to attract attention. For this very reason one suspects that power is more visible than it deserves to be and less important than most people think. That it is often important, however, cannot be denied; hence, of course, it deserves most careful study. It is particularly important to the people who exercise it and those on whom it is exercised. One can be fairly sure that locally in particular times and places power is much more significant than it is in considering the totality of the pattern through time. It is in these local times and places, however, that we all live, so we certainly cannot be blamed for being interested in power or even for overestimating its significance. It is not much comfort to us to think that what we do matters less than we thought.

TYPES OF POWER: THREAT POWER

There are many different kinds of power. We can distinguish roughly three types of power corresponding to the three major social organizers of Chapters 7, 8, and 9. The first of these is threat power, often identified with what is called "force." The second is exchange power, which is the power of wealth or riches. The third is integrative power, which is the power of legitimacy or status. In popular thinking, power is often exclusively associated with threat power both on the right and on the left. This, however, is a great mistake. Threat power is only one form of power and is in and of itself by no means the most powerful. Exchange power in its various forms is at least as important, and integrative power is probably the most important of all. Without integrative power, that is, some kind of status, role structure, or legitimacy, the other forms of power have very limited horizons and are very weak. This is often not generally recognized.

Threats, as we have seen, can be of many kinds. There are those associated with weapons, that is, with artifacts designed to give the possessor or the wielder the capability of doing harm to others. Threats only lead to power in the threat-submission system, in which case the threatener has the power to change the behavior of the threatened in what the threatener perceives as his favor. The threatened party then perceives his freedom as being diminished. Threat power is least effective when the threats are highly unspecific and generalized as, for instance, when minority groups use bombings at rather unspecified targets. Threats are most effective as power when they are specific and especially when they are not carried out but held, as it were, in reserve. Threat power is generally very ineffective unless it is linked intimately with some form of integrative power to legitimate it, as is the case, for instance, with the tax system and the law. The state has a great deal of threat power precisely because it is regarded by most people as legitimate. If the legitimacy decays, the threat power decays also. If the legitimacy of a taxing authority, for instance, is denied by a large majority of those who are liable for taxes, the authority collapses even in the face of severe sanctions, and the cost of collecting taxes rises to the point where they are not worth collecting.

Physical threat and weapons are by no means the only kinds of threat. Spiritual threats, as we saw earlier (p. 146), were an important source of the power of a priesthood, and even in the European middle ages the threat of excommunication by the pope could bring an emperor literally to his knees. Threats of exclusion or social disapproval and rejection are very powerful organizers of society. Most people are kept in line to follow the social mores and to obey the law more by the subtle threat system of exclusion from society, community, or valued social intercourse than they are by the sanctions of the law.

THE POWER OF NONVIOLENCE

The theory of the power of nonviolence as developed, for instance, by Gandhi and expounded in the United States by Richard B. Gregg[3] and Gene Sharp[4] is a very interesting example of the development of subtle forms of threat. The use of nonviolent threats as an instrument of political power is an important social invention. We have seen it used in struggles for independence, as in India, or for the rights of minorities, as in the United States with Martin Luther King and the civil rights movement. There are many different forms of nonviolent threat. The most common perhaps is that of simple withdrawal, that is, a passive defiance of the threats of the authorities whose legitimacy is being challenged, coupled with the willingness to suffer the consequences. Threat power is limited by the phenomenon noticed before that the carrying out of a threat is often highly costly to the threatener and that, where this is so, threat-submission systems are apt to be unstable and slip into defiance. Defiance, especially if it is well organized, may be quite successful in undermining the credibility and the legitimacy of the original threat system of the authorities. Strikes, boycotts, sit-ins, demonstrations, tax refusal, and so on are as much a part of threat power as guns, bombs, and armies. The development of organized nonviolence, indeed, is perhaps one of the most significant political inventions of the twentieth century, even though it has been known in a sporadic way for a very long time. It operates partly in undermining by calm defiance the threat system of the authorities; this operates to undermine their legitimacy, particularly their internal legitimacy, that is, their morale or self image. An army or police force faced with disciplined and organized nonviolence is a little bit like the personal attacker faced with jujitsu. The violent expect violence in return. When they are met with nonviolence they are thrown off balance and their self-confidence and legitimacy tend to be undermined. Without legitimacy, however, as we have seen, threats are very ineffective, even violent threats.

It is a paradox of nonviolence, however, that it is much more effective for aggression than it is for defense. Aggression may be defined as activity directed to produce change wanted by the actor. The word aggression carries considerable overtones of illegitimacy in the English language, but it is hard to think of any other word that means the effort to produce a wanted change. Defense, on the other hand, is effort designed to prevent unwanted change. This is just as common and just as legitimate as aggression, though, as we shall see later, it always seems to produce pathological results. Nonviolence is almost always aggressive in this sense, that is, it is designed to produce the change desired by its organizers. Defense against it is often very difficult, which is why one suspects that nonviolent action in organization quite often produces violence as a reaction, though often rather ineffective violence. The effectiveness of nonviolence depends a good deal on the particular structure of the integrative system within which it is operating. It is most effective where the wielder of established threat systems, such as an occupying power or an imperial power, is in a weak integrative position. We will look at this problem a little further when we discuss integrative power.

ECONOMIC POWER

The second major source of power is economic power. This is not quite the same thing as exchange power, although, of course, it is closely related to it because exchange is such a central institution in economic life. Economic power is the power to command or control human artifacts, particularly those artifacts which are commodities and which participate in the processes of exchange, that is, economic goods. We do not have to limit these to goods that actually participate in exchange. There may be "provisions" (economic goods) that are human artifacts of value and significance to those who possess or control them. These may be produced for consumption and used domestically, rather than for exchange. But it is, as we have seen, the exchange phenomenon that leads to the division of labor, increase in productivity, and the massive expansion of human artifacts.

Economic power, that is, command over economic goods, comes from a number of different sources. It comes mainly from control over the factors of production that enter into the process of production of economic goods. As we have seen earlier, these consist essentially of knowledge or know-how, energy, and materials. The greatest of these is knowledge, although there are occasions in which the power to produce economic goods is limited by lack of access to energy or to materials. It is these three factors that largely determine the productivity of human activity in the production of economic goods. This is particularly true of larger groups or societies. Today, for instance, the rich countries are rich and the poor countries are poor mainly because the rich countries have large accumulations of knowledge and capital, which is essentially human knowledge imposed on the material world by past production, and access to large energy sources and material sources. The poor countries lack knowledge and, because of this, they also frequently lack access to energy and materials. In the rich countries the capabilities of production rest on a vast infrastructure of scientific and technical knowledge that permits these countries in these days to draw on fossil fuels through elaborate mechanisms of production and exchange, and with these to transform large quantities of materials into large quantities of economic goods. The poor countries, relying on their traditional folk knowledge, on human and animal muscles as energy sources, and on purely local materials are able to produce very little.

A rough measure of economic power is the net output of economic goods per head or per capita real income. For any group or even any arbitrary set of people, the total income of economic goods depends on the division of total activity among (1) production for domestic use, (2) production for exchange, and (3) nonproduction, such as activity devoted to leisure or sleep, or time spent in unemployment. Suppose that out of a group of L persons we have the equivalent of L_d persons producing for domestic use, L_e producing for exchange, and L_u not producing. Then

$$L = L_d + L_e + L_u \qquad (1)$$

If p_d is the productivity of domestic activity, p_e the productivity of production for export, T the terms of trade (that is, how many imports are obtained per unit of exports), and G the total of grants, gifts, or transfers (which may of course be positive or negative), the total real income Y is

$$Y = L_d p_d + L_e p_e T + G. \tag{2}$$

Then we have the per capita real income or economic power,

$$y = \frac{Y}{L} = \frac{L_d p_d + L_e p_e T + G}{L_d + L_e + L_u} \tag{3}$$

This is an instructive equation, showing the sources of an increase in economic power. A shift out of L_u, that is, unemployed potential, into either L_d or L_e will increase economic power, y. Shifts into production for export out of domestic production will increase only if p_e is greater than p_d. An increase in positive grants, of course, will increase economic power and so will an improvement in the terms of trade, T, that is, how much we get in imports per unit of what we give up in exports. The major long-run source of increase in economic power, however, is increase in productivity, that is, in p_d or p_e. This is the only source that can be sustained for very long. An improvement in terms of trade easily reverses itself. Shifts into more productive occupations soon exhaust themselves. The horizon on the increase of grants is fairly low. Rich countries have become rich because their productivity has been increasing so rapidly for so long. Any improvement in their terms of trade has been a minor factor, occasionally significant for short periods. Even exploitative grants to them from the poor countries have been quite small.

This formula can be applied to a single individual or family as well as to a nation or group. Here again, if in a particular occupation there are good terms of trade and good productivity in production for exchange, the individual may get richer by shifting from domestic production into exchange production such as, for instance, going to work for an employer and getting wages with which he or she buys other things rather than trying to produce these other things at home. Increase in productivity often comes from education, training, or an increase in skill. The grants factor in the case of an individual would include income received without any activity, which could include either welfare payments or income on property, especially pure interest or dividend income, which does not involve any management or activity factor. The richest individuals tend to have a larger income from property than they do from their own labor or activity.

PRODUCTIVITY AND REALLOCATION AS SOURCES OF ECONOMIC POWER

Equation 3 really points us to four types or sources of economic power. The first might be called "productive power," as reflected in the productivity coefficients p_d and p_e. This is very largely a function of the knowledge stock, although it is also a function of the availability of energy and of materials of various sorts. This is reflected, for instance, in the fertility of the land a group occupies, the natural resources to which it has access, and so on, but over the long haul the knowledge factor is really dominant. A good example is the case of Germany and Japan after the World War II. The destruction of a large amount of the material base in terms of buildings, machines, and so on can be recovered very easily if the knowledge factors are not affected. Both Germany and Japan had remarkably rapid recovery from the defeat and devastation of World War II. Defeat in war may even have improved the knowledge base of the society in the sense that it got rid of a lot of powerful people, like Hitler and the Japanese military, who had very imperfect knowledge, that is, whose images of the world were very unrealistic. Many countries that in 1945, let us say, had not been devastated and had their material capital unimpaired nevertheless stagnated or developed very slowly in the next generation because the knowledge stock simply was not there.

A second rather minor source of economic power is what might be called "allocational efficiency," that is, the ability of either a person, group, or society to allocate its resources properly first between production for domestic use and production for exchange, and then in a larger sense between the lines of production among the different industries. A society willing to take advantage of the terms of trade that the world market offers is likely to develop more rapidly than one that goes in for import substitution, protecting often very inefficient domestic industry, and so on. This is not to say that absolute free trade is always the best road to riches. There are disadvantages of producing for exchange as well as advantages. Both an individual and a society have to find a proper balance between domestic production and production for export and exchange.

It is hard to assess the actual impact of this factor because it is associated with certain psychological factors that also have an effect on the growth of knowledge and productivity. "Protectionist" individuals and societies, which are suspicious of intercourse with the outside, exchange, foreign trade, and producing for others and become ingrown, inward looking, and hostile to the outside world, are very often also individuals and societies that inhibit the growth of knowledge in themselves, are afraid to take risks, and stagnate in their own little self-contained package. The hippie, the drug addict, the withdrawn communitarians, the agrarian simple lifers, and the nationalist protectionist nations all have this element of withdrawal in common. They all are likely to suffer from it in the long run.

TERMS OF TRADE, MONOPOLY, AND
GRANTS AS SOURCES OF ECONOMIC POWER

The third source of economic power is reflected in the terms of trade higher the price of the things we sell and the lower the price of things we buy, the richer we are. Control over the terms of trade, however, is only achieved through monopoly power, which in turn is only achieved through control of the total sales and ultimately the total output of the export commodity. Monopoly power is very widespread in society, but in a certain sense it is not very large. For one thing, monopolies often tend to be fragile, especially when they are based on some "organization of organizations" like a cartel, which are difficult to maintain unless they are upheld by the threat power of the state. Monopolies frequently tend to be undermined by technical change, which they may indeed stimulate, in the invention of substitutes for the monopolized commodity. There are fairly strong limits to the degree to which terms of trade can be manipulated. It would be very hard, for instance, even under the most favorable circumstances such as OPEC, the monopolistic association of the oil producers, to raise the terms of trade by much more than a factor of 2 or 3. This is a one-shot operation—once done it cannot be repeated. Productivity coefficients, on the other hand, have been doubling each generation in what are now the rich countries for a number of genera- tions and in some fields are more than 50 times what they were 200 years ago.

Nevertheless, monopoly is important especially in the short run, and it is quite pervasive. Labor unions, especially craft unions, insofar as they can restrict entry into their occupation, exercise monopoly power, some of which they usually pass on to their employers. This is obtained at the expense of the purchasers of the commodity that they jointly produce. Professional associa- tions like the American Medical Association also create very substantial monopoly power for the medical profession by restricting entry into medical schools. Cartels and commodity agreements may create monopoly power for the producers of particular commodities. In the past these have not been very successful, except for short periods. The oil producers are a notable exception to this rule. When the last of the oil is all gone, this will have been a very temporary episode in human history. It may have long-run results if the oil producers can invest their monopoly gains wisely. "Natural monopolies" are important in some fields, like telephones and electric utilities, where there are great technical advantages in having a single firm in one area. These are usually subject to some kind of public regulation.

Monopoly power frequently tends to be mixed with threat power. The monopolist says in effect to his customer, "If you do not pay my price, you will not get the commodity." Monopoly power can be regarded, therefore, as a use of organized threats to push the terms of trade, where there is a range of mutual benefit, toward the high price or the sellers' end of the scale. As we have seen, there is both a community and a conflict of interest in exchange, and monopoly power is a way of organizing the conflict of interest. On the other side of the picture, monopsony power is more rare, but not unknown.

This is the power of organized buyers who refuse to buy from the sellers except at a price toward the buyers' end of the range of mutual benefit. Tacit or sometimes open agreements among employers in an area not to bid up wages, which Adam Smith noted,[5] are an example. When a large corporation purchases a commodity produced by large numbers of individual producers or by a considerable number of individual countries, it may be able to set a "take-it-or-leave-it" price, which the producers simply have to follow. In the absence of organized political power, however, both monopoly and monopsony power are hard to sustain simply because the more the power is exercised by the collective organization, the greater are the incentives for the individual member to break away.

Threat systems, as we have seen, are costly to the threatener as well as to the threatened. Monopoly power is most sustainable when there are few producers of a commodity that has very few substitutes. Petroleum, of course, is a very good example of this. On the other hand, if the monopoly power is exercised too vigorously, there are strong incentives both to discover substitutes and to increase the efficiency of the use of the monopolized article; hence the monopolists find their market shrinking. The weaker ones among the associated producers find themselves in an increasingly difficult position with shrinking markets and hence they have increasing incentives to break out of the monopoly and to offer to sell at a lower price. This has been the history of innumerable monopolies in the past; it would be a little surprising if it does not happen to OPEC in the future.

The most secure monopolies are those supported by the organized political threat system of the state, such as the monopoly of the communist party in communist countries. An interesting historical example was the sovereign monopoly of the British East India Company in India and similar state trading companies especially in the sixteenth and seventeenth centuries in Europe. Even the history of these, however, is full of disaster and collapse. The monopoly may have aroused enough antagonism to undermine the legitimacy of the political organization that supports it. This happened with the British in India. The monopoly itself may generate so much internal inefficiency, because it relies on threat power rather than exchange power, that it collapses internally in spite of its monopoly power. Most of the monopolistic trading companies suffered this fate. Even the powerful East India Company was virtually bankrupt around the mid-nineteenth century.

The fourth source of economic power is grants (G of the formula on p. 244). They are a product partly of the threat system in the form of tribute, theft, and taxes, and partly of the integrative system in the form of gifts. Taxes are essentially part of the redistribution of economic power through the threat system, although there are elements of integrative power here as taxes, for instance, can only be collected if the threat behind them is widely regarded as legitimate. Tribute and armed robbery arise out of almost pure threat with a very small integrative component. Grants in the form of gifts belong mainly to the system of integrative power, such as grants within the family from parents to children and in old age from children to parents, charitable grants to beggars, contributions to worthy causes, foundation grants, welfare payments, foreign aid, and so on.

INTEGRATIVE POWER: ROLE POWER

Integrative power is one of the most subtle and least understood of the forms of power, yet in terms of long-run social dynamics it is probably the most important. It is, however, a very heterogeneous collection of types of power, and the question could legitimately be raised whether it is too heterogeneous to deserve a name. It is, however, convenient to have a category of relationships and types of power that does not fall easily into the other two categories of threat power and economic power, recognizing that we may want to subdivide it into various sub-categories.

Perhaps the most important category of integrative power is what might be called "role power." This is the power that comes to an occupant of a role simply because he or she occupies it rather than because of any personal characteristics of the occupier. Role power is closely bound up with the legitimacy of the role, that is, the degree to which it is accepted by those who occupy it and by those who are related to it. Thus, anybody who becomes president of the United States increases his personal power because of the role he occupies. When President Nixon resigned from office, his personal power diminished enormously. When Lenin became in effect czar of the Russian Empire, even though he did not adopt the title, his personal power increased enormously. It is the role, however, that gives the power, not the person, though the behavior of the person may affect the power of the role and frequently does. If the person performs very badly, the role itself may be delegitimated and its integrative power lost.

The exact dynamic process by which powerful roles are created is a complex, puzzling phenomenon. Roles evolve essentially in the human learning process. It is the images of roles in the minds of the human race that give them their power and nothing else. Repetition is an important element in this learning process. It is constantly drilled into us that certain roles are powerful, and if we never hear anything to the contrary, we come to believe it. Once we believe it, the sheer force of habit makes it hard to disturb that belief, except under conditions of extreme dislocation.

SYMBOLIC POWER

Another important aspect of integrative power is symbolic power. This is significant mainly perhaps because it is part of the learning process by which role power is developed. The symbols of role power are an important part of the process by which it is established. These are such things as the ideology of the revolutionary, the crown and the robe of the monarch, the sword of the noble, the gown of the scholar, the collar of the cleric, the vestments of the priest, the flag and the anthem of the national state, the ritual of the church, and ceremonies of all kinds such as coronations, investitures, convocations, commencements, religious rituals, marriages, funerals, festivals, holidays. These are all part of the learning process by which the structure of role power is created. Art and architecture are important in creating the settings by which symbolic power is reinforced; temples, palaces, cathedrals, and campuses are all part of the symbolic learning process—what Adam Smith called "state" in the sense of "stately." Pageants and processions and the architecture, art, and music accompanying them all reinforce the distinction and legitimacy of important and powerful roles. Much of what the American Institutionalists like Thorstein Veblen[6] and Clarence Ayres[7] despised as the extravagant, conspicuous-consumption, ceremonial aspects of life are in fact extremely important elements in establishing role structures. The Capitol in Washington, D.C. proclaims at the top of its silent voice, "I am important and what goes on in here is important." Nobody would pay much attention to a government that met in a mud hut or a chief executive that lived in a hovel—unless, of course, these too become symbols of power, as they well may.

As legitimacy becomes established through age and habit, it may no longer be necessary to symbolize it by extravagant buildings and expenditures. State universities, for instance, are now such well-established legitimacies that they tend to abandon the gowns, processions, and elegant architecture with its associations with past legitimacies, and turn to building hideous shoeboxes and granting mail-order degrees. Titles are also important symbols of legitimacy. The loss of legitimacy of a role indeed through misbehavior or incompetence on the part of previous occupants can sometimes be restored by simply changing the title—the king or emperor becomes president or chairman, or challenged by women's liberation, a chairperson. Titles, "good words," and fashionable expressions, like "the name of the game," have a kind of ecology of their own. Those who use the right words and adopt the right gestures often achieve the powerful roles.

COMMUNITY POWER AND MORAL POWER

A very important form of integrative power, which has a considerable impact on the grants economy, might be called "community power." This is the power that people or groups have because they are recognized as belonging to a larger community. The smallest community is of course the family. Membership in a family confers very substantial power on the individual, which is greater, of course, the greater the wealth and power of the family to which the individual belongs. This is reflected in the importance of the family grants economy, which may be as much as 30 percent of the gross national product in the United States.[8] The national community is of increasing importance, particularly in the grants economy, in effecting redistributions. Belonging to communities within the larger community, like a governing class, may be of considerable importance in determining the power of an individual in obtaining grants and privileges. On the other hand, as national states are moved toward a larger basis of participation, the poorer classes within them have tended to benefit from redistributions, especially those classes perceived as victims of discrimination, but who are recognized as being part of the community.

This might almost be called "hypocrisy power," because when the practices of a community do not conform to its professed ideals, as has been the case in the United States for instance in regard to racial, cultural, and sexual discrimination, the victims of this hypocrisy can use it as a moral weapon to increase their own power in the community. Thus, whatever "black power" exists in the United States is mainly integrative power of this kind. It does not rest very much on threats or economic power, but on the appeal to the principle of community that "we are all Americans together." One sees this dramatically in comparing the United States, for instance, with a country that does not make these professions of community. The blacks in the United States are Americans, even if as a group they may be somewhat underprivileged citizens. The blacks in South Africa are not South Africans at all and are excluded completely from the political community as aliens in their native land. We see the exercise of community power in a very interesting way also in the disbanded empires. The French community, for instance, has a great deal of community power. The outlying parts of the remaining French Empire, such as Cayenne, Reunion, and until recently the territory of the Azars and Issas, extract large grants from metropolitan France because they belong to the French community. Even the British Commonwealth—a weak community—had its Columbo Plan for economic aid.

In general social dynamics it is important to identify something that might be called "moral power." The development of professed moral ideals is part of the larger dynamic of symbolic and persuasive systems, which has a strong, though poorly understood dynamic of its own. Moral power arises with the development of the perception of inconsistencies between these professed moral ideals and the actual practices of a society. This can be particularly important when the professed moral ideals are enshrined in sacred documents, like the Bible or the American Declaration of Independence, with which the hypocrite can be confronted.

Role-filling Mechanisms

The problem of who gets into powerful roles is another very interesting question that is important in all large organizations, whether they are institutions of political life like the state, of economic life like the corporation or bank, or of religious life like the church. It is indeed large organizations that create powerful roles. Constitutions usually specify the mechanism by which role occupants are selected. It may be by appointment in the hierarchy, as the pope appoints cardinals or the president of the United States appoints justices to the Supreme Court. It may be by election, with all sorts of conventions about who votes and how many votes are necessary, as in the case of parliamentary or congressional democracy or in the case of the cardinals electing the pope. It may be by direct threat, as in a military coup, a revolution, or the capture of the police or armed forces by an ambitious and charismatic figure. Role occupancy may also be determined by inheritance, as in the hereditary monarchy. Even when there is no inheritance by persons, as in the case of the monarchy or hereditary aristocracy, there is often a hereditary class in the sense that children born of certain parents have a much better chance of achieving powerful roles than children born of others. Another important source of role power is sacredness, as an aspect of symbolic power. How this is created and destroyed we do not really know, but historically it has been of great importance. The interaction between the icon builders and the iconoclasts throughout human history has been of considerable importance. All these methods of role occupancy must find their own legitimacy and their own place in integrative structures, in interactions which may be of great complexity.

ALL FORMS OF POWER INTERACT

It is very important to stress that all the forms of power interact with each other. It is very rare indeed to find any of them in a pure form. Power indeed is an ecological system. It is hard perhaps to think of its many forms and manifestations as populations, but they do interact in a highly ecological way—sometimes reinforcing each other, sometimes competing with each other, sometimes in a predative relationship. Political power is an intricate mixture of threat power, economic power, allocative power, organizational power, monopoly power, and role power. Economic power likewise develops in a complex matrix of threat and integrative structures. Role power is closely related to threats on the one hand and to economic power on the other. No single form of power is dominant at all times and places, although the importance of different forms of power varies widely from place to place and from time to time. Sacred power was important in the European Middle Ages and is still important in communist countries today. This is the power of ideology and of the unquestionable and the untouchable. Economic power rises in importance under capitalist development and occasionally subordinates the political power. The power or weakness of classes and groups, of minorities, of blacks, of women, and of the poor of the third world are all bound up in an intricate dynamic that all the forms of power interweave.

Invoking a power that does not exist may be very dangerous to the invoker and actually diminish his power. Thinking of power in terms of a single form, such as threat power, may be highly unrealistic. On the other hand, imaginative leaders may create new forms of power. The more we appreciate the subtlety and yet at the same time the very persistent patterns of the dynamics of power in society, the more likely we are to move toward those forms of power that are in fact fruitful and can move us toward the better rather than toward the worse.

NOTES

1. For a further discussion, see Kenneth E. Boulding, "The Dimensions of Economic Freedom," in *The Nation's Economic Objectives*, Edgar Edwards, ed. (Chicago: University of Chicago Press, 1964), 107–122 (reprinted in *Kenneth Boulding/Collected Papers*, Larry Singell, ed. (Boulder: Colorado Associated University Press, 1973), Vol. III, 201–218.

2. Stoke Poges is supposed to be the site of Thomas Gray's "Elegy Written in a Country Churchyard." The verse quoted is:

Some village Hampden that with dauntless breast
The little tyrant of his fields withstood,
Some mute inglorious Milton here may rest
Some Cromwell guiltless of his country's blood.

3. Richard B. Gregg, *The Power of Nonviolence* (New York: Schocken Books, 1966).

4. Gene Sharp,, *The Politics of Nonviolent Action* (Boston: Porter Sargent. 1973).

5. Adam Smith, *The Wealth of Nations* (New York: Modern Library Edition), 66.

6. Thorstein Veblen, *The Theory of the Leisure Class* (New York: Modern Library, 1934).

7. Clarence E. Ayres, *Towards a Reasonable Society* (Austin: University of Texas Press, 1961).

8. Nancy Baerwaldt and James N. Morgan, "Trends in Intra-Family Transfers," in *Surveys of Consumers, 1971-72*, Lewis Mandell, ed. (Ann Arbor: Survey Research Center, Institute for Social Research, University of Michigan, 1973).

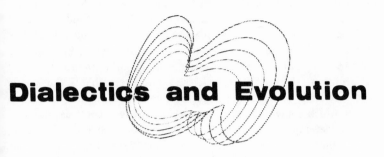

Chapter 12

Dialectics and Evolution

DIALECTICAL (CONFLICTUAL) VERSUS NONDIALECTICAL PROCESSES

The word "dialectics" has a confusing variety of meanings. When it is used simply to mean dynamics, as it sometimes is in ideological discussions, it really ceases to have any distinctive meaning. It is a word, however, that can be used to distinguish two important categories of processes in dynamic systems, especially in social systems, which can be termed dialectical processes and nondialectical processes. The concept of the dialectical process goes a long way back in human history, certainly to the Greeks, because the word is a Greek word meaning conversation or "speaking across." It comes into prominence in Western philosophy, however, with Hegel and it acquires great emotional and ideological significance in Marxism, in the doctrine of dialectical materialism, which in effect denies any significance to the nondialectical processes. The distinction between dialectical and nondialectical processes may not be wholly clear—very few important distinctions are—but it is something real, and the problem of assessing the relative importance of these two broad categories of processes in the larger dynamic process of the universe, and especially in the processes of society, is a problem of some importance.

We can perhaps arrange the dynamic processes of the universe in an order of the degree to which they exhibit dialectical or nondialectical elements. I define dialectical processes, for the purposes of this distinction, as those which involve conflict or struggle as an essential element. The more conflict a process involves, the more dialectical it is. Ranging from the least dialectical to the most dialectical processes, we then have: (1) Processes that involve simple dynamic or cyclical equilibrium, such as celestial mechanics in which there is interaction, but nothing that can reasonably be called conflict because, unless we are astrologers, there is no sense at all in putting valuations on the different positions of the system. (2) Prebiological evolution involves very little that one can think of as conflict, involving as it does simply the generation of complexity under the appropriate physical conditions by a series of phase transformations. There may be interaction among physical and chemical species of different kinds that causes a diminution in some and expansion of others, but to call this conflict is invalid anthropomorphism. (3) Biological evolution, the process by which the genosphere, that is, the genetic structure of the earth, increases in complexity, involves an intense interaction of species in which some expand, some decline, some become extinct, and new ones are developed, but there is very little here that can be called organized conflict. Processes of production from the fertilized egg to the mature animal are still less conflictual. There may be conflict of siblings in a nest or a litter for a limited food supply in which not all of them will survive, but there is nothing conflictual about the actual dynamic process by which the fertilized egg becomes a mature animal. (4) In the ecological interaction of populations there is competition in the sense that the more there is of one species, the less there will be of another, but this is not the same thing as conflict. It would be perfectly possible, for instance, for two species to be in competition without ever seeing each other or being aware of each other's existence, if both fed on a common food supply at different times. As we have seen (p. 92), even mutually competitive relationships may produce an equilibrium for both species or they can also lead to the extinction of one species. Relationships of predation are likely to be favorable to both species and fairly stable. Relationships with mutual cooperation are likely to be highly favorable to both species. The "struggle for existence," as we have noted earlier, is an entirely inappropriate, anthropomorphic metaphor derived essentially from human experience.

Conflict in the Biosphere

There only seem to be three places in prehuman biological systems in which conflict systems have much significance. One is in the development of territoriality. A group or a pair of some species stake out a territory and defend it by fighting off invaders from the same species. This behavior is noted even in fish in the case of the stickleback; it is also fairly common in birds, the robin being a good example. There may be cases of it among insects such as ants, and it is fairly common among animals. The great advantage of territoriality in evolutionary strategy is paradoxically that it creates a smaller niche for the animal in question than it would have if the population were limited only by the food supply, but it probably leads also to better fed and healthier individuals that are able to survive disease and can adapt more easily to a worsening of the environment. There is a certain cost to territoriality, however, in terms of fighting and, if this becomes too severe, it can be adverse to survival. The animals that do not find a territory of course do not survive.

On the whole territoriality does not seem to lead to very extensive armament because that would be adverse to survival if it did. The fighting for territory is often highly ritualized so that it causes very little damage to the winner, although the loser of course may not survive, not because he is damaged in the fight, but simply because he cannot find a territory. Group territoriality, which is occasionally found, is the worst of all possible strategies because it involves fighting, which may be damaging, and it also means that the population of the species will be limited by the food supply rather than by the territory. Such species are in the worst of all possible worlds.[1]

Another pattern in the biosphere in which conflict is of some importance is in establishing pecking orders in animals that live in groups. Even here, however, natural selection seems to have produced methods of establishing these dominance orders that are ritualized and not very costly in terms of actual damage done during a fight. Many animals, like the wolf for instance, have behavioral mechanisms that bring fights to a termination before serious harm is done to either party. The wolf exposes its throat to its opponent, which is taken as a signal that it has lost the fight and is going to accept an inferior-dominance order. Any animal whose genetic code instructed it to take fighting seriously would soon be eliminated. The pecking order itself is no doubt useful for survival of the total species, but these are obvious payoffs for instinctual limitations on behavior, which enable a group to establish a pecking order at the least possible cost in terms of fighting damage. Diplomacy rather than war is the norm in nature.

Yet another situation in biological dynamics in which fighting occurs is in sexual selection where usually the males fight for the favor of the females. Here again, there seems to be a strong tendency in natural selection to ritualize this kind of fighting and it often ends up in courtship displays of plumage and even in the excesses of the lyre bird, the bower bird, and the peacock. It is an interesting question whether a species that gets into sexual selection too much may not be on the road to extinction. What the girls (or occasionally the boys) like is not always what leads to survival. The Irish elk seems to be a case in point in that sexual selection made the horns longer and longer until they caught in the bushes and the animal became extinct.

Neither of these three types of conflictual behavior is very fundamental in the overall evolutionary process, although it may affect certain parts of it. The image of the biological realm as a kind of Hobbesian nightmare full of snarling species fighting to the death is a gross misunderstanding. Nature certainly has a dab of red on the tooth and claw, there are food chains, there is competition, and there is a constant turnover of species, but conflict in the sense of fighting is really quite rare, though it does increase as one goes up the evolutionary scale. One can watch almost any ecosystem for months and never see a fight. What one observes is growth, decay, birth, death, respiration, excretion—none of them conflictual processes. It is the very rarity of conflict processes that in part makes them so interesting and exciting, drawing our attention to them and hence perhaps leading us to overestimate their importance.

Conflictual and Nonconflictual Processes in Human History

As we move into social systems and human interactions, conflictual processes and fighting becomes much more common, simply because decisions become more important. Power becomes more important, as we have seen in Chapter 11. Human beings have elaborate images of the future from which they make choices. These images often include perceptions of redistributions of welfare with some people or groups getting better off and some worse off. When competitive relationships are so perceived, they become conflict and decisions may be taken accordingly.

Even in human society, however, a very large part of human activity is nonconflictual. Getting up in the morning may involve a bit of a struggle between physiological desires to stay in bed and get some more sleep and social drives to get up and take on the business of the day. A great deal of human activity, however, does not involve even internal struggle. Even though we can think of any decision as a resolution of the conflict of alternative choices, the resolution may come without struggle by simple ordering. Struggle comes in the dilemma where we are choosing the lesser evil. But most decisions are not dilemmas. Many people even get up in the morning without struggle. They get through the day: eating breakfast, going to work, doing a job, eating lunch, going back to work, coming home, having dinner, watching television or going to a movie, reading a book, and going to bed. Some of these activities have conflictual elements in them, but for the most part they are almost entirely nonconflictual. The process of human growth and learning is for the most part nonconflictual. This is what I have called "unviolence," the great bulk of human activity that is neither violent nor nonviolent, simply because it is not at all conflictual, perhaps because it is involved in production rather than distribution. Productive activities only get into conflict when they involve dilemmas over alternative costs, that is, where production of one thing involves not producing another thing that is almost equally valued. But these relationships are often remote and rarely get expressed in organized activity. Alternative costs very rarely lead to fights.

In the evolution of human artifacts and the growth of the noosphere there is a good deal of competition, as in biological evolution, in the sense that some artifacts displace others, some occupations displace others, and some methods displace others. Competition, however, as we have seen, is not at all the same thing as conflict, although it may lead into conflict and provide the ground for conflict. The great movements of the social species—the rise of domesticated crops and livestock, the improvements in transportation, the shift out of agriculture, the rise of the service trades—involve competition, but it is only rarely that this breaks down into conflict. If resources are mobile, indeed, competition need not lead to conflict at all. As horses decline, the blacksmiths and farriers and harness makers flit easily and quietly into the automobile factories and change their occupations without any massing of forces or any defense of the old methods of production. It is only where resources are immobile, that competition tends to lead to conflict, protectionism, subsidies, and political activity.

Inner Conflict in Decision-making:
The Dilemma—Avoiders versus Approachers

Finally, however, we do get to those dynamic processes in which conflict is an essential element. We have first of all inner conflict within the personality. The simplest of these is the dilemma, a situation in which we find it hard to make a decision between two alternatives and hence we become conscious that decision is a conflictual process rather than simply the process of selection. This is likely to happen, as Neal Miller[2] pointed out, when people are "avoiders" rather than "approachers." Faced with an agenda for decision, the approacher ranks these in order of the best, second best, third best, and so on; once this ranking has been performed, he simply selects the best and chooses that. The avoider, on the other hand, starts the ranking from the bottom—the worst, the next worst, and so on—and eliminates successive diminishing dislikes until he is left with only one alternative, which he dislikes the least, and so chooses that. These two processes seem very similar, but they may have very different results, especially when it comes to a dilemma, that is, when the top two alternatives on the agenda look equally attractive, but we have to decide between them.

The problem is illustrated in the famous story of Buridan's ass. A donkey is equidistant between two equally attractive bales of hay; the question is: "Will he starve to death?" The answer is no, because random forces will move him slightly toward one rather than the other; the one he is closest to will smell a little sweeter, he will go and eat it, and then come back and eat the other one. Buridan's ass is a typical approacher. Put Buridan's ass between two skunks, however, and he becomes an avoider. As he moves toward either one he is driven back to the center and he ends up kicking and screaming in a complete nervous breakdown as a result of unresolvable internal conflict. Approachers, therefore, resolve internal conflicts easily and enjoy excellent mental health; avoiders constantly get into internal conflicts and waste an enormous amount of time on internal frustration and arguing with themselves. Avoidance also tends to lead into malevolence, which as we have seen easily becomes a negative-sum game that leaves everybody worse off. This again often leads to the intensification of external conflicts, so that internal conflict easily moves over into conditions that give rise to external conflicts.

Whether approachers and avoiders represent two different psychological types, how they are produced through learning experiences, and even whether they have any genetic bases, I do not know, and unfortunately psychologists seem to have done very little work on these problems. It is, however, a very critical question for the development of conflict in society because internal mental conflict is costly not only to the individual, but also to the whole society insofar as it produces unnecessary external conflict. There is a school of psychologists[3] which argues that externally aggressive behavior is the result of internal frustration—the famous frustration-aggression thesis. This has been challenged, though up to a point it certainly seems plausible and again would relate internal to external conflicts. I have often thought it curious that what an economist calls equilibrium, the psychologist calls frustration, these being virtually identical concepts—namely that of proceeding to the most highly valued point on the opportunity boundary and staying there. Economic man seems to stay there very calmly and psychological man seems to stay there kicking and screaming, because economic man is essentially an approacher whereas psychological man seems to be an avoider, moving away from hunger and unsatisfied desire rather than toward being well fed and fulfilled.

FIGHTING IN THE BIOSPHERE AND IN HUMAN HISTORY

External conflict between human beings, that is, fighting, undoubtedly begins very early in human history. It predates the human race, as we have seen. There is a very wide variety of patterns, even among the near relations of the human race such as the apes and monkeys, ranging from the gentle and unconflictual gibbon and even the highly ritualized conflict of the gorilla to the possessive pomposity of the snarling baboon. What our own simian ancestors were like we really do not know because there are none of them now around. It is clear, however, that genetically even the apes and monkeys were capable of a wide variety of cultural expression in regard to conflict, and the human race has an even wider repertoire between gentleness and ferocity. It is the enormously wide range of patterns of social dynamic processes that permits us to observe the fantastic variety of humankind. It is as if the human race started on top of a mountain and by chance forces took different paths down different valleys to extremely different destinations.

Fighting, however, is a common form of human behavior. It is almost universal among children, though here again there do seem to be built-in mechanisms for keeping it from going too far and being too injurious. Indeed, part of the reason why pain has been selected for almost universally, at least among the higher animals, in the course of natural selection is that it is an avoidance mechanism not only for natural hazards but also for fights. If fighting did not hurt, there would be much more of it, it would be much more dangerous, and there would be a good deal less running away, which, as the proverb tells us, enables us to fight another day.

Among adults fighting tends to be concentrated toward the "outgroup." If there is too much fighting in an ingroup, it tends to disintegrate. Selective factors, therefore, will limit the tendency toward infighting, although they will not eradicate it altogether. There does seem to be an historical tendency to form larger and larger groups within which infighting is discouraged, as conflict tends to be channeled toward the outsider. The larger the ingroup, the less fighting there is in general simply because fighting is confined to the borders of groups, and the bigger the groups, the fewer borders there are, culminating, of course, in the group of all mankind, which has no borders, except for some hypothetical invaders from outer space.

The amount of fighting that has gone on in North America in the last 100 years must be much less than in the previous 1,000 years because of the consolidation of the continent into three states, which have maintained relatively stable peace for well over 100 years. Even if we count the wars of the eighteenth and nineteenth centuries, these probably represented a smaller proportion of total resources than the constant fighting of the Indians among themselves in the previous period. The very sparse population indeed of the period before European settlement in North America, in spite of the fact that agriculture was widely known, suggests that the human niche was limited far more by the small size of the political community and the constant warfare between them than it was by food supply. The European settlers, as Adam Smith remarked with extraordinary insight, brought with them "the habit of subordination"[4] and thus were able to organize themselves into much larger communities with a tremendous diminution of internal fighting and the ritualization of conflict in the form of elections, logrolling, and the whole game of politics.

War as Activity of the State; Conquest and Deterrence

The most striking conflict phenomenon in human society is of course war, that is, organized conflict between groups. Before the development of cities and states there was undoubtedly a good deal of intergroup and intertribe violence and hostility. It is virtually impossible to assess how much there was and what proportion of human resources were devoted to it. Many neolithic villages seem to have been undefended, suggesting at any rate that in the great age of neolithic expansion tensions were easily relieved by migration. With the closing of the neolithic frontier and the development of urban civilization, however, war became a virtually continuous form of human activity, requiring the development of specialized armed forces, which involved a fulltime job and lifetime career for many. This indeed marks the beginning of empire, which is, as we have seen (p. 151), an organized threat system able to extract tribute from subject populations mainly in the form of foodstuffs, which the king or the emperor can then feed to the armies that constitute the capability for carrying out threat. This looks like a very stable system, except that it is governed by the cost of transport, as we have seen (p. 152), which limits the size of the state or empire and makes it possible for two or more such organizations to exist simultaneously at some distance apart. Conflict then becomes endemic. It is the principal activity around which revolves the ruler and his armed forces. Specialized armed forces have to justify their existence and their very existence provides a constant incentive to put them to use. It is not surprising, therefore, that with the development of specialized forces war becomes an endemic activity of the human race. A system of this kind may be called an "international system" even though the city states and empires among which the system originated were different in many respects from the nation states of today.

War can be divided into two large classes: wars of conquest and wars of deterrence. Wars of conquest are mainly for the purpose of bringing new areas of land and most of the people living in these areas under the control of the war-making polity. At one extreme of this we have wars of extermination designed simply to eliminate another group and settle their land with the people of the invading state. These are most likely to take place where an aggressively expanding society with rising population and an advanced technology for the day expands into territory previously controlled by less numerous and less technically advanced people. The invasion of the Americas and Australia by Europeans is a case in point. The original inhabitants were for the most part not exterminated, but they were driven off their own lands and forced into reservations. A quite common pattern is the enslavement of the conquered populations or at least their demotion to the position of a lower class. Slaves are also frequently part of the booty of war and a conquered population may be transported to other places where they are more useful to the conqueror than on their previous territory. The Greeks and Arabs did a good deal of this. The African slave trade of the seventeenth and eighteenth centuries is a singularly painful blot on the human record.

At the other end of the scale of wars of conquest, we have wars of liberation intended to undo a previous conquest or to dismantle an old empire and create new sovereign states. A variant to this is the internal split, where a portion of an old state breaks away to form a new one, even though they may not have had a history of conquest. The American Revolution was something like this, although the status of the American colonies before the Revolution had something of the aspect of a conquered territory.

Once an international system has been established for a number of different and sovereign states of approximately the same technical level, wars of conquest become too expensive and unrewarding and the system tends to drift over toward deterrence, as we have seen in Chapter 7. Deterrence is a system of threat-counterthreat, but it has a certain fundamental instability because of the depreciation of credibility with time, to the point where it is almost bound to be challenged. A war of deterrence is designed, therefore, to reestablish the credibility of the threats of the various parties and so restore an unstable peace, stable until the threat credibility deteriorates again.

THE FOUR PHASES OF A WAR-PEACE SYSTEM

I have argued that there are four "phases" of an international system.[5] The first is stable war, in which war is virtually continuous and regarded as the normal state of affairs between the parties. In tribal societies this is not uncommon and in civilized societies there have been certain periods that could be described in this way, like the Hundred Years' War between Britain and France, the Thirty Years' War in Central Europe, and indeed the Vietnam war, which lasted for a whole generation. War is costly to both parties, however, and it is not surprising that efforts to moderate it began quite early. Diplomacy begins in the international system certainly by the time of the Hittite Empire and probably long before. Ambassadors are exchanged, royal marriages are arranged, and treaties are signed. Stable war thereby passes into unstable war in which war is interrupted by periods of arranged peace, but war is still regarded as the norm. The situation in the Middle East has been close to this phase in the last generation.

As the intervals of peace get longer and the costs of war rise, unstable war imperceptibly shades over into unstable peace, that is, a situation in which peace is regarded as the norm although interrupted by occasional war. The central international system of Europe and its appendages since 1648 has approximated this condition. Unstable peace often may slide imperceptibly over into stable peace, a situation in which the probability of war between the parties is so low that it really plays no part in the calculations. North America and Scandinavia achieved this in the nineteenth century. It may be that we will achieve it in the whole temperate zone before the year 2000, but we do not really have it yet. These phase changes in the international system represent in the main growth of integrative structures. This involves diminishing the costs of conflict by transforming the nature of threats and substituting legal procedures, arbitration, reconciliation, and so on (in other words conflict management) for systems of conquest and deterrence.

We see the same thing happening in other fields of conflict. Industrial conflict develops partly because of cultural differences between employers and employed, making for failures of empathy and understanding, and also because of the perception of real conflict in which power can be used to alter distribution of welfare. In the initial stages of industrialization there is little overt conflict between employers and employed, perhaps because the psychological status of the employed may still be that of an internally conquered people. With rising wealth and education, however, labor organizations get underway and strikes for recognition and for contracts appear, which have some parallels with "wars of liberation," though they are usually much less damaging. Sporadic disaffection and sabotage often precedes this, which is a little parallel to the sporadic revolts of individuals and small groups in a conquered society. With the development of a system of industrial jurisprudence, however, industrial conflict tends to diminish in intensity, though not necessarily in extent. We can trace the four stages, which are somewhat similar to the four stages in international conflict; however, stable war would be almost impossible because of its immense destructiveness to both parties. Unstable peace, however, is very common, that is, agreements of "treaties" punctuated by recurring strikes. In many industries this does lead into stable peace in which strikes are virtually unknown.

Other forms of conflict, such as marital conflict, do not exhibit these clear phases. Marital conflict in its extreme form is rather like stable war. There may be a sharp systems break in divorce, which really represents a solution of conflict by increasing distance. The flight of refugees from a country that has become intolerable to them is a rather similar phenomenon. Just as divorced persons occasionally remarry, refugees return to their homeland, but both of these phenomena are rather rare.

DIALECTICS AS "WHEN IT MATTERS WHO WINS"

Exactly where we draw the line between what we call dialectical processes and what we want to call nondialectical processes in this broad spectrum of social dynamic patterns from the nonconflictual to the conflictual is a linguistic rather than a substantive question. Those who see dialectics as virtually synonymous with dynamics would want to draw the line very far over to the conflictual side and identify unconscious competition, for instance, as a dialectical process. Evolutionists, on the other hand, perceive dialectical processes on the whole as peripheral and want to draw the line between those processes that involve conscious conflict and those that do not. This is a matter of symbolic rather than substantive importance, although, as we have seen earlier, symbols are sometimes a very significant element in social dynamics. The substantive question, which is very difficult to answer, is just what is the quantitative or even qualitative significance of dialectical processes, interpreted narrowly as involving conscious conflict, struggle, victory and defeat, winning or losing, revolution and counterrevolution, war and peace, in the great four-dimensional tapestry of the universe?

In physical and chemical evolution I would argue that these processes are of no importance; in biological evolution I would argue that they may be of occasional importance, but on the whole are peripheral to the nonconflictual processes of ecological interaction. We can perhaps frame the question by asking, "When does it matter who wins?" In physical and chemical evolution the question is meaningless; in biological evolution it is not wholly meaningless because sometimes it does matter who wins the fights between animals because it is the winning animal who transmits its genetic structure to the next generation, so that fighting is part of the selective process and the ability to win fights may be favored in selection. On the other hand, this form of selection can easily be adverse for the survival of the species. When the individuals of the species get continually better at winning fights, it may mean they get worse in all other innumerable things that are significant in the survival function. On the whole, therefore, I would be prepared to defend the proposition very vigorously and indeed even fight for it dialectically and argue that it mattered who won, that dialectical processes in biological evolution are peripheral and have had very little effect on the biological history of the earth.

DIALECTICAL PROCESSES AFFECT THE DETAILS RATHER THAN THE LARGE PATTERNS OF HISTORY

When it comes to social systems, the problem of assessing the impact of dialectical processes is much more difficult. In social systems fighting and struggle are more important and, for a good many people in a good many times and places, it has mattered very much who wins. Nevertheless, the question whether it "really" matters who wins, especially in the larger perspective of the movement of the system through time, is by no means clear. We can perhaps take an analogy from sports. It undoubtedly matters a great deal to the teams who are playing and their supporters who wins a particular match, otherwise the activity would not arouse the enthusiasm it does. In considering the history of sport as a whole, however, it is clear that who wins any particular match is practically irrelevant. If one team becomes so superior to the others that it wins every time, this may destroy the interest in the sport, which would be destructive to it. In order to sustain interest, each team should have at least an approximately equal number of wins and losses over a period of years. A competitive sport seems to be clearly a dialectical process. Nevertheless the outcome of the dialectic really does not matter in terms of the survival of the sport. The sport will only survive if it can sustain interest and be exciting, and this can happen only if winning has a strong random element.

Sport no doubt is an extreme case. If we look at something like the spread of languages, we find that the dominance of a particular language in an area may depend a good deal on "who wins," because the dominant language tends to be that of the dominant culture, and cultures frequently establish dominance by some dialectical process in which they have won over their competitors. Thus, if we ask ourselves why English is the predominant language of international intercourse today even though Chinese is spoken by probably the largest number of people, the answer is partly that the English "won." For instance, they took Canada from the French, certainly by a dialectical process, and this probably led eventually to the sale of Louisiana to the predominantly English-speaking United States. Australia probably speaks English because the English wrested command of the seas, again a dialectical process, from the Dutch, Portuguese, and later the French by the end of the eighteenth century. Or perhaps Australia speaks English partly because the English *lost* command of the seas to the French at the time of the American Revolution, which permitted that revolution to proceed, and caused England to look for other places to dispose of its criminals and unwanted populations, at least in the early stages of settlement.

Russia is certainly a centrally planned economy today because of a whole series of dialectical processes that began with World War I which Russia lost. With the ensuing loss of legitimacy of the old regime, it was possible for a determined power seeker like Lenin to seize power, and in effect to take the role vacated by the czar and expand it by bringing Russian industrial organizations under the control of the state. Europe became Christian because in a certain sense the Christian church "won" over its adversaries and became the receiver of the bankrupt Roman Empire. In detail, it is clear that human history has been profoundly influenced by some dialectical processes.

If the dialectical processes had gone the other way, however, and somebody else had won, would it have made very much difference to the larger patterns of human history? This is a question that is very hard to answer, but one suspects it would have made much less difference than most historians think. If England had been less successful in winning wars and establishing naval power after Queen Elizabeth, if Spain had not declined under the debilitating burden of empire achieved too soon, or if France had not committed the terrible mistake of driving out the industrious Huguenots, but had tolerated nonconformity as England did and so perhaps might have pioneered the Industrial Revolution, then the Spanish or French, which encapsulated themselves as regional languages, might have been the world language instead of English. If all this had happened, would the general pattern have looked very different? The answer is almost certainly "No." It would have been a little better for the world if Spanish, which is easier for most people to pronounce and spell than English, had become the world language. But that some language would become a world language by the end of the twentieth century through the essentially nondialectical processes of the general growth of knowledge was highly probable. This led to the improvement of transportation and communication. It also led to the development of a world-wide "superculture" of science and science-based industries and artifacts. This in turn has produced a great breakdown in isolation, especially in urban and industrial centers. This therefore created a situation in which some language understood by a majority of people in the superculture became a world language simply because it had the most payoffs for learning on the part of people who did not speak it as a native language.

Similarly, after the breakup of the Roman Empire and the consequent increase in the isolation of its various parts, it is not surprising that Latin developed into a number of rather different but related languages from Rumanian to Portuguese by processes that are only indirectly connected with dialectics. On the other hand, if the official language of France is that of Paris rather than that of Avignon, it is because the dialectical processes of French history led to situations in which Paris "won" and became the dominant power and therefore the dominant language. Similarly, if standard Spanish is Castilian, it is for exactly the same reason. But if we ask, "Would it have mattered much if it had gone the other way?" the answer is "No." It really matters very little what particular language people speak. What does matter is what they have to say and how well they can say it. While, as we have seen, this is in some small degree a function of language, other cultural factors are much more important in the overall skills and potentialities of communication.

DIALECTICS MATTERS ON "WATERSHEDS"

It would seem that a strong case can be made from the point of view of the larger perspectives of the universe and even from the perspectives of human history that dialectical processes are mainly peripheral and of local importance only. There is one possible exception to this principle. We have to allow for the possibility that there are times in the larger dynamic process when there are "watershed systems," that is, situations in which relatively small changes at the moment will cumulate into much larger changes later on. These are the moments especially at the beginning of the great phyla of development. At these moments dialectical processes may be of great importance. It really does matter who "wins," because that may determine on which side of the watershed the system will fall. These watershed moments, however, are extremely hard to identify, almost impossible to identify at the time. The creation of evolutionary potential at the beginning of a phylum is apt to be an event of low probability that in fact comes off. It is impossible to plan for, usually impossible to recognize at the time, and therefore quite impossible to have a conflict about. Even at these moments therefore, if dialectical processes are important, it is only because they are part of a generally random structure of these critical moments. Furthermore, it is often those who lose fights and flee who become founders of a new phylum elsewhere (compare the so-called "founder effect" in biology), or who are stimulated by defeat to reorganize themselves and create new evolutionary potential.

The general conclusion is therefore that struggle is peripheral, that if we push something up the wrong hill, it will slide down again, and that activity in organizing conflict—forming political parties, agitating, fighting wars, and making revolutions—although certainly very important to the people who participate in it, has very little long-run effect. It is the processes of growth and production rather than of conflict that are really significant. The man who makes the better mousetrap, who makes two blades of grass grow where one grew before, who really pushes the human race along the road that it is going, is really more significant than the conquerors, the revolutionaries, the Alexanders, the Napoleons, the George Washingtons, the Lenins, and the Maos. These people create eddies in the stream, but contribute very little to its progress.

DIALECTICS OVERESTIMATED BECAUSE IT IS DRAMATIC

The case for the above view is very strong. Why then do so few people believe it? Dialectics in many different forms has a surprisingly good press. Most people believe that struggle is very important and that it is important also to be on the right side in a conflict. We must strive, stripped for action, to build up stress and cultivate strength (Why do all these words begin with "str"? Is there something peculiar here about our Anglo-Saxon heritage?). Religion adds its own commendations—fight the good fight with all thy might, conquer evil, struggle with Satan. The whole vocabulary of sport adds to the dialectical rhetoric—fight, fight, fight for dear old whatever it is; play the game, yes, but win; nice guys come in last. Political rhetoric adds its own notes to the chorus—the war against poverty, freedom fighters, the cultural revolution. In all this uproar it is pretty hard for any other point of view to be heard.

Part of the difficulty is that the human race has an enormous and by no means unreasonable passion for the dramatic, and conflict is much more dramatic than production. Nobody ever wrote a great poem about how a hen is produced from an egg or a great play about an automobile being produced on the assembly line. The awful truth about the universe—that it is not only rather a muddle, but also pretty dull—is wholly unacceptable to the human imagination. Nevertheless, it is the dull, nondialectical processes that hold the world together, that move it forward, and that provide the setting and the media within which the dialectical processes take place. Evolution is the theatre, dialectics the play. It is a tragic error to mistake the play for the theatre, however, because that all too easily ends in the theatre burning down, and then it would be pretty hard to have another play. Unless there is reasonably widespread appreciation of the proper role of dialectical processes, these tend to get out of hand and become extremely destructive.

I have argued indeed that dialectical philosophies are catastrophic because they divert far too much effort into dialectical processes that do more harm than good.[6] It is only as we develop nondialectical philosophies stressing productivity rather than conflict, integrative systems rather than threat, economics rather than politics, that the dialectical processes—which are a necessary part of the human enterprise—will become fruitful rather than pathological.

Appendix to Chapter 12:
THE HEGELIAN-MARXIAN DIALECTIC

Dialectical philosophers, and especially Marxists, may object that I have not been fair to them in confining dialectical processes to those in which there is a struggle and conscious conflict. In the Hegelian philosophy the dialectical process is seen as a pattern of successive systems. Whatever it starts with is the "thesis." The thesis, because of inner contradictions in its structure, produces the "antithesis." It is the interaction between the thesis and the antithesis that produces the synthesis. This interaction may not necessarily be conflictual, although it is usually thought of in this way. The synthesis now becomes the new thesis, and the pattern starts over again. The role of contradiction in this process is very important. The whole theoretical scheme looks at times like an attempt to impose the principles of formal logic on the empirical world.

In Marxism this schema appears as a succession of systems—feudalism, capitalism, culminating in socialism and communism—in which the inner contradictions of each system produce the changes that create its successor, almost in a deterministic ·manner. Contradiction is supposed to stop after the final revolution; as contradictions arise out of the class structure, there will be no more contradictions. This schema finds it hard to accommodate the historical fact that all revolutions have produced a *new* class structure.

I have to confess I find this whole schema very unappealing. It is hard to fit the enormous interactional or complexity of the real world into it. The whole idea of a dialectical succession of systems seems to me to be arbitrary in the light of the essential continuity of the real world. There are, of course, clusters of ecosystems, habitats, and so on, which exhibit ecological succession, but the movement from one to its successor is usually not the result of any contradictions; it is simply the result of cumulative processes of erosion and deposition, coupled with constant mutation and selection. The dialectical schema does perhaps throw some occasional light on reality where we have two related processes that have a degree of independence in their dynamic patterns, but do at times intersect and interact and perhaps contradict each other. The tension between two contradictory tendencies, as we shall see in the next chapter, is occasionally an important explanatory model. This is about as far as I am prepared to go toward Hegel, because I am pretty scared of venturing toward what looks to me like an intellectual disaster area.

NOTES

1. Robert Ardrey, in *The Territorial Imperative* (New York: Atheneum, 1966), completely misses this point (see Chapter 7 of this volume).

2. Neal Miller, "Experimental Studies of Conflict," in *Personality and the Behavior Disorders*, J. McV. Hunt, ed. (New York: Ronald, 1944).

3. John Dollard, et al., *Frustration and Aggression* (New Haven: Yale University Press, 1939).

4. Adam Smith, *The Wealth of Nations* (New York: Modern Library Edition), 532.

5. Kenneth E. Boulding, "The Balance of Peace," *Papers*, Peace Research Society (International), Vol. XIII, 1970, 59-65 (reprinted in *Kenneth Boulding/Collected Papers*, Larry Singell, ed. (Boulder: Colorado Associated University Press, 1975), Vol. V, 371-81).

6. Kenneth E. Boulding, *A Primer on Social Dynamics* (New York: Free Press, 1970).

Chapter 13

Evaluative Change

SELECTION IMPLIES EVALUATION

The dialectical processes of conflict, struggle, winning, and losing discussed in the previous chapter are for the most part short-run disturbances in the larger processes of dynamics of the universe. Even in the dynamics of social systems, where they play a considerable role, they are only occasionally of long-run significance. Nevertheless, these dialectical processes should be regarded as a special case of the larger and more significant class of processes, which might be described as "evaluative change." These processes are not unknown in biological evolution. The process indeed by which a fertilized egg carries out its program clearly contains evaluative elements in that the know-how of the genetic structure is able to select those operations which will carry out the program and reject those which will not. There is a kind of dynamic cybernetics at work here guided by deviations from the "creode" (see p. 108). There is also the larger phenomenon of emergent evolution, which we noted earlier, in which certain general end results, like the improvement of the eye as a means of perception or the development of adaptability through increased complexity in the nervous system, have a generalized survival value, which may lead to their development by a number of different but converging paths.

THE "GOODNESS FUNCTION"

In social systems evaluative change takes on dimensions far beyond what it has in biological systems because of the extraordinary capacity of the human nervous system for imaging the future and evaluating complex structures.

Human behavior, as we have seen in Chapter 10, is profoundly affected by decisions, which in turn affect the dynamic course of the total system. Decisions involve constant evaluation and reevaluation of both past experience and future projections.

All evaluations involve what might be called a "goodness function,"

$$G = g(A, B, C, etc. . .).\tag{1}$$

What we know about G is that it is some indicator that goes up when we perceive things are better and goes down when we perceive things are worse. It is a qualitative indicator rather than a quantitative one, but it is a capacity everybody possesses in their minds and constantly uses. The variables A, B, C, etc. in the argument consist of anything relevant to the evaluative process, and everything in which change is perceived as altering the total state of affairs either for better or for worse. Decisional behavior consists of moving from a condition in which things are perceived as worse to a condition in which they are perceived as better. This is found in animal behavior as well as human behavior, though of course in human behavior it is much more dominant and elaborate.

"STATE" AND "GOAL" EVALUATIONS

The situation is complicated by the fact that there are many goodness indicators and correspondingly many·different goodness functions. A given change may be evaluated as better for this and worse for that, depending on the goodness function we use. One important distinction is between what might be called "state evaluations" and "goal evaluations." In state evaluations we are using an indicator, call it G_1, which is an estimation of whether we are better off or worse off in our immediate condition. It is the kind of indicator we think of when asking the question, "Am I better off today than I was yesterday?" If my house has burned down, I am pretty clearly worse off; if I have lost my job, I am worse off; if I have found a better job, I am better off; if I have married, I am better off; if I have been put in prison, I am worse off; if I have been freed from prison, I am better off. Evaluations of state are extremely important. They do have a profound effect upon decisions of human behavior. If I perceive myself as getting continually better off day by day, I am much less likely to change my patterns of life than if I perceive myself to be getting continually worse off.

There is another indicator of goodness, G_2, however, which is goal-oriented evaluation. This goes up when we are closer to some goal, and down when we are further from it. G_2 can easily be going up when G_1 is going down, and vice versa. If I am a Moslem making a pilgrimage to Mecca, I leave the comforts of my home and my actual state may get worse every day with the discomforts and dangers of travel in increasingly unfamiliar surroundings, but every day brings me nearer to the goal, so G_2 is rising all the time. After I get to Mecca and start on the homeward journey, there is another goal—getting home—here again my G_1 state may get better or worse along the way, as I stay in comfortable inns or wretched ones, encounter storms or fair weather, and so on; but G_2 rises all the time until I get home. A graduate student may exchange a well paid job for the poverty and occasional indignities of student life; again his state evaluation G_1 may go up and down, but G_2 continually rises as he moves toward the goal of a Ph.D. The dialectical processes of conflict can be seen as a special case of goal-oriented behavior and evaluation in which the goal, of course, is to win, to overcome the opponent, to seize power, and so on.

SCOPE OF EVALUATIONS AND THE "DECISION GOODNESS" FUNCTION

There is another set of goodness indicators and functions arising out of the existence of integrative relationships, which depends on the scope, range, or size of the system on behalf of which we are evaluating. Thus, I perceive a given change as being better for me and worse for my family, or better for my family and worse for my country, or better for my country and worse for the world. Here again we are postulating goodness indicators and goodness functions, G_i shall we say for the individual, G_f for the family, G_c for the community, G_n for the nation, G_w for the world, and so on. Just as we may perceive that a worsening of our immediate state brings us closer to our final goal (when G_1 goes down and G_2 goes up), we may also perceive that a worsening of our personal condition, for instance a tax increase, may be better for the country as a whole, so that the same change produces a decline in G_i and a rise in G_n.

How these perceptions affect our behavior depends, of course, on our structure of integrative relationships, particularly on our structure of benevolence or malevolence, as seen in Chapter 9. If I have to make a decision between two alternatives, A and B, and I perceive A as being better for me (increasing G_i) and worse for the country (diminishing G_n), but I perceive B as being worse for me and better for the country, which will I choose? This depends, of course, on the degree to which the other indicators are part of the argument, that is, determining variables of my own goodness function. A patriot will sacrifice his own welfare for the welfare of the country to a degree which depends on the extent of his patriotism. We could postulate what we might call a "decision goodness," G_d, which is always higher for what we choose than what we do not choose and in which the criterion of betterness is choice itself. We can then postulate a decision goodness function,

$$G_d = g_d (A, B, C, \ldots \text{etc.}, G_i, G_f, G_c, G_n, G_w, \text{etc.}) \qquad (2)$$

Any variable in the argument, that is, any "subordinate good," which affects the goodness indicator is a "good" if a rise in it raises the goodness indicator, or a "bad" if a rise in it lowers the goodness indicator. The extent to which any particular variable is a good or a bad is measured, of course, by the size of the change in the goodness indicator per unit of change in the variable produced.[1] Thus, if when a increases by one unit and our perception of goodness in the situation (G) increases a large amount, then a is clearly a very "good" good. If when A increases by one unit, our perception of goodness decreases by a large amount, A is clearly a very "bad" bad. If an increase of one unit in A does not change our perception of goodness in A, then A is neither good nor bad but neutral. Whether A is a good or bad and by how much depends on its "marginal goodness," that is, the amount by which a unit increase in A will increase the "total goodness," G.

There is every reason to suppose that the marginal goodness of virtually any subordinate good or bad diminishes algebraically as we increase the quantity of the subordinate good or bad. This is a generalization of the famous economic principle of diminishing marginal utility. A small quantity of almost anything tends to be a good, though there may be some exceptions to this. As the quantity increases, however, the marginal goodness of the good will diminish until it reaches zero, at which point an increase in the subordinate good is making no contribution to the general good (G) and the general good is at a maximum with respect to the subordinate good. As the subordinate good increases beyond a certain point, its marginal goodness becomes negative and the general good declines. Thus, all goods become bads if we have too much of them and many bads may become goods if they are diminished sufficiently in quantity. This is, of course, the famous principle of the Aristotelian mean. We see this even in regard to the virtues and vices—too much pride is arrogance, too much dignity is pompousness, too much probity is overscrupulousness, too much courage becomes foolhardiness, too much caution becomes cowardice, too much vigor becomes aggressiveness. It is remarkable what a deep sense of this moral nonlinearity is implanted in the language. The fact, however, that our experience of variation in these variables may be rather small often leads us into delusions of linearity. If our range of experience is very limited, for instance, we may not realize that marginal goodness diminishes and therefore fall under the illusion that, if anything is good, more of it is always better.

JOINT PRODUCTION OF GOODS AND BADS

The situation is further complicated by the fact that quantities of goods and bads themselves may be interrelated. An increase in A, which is a good, may produce an increase in B, which is bad. Our evaluation of the increase in A, therefore, must be offset by our evaluation of the increase in B that goes along with it. This is a very large part of the problem of pollution. We have pollution because goods and bads are produced in joint production. We cannot have the goods without also having the bads. We cannot have electric power, which is certainly a good, without producing air pollution at the power station, which is a bad, and without perhaps using up irreplaceable fossil fuels, which is the diminution of a good. We think we cannot have national security, which is a good, without occasional war, which is a bad. We cannot have a strong community, which is a good, without frustrating many individuals, which is a bad. As we shall see later, this joint production of goods and bads is not something accidental, but is very fundamental in the whole evolutionary process and must be accounted for in our evaluations. When goods and bads are interrelated, therefore, we have to face the problem of tradeoffs. No single variable in the argument can be used as a measure of goodness, no matter how good it is, because an increase in it will produce diminutions in other goods and increases in other bads.

The problem of tradeoffs between goods and bads, and also between goods and goods and bads and bads, is one of great difficulty both in theory and in practice and is discussed further in the appendix to this chapter. Perhaps one of the most dangerous illusions of the human race is that of "absolute value," which boils down to an assertion that for some things at least there are no tradeoffs. We can certainly suppose that some things have an infinite price in terms of life; otherwise we would not have martyrdom and war. These occasions are rare, however, and the fact that they must be respected does not mean that they can be generalized. It is particularly dangerous to assume that just because something is bad it should be prohibited. Trying to get rid of one bad often increases another bad or diminishes another good. The great fallacy of moralism is that the moralist tends to assume that, if something is proved to be bad, that is a sufficient argument against it and it should be gotten rid of at all costs. It does not prove anything, however, to show that something is bad unless we can show that something else, and particularly some achievable combination of things, is better.

EVALUATION OF WHOLE SOCIETIES: MORAL GOODS

Because of the existence of integrative structures, evaluation of the qualities and properties of larger groups and whole societies plays an important role in both the dialectical processes among them and the larger emergent evolution patterns that transcend these dialectical processes. A society perceived by its own members as "bad," or at least low on the goodness scale, has a much worse chance in winning in dialectical processes than a society perceived as good or high on the goodness scale. Dialectical processes themselves, of course, tend to polarize these valuations. That is, people tend to think of their own society as good and other societies as bad, unless they happen to belong to a subculture that encourages ethnophobia and xenophilia, i.e., hatred of the in-group and love of the out-group, like W. S. Gilbert's[2] "idiot who praises in enthusiastic tone, Every century but this, and every country but his own." These cultures are rare, however, because selective processes lead to their nonsurvival; ethnophilia and xenophobia seem to be a more general rule, though this too in excess leads to nonsurvival. The processes of conflict often reinforce the conflict no matter what it is about, if only because conflict tends to produce negative identities based on what we are not rather than on what we are (p. 191).

Looking beyond dialectics, however, to the larger processes by which people evaluate groups and larger societies, evaluations may be subject to some kind of long-run evolution that gives certain patterns a bias toward survival. We do perceive what might be called "moral goods," that is, large-scale characteristics of different groups and societies such as wealth, power, justice, equality, freedom, meaningfulness, friendliness, health, excitement, creativity in architecture, music, the arts, religion, sobriety, stability— the list might be considerably extended. We then postulate an overall goodness of society function, G_s,

$$G_s = g_s(W, P, J, E, \text{etc.})\tag{3}$$

which is written as a function of W, P, J, and E, that is, wealth, power, justice, equality, freedom, and so on.

For some of these attributes we have at least moderately good measures. The gross national product, for instance, is at least an approximate measure of the riches of a society, though it is not a very good measure and better measures may be forthcoming.[3] Power in the military sense may be measured by the amount in real terms spent on national defense. At least some statistical measures are available for equality, though they are not very good, as we shall see later. Health can be measured in terms of expectation of life or the proportion of the working force incapacitated by sickness. For education we have statistics about the number of schools, pupils, and amounts of money spent, for what these are worth. When it comes down to such things as justice, freedom, meaningfulness, friendliness, and creativity, indicators are very hard to get and the impressions of most people are fairly vague. If we were to do a world survey asking people to rank the countries of the world in the order of justice, freedom, and creativity, we would probably come out with some very different sets of answers even after we had discounted ethnophilia. Nevertheless, these impressions, vague as they are, are extremely important in developing final assessments, particularly in increasing or decreasing legitimacy. The widespread perception that a particular society is unjust, for instance, diminishes the long-run survival probability of that society, though nobody is really sure what justice means or how to measure it. Looking at the long-run patterns and especially at the future, therefore, these evaluative perceptions are of great importance in giving a constant bias to the selective processes, whether dialectical or nondialectical, as they introduce a bias into the long-run decision-making process.

TRADEOFFS OF MORAL GOODS

In the overall goodness function, some of these moral attributes are cooperative with each other and some may be competitive. Up to a certain point riches are not only very clearly a good, in the sense that getting richer is perceived as getting better, but it is also cooperative with a good many of the other attributes; the richer a society gets, the easier it is to be powerful, just, equalitarian, healthy, well educated, creative, courteous, and friendly. There seems to be a level of grinding poverty at which it is virtually impossible to have any of the other virtues. The Ik tribe in East Africa may be an example of this.[4] On the other hand, there may be a level of moderately stable poverty above the level of destitution in which people are more friendly, more willing to help each other, and more able to be creative in personal relations than they are at a somewhat higher level of riches, where a grasping commercialism may destroy some of the simpler virtues. On the other hand, again, periods of great creativity in the arts, architecture, painting, music, and so on have often coincided with periods of fairly rapidly increasing wealth and the development of a class able to support these achievements, although sometimes again increasing wealth goes along with bad taste and corruption of the arts.

A particularly difficult problem is the interaction between justice and freedom, or between equality and freedom, and among all of these and riches. Freedom in the sense of the absence of governmental intervention and redistributions has a strong tendency to produce inequality, and this may lead to institutions that violate ideas of justice such as excessive subordination, labor peonage, and the like. In the search for equality the Chinese have certainly destroyed the freedom to be different and seem to be producing a cultural monoculture, which may turn out not only to be dull and uncreative, but dangerous in the sense that it destroys reserves of adaptability to meet unforeseen future catastrophes. All oppressive regimes gradually erode their own legitimacy as they fail to conform to emerging moral values.

It is a precarious enterprise to try to identify these emerging moral values; we are always very much in the middle of the process, and the patterns are by no means clear. Nevertheless, certain patterns can be traced and it is important to try to trace them. The better these are understood, the more likely is the human race to direct its attention toward those systems of evaluation which themselves have survival value and conform to the underlying patterns of the dynamic system. Personal and public activity devoted to promoting institutions and systems that do not in fact conform to the underlying dynamics will result in frustration, wasted effort, and movements from better to worse, instead of from worse to better.

THE DRIVE TO WEALTH AND POWER AND ITS DANGERS

There is clearly a long-run drive to wealth and power. Very little can be achieved by poverty and impotence. It is now becoming apparent, however, that the law of diminishing returns applies to this as to any other value. At low levels of wealth and power it is very clear that these are goods and increasing them makes things better. At higher levels, however, we begin to move toward the maximum point M (Figure 13A.1) and beyond this an increase in wealth and power makes things worse rather than better. Poverty and impotence have been so long the lot of the mass of mankind that it is hard for us to accept the possibility that wealth and power might become bads rather than goods. We may now, however, be close to the turning point in the richer countries. No one has any doubt that an increase in per capita real income, say from $100 to $200 to $400, is clearly movement from worse to better. An increase from $5000 to $10,000 to $20,000 to $40,000 is much more dubious, not only because of the environmental consequences, which really should be taken into account in the measure anyway, but also because of the consequences for the overall quality of life and society.

We have to think of wealth not just in terms of some dollar number but also in terms of the structure of what various levels and kinds of wealth really involve and how far the structure is generalizable. Up to a point increasing wealth seems to go along with increasing equality. At low levels of average per capita real income it is almost necessary to have a sharp inequality with a very small group of rich and powerful fulfilling some of the larger potentialities of the human race in architecture and the arts, and the large mass of the poor barely producing enough surplus to sustain their own lives with a little left over to support the rich. The coming of the science-based economy with its enormous increase in the production of almost everything leads to a mass consumption society in which the elimination of poverty becomes possible. Everybody can have enough to eat, good health, attractive clothing, a decent house, opportunities to travel, and the enjoyment and practice of the arts. We are not too far from this in some of the richer countries. Beyond a certain point, however, we run into the problem that increased productivity tends to be confined to the goods-producing sectors where equality is moderately feasible (it is easy for every household to have a TV set), and the released resources increasingly go into personal services where equality is not feasible (maids cannot have maids) and into areas of public goods, like the enjoyment of nature, where equality and the subsequent congestion destroy the very thing we seek to enjoy, as we see in the overuse of our national parks.

We further face the problem acutely in the twentieth century that knowledge, which increases our powers of production, also increases our powers of destruction. Threat systems therefore become increasingly dangerous and we are to the point now indeed with nuclear weapons and the possibility of what Herman Kahn calls the "doomsday machine,"[5] which would destroy all life on earth, where the carrying out of threat, which is an almost essential element in threat systems, becomes so dangerous to the threatener as well as to the threatened that the threat systems themselves must be replaced by other methods of organizing society, or at least limited and legitimated to the point where they are no longer threatening to the society as a whole.

MOVEMENT FROM THREAT TO EXCHANGE TO INTEGRATION

One of the patterns we can discern, therefore, is a movement from threat power toward exchange power toward integrative power. This is not to say that integrative power and integrative systems will absorb all the others. Almost any system, as we have seen, is a mixture of all three. It is abundantly clear that we must move toward diminishing the role of threat in human systems and in social systems. It is less clear that we have to move toward diminishing the role of exchange, although this can be argued. Exchange, as we have seen, is extremely difficult to sustain in the absence of integrative structures. It is an exaggeration, but not wholly untrue, to say that threat is associated with malevolence, exchange with selfishness, and integrative systems with benevolence, because all these things overlap. There can be benevolent threats, as in childrearing. Exchange, as we have seen, requires a small amount of benevolence, or at least no malevolence among the parties, because malevolence and especially mistrust would soon destroy it. Integrative structures go both ways and include both malevolence and benevolence, hate as well as love. Even war has integrative aspects because each side in a fight needs the enemy and cannot fight without it. Still, we shall not go far wrong in supposing that a move toward increasing the importance of integrative structures is also a move toward benevolence.

The weakness of exchange, as we have seen, is that it may produce alienation and a lack of sense of community. Exchange is a simple, rather stripped relationship that involves courtesy but not a deep commitment or a highly meaningful relationship. This means that a society based too much on exchange may fail to develop those integrative structures, that sense of legitimacy and community, necessary to sustain it. The passionate hatred of exchange that we find in Marx may have originated psychologically in his revolt against his father and in what he felt to be an undeserved lack of exchange power in his life-long genteel poverty; but it strikes a responsive chord in those who yearn for the warmth and conviviality of reciprocity. I recall a high school teacher of mine, a historian quite innocent of economics, saying, "Why can't we all just go down to the stores and get what we want without all this nonsense about paying for it?" In complex societies, however, integrative structures are not now capable of taking on the burden of economic and political organization. Even in the socialist countries exchange is a very important part of social organization, because it is not possible to organize large-scale systems without it.

CONCEPTS OF JUSTICE

Justice is such a vague concept that one despairs of ever being able to define it much less measure it. Nevertheless, it has some components that are more susceptible to clear definition and measurement than justice itself. We can perhaps postulate a justice function as we have postulated a goodness function:

$$J = j(A, B, C...)$$ (4)

with J as a function of A, B, C, etc., whatever these may be. Sometimes indeed justice is viewed as almost equivalent to goodness. The justice function would then become identical with the goodness function, but this seems to be a mistake. Justice, for instance, is certainly not the same as freedom, and neither of these are the same as mercy. The proposition that things would be better if we had a little more justice and a little less freedom, or a little less justice and a little more freedom, is a proposition that cannot be brushed off as meaningless and yet it certainly suggests that justice is part of the argument of the goodness function and is not in itself a measure of it.

A good many different concepts of justice have been propounded since Plato and all of them perhaps constitute variables in the argument of the justice function. We have first of all the idea of equality and that of the optimum degree of equality or inequality as constituting justice. Gross inequality is clearly unjust; complete equality regardless of merit is also unjust.

A second concept of justice is that of desert—people should get what they deserve. This is a problem in terms of social exchange or reciprocity. Exchange should be of equal value in some sense, though this is by no means easy to define. Everybody makes positive or negative contributions to society and in return receives a contribution from society. One concept of justice is that this overall personal exchange of the individual with society should be on reasonably equal terms. Anyone who gives a great deal to society and gets very little back is being treated unjustly. Similarly somebody who does nothing for or even damages society, but receives a lot from it, is also an example of injustice, though it is hard to call him a victim. The theory of punishment and legal justice emerges out of this view that, if a person makes a negative contribution to the society, society should make a negative contribution to him.

Yet a third concept of justice is related to alienation and community. A just society in this view is one from which nobody feels alienated, and of which everybody feels themselves to be a member. Alienation is a psychological phenomenon and its sources are obscure. It is related to the processes of legitimation and delegitimation. People are alienated from institutions, which they feel in some sense are illegitimate, but to which they have to relate. There has really been very little empirical study of this phenomenon, which tends to be used as an instrument of rhetoric rather than of knowledge, but it undoubtedly exists and at certain times and places can be quite important.

Different people undoubtedly give different weights to these three variables in the justice function; conservatives tend to give more weight to the second and radicals to the first and the third. What determines these weights we really do not know, which is one reason why justice is so extraordinarily difficult to measure.

OTHER MORAL GOODS: HEALTH, MEANINGFULNESS

Some of the other attributes of society may be mentioned briefly. Health is one of these variables where an improvement from low levels is unequivocally good, but where beyond a certain point difficult evaluative problems arise. Health is not measured by the mere preservation of life. The ideal is for everybody to maintain good health to the day of death, though this may not be possible. For some people at any rate ill health may be a stimulus to a creativity that otherwise might not have been realized. The medical profession and the health industry in general may push their activities to the point where they diminish the amount of health rather than increase it, simply because too many sick old people are kept alive beyond the allotted span of their potential. The prolongation of an active human life beyond the present genetically determined span is not wholly off the human agenda if we can discover what the mechanism of aging is and act to correct it. Any effective prolongation of active human life, even say to 100 or 200 years, would present a very deep crisis for existing institutions, all of which are geared to the present level of life expectancy.[6]

Meaningfulness is another tricky concept that cannot be left out of the goodness function. It is precisely in societies that have lost their meaning to people that people become alienated and legitimacy decays. Meaning is often given by identification with goals. This is one reason why the morale of a society is often high in what is perceived as a struggle, such as a war. Dialectical processes indeed insofar as they produce goal-oriented behavior that is perceived as important, in which for instance the goal of winning becomes overriding, often tend to increase the sense of meaning and to diminish alienation. Tennyson's vision of the future peaceful world in "Locksley Hall": "There the common sense of most shall hold a fretful realm in awe, and the kindly earth shall slumber, lapt in universal law," is a vision of the future frighteningly reminiscent of a wet Sunday afternoon in Dullsville.

Meaningfulness is related to the problem of excitement and dullness. Almost all visions of utopia and indeed of heaven sound rather dull. The socialist countries indeed are dull. They lack creativity in the arts or any sense of intellectual excitement. They are both imitative and pedestrian. Here again, there may be a role for a continuing dialectic, if only to keep people from falling asleep in the great theatre of the world. There is a challenge here for the artistic community to perceive exciting and interesting patterns of drama in the nondialectical as well as in the dialectical processes.

WHY EVALUATIVE DYNAMICS FAILS TO CLOSE GAP BETWEEN IMAGES OF THE REAL AND IDEAL

The dynamics of evaluational systems always begins with some perception of a gap between images of the real and the ideal. There must then be some cybernetic system that sets in motion processes of change intended to close the gap. If the gap is closed, that ends the process. In continuing dynamic processes, however, the gap fails to close for one of two reasons. The decisions that lead to the activity designed to close the gap may be unrealistic in the sense that the dynamics of the situation do not respond to decisions in moving the world in the way the decisions intend. A thermostat will not maintain the temperature if the furnace is broken no matter how good the instructions are that the thermostat sends down to it. The second reason is that the ideals themselves may change so that, as the real pursues the ideal, the ideal retreats before it and the gap remains. This can happen because ideals have a dynamic of their own, which does not respond sensitively to perceptions of a failure to close the gap. The reverse may also happen in that failure to close the gap between the real and the ideal may result in a movement of the ideal toward the real rather than the real toward the ideal. This might be called the "sour grapes principle." The fox, we recall, who could not reach the grapes, decided that they were no good and he did not want them anyway. This is also Buddhist economics—if we cannot get what we want, we decide to want what we can get; if we cannot get much, we decide to be content with little. The dynamics of the ideal are often a very complex interaction between these two opposing forces, with the sour grapes principle tending to bring the ideal toward the real and the processes of emergent evolution tending to push the ideal still further from the real, as the realization of one ideal creates a demand for a new one. The gap itself indeed may be a positive value (some people prefer a cheerful hypocrisy to a dour morality), and if we are too successful in closing it, there will be pressures to reopen it.

The current patterns of economic development show many examples of failure to close the gap between the ideal, which is rapid growth toward riches, and the realities of poor and relatively stagnant societies. Some societies like Burma abandon the game, shut themselves off from the world so that expectations will not be aroused, and try to develop falling expectations rather than rising achievements. Two patterns seem to make for rapid development. One is a well-governed free-market pattern like Japan and West Germany, in which the government provides the framework but the main developing institutions are private. This pattern seems to have produced the highest rate of economic growth. The other pattern is the tight, centrally planned economy with a large proportion of resources devoted to investment by the state and with low consumption levels imposed on the mass of the people. The Soviet Union and the eastern European countries are examples of this.

The failures of development seem to be those societies that fall between these two stools in that they have enough socialism to prevent private development but not enough to create public development. Uruguay, Argentina, Chile, Indonesia, India, and Egypt are good examples in the last generation. Here the failure to understand the real dynamics of development on the part of government decision-makers especially may lead to severe failure to narrow the gap.

The Vietnam war was a good example of failure on the part of the United States to understand the patterns of political power in the international system, particularly the failure to understand the relations between power and legitimacy. The United States had an enormous threat power and economic power in Vietnam, but it was ultimately helpless because it failed to establish its legitimacy.

THE DIFFICULT DYNAMICS OF EQUALITY

Thy dynamics of equality is particularly subtle. Attempts to create greater equality are often frustrated as a result. Equality is always the property of some kind of distribution, for instance, of wealth, income, power, or even beauty and brains. It is not always easy to say whether one distribution is more unequal than another because distributions have many dimensions. Two distributions can have the same Gini index and still be very different in other respects, for instance in terms of skewness or of class structure. These are rather secondary considerations, however, because our perceptions of inequality are usually quite gross and statistical refinements make very little difference to them.

Distribution of anything at any given moment of time is just a cross-section of the total distributional process by which the distribution changes. We must understand the process of distribution through time, therefore, if we are to produce change that will move distributions toward our ideal, whatever it may be. Too much thinking in this area is of a static nature in that it simply contemplates an existing distribution, criticizes it, and then proposes a once-and-for-all change. Insofar as distributions are the result of equilibrium processes, a change may be simply a disturbance and the old distribution will reestablish itself. If we are to establish a new equilibrium distribution, we have to understand the dynamics by which distributions change and by which equilibria are maintained.

In biological systems there seems to be a rough approach toward equilibrium in the distribution of the sizes of living organisms. This is dependent in turn on the niches available for different structures. For instance, within a given ecosystem there may be niches for microorganisms, insects, birds, mammals, trees, grasses, bushes, and so on. There are different niches for different sizes—small things live in the cracks under the shadows of large things, and so on. Somewhat the same principle goes for the sizes of social organizations. Size is limited as in biological systems by the principle that there are diminishing returns to scale for each type of structure beyond a certain point. Large corporations have mostly expanded to the point or even beyond the point where there are no longer economies of scale. Any further expansion would weaken their position. In the cracks between the large corporations, many small organizations flourish with different structures, like the gas station and the corner grocery. Somewhat the same principle applies to nations. Here perhaps the diseconomies are those of heterogeneity rather than of scale, so that relatively homogeneous countries like the United States, Russia, and China can thrive—often with small buffer states on their borders—whereas India might well be better off if it broke up into smaller, more homogeneous states. In any case, the condition of equality of size seems to be unstable and will move toward some kind of equilibrium inequality.

The dynamics of distribution of wealth and income is much more complex than that of organizational size. What happens to the distribution of wealth depends partly on the laws and customs of inheritance. If an inheritance is broken up among a larger number of heritors, this tends toward equality; if it is passed on intact to the eldest son under primogeniture, for instance, this tends to perpetuate inequality. There is also what is sometimes called the "Matthew principle"—for whomsoever hath, to him shall be given[7] —that is, the more wealth one has, the easier it becomes to accumulate more. If this model were to work unhindered, a position of equality in distribution would be an unstable equilibrium. If there were some random movement that made some people a little wealthier than others, the wealthier ones would increase in wealth faster than the less wealthy ones, and the difference between them would widen. Those that got started earlier would end up being the richest; those who fell below the line at which accumulation was possible would find themselves getting poorer and poorer until they reached the subsistence level. If they fell below that, of course, they would simply die. Such a system is likely to reach an equilibrium with part of the society very rich and part of it very poor.

There are, however, offsetting principles to the Matthew principle. One is that wealth, and especially inherited wealth, makes people careless and they tend to lose it. This is the "shirtsleeves to shirtsleeves in three generations" syndrome. There is not much longitudinal empirical study of this process to see how important the phenomenon really is in different societies. There may be a heavy random factor, for instance, in stock market capitalism; people lose wealth in the lottery just as easily as they gain it, and those who lose it then find by the Matthew principle that it is hard to get back. Another corrective to the Matthew principle is the development of a grants system from the rich to the poor. This begins as private charity arising out of personal pity-gifts to beggars, for instance. In modern states it becomes systematized in the form of progressive taxation, welfare payments, negative income taxes, and so on. If this is sufficient to offset the Matthew principle, there may then be a dynamic movement toward equality. In the United States we seem to have reached something of an equilibrium between the Matthew principle and its offsets, because the distribution of wealth and income in proportional terms has remained virtually stable for the last 25 years.

EQUALITY IN THE DISTRIBUTION OF POWER

The distribution of power is an even trickier problem because of the many different kinds of power. In socialist countries the distribution of wealth is more equal than it is in capitalist countries. The distribution of income is not very equal, mainly because in modern society one of the most important forms of wealth is skill and knowledge embodied in the individual mind and body. This could only be expropriated in a socialist slave state. As long as individuals are free to own their own bodies and minds, this will be a source of substantial inequality of income. Inequality of political power in socialist states is very great because of the concentration of organization in the hands of the state and the party. A socialist state is a one-firm state and power, which in capitalist societies is distributed among government, business, and other social organizations, is heavily concentrated in the state in socialist societies. Stalin had power far beyond that possessed by an American president or the president of General Motors and he used that power to create a very large amount of human misery.

The Matthew principle applies to the concentration of power as well as to the concentration of wealth up to a point, because the powerful find it easier to add to their power than do the impotent. Limiting factors come into play, however. One of these is again inheritance, as when Alexander or Charlemagne divided their empire among their successors. Another is grants of power to others from those who have more power than they know how to manage, as William the Conqueror granted much of the land of England to his knights, or as a socialist state may decentralize operations into semi-independent trusts or regions. The growth of democratic institutions represents another possible source of wider distribution of power. It arises mainly out of the dynamics of the integrative system, which lead to the gradual inclusion within the national community of groups of people of lower status, as in the extensions of the franchise.

We thus see the total dynamic of equality as the interaction between two long-run opposing broad tendencies. The larger dynamic makes equality unstable and leads into inequalities of all kinds, of which the Matthew principle is only a part. The countervailing tendency is the growth of integrative structures and sentiment that lead to the eventual inclusion of all human beings into a common human community. It is this latter tendency that leads to structural changes which offset the forces leading toward inequality. This is by no means easy and very often the things that are done in the name of equality actually turn out to reinforce the dynamic that leads to inequality, as socialism, for instance, enormously increased the inequality of power. Socialism in the form of centrally planned economies concentrates the three major forms of power in the hands of a small group of party leaders, with high concentration of threat power because they control the state, exchange power because they control the capital of the society, and integrative power because they control the party and the propaganda machine.

In the United States the drive toward equality led to the doctrine of the separation of powers and a polycentric society. Even here, the Matthew principle operated to concentrate wealth, and wealth was frequently able to buy political power. Nevertheless, in spite of some concentration of power in the hands of the president, the system of checks and balances is by no means dead, as the Watergate episode showed.

We are dealing here with systems of great complexity and some dynamic instability, so it is often very hard to know which way the cat will jump. Nevertheless, as we understand them better, we have a better chance not only of survival, but also of moving toward a better world rather than a worse world as judged by constantly emerging moral values.

Appendix to Chapter 13:
THE THEORY OF THE GOODNESS FUNCTION

The mathematical properties of the goodness function in all its various forms are crucial in human evaluations, decisions, and policies. This appendix is a brief introduction to the complexities of the problem.

If we take any variable in the goodness function, say A, and we hold all the other variables constant, we can postulate a section of the goodness function in the G-A plane, which will look something like Figure 13A.1. Here we measure A horizontally, G vertically, the section of the goodness function as the line LMN; when A is zero, there is likely to be some positive level of goodness, OL, depending on the other variables; as A rises, goodness rises at first from L to M, reaches a maximum at M, and as A rises still further goodness declines. If A is very large, goodness may even decline to zero at N, which would represent perhaps death. Between L and M, that is, as A rises from zero to L, A is a good, that is, an increase in A increases $G; \frac{dG}{dA}$ is positive. When we expand the problem even to two subordinate variables, it becomes much more complex, as illustrated in Figure 13A.2. Here we take two of the variables of the goodness function, A and B, measuring A horizontally and B vertically. Any point in the field then represents a combination of quantities of A and B. For each of these combinations we can postulate a goodness measure, G, rising vertically above the field, so that we have as it were a mountain of goodness rising above the plane of the diagram. This could be represented by contours. Let us suppose just for the sake of the exposition that we can measure goodness in a cardinal number. We suppose a maximum position of a goodness of 10 at point M; around this is a contour labelled 9, meaning all points representing combinations of A and B with a goodness of 9. Around this again would be a contour 8, and so on down to zero, which again may represent death. If we take a section of this figure along the horizontal line RST, B is constant equal to OR and A is increasing from R to T; this will be something like Figure 13A.1. As A increases, goodness rises from 5 to 6, reaches a maximum of 7 at S, and then declines to T. S, where the horizontal line touches contour, is the point of maximum goodness along the line RT, where the contour is horizontal. Line M_aM_a' goes through all these points on the different contours and shows all the points where for a given value of B, A is at the point where goodness is at a maximum. Similarly, the line M_bM_b' goes through all the points where the goodness contours are vertical and B is correspondingly at a maximum. These two lines divide the figure into four quadrants. In the quadrant bounded by M_bMM_a, both are goods, that is, an increase in either increases G. In the quadrant bounded by M_aMM_b', B is a good but A is a bad. In the quadrant bounded by $M_b'MM_a'$, both A and B are bads. In the quadrant bounded by $M_a'MM_b$, B is a bad and A is a good.

Now let us suppose that the line OK_1L_1 shows how much B has to be associated with each quantity of A, or how much of A for each quantity of B. This is the joint production function. The best position we can reach on this line is K_1, where it touches the goodness contour, in this case being the contour 8. At K_1, however, we notice that B is a good, that is, an increase in B still increases goodness, but A is a bad; A, that is, is a pollutant and B is a good. If, however, the joint production line is OK_2L_2, with an optimum at K_2, in this case A is the good and B is the bad. The difference in the two cases, of course, is that in the first case we have to have a lot of A in order to get a little B, so that A is likely to be the pollutant. In the second case we have to have a lot of B in order to get a little A, so B is likely to be the pollutant. This is a conclusion that intuitive thinking would be unlikely to

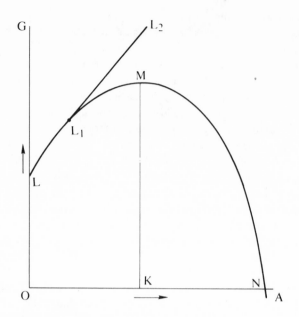

Figure 13A.1: The Goodness Function of One Variable

reach, especially because it is very rare to find major changes in joint production functions, and our experience only ties along the one with which we are familiar. There have been cases something like this for instance in oil refining, however, where in the early days kerosene was the main product and gasoline was a nuisance; later gasoline became the main product and kerosene became the nuisance. In this case it was because of the shift in demand. If the joint production line goes through the maximum point of satiation, that is, an increase in either of them makes no difference to us. What is particularly interesting about this analysis is that with joint products we are best off where one of them is a pollutant and does become a bad. If, of course, we stay in the quadrant M_bMM_a, that is, with small enough amounts of both variables, both of them are goods. If we can expand beyond this to where one of them becomes a bad, however, we will be better off. It is not surprising, therefore, that pollution is a universal problem.

Suppose now that the two variables are not joint products but competitive products, that is, the more we have of one, the less we can have of the other. Our production curve looks like $C_1D_1E_1$, where the optimum position is D_1 in which the line touches the goodness contour. In this case both of the variables are in such quantities that they are goods at the optimum point. Suppose now we have very large amounts of these alternative goods, so that the production line is $C_2D_2E_2$. We get the extraordinary result that the optimum position is where they are both bads. If we try to limit them to the

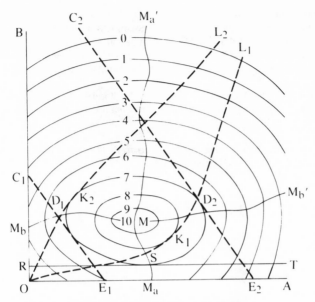

Figure 13A.2: The Goodness Function of Two Variables

point where one of them is a good and the other a bad (as at C_2 or D_2), we will be worse off than if we permitted one to expand and the other to contract to a point where they were both bads. It is virtually impossible to think of examples of this situation, however, because we live for the most part in a world of scarcity in which extremes of overabundance are virtually unknown.

The tradeoff problem as represented by the line $C_1 D_1 E_1$ is very real. It is indeed at the very core of economic life, where the facts of scarcity mean that, if we want more of one good, we have to have less of another. The price system and the market indeed reflect the alternative cost structure and the productive process. In order to get one more unit of A, we have to attract resources that will diminish our production of B by two units. Two units of B is the alternative cost of A, and if the ratio of exchange in the market is not the same, there are likely to be shifts in the size of the A-producing industry and the B-producing industry, which will bring the market price toward the alternative cost ratio.[8]

NOTES

1. In the language of economists, we would think of these variables as factors of production of goodness and their goodness or badness as measured by the marginal goodness product, such as $\frac{dG_d}{dA}$.

2. W. S. Gilbert, The Mikado.

3. James Tobin and William Nordhaus, in *Economic Growth* (New York: Columbia University Press, for the National Bureau of Economic Research, 1972), have developed a "Measure of Economic Welfare" (MEW), but it has not yet come into general use.

4. Colin M. Turnbull, *The Mountain People* (New York: Simon & Schuster 1972).

5. Herman Kahn, *Thinking About the Unthinkable* (New York: Aron Books, 1964).

6. Kenneth E. Boulding, "The Menace of Methuselah: Possible Consequences of Increased Life Expectancy," *Journal of the Washington Academy of Sciences*, 55, 7 (Oct. 1965), 171–179.

7. Matthew 13:12.

8. See Kenneth E. Boulding, *Economic Analysis* (4th ed.; New York: Harper and Row, 1966), Vol. I, Ch. 4, for further details.

Chapter 14

Limits

"OVERSHOOT" SYSTEMS

The publication of the Club of Rome reports[1] has drawn attention in a dramatic way to the problems that are likely to emerge in the twentieth and twenty-first centuries because of expanding population, the exhaustion of presently known resources, and increasing pollution. The models used by these reports in making their projections are not different in principle from those of celestial mechanics. They rely on a set of interrelated difference equations with constant parameters derived for the most part from past experience. The computer has enabled us to handle large numbers of these equations simultaneously, which would be difficult to do in pencil and paper mathematics, though not necessarily impossible. The computer "spaghetti," that is, a printout in the form of time charts, is a picture of the future that is implied in the assumptions and the constant parameters. These are projections rather than predictions. They tell us what will happen if certain things go on much as they have been going on without change.

The picture these models present is one of a system approaching certain limits on some fairly plausible assumptions. In most of the models it does not approach these limits gradually and gently, but has an "overshoot" followed by subsequent collapse. An overshoot is what happens when a system that is moving toward some sort of equilibrium gathers sufficient momentum on the way and shoots past the equilibrium point, then eventually is pulled toward the equilibrium point again, which it again overshoots, and so on, repeating this in a cyclical movement that is usually convergent to the equilibrium. The oscillations of a pendulum about its lowest point, which is the point of equilibrium, or the twang of a plucked string around its point of ultimate rest are good examples of systems of this kind. They are very common in the physical world, much less common in the biological world, and by no means unknown though infrequent in social dynamics. In the biosphere the cyclical fluctuations of predator and predatee, which are observed in very simple systems, and the population overshoots of the lemmings, which lead apparently to mass suicide, are interesting examples. In human history there are examples of collapse of societies such as that of the Mayans around 900 A.D. and the Khmers in the 1300s that look in retrospect very much like an overshoot. In John B. Calhoun's "rat utopia,"[2] uncontrolled population growth under conditions of abundant food supply in a limited area produces overcrowding, catastrophic "behavioral sinks," and withdrawal from the normal patterns of reproductive behavior, which leads eventually to decline in fertility to the point where the population no longer reproduces itself and dies out. Calhoun's utopia, however, is highly contrived and is a sort of situation that is almost unknown in the wild because any species that got into these kinds of patterns would have become extinct long ago. Whether any of the great extinctions that have occurred in the past represent overshoot patterns or whether they simply came from subtle changes in the climate or topography, that is, the physical environment to which we all need to be adaptable to survive, we do not really know, though physical environment change is by far the most plausible hypothesis.

AVOIDING OVERSHOOT BY NICHE EXPANSION

A number of recent writers, particularly Ester Boserup[3] and Richard Wilkinson,[4] have suggested that under certain circumstances rising populations may not lead to overshoot, but may lead to adaptations that expand the niche through inventions. Calhoun[5] even observed something like this in an earlier experiment with rats, in which rats invented a new way of digging burrows by rolling the dirt up into balls and rolling the balls out. In the history of the human race the phenomenon of niche expansion is very striking. The invention of agriculture, for instance, may have been in part a consequence of the crowding produced by the last ice age in paleolithic societies, when the more northerly members of the human race were pushed down into the narrow peninsulas of North America, the Mediterranean, and Mesopotamia. Agriculture and especially the domestication of animals that went with it increased the energy input into human productive processes very substantially and this expanded the niche of the human race by orders of magnitude, perhaps from ten million in the paleolithic to hundreds of millions. On the other hand, population pressure is only one of many processes of niche expansion. The great expansion due to science was not due to any immediate population pressure. The scientific revolution indeed went along with a large expansion of the land area and the resource base of the science-producing European populations. Rather, the great niche expansion was a result of the development of the subculture of science, producing self-generating expansions in the knowledge structure, due more to idle curiosity rather than to population pressure.

THE EXPLOSION OF SCIENCE AND THE CLOSURE OF EARTH

The critical question facing the human race as we look forward into the next century or two is whether we are indeed facing a catastrophic overshoot, whether we can go on expanding the human niche in the face of increasing population, or whether we can move beyond large-scale catastrophe to a high-level equilibrium at the ultimate niche of the human race.

The last 200 or 300 years have been quite unprecedented in the history of the planet earth. There has been an explosion of human knowledge and a great expansion of the noosphere. Even 300 years ago the human race was still divided into relatively small groups, each knowing a good deal about its own locality, but very little about the earth as a whole, though this knowledge was growing rapidly. Today the earth is almost completely mapped. This knowledge is enshrined in globes and atlases in almost every schoolroom of the world. We are now going out into the solar system and we know the topography of the moon and Mars. Even 200 years ago we did not know the structure of physical matter, the elements that are its building blocks. We knew very little about the forms of energy. The first electric power station was built less than 100 years ago. The great period of the application of science to technology occurred during my grandfather's life from about 1850 to 1920. The railroad and the steam engine preceded 1850, but the steam engine owed very little to science. It was really the tag end of the great development of folk technology in the European Middle Ages. From 1850 on, however—perhaps the great exhibition of the Crystal Palace was the signal—there is a great explosion of science-based technology. We get the chemical industry, beginning with analine dyes, which would have been impossible without Dalton, Kekulé, and Mendeleev. The electrical industry, which begins in the 1880s, would have been impossible without Faraday and Clerk Maxwell. The nuclear industry of the twentieth century would have been impossible without Bohr and Rutherford. Watson and Crick, who discovered DNA, may be the fathers of biological industries yet unborn.

With this explosion of human knowledge there also comes an enormous upsurge in population partly as a result of increased knowledge of medicine, nutrition, and pest control. The chemical industry probably did more to create the population explosion than any other simply by the development of chemical controls for malaria. The expansion of human artifacts has been even more spectacular than the population expansion. So far the artifact explosion has outdistanced the population explosion, and the average output of human artifacts per capita continues to rise, though only a portion of the world's population has really enjoyed this rise.

THE RISE OF WORLD INEQUALITY
BY DIFFERENTIAL DEVELOPMENT

The developmental process of the last 200 years has increased strikingly the disparity between the rich and the poor. We have no national income statistics for the eighteenth century, but it is doubtful whether 200 years ago the richest country had a per capita real income more than five times that of the poorest. In the 1500s certainly India and China must have had per capita real incomes not very different from Eruope. Even in the 1730s Britain seems to have had a Malthusian equilibrium population of sheer misery and malnutrition aided by gin. Today the difference between per capita income for the richest countries and for the poorest is of the order of 1 to 50 rather than 1 to 5. Rich countries in the temperate zone are 20, 30, 40, 50 times as rich as countries at the bottom of the list like Haiti or Botswana. The reason for this is not exploitation in any simple sense; it is not that the poor countries produce a lot and the rich countries take it away from them. The income differences must be explained mainly by differential development. That is, the rich counntries have been getting richer faster and longer and the poor countries have not been getting richer at all. For six generations in the rich countries income has been doubling roughly every generation. It has gone, say 100, 200, 400, 800, 1600, 3200. In the poor countries it has gone 100, 100, 100, 100, 100, 100. The widening gap is again a partial application of the Matthew principle that "to him that hath shall be given" (p. 282), that once the essential development has gotten underway and knowledge has started to increase, it becomes easier to increase it; once capital has started to accumulate, it is easier to accumulate it. At low levels of output, the whole output has to be used just to maintain the society and to keep people alive to reproduce themselves. There is no surplus left over for accumulation of either knowledge or artifacts. Only about a quarter of the human race has participated in this process of expanding wealth to varying degrees. About three quarters of it has not. A quarter, perhaps a third, of the human race has moved toward a kind of world superculture of skyscrapers, automobiles, airplanes, and intercontinental hotels. The rest of the human race still remains close to subsistence.

The superculture is now spread all over the world in urban enclaves. Johannesburg, Singapore, Nairobi, Tokyo, Caracas, and Delhi all have skyscraper skylines. The older cities are likewise being transformed. In London one can hardly see St. Paul's for the new office buildings. Paris is breaking down into skyscrapers. Melbourne, which must have been a charming Victorian city in 1920, is now a mish-mash of skyscraper shoeboxes. Even the socialist countries, those bastions of Victorianism, are breaking down. There is an intercontinental hotel in the neo-brutal style in the middle of Edwardian Bucharest. Belgrade looks increasingly like the Bronx.

Over most of the tropics, however, these cities are only enclaves. A few miles outside of them one is back in subsistence agriculture and grinding poverty. The shacks of the favela in Rio de Janeiro, the barrios of Lima and Caracas, the flimsy huts and the sacred cows that press in on the Delhi skyscrapers symbolize the great gulf between the superculture and the exploding subsistence populations of the poor. There is evidence indeed that economic development in the tropics, with a few exceptions like Singapore and Taiwan, has actually worsened the condition of the bottom 25 percent of the population. As the traditional societies are eroded and traditional skills are made less valuable, the poorer people are unable to make the jump into the factories and the farms of the superculture. The labor unions in the poor countries accentuate this gap, creating a labor aristocracy at the cost of keeping the poor out of it.

THE ROLE OF ENERGY IN DEVELOPING THE
"SUPERCULTURE": ALTERNATIVES TO OIL AND GAS

The development of the superculture is the result of the knowledge explosion, which led not only to new theories and processes, but also to new discoveries, especially of fossil fuels and rich ores. In 1859 the human race discovered a huge treasure chest in its basement. This was oil and gas, a fantastically cheap and easily available source of energy. We did, or at least some of us did, what anybody does who discovers a treasure in the basement—live it up—and we have been spending this treasure with great enjoyment. It has now dawned on us that the bottom of the barrel is no more than a lifetime off. The Arabs put in a false bottom by extracting a monopoly price, and for this we should be grateful, because it has forced us to think about things now that we might not have thought about until it was too late. It is a very fundamental principle of the dynamics of the price system that, if we have something that is plentiful now but is going to be scarce later on, the sensible thing to do is make it expensive now, which will force us into improvements that will save and economize the expensive item, so that by the time it becomes really scarce we will have found means to use it much more efficiently and we will also have found substitutes. One would prefer to do this through the tax system rather than to have the OPEC countries reap excessive monopoly gains, as they are doing, but even this is better than having gas remain too cheap, in which case we might not bother to work on substitutes and economizing it until it was all gone and we would suddenly be in a very severe crisis.

Fortunately, the possibilities both for economizing fossil fuels and for finding substitutes are quite large. Nuclear fission and especially breeder reactors are a possible stop gap, but they are very expensive and dangerous and produce a negative inheritance in terms of atomic wastes of long life. The disposal of these is already a serious problem and, if an attempt were made to make fission and breeder reactors the principal source of energy for the developed societies, and still more for the poor countries, the problem of nuclear waste might become insoluble quite rapidly.

Nuclear fusion is another candidate for a major energy source. There is enough deuterium in the top foot of the oceans to keep us going for perhaps half a million years if we could produce the desired reaction. This would enable us to go burning up our "spaceship earth" for a long time. The problem in an engineering sense is still not solved, however, and may be insoluble. One is reminded of the alchemist who was trying to find a universal solvent until someone asked, "What are you going to keep it in?" Fission at ten million degrees is an extremely universal solvent and is hard to contain. The problem may be solved by means of magnetic fields and so on, though we still seem a fair way from it and it may turn out to be very intractable. Furthermore, over a few centuries the released heat could well make the earth uninhabitable. Geothermal energy, that is, from the heat of the earth itself especially where it is concentrated in volcanic magmas, is already in use in several places such as New Zealand and California. This has its own problems of pollution, for instance, where the heat is pumped up in water, which dissolves minerals along the way. It is, however, a relatively minor potential source of energy.

The last resort, of course, is solar energy, which is very abundant but also very diffuse. The whole biosphere uses much less than one percent of the solar energy that falls on the earth and, if we can get this up to two percent, we would probably be all right for energy for a long time. One source for optimism in this regard is that there are many lines of attack on this problem—mechanical, electrical, chemical, biological—so that it will be a little surprising if none of them work. Other forms of continuous energy can also be expanded. Hydroelectric power, especially in the rich countries, is by now mostly developed but it contributes only a small amount of the total energy supply. Tidal energy likewise has some potential, but compared with the total energy used even today this is very small.

A promising source of continuing energy is wind, which derives ultimately from solar energy but in some areas is fairly continuous and concentrated. The main problem with wind is its discontinuity and variability. If it can be combined with pumped storage of water, however, this difficulty would be taken care of. Suggestions have even been made for large concrete flywheels to store the energy for use when the wind is not blowing hard enough. If windmills were also tied into a large electric grid, the wind would probably always be blowing somewhere within its range. One could even visualize in windy areas a very efficient windmill on the rooftop pumping water from a tank in the basement to one in the attic, the water then running down to the basement through an efficient small generator, which would provide electricity for all domestic uses. These are technologies that are not remote from human experience. Windmills have been known for nearly 1,000 years in Europe and even longer in China, and if it had not been for the extraordinarily cheap energy provided by fossil fuels, it is likely that this technology would have been developed very substantially in the last 100 years. Even a generation ago almost every farmer in the middle west had a windmill pumping water.

EXHAUSTION OF MATERIALS

The exhaustion of concentrated materials in the form of ores may turn out in the long run to be a more intractable problem than that of energy. Most economic operations increase material entropy, that is, they diffuse concentrated materials. There are a few processes, notably the Haber process for the extraction of nitrogen from the air and the Dow process for extracting magnesium from the sea, which reverse this and concentrate the diffuse instead of diffusing the concentrated, but these are rather rare and they require large energy inputs that are now coming mainly from fossil fuels, so that at the same time we are concentrating materials, we are also running down our fossil fuel stock. If inexhaustible energy can be obtained from the sun, however, part of this can be used to concentrate diffused materials, both those which have been diffused by human activities in innumerable dumps throughout the world, and those which exist in low concentrations in the rocks, the atmosphere, or the oceans. We really do not know how much energy will be necessary to concentrate materials in the absence of natural concentrations of ores. It might turn out to be quite large.

The human race has indeed been fortunate in that at the time when its knowledge grew to the point where it could utilize fossil fuels and ores, it discovered these things in relatively large quantities. The geological history of the earth might have been different. The metals, for instance, might have been widely diffused through the crust instead of being concentrated in mines. If the earth had not had the extraordinary history of tectonic continental drift, there might not have been any great concentrations of metals as in the Mesabi Range. The fossil fuels again are in a sense an accident of geological and biological evolution that gave the earth large areas of shallow warm seas, which produced the oil-forming organisms and swampy lowlands that produced the carboniferous forests. The earth presumably might have had another kind of history that would not have produced any ores or fossil fuels. If that had been the case, all the knowledge in the world would not have discovered them, and the history of the last 100 years or so would have been very different.

POLLUTION: THE JOINT PRODUCTION OF GOODS AND BADS

Another possible limit to growth is the growth of pollution. As we saw in the previous chapter, most processes of production involve joint production in which a number of different things are produced in the same process. Again, we do not seem able to do only one thing. Even a chemical reaction that produces only a single product, like the burning of hydrogen and oxygen, also produces heat. Many chemical reactions produce two or more products, like the Solvay process reaction, which produces sulfuric acid and calcium chloride. When we include social products, it would be extremely hard to find any process in social life or any activity that produces only one product. An automobile factory that produces a particular make of car also produces air pollution and water pollution from the physical and chemical byproducts of the production, and it will also produce a great range of positive and negative social products—jobs for workers, taxes for governments, injuries, perhaps alienations and political dissatisfaction. The list could be extended.

The proportions in which these multiple products are produced are not wholly inflexible and indeed it is always the hope of technology to move toward processes that produce more goods and fewer bads, but there are quite confining limits within which this can be done, and because we want the goods we put up with the bads. Indeed, as we saw in the previous chapter, we are likely to expand joint production until one of the products becomes a bad. That is, we are better off with larger amounts of the goods and larger

both, which would turn the bad into a good. Pollution therefore is no accident; it is built very deeply into the processes of the world and occasionally it produces great transformations. As we noticed earlier (p. 30), the earliest forms of anaerobic forms of life produced oxygen as a pollutant, thereby largely sealing their own fate, but opening up the evolutionary process to more efficient oxygen-using animals. This was a pretty rare occasion, however, and it is hard to think of another one of similar magnitude. It is very doubtful, for instance, whether the dinosaurs died and became extinct because of accumulations of their own excrement.

RECYCLING AND SEGREGATION

On the whole, the biosphere deals with the problem of pollution by recycling. The excrement of one animal, for instance, is the food of another. The carbon dioxide that animals excrete, plants ingest and turn back into oxygen, which the animals breathe in and use and then again turn into carbon dioxide. Nitrogen passes through plants into the atmosphere where it is fixed in the soil by nitrogen-fixing bacteria associated with other plants and is again available for protein formation. Carbon is constantly recycled from the atmosphere to the soil, through the biosphere, into the atmosphere and the soil again. Many other elements are recycled in a similar way. The human race indeed is almost the only living being that has developed a linear economy, moving materials from wells, mines, and soil into products that are then distributed into dumps or flushed down to the oceans or burned in the atmosphere. This is obviously a temporary arrangement, but exactly how temporary is a little hard to say. Ultimately, if the human race is to survive, it must develop a cyclical economy in which all materials are obtained from the great reservoirs—the air, the soil, the sea—and are returned to them, and in which the whole process is powered by solar energy.

Where the pollution problem cannot be solved by recycling, it can only be solved by segregation, that is, by concentrating the pollutants in some locality where they are not in the way of the human race. We might shoot radioactive waste off into space. We segregate economic waste and garbage in dumps. We may be running out of easily available depositories in the course of the next century or so. It has suddenly dawned on us that neither the ocean nor the atmosphere are infinite. In particular places the human race has always polluted the atmosphere, whether this was inside a smoky tent or cave, a smoky industrial city, or the automobile smog of Los Angeles or Denver. We are now beginning to worry that human activity might produce adverse, irreversible changes in both the atmosphere and the oceans as it has in various places in times past produced irreversible adverse changes in soils and in water supplies. While not all the deserts are man made, at least some of them are, and soil deterioration, especially in the tropics, may have been the factor behind the "overshoots" leading to phenomena like the Mayan and the Khmer collapses.

We are worried about the atmosphere because we are putting a lot of previously unknown substances into it—nitrous oxides, carbon monoxide, sulphur oxides, as well as the familiar carbon dioxide. The latest anxiety is over freon, a chemical the earth had never known before the advent of man. It is used in sprays and refrigerators and is escaping into the upper atmosphere where it evidently undergoes complex chemical reactions that may destroy the ozone. It is the ozone layer in the upper atmosphere that protects the earth from the dangerous ultraviolet radiation of the sun and, if it disappears, we will be in a bad way. All the evidence is not yet in and the ordinary fluctuations in the ozone content are large enough that it is hard to evaluate what the exact effect of human activity has been, but there is enough evidence to be very worrying.

The increase in carbon dioxide in the atmosphere is supposed to warm it up. This is the greenhouse effect, which we have noticed. The fact that it is not doing so suggests we are still very far from complete knowledge of the earth's systems. The awful truth is that the physical sciences are really very backward, particularly when it comes to dealing with middle-sized systems like the earth. We know a lot about mesons and quasars, but the total system of the earth exhibits a degree of complexity that is very hard to handle with the present apparatus of the physical sciences. We still do not know what really produced the ice ages. The earth is clearly in the grip of very large systems in relation to which human activity is still something of a pipsqueak. Nevertheless, there may be "trigger systems" in which quite small changes induced by human activity could cause very large changes in the end result; and this is frightening.

The more obvious forms of pollution do tend to be dealt with, particularly when they become scandalous enough. We have cleaned up Pittsburgh remarkably and we are cleaning up Lake Erie. The English cities and rivers are far better than they were 40 years ago. The Dust Bowl no longer deposits inches of dust in Chicago as it did in 1934, and though some of this may have been a long stretch of good luck in the weather, some of it is due to changes in agricultural practices. I sometimes scandalize my young friends by telling them that I have lived through a period of great improvement in environment. On the other hand, the things that are worrying are the unknowns, the trigger effects, and the novelties. Perhaps the most disturbing thing about human activity is that it has introduced large numbers of new chemical and radioactive substances into the earth with which the biosphere never had to deal before. There are no bacteria, for instance, that know how to eat nylon and dacron. These substances are here to stay. They may not cause much damage; on the other hand it is a bit alarming to find that nylon fragments from fishing nets are getting into the digestive systems of a good many marine animals, and it is not altogether clear that they will know what to do with it. We should be careful of delusions of grandeur on the part of the human race, because we are still a very small influence. But we must also be on the lookout for the invisible dangers, where our small activities may turn out to have large effects.

THE NECESSITY FOR POPULATION CONTROL

The ultimate outcome of the present dynamic may depend more than anything else on the ability of the human race to control its own population. We are in a period now of uncontrolled population growth, which has followed from the improvement of food supplies, the improvement of health, and the decline in mortality, especially infant mortality. This all follows from general easing of the conditions of life, which the great expansion of human artifacts has produced. The human population has been expanding for a long time, as we have seen, despite relatively brief periods of contraction such as following the fall of the Roman Empire, following the Black Death in 1349 in Europe, resulting from the Thirty Years' War in Germany, or resulting from the Mexican and Russian Revolutions of the twentieth century, but these have usually been temporary and the losses are very soon regained once conditions improve. It is a rare period of decline that is not made up in a generation or two simply because of the enormous power of exponential growth. A growth rate of one percent per annum is not hard to attain. It is consistent with death rates up to 30 and 35, birth rates of 40 and 45 per thousand, and an expectation of life of under 30. Still it can produce a doubling of the population in 70 years, which is a short time in human history.

In the last 200 years or so there have been two great surges of population. The first, of European population from about the middle of the eighteenth century, was largely a result of improvements in nutrition originating in technical improvements in agriculture. This explosion of European population led to the settlement of the Americas, Australia, New Zealand, South Africa, and Siberia with European populations. The indigenous populations in the areas of European immigration often declined, and in most cases were very small to begin with, though often with a subsequent recovery as in the Americas. The European population explosion diminished substantially after about 1880, and in the twentieth century populations of European origin have been expanding relatively slowly.

In the tropics the great population explosion begins about 1950, with the introduction of DDT and the control of malaria, producing a spectacular decline in the death rate, especially the infant death rate, which as we have seen is the most significant because it is virtually equivalent to an increase in the birth rate. There was even some rise in birth rates as populations became healthier. In many tropical countries around 1950 death rates dropped from about 1880, and in the twentieth century populations of European origin have been expanding relatively slowly.

In the tropics the great population explosion begins about 1950, with the introduction of DDT and the control of malaria, producing a spectacu 30 to under 10 per thousand in two years. The result has been a population expansion at rates of three, percent and over per annum, which means doubling every generation. This kind of rate of increase was prevalent in the American colonies in the eighteenth century, but then these populations had an enormous land area, which they were in a position to occupy, and which could support with the European-type techniques a very much larger population than it had before the European expansion. Now, however, we are having the same kind of population increase without any great empty spaces. The formerly empty spaces of the world are now all full with a few possible exceptions such as the Matto Grosso in Brazil and northern Queensland in Australia, and even these are doubtful. The present population explosion is taking place in areas that are either already very crowded like South Asia, or are unfriendly to human habitation, like large parts of South America and tropical Africa. We are now having a population explosion, therefore, in a very confined space and this bodes ill for the future.

THE HIGH PROBABILITY OF DEMOGRAPHIC CATASTROPHE

There have been similar experiences in the past. One of the most recent was the Irish famine of 1846, which is indeed a classic example of an overshoot followed by a catastrophe. In 1700 Ireland had a population of about two million, living mainly on barley and small grains; then somebody introduced the potato, which produced much more food per acre than any previous crop. Under these favorable conditions the population, living largely on potatoes, expanded to eight million by 1840. One-crop economies are subject to blight, however, and this happened to the potato in 1846. Roughly two million Irish starved to death, two million emigrated, and the four million that were left seem to have comprised a moderately equilibrium population. There are still about four million in Ireland today. Ireland indeed is a good example of a recovery from overshoot catastrophe and the attainment of something that is reasonably like a steady state. In the last 40 years indeed the condition of the Irish has improved noticeably, especially in regard to housing. In part, the relatively stable population has been achieved by emigration; this, of course, is something that cannot take place on a world scale unless we populate outer space with revolving spaceships as Professor O'Neill of Princeton[6] has suggested. This seems somewhat implausible, though not impossible. In any case the problem of the expanding populations of the tropics cannot be solved by emigration. If there were somewhere to go and even if the countries of the temperate zone would let people emigrate in unprecedented numbers, there are not enough ships to transport the 80 to 100 million people who are added to the earth's population every year.

There is no acceptable solution to this problem short of bringing the birth rate down to the death rate. There is an unacceptable solution, which is to bring the death rate up to the birth rate. The forces that underlie human fertility, however, are a considerable mystery. We do not really understand, for instance, even in the United States why fertility was so high between 1947 and 1961 and why it has fallen so dramatically since. It is to the point now indeed where native-born Americans are close to being an endangered species, in that they are no longer reproducing themselves, though this may not last. Even at the present fertility rate it would take a very long time for Americans to become extinct! In a country like India, which has made a determined effort to reduce the birth rate, these efforts have not been very successful. A brilliant essay by Mamdani[7] suggests why in the Indian village with sharp class and caste distinctions the only hope of the poor or moderately poor peasant for rising in the world is to have about four sons who can enable him to expand his holdings, with perhaps one or two going to the city to send back remittances, and so on. It is hard to have four sons without also having four daughters on the average, and this leads to a great population expansion catastrophic for the society.

We have here almost a classic example of the failure of the "invisible hand," that is, a situation in which the rational private interest is directly opposite to what is necessary for the long-run public good. A catastrophe that will make the Irish famine look like a minor episode, in which perhaps over a relatively short period a 100 million people will starve to death, is by no means impossible in south Asia. The potentialities for demographic disaster in tropical Africa and Latin America are perhaps a little further off than they are in south Asia, but these parts of the world are now on a course that will either be changed or lead to catastrophe.

MANKIND–TURNING POINT OR LIFEBOAT ETHIC?

The second Club of Rome report, "Mankind at the Turning Point" by Mesarovic and Pestel, by breaking down the world into regions adds a good deal to the very broad scenario of the first report, "The Limits to Growth." Its conclusion was that, if a major demographic catastrophe in the tropics were to be avoided, there had to be almost immediate reduction of the birth rate in the tropics on a large scale and there also had to be very substantial transfers of economic goods from rich countries to the poor, an order of magnitude larger than the present flow of investments and foreign aid. Unfortunately, neither of these events seems to be very likely. The expansion of grants from the rich countries to the poor ones depends first on the development of an increased sense of community, that is, a stronger world integrative structure. In the second place, it depends on the perception that these grants will be efficient. The perception of the efficiency of grants is a very important element in their supply. If by giving up $1, I can benefit another by $100 or even possibly save another's life, I am very likely to do this. If by giving up $1, I only benefit the recipient by 10 cents, I am very unlikely to do it.

Unless grants from the rich to the poor countries can be tied to an effective method of population control, they are likely to be ineffective and may simply increase the ultimate sum of human misery and the size of the eventual disaster. On the other hand, up until now we have simply not devised any social technique for tying grants to birth reduction. There are very good reasons for this failure. Grants are often perceived as degrading to the recipients. There is always a status gap between the recipient and the donor. Grants in the form of gifts are usually handed down the social scale, though if they are in the form of tribute obtained through threat, as they sometimes are, they may go from the poor and lowly to the rich and powerful. Furthermore, procreation is regarded rightly as one of the most private and sacred aspects of human life, and to turn it into an object of exchange or even reciprocity is deeply repugnant in most cultures. We can see the moral dilemma in extreme form if we postulate that the method of control is infanticide; are we going to offer $1,000 for every dead baby? That I think would carry rationality almost to the point of Dean Swift's "modest proposal."[8]

The appalling moral dilemmas of the present situation are reflected in the "lifeboat model" of Garrett Hardin.[9] If we have a lifeboat with 20 people in it and enough food for only ten to survive until land is reached and if they all share the food, none will survive, and for every one thrown overboard up to ten, the better the chances are that the rest will survive. The question is: "Who will be thrown overboard and who will decide?" The most obvious solution is a lottery; perhaps the most just solution is that the virtuous and deserving should survive. The less virtuous should certainly be thrown overboard, although this again raises the question, "Who will decide?" The most probable solution, unfortunately, is that the most powerful will survive. If indeed we are in this scenario in the world (and we cannot be sure that we are not), the inference is that the powerful temperate zone will simply let the tropics sink. The abandonment of the European empires may indeed be a prelude to an abandonment of responsibility. Independence might be construed as simply prying the clutching fingers of the old colonies off the gunwale of the lifeboat.

THE LIMITS OF HUMAN ORGANIZATION IN THREATS AND EXCHANGE

So far the limits we have been discussing have been mainly physical and biological limits, the critical question being that of the carrying capacity of the earth in terms of human beings at different levels of affluence. These kinds of limits loom very large in the background. Nevertheless, there are other limits we might reach before the physical limits, although we know very little about them. There are limits, for instance, to the capacity of threat systems, exchange systems, and integrative systems to organize society. The limits of threat systems have been apparent many times in human history and, while these like all limits are subject to expansion under new technologies, it is pretty clear that, while threat systems can establish civilization, they cannot do any better. Mere civilization—the kind of society that stretches from ancient Sumer to, shall we say, Amin's Uganda—is not good enough. Its achievements, great as they were and are, have been paid for at a very high cost in human degradation, suffering, inequality, and dominance.

The last 100 years or so have shown us that something better than classical civilization is possible, though we may have some doubts as to whether it is sustainable. In other words some systems have a rather low evolutionary horizon, which they soon reach. A feeling prevalent in post-Roman Europe even as late as the early eighteenth century was that civilization had reached its peak in the West, at any rate in Greece and Rome, and had been declining ever since. Cycles of rise and fall are frequently observed by philosophers of history, though the complexity of interaction of different segments of society destroys any simple pattern. Nevertheless, it is a very interesting question whether once a society has reached the limits of a given system it can stay there in a stable equilibrium, or whether a process of decline does not inevitably set in as the impetus gained from rising is lost. Many systems seem to exhibit what might be called a "balloon pattern" of rising to some kind of ceiling, but then losing buoyancy and sinking slowly but surely below the maximum point.

Exchange systems have a much wider horizon than threat systems and have helped to produce the enormous increase in wealth and variety, which the last 5,000 years has seen. It was the merchants, the manufacturers, the inventors, the entrepreneurs, and the scientists, who created this great horn of plenty, not the kings, the conquerors, the generals, and the revolutionaries. The exchange system also has its limits, however. It may fall into deflations and depressions as in 1929 to 1932. It may be unable to solve the problem of maintaining full employment without inflation, which is the fix we find ourselves in today. Most of all, it may be unable to generate the integrative structures, the legitimacies, the acceptances, the sense of community, which are necessary to sustain it. The fact that the old stock exchange in Leningrad is now a Palace of Culture and Rest is a reminder of the precariousness of certain types of exchange, at least under conditions of loss of legitimacy.

It could be indeed that the exchange system reached its peak in the nineteenth century and that a long decline is facing it as it loses buoyancy. The virtual disappearance of foreign investment, for instance, is an indicator. In the nineteenth century Britain invested something like three percent of its GNP abroad for long periods. Now the United States is making virtually no net investments abroad at all and is even repatriating capital. The United States' net exports, which are some indication of its overall contribution to building up the rest of the world, have been less than one percent of the economy ever since the end of the Marshall Plan and have actually become negative, turning into net imports in 1972. This is disturbing because it suggests that the old machinery of foreign investment by which the rich helped both the poor and the rich to become richer is no longer working because it has been completely delegitimated. There is unfortunately no substitute to take its place. The grants economy on the international scale is quite small and incapable of performing the task that is necessary if the poor countries are to avoid disaster.

Internally also the tendency for the exchange system to be paralyzed by politicization is very noticeable in many societies. Rent control, for instance, often leads to a decay of the cities, as it has done in New York and in France. Licensing, regulation, and sporadic price control further debilitate the exchange system. The most striking examples of this are the three temperate zone countries, Uruguay, Argentina, and Chile, which in 1910 or 1920 were among the rich countries of the world and have been drifting downhill ever since, mainly because the exchange system has not been allowed to function and nothing else has been put in its place. The problem here is what H. G. Wells has called the problem of the receiver[10]—that it is all very well to claim capitalism is insolvent, but we cannot bankrupt it unless there is a suitable receiver! Where the state is incompetent and corrupt, as it frequently is, this problem of the receiver becomes extremely acute. To put the same problem in somewhat different terms, it is very dangerous to delegitimate one system if we do not provide a substitute legitimacy.

LIMITS OF THE INTEGRATIVE SYSTEM

The problem of the limits of the integrative system is very puzzling and in the long run may be very important. We are pretty sure we have not reached these limits in general. Nevertheless, we do run into partial and local limits. This happens, for instance, when a marriage breaks down or when there is a civil war or revolution, or even when there is widespread apathy and the lack of developmental activity of all kinds, which seemed to characterize Portugal for nearly three centuries. The rise and decline of the morale or the "nerve" of a society is an extremely puzzling phenomenon, and yet a tremendously important one. It is a great harbinger of change. It is a loss of nerve on the part of the powerful that leads to their distributing their power, which is by no means an infrequent phenomenon. Often indeed this may be very desirable, because redistribution of power leads to new bursts of energy, even in the society that has abandoned the power. Power frequently corrupts, as Lord Acton so sagely observed.[11] One sees this, for instance, in the flowering of a society, which frequently follows its military defeat. France after 1870 became the center of world culture in the arts; Germany after 1918 produced the Bauhaus, as well as Hitler, and set the style in architecture for the whole superculture. Knowledgeable future archeologists digging up our own remains in 3000 A.D. might decide that North America was conquered by the Germans and Japanese in the middle twentieth century, having previously been an outpost of the Roman Empire and having gone through a brief Medieval Gothic period. A walk around the Princeton campus provides convincing evidence that the United States has suffered three periods of colonization from abroad.

We know something about the limits to growth. What do we know about the limits to love? The limits to community? The limits to benevolence? The limits to the grants economy? The limits to dedication? The limits to freedom? The limits to justice? The answer is very little. We hope these limits are a long way from where we are now.

It is important to realize, however, that no limits are absolute. The evolutionary process is one in which existing limits have constantly been transcended because of the evolutionary process itself, first in the growth of complexity in the genosphere and now in the growth of complexity in the noosphere. The classical economist saw economic development as the race between capital and population. We might broaden this to see it as a race between increasing knowledge and increasing scarcities. For the last 200 or 300 years knowledge has been winning hands down. The ultimate limit, however, is the limits to knowledge. These we obviously cannot know. For this reason the future must always remain mercifully uncertain, as we shall see more clearly in the next chapter.

NOTES

1. Donella and Dennis Meadows, et al., *Limits to Growth* (First Report to the Club of Rome) (Washington, D.C.: Potomac Associates, 1972); and Mihajlo Mesarovic and Eduard Pestel, *Mankind at the Turning Point* (Second Report to the Club of Rome) (New York: E. P. Dutton/Reader's Digest Press, 1974).

2. John B. Calhoun, "Population Density and Social Pathology," *Scientific American*, 206 (Feb. 1962), 139–148.

3. Ester Boserup, *The Conditions of Agricultural Growth* (Chicago: Aldine, 1965).

4. Richard G. Wilkinson, *Poverty and Progress: An Ecological Perspective on Economic Development* (New York: Praeger, 1973).

5. John B. Calhoun, "What Sort of Box?" *Man Environment Systems*, Vol. III, No. 1. (Washington, D.C.: U.S. Department of Health, Education and Welfare, National Institute of Health, Jan. 1973).

6. Gerard O'Neill, "Testimony," *Co-Evolution Quarterly*, No. 7 (Fall 1975), 10–19.

7. Mahmood Mamdani, *The Myth of Population Control: Family, Caste, and Class in an Indian Village* (New York: Monthly Review Press, 1972).

8. The proposal was, it may be recalled, to solve the Irish population and nutrition problem by eating the babies.

9. Garrett Hardin, "Living on a Lifeboat," *Bioscience*, 24; 10 (Oct. 1974), 561–567.

10. H.G. Wells, *An Experiment in Autobiography* (New York: Macmillan, 1943).

11. "Power tends to corrupt and absolute power corrupts absolutely," Lord Acton, *Essays on Freedom and Power* (Boston: Beacon Press, 1948).

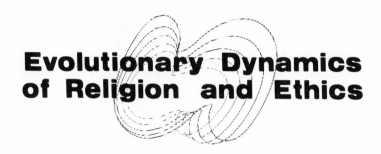

Chapter 15

Evolutionary Dynamics
of Religion and Ethics

RELIGION IN HUMAN HISTORY: IN THE INTEGRATIVE SYSTEM

The earliest records of the human race suggest that religion has always been a part of the distinctively human experience. Even the Neanderthals buried their dead with some ceremony, and there is little doubt that the cave paintings of the Cro-Magnon had religious significance. It was probably the capacity of the human nervous system for language that evoked the capacity for religion, which is very deeply embedded in the symbolic systems of the human race. It is hard to imagine even the most intelligent chimpanzees going to church.

From the very beginning, therefore, religion has played a part in the great phyla of human and societal evolution. It has occupied a complex set of niches in the noosphere relating to humans' images of themselves and their larger environment. These images have produced artifacts such as tombs, temples, churches, and ritual objects. Many of these have turned out to be highly durable, perhaps because the search for the durable has been one of the motivations behind religion. Hence, it tends to be embodied in durable artifacts like sacred songs, poems, literature, pyramids, painting and sculpture, cathedrals, and so on. One of the by-products of religion, therefore, has been to increase our knowledge of the early history of the human race. Religion has also played an important part in organizational phyla—temple organizations, hierarchical priesthoods, monasteries and nunneries, organized churches, and so on. This also probably begins very early. The shaman or the priest may have been the first specialized human occupation. Similarly, religion has played an important role in molding the character of human beings not only in specialized religious occupations such as priests, acolytes, monks, nuns, hermits, missionaries, and the like, but also in forming the behavior of uncountable numbers of ordinary humans as they have been moved by fear or love and inspired by religious ideas and images to do things they might not otherwise have done or abstained from doing things that they might otherwise have done. The relation between religion and morality, while it is often loose and tenuous and shifts from time to time under different forms of religion, nevertheless, has probably been there from the start.

Religion has had an important role to play in the integrative system, as the very name suggests. "Religion" and "ligament" come from the same Latin word meaning something that binds together. It is equally part of the integrative system because it has kept people apart. Differences in religion have been an important source of human division and conflict, probably from the very earliest days right up to the Protestant-Catholic split in Northern Ireland, the Hindu-Muslim split in India, and even one might say the Russian-Chinese split within Marxism. Within a group holding a common religion, however, religion has been a very important bond of union in many periods of human history, although a common religion has never been any guarantee of avoiding conflict. None of the great religions have been able to prevent wars among their adherents. Christendom, Islam, and the Hindu and Buddhist areas have usually been divided into warring states. Nevertheless, the alliance of church and state has been common in history, mainly because religion has given the state an integrative structure that it otherwise might have lacked.

RELIGION IN THE THREAT AND EXCHANGE SYSTEMS

Religion is not, of course, exclusively confined to the integrative system. It is often part of the threat system and it has used the motivation of fear, especially perhaps in its earlier days, as much as if not more than it has used the motivation of love. Religion originated, at least partly, in a fear of the unknown and an attempt to propitiate it. Even in the developed religions, shall we say, of the European Middle Ages the fear of hell was by no means an unimportant element, as the great stained glass windows and paintings all over Europe representing the Judgment testify.

There is an exchange element also in religion. This is particularly apparent in its more magical aspects, when the believer pays the priest in money or in kind to perform rituals believed to be efficacious in producing what the believer wants—sons, good crops, good weather, success in war, health, or a good time after death. The Catholic Church in certain periods of its history was particularly exchange minded and charged a regular tariff for indulgences, for the rescue of departed souls from purgatory, and so on. Even today it is questionable whether we should count most of church contributions as part of the grants economy or whether we should not regard them as some form of collective exchange. If a group of people get together to build a fine, expensive church, apart from its community aspects, this is not so very different from enjoying a fine, expensive house, so that in the matter of most church contributions, there is a considerable quid pro quo. Nevertheless, the integrative element is always there as well, as indeed symbolized in the fact that churches usually take up collections; they rarely charge admission or provide benefits upon explicit contract. The exchange here verges over toward reciprocity, which has larger integrative elements than contractual exchange.

THE DEMAND FOR RELIGION

A critical question, therefore, is what are the characteristics of the human race that have given religion its place in the evolutionary dynamics of society and have made it such a large and significant phylum? Why does religion have such a large niche not only in the human cognitive and evaluative structure, that is, in the noosphere, but also in the great phyla of human artifacts, organizations, and people? This comes down for the most part to the question what is the nature of the demand for religion, bearing in mind the possibility that, like many other demands, the demand may be induced in part by the supplier, because religious ritual and propaganda are perhaps the earliest examples of the activity of selling. Nevertheless, even the most persuasive salesmanship cannot be successful unless there is an underlying potential demand to be realized. In the case of religion, this underlying demand is clearly of great human importance.

It is a demand both for theory and for practice. The theory and the practice may be quite loosely related and may not even have very much to do with each other in terms of overall social ecology, although they are supposed to have a one-to-one relationship. The demand for theory is a demand for some kind of structure within the human consciousness that forms a satisfying gestalt and helps create a satisfactory image of personal identity. Just what gives religious ideas their power is a puzzle. This is part of the general puzzle of symbolic systems as to why symbols, for instance, may have great power at one time and very little at another. There is no doubt, however, that within a given religious culture an evolutionary process in religious symbols takes place. A given culture is an ecosystem of ideas and images and exhibits a kind of ecological succession within which certain combinations grow and flourish and eventually decline while others take their place.

Underneath all the rise and fall of particular forms, symbols, and expression, however, there are some fundamental underlying demands. One of these is for an image of order or nonrandomness. Human life is subject to innumerable accidents. Human beings have always found themselves to be in the grip of great processes over which they have no control, like the weather, disease, mishaps, getting lost or found, finding things and losing them, encountering love and engendering hate, community and conflict, peace and war—all the great drama of human life. Whether some image of a transcendent governor of luck or fortune was the first deity to be worshiped we do not know, but the search for order in a bewildering and seemingly random environment and for some chance of protection against ill fortune has undoubtedly been one of the main sources of demand for religion.

MAGIC

A very early form the religious impulse takes is magic, which could almost be defined as an attempt to control nature by the same methods by which we try to control other people, that is, by threats, gifts, sacrifices, exchanges, and persuasions. With the development of language, the human race soon found it could use this great art to change the social universe and to persuade others to move closer to our will. It is not surprising that by analogy this power was also postulated for the nonhuman universe, so we get incantations and sacrifices, rain dances and magic spells, petitions and prayer wheels, in spite of little in the way of conclusive evidence that these activities are effective. They arise out of our desperate desire to do something in the face of the vast incoherence and randomness in nature. If another person will respond to an entreaty, why should not the "weather" or the dim, vague forces that govern success in any human endeavor?

The attempt to intervene into highly complex systems, where the effects of the intervention are so complex and uncertain that they can be interpreted in a great many different ways, produces a phenomenon of self-reinforcing images. The theory behind magical intervention is presumably that there are unseen forces or beings in the world of nature that can be affected by it. This is not very different from a scientific hypothesis, that if we do A, then B will follow. If we do A and B does follow, then of course our hypothesis is confirmed, although not proved. Our belief in it tends to be reinforced, but there may still be alternative hypotheses. One is that B happened because of something else, not because of A. Another is that we misperceived B. Another is that we did not do A right. If A is perceived to produce B, these alternative hypotheses are rarely invoked. If A does not produce B, however, they frequently are invoked. For instance, if a rain dance is followed by rain, this reinforces the belief that rain dances are efficacious in producing rain. If the rain dance does not produce rain, however, the alternative hypotheses are invoked. It is a little hard of course to avoid perceiving rain or drought, but it is easy to argue that something went wrong with the rain dance and it was not performed properly. I must confess that my experience in laboratories as a student was not very different from this. My experiments rarely seemed to produce the results my instructors were expecting, but instead of writing this up as a scientific discovery, they would always say, "Go back and do the experiment and get it right."

In social life magic is a good deal more common than we often like to think. The proposition, for instance, that a neutron bomb will increase national security is more a magical than a scientific hypothesis. It may make us feel more secure, but this does not disprove the alternative hypothesis that our perception of security is in error. If the introduction of a new weapon is followed by a disastrous war, the inference is rarely drawn that the original hypothesis was incorrect. On the rain dance principle we argue that we did not do it quite right, and so do more of the same. There are so many examples, indeed, of this principle of self-reinforcing images that one has moments of doubt about whether it is ever possible to move images toward correspondence with the real world and the truth. Why should the plausible but false hypotheses of magic ever be shaken? The answer seems to be that there is a certain asymmetry between error and truth and that erroneous images are more likely to be changed than true ones. Error can be found out, but truth, one hopes, cannot, though under some circumstances we have to admit that images might shift from those that have less error to those that have more. The common sense pragmatic view that what clearly works is more true than what does not has been an important and constant pressure that makes us substitute truer images, no matter how implausible, for falser ones, no matter how superficially plausible.

THE ROLE OF METAPHOR AND THE
DYNAMICS OF RELIGIOUS SYMBOLS

In both religion and science we run into the difficulty that images are metaphors. This is almost the same as saying they are models that do not correspond in a one-to-one relationship with external reality, but represent some aspect of that reality that is significant for us. Sometimes indeed the model or the metaphor is worshipped as a reality. This is idolatry from which even econometricians may not be wholly exempt. Idolatry, however, like magic has elements of instability in it in that it can be found out. In all developed religions we observe the use of religious language as metaphor, which facilitates the experiences and the practices in which religion really originates. This accounts for much of the vitality of institutional religion in the face of Copernican and Darwinian challenges to its traditional images of the universe and the Marxist challenge to its morality. An American humorist raised in the Jewish faith quipped that he had thought of becoming an atheist until he found out that they didn't have any holidays.[1] There is a profound truth in the jest. There is a strong demand in the human organism for a view of the world that will permit both consolation and celebration. Neither the subculture of science nor that of atheistic materialism can really supply this need. The attempt to form artificial religions, like that of the Goddess of Reason of the French Revolution, have been dismal failures. They represent mutations in symbolic systems that did not survive.

Just what does lead to survival in religion is puzzling. Why did Mithraism and the mystery religions of the late Roman Empire lose out to the more austere, materialistic, and earthy Christianity with its outrageous claims of a real carpenter born in a stable, who was observed to have risen from the dead? Why within the Christian church did the trinitarian orthodoxy of Anathasius survive and thrive while the more intense and esoteric Gnosticism and the more bland and rationalistic Arianism faltered and became virtually extinct? Why was iconoclastic Islam successful with its almost incomprehensible Koran when Byzantine iconoclasm was extinguished? These are real puzzles of societal evolution. Part of the difficulty is always the imperfection of the record, which makes it hard to pinpoint the exact parameters of ecological interaction at this level. Part of the problem perhaps is the absence of an adequate theory of symbolic evolution that can guide us toward what is really interactive.

The problem of cultural conversion is particularly puzzling. Why are some cultures stable for so long, transmitting themselves with only minor modifications for generation after generation, while others are transformed in a single generation? The conversion of the Anatolian Greek Christians to Islam and to the Turkish language is one such transformation. The conversion of Latin America to Catholicism is another. The conversion of China to Maoism is still another. Evolutionary theory certainly provides an existence theorem for such transformations, because complex ecological structures can reach some kind of catastrophe point in their parameters in which very radical restructuring can take place. Just what the conditions are that produce these restructurings, however, we do not really know, which makes it virtually impossible to predict them.

ETHICS AND THE LEARNING OF VALUES

The history of ethical ideas and practices is an integral part of societal evolution and is governed by the same general principles. Ethical ideas and practices, like those of religion, are part of the noosphere, the genetic structure of social institutions and artifacts. They arise by some sort of mutation and they survive or become extinct depending on how they fit into the overall social ecosystem. They are, of course, very much bound up with the integrative system, though the extent to which they are embodied in cultural subsystems, the survival of which is affected in some degree by threats and exchange, should not be overlooked. It is pretty safe to say that no human society has ever existed without some kind of ethical base or ethical ideas, formulated in a rhetoric that is passed from generation to generation. This was undoubtedly one of the first uses of language and probably set up one of the feedback processes in the development of language. Ethics, at least in the form of socially controlled behavior, is found in many prehuman species that exhibited the phenomenon of community, but it is perceived only in those cases where an individual fails to perform and is killed or expelled from the community for this reason.

We have still not defined ethics, and perhaps that should be left to the philosophers. Within the field of human images and activity there is a subfield of images and activities related to evaluation. All behavior insofar as it involves decision rests on the ability to evaluate alternatives. We can study the effects of given valuation structures, as we do in economics. The theory of economic behavior usually assumes a given structure of preferences. The moment we begin to inquire how these preferences are formed, whether in an individual human learning process or whether in the larger evolutionary process by which the whole ecological system of the noosphere changes, we begin to get close to the traditional purview of the moral philosopher and the student of ethics. We learn our preferences in the course of growing up just as we learn everything else. These preferences have a certain genetic base in, for instance, sensations of pleasure or pain, in our preference for pleasure over pain, and in the various structures of the nervous system that lead to and from the pleasure center, whatever it is, the activation of which creates the sensation of pleasure. The newborn baby has certain genetically created preferences—for milk, for warmth, for being held securely, for bodily contact with a mother, or for a reasonable substitute such as a blanket. Building on this primitive genetic structure, we add increased complexity by an evaluative learning process that includes feedback from perceived activities, symbolic communications, joint products, and associative identification, in which something is valued because it goes along with something else that is highly valued, and so on.

The exact process by which values are learned is imperfectly understood. There is indeed a very inaccessible element in it, which is the internally generated information and feedback within the person. Different people clearly have different capacities for dealing internally with unfavorable external inputs. Learning is not a purely "behavioral system" with stable relations between the external inputs (stimuli) and the resulting structure of external outputs (responses). The internal inputs are an important part of the process, and it is hard to find stable parameters in them. Some children who grow up in very unfavorable environments are able to handle this by their internal inputs and become adaptable, creative kinds of people; other children who grow up in the most favorable environments can develop character disorders, impose very high costs on their society, and contribute very little to it. Whether genetic factors have any role in this internal response we do not know. These differences in internal response may cancel out over a large number of cases, and the external environment of inputs may be the dominant factor; but it is always hard to evaluate the relative importance of the external and internal environments.

THE PUBLIC ETHIC

Just as we can distinguish between private images of the world and a widely shared public image, so we can distinguish between a private ethic and a public ethic. The public ethic is a set of valuation principles or value functions that are widely shared. The public ethic indeed is the principal determining characteristic of a culture or a subculture. This extends even to matters of consumer choice and aesthetic taste. Each culture defines the limits within which individual variation is permissible. In our culture, for instance, a taste for going around naked in public places is severely frowned upon and a taste for wearing crowns and ermine robes to the supermarket would similarly soon put an individual in a mental institution. Just what determines the limits of tolerance of a culture is a puzzling question. On the whole, the larger the area and population of a culture, the more tolerant it is of diversity, but even within cultures that are otherwise similar there may be considerable divergence in the degree to which eccentricity is tolerated.

When one looks at the overall evolution of ethical ideas and behavior, it is clear that this divides into two very different, somewhat independent processes. There is first the evolution of ethical ideas within a single culture. It is not always easy to define the limits of a single culture historically. When, for instance, in the course of constant change does one culture become a different culture? There are historical continuities, however, of which language is perhaps the most outstanding feature, but in which many other cultural traits can be included. Just as language changes in the course of time, so does the public ethic. In the European culture stream, for instance, duelling, which had been very much part of the ethic for several hundred years, became unacceptable in the nineteenth century, as did slavery and many unrestricted rights of property, all within an essentially continuous culture. The rise and decline of the temperance movement is an interesting example of an attempted ethical change that failed, perhaps because it had a premature success in prohibition.

The Example of Alcoholism

Alcoholism indeed is a very interesting case study of the complexities of ethical dynamics within a single culture. Moderate consumption of alcohol does not seem to be attended with any grave personal or social consequences, and indeed seems to be much less injurious to health than smoking. Drunkenness, however, is widely looked upon with ethical disfavor as demeaning to the dignity of the human being by producing behavior that is damaging to the drunkard and to others. Alcoholism is a serious social pathology, producing severe damage to the health of the alcoholic and to the welfare of his family, to his work environment, to the safety of the roads, and to other things. Responses to this problem have been highly various. Some subcultures, such as Protestant nonconformity in Britain and America, Islam, Ghandianism in India, responded to this with strong moral condemnation of alcohol consumption in any form, and have gone in for teetotalism and prohibition. Other cultures have tolerated the problem and tried to deal with it by laughing it off, making it a matter of jokes or tolerant amusement, and developing an ethic of conviviality condemnatory of the austerities of teetotalers. The English writer, G. K. Chesterton, is perhaps one of the most eloquent exponents of this school. A third approach is the medical, which tends to see alcoholism as a disease subject to cure by psychoanalysis or some other therapeutic regime rather than as a moral defect. Alcoholics Anonymous somewhat straddles the medical and the ethical, emphasizing therapy, especially group therapy, as well as the moral responsibility of the individual to seek the inner resources that will make the therapy effective.

The alcohol problem is an almost classic case where what would seem to be persistent ethical failure on the part of individuals resulted in varied attempts to achieve political and legal solutions ranging from early closing of state liquor stores, to heavy taxation, to downright prohibition. Alcoholism seems to be about as responsive to all these solutions as rain is to rain dances. They seem to exhibit a cycle of imposing increasing restrictions in a desperate attempt to deal with a very real problem, to a recognition of the failure of these restrictions, and then to their abandonment. This does not solve the problem either and new restrictions may be reimposed.

PUBLIC GOODS AND THE TRAGEDY OF THE COMMONS

The tendency for ethical failure to lead into restrictive legislation is very strong. There is a very good reason for this in what economists call the "public goods problem." A public good in its most extreme form is something that can be enjoyed by one person without a diminution of its enjoyment by another. Enjoyment of environmental amenities, the ability to drive on uncrowded roads, the general security of life and property, are all examples. There are also public bads, in which one person experiencing some disutility does not diminish the disutility of another, such as air pollution and environmental decay. Public goods and bads cannot be handled by the institution of private property, which up to a point is probably the best way of handling private goods. Private bads can be handled to some extent by the law of torts. If someone drives his car into my living room and pollutes it, I can sue him for damages; this is a private bad. If someone congests the road or pollutes the air, however, there is not much I can do about it as a private individual.

The appeal to ethical behavior has been an important element in the attempt to deal with public goods and public bads, and it is by no means wholly ineffective. If it were not, indeed, for the voluntary restraints imposed by the standards of courtesy, the motives of charity, and the practice of decency, the problem of public goods and bads would be virtually insoluble. Nevertheless, there comes a point in many cases at which the appeal to ethical behavior breaks down, simply because the conflict between individual values and community values becomes too great and individuals follow their own values and exploit their own privileges to the detriment of the community. This leads into what Garrett Hardin has aptly called the "tragedy of the commons."[2] When a public good such as a grazing common is inadequately regulated, there is constant danger of overgrazing. The virtuous individual who restricts the number of cows he puts on the common will lose to the benefit of others from whom he cannot get compensation. Exchange therefore breaks down.

The ethical appeal to benevolence may have some impact, but it is often not strong enough to overcome the strong individual self-interest. This is particularly true when the community is rather large and diffuse. In a small group of ten men on a battlefield the willingness to sacrifice for the group becomes very strong and the identity of the individual becomes bound up with that of the group. In the case of a large, diffuse community it is hard for the individual to see that his sacrifice does very much good, even to the community, and it is unlikely to be made. The problem of population control, as we noted earlier (p. 300), falls into this category. The individual interest in having a large family may clash catastrophically with the social interest in population control, especially where the gap between the individual's perception of his own interest and the public ethic of the larger interest is large. Exhortation and other forms of ethical learning may then be ineffective, and other devices must be used.

These other devices usually take the form of penalties for what is regarded as unethical behavior, which then becomes illegal. Even the power of legal penalties to change the system, however, runs into severe limits, as the persistence of crime, and even in the last ten years or so its expansion in the face of increased crime prevention expenditures, suggests all too poignantly. Psychologists assure us that rewards are more effective in learning than punishments, yet we seldom seem to apply this principle in society, especially in regulating the private sector. And it is, of course, precisely the rewarding of productive behavior that benefits both the individual and society and constitutes the famous "invisible hand" of Adam Smith. In handling the problem of public goods we use rewards very sparingly. These somehow seem to smell of bribery and corruption, of tribute rather than defense. Nevertheless, there are often situations in which this is the most rational way to handle the problem and even is most likely to lead to moral learning.

THE SINS OF OMISSION—"DOERS AND STOPPERS"

A problem that has received too little attention from modern moralists and political actionists has been that of "sins of omission," a famous subject of Christian moral exhortation. The English prayer book says, "We have done those things that we ought not to have done and left undone those things that we ought to have done." The sins of commission, doing those things that we ought not to have done, are fairly easy to identify and legislate against. The sins of omission, leaving undone those things that we ought to have done, are hard to identify and even harder to legislate about. Unfortunately, however, they may be very important. The difference in dynamic between the developing and stagnant societies may easily lie in precisely the sins of omission, in that in the stagnant society people are not doing things that ought to be done. One of the dangers of moralism is that it tends to overemphasize the sins of commission. If it sets up too many sanctions, either of public opinion or of legislation against these, this may have the effect of increasing the sins of omission; people will avoid doing anything for fear of doing wrong, which may easily produce a worse state of affairs than if the society had been a little more tolerant of wrongdoing in order to gain more of what may be the associated activity of rightdoing.

One has rather an uneasy feeling that society is divided roughly into two classes of people—the doers and the stoppers. The doers include those who do right as well as those who do wrong. These are the bankers and the businessmen, the organizers, the entrepreneurs, the inventors, the investors, the developers, the builders, and so on, some of whom are doing right and some of whom undoubtedly are doing wrong. The stoppers are those who are concerned to stop the doing of wrong. Up to a point this is highly desirable if the innumerable tragedies of the commons are to be prevented. Too much stopping may lead to a kind of paralysis, however, in which the doer is stopped from doing right as well as from doing wrong. Unfortunately, it is very hard to detect this situation. It is as hard to detect what is not being done as to detect what is not there, and from the point of view of the total system, what is not there and what is not being done may be more important than what is there and what is being done. This could well turn out to be one of the most significant long-run problems of social organization. Unfortunately, nobody worries about it, and I am certain that very little work is being done on it.

THE "TAKERS" AND THE "PRODUCERS"

Perhaps to these two categories we should add a third—the "takers." These are the people who do not do very much that is productive or that adds to the total welfare of society, but who take from society what others have added to it. These are the wrongdoers, thieves, embezzlers, cheaters, exploiters, as well as at any one moment of time the young and the old who have taken from society what those in middle life and working age are producing without giving back immediately to it. Over a longer perspective, of course, the young are taking what they will later return when they come to be of working age; the old are taking what they have previously given in some sense. As we have seen, a society with a very large proportion of old and young will find itself in real difficulties.

Then we have a group regarded by the Marxists as pure takers and by non-Marxists as in some sense legitimate takers—those who receive income from property pure and simple. Interest receivers are the most obvious example of this. It is not surprising that the ethics of interest have been for a very long time a difficult moral problem. Receivers of profit and rent may be more actively engaged in risk-bearing and ultimate decision-making. Here again, the absentee landlord and the absentee shareholder are in a dubious moral position. The great ethical dilemma that underlies the ideological split in the world today is that private property encourages the doers. This is the famous magic of property, simply because under a regime of private property a person benefits from what he does. Additions to his property produced by his own activity accrue to him. On the other hand private property, especially when not well regulated, also produces the takers, that is, a class of idle rich who contribute very little to the society from which they take. Thus, the institution of property may benefit us all at the cost of an especially undeserved benefit to some. On the other hand, the alternative of a centrally planned economy produces on the whole a society of stoppers. The great bureaucratic apparatus only does the thing it knows how to do and it stops ruthlessly the productive activities that do not conform to its rules. This may be the explanation of why the cost of socialism seems to be so high. One hopes that social invention is not over and that the moral dynamic of society will continue toward a solution of this intractable problem.

ETHICS AND THE COMPETITION OF DIFFERENT CULTURES

Another aspect of the evolution of morals is the evolutionary patterns of the interaction of different cultures and societies by which some of them expand and flourish and others contract and become extinct. It is the internal moral dynamic of the most successful and expansive societies that comes to dominate the total system. The moral dynamic of societies that have become extinct indirectly affects those societies that prosper, but it does not seem to have a very good evolutionary future. That the ethical principles of a society, especially its ethical dynamic for adaptability, have something to do with its survival can hardly be doubted, but the exact relationship is very hard to spell out. This actual system of ethical principles and social mores, which prevails in any particular society at any particular moment, is clearly the result of its evolutionary process. In any particular society it is a result of its internal evolution; the society exists because its internal evolution produced something that gave it survival value in the past, although this by no means guarantees survival value in the future.

The capacity of any given society to survive depends first on its ability either to prevent declining population, which will carry it to extinction, or to control an expanding population, which will give it an "overshoot" that again may lead to extinction. The recipe for survival, therefore, would seem to be high potential fertility, which would enable a society to overcome temporary setbacks by rapid restoration of population, coupled with great restraint in the exercise of this potential fertility, so that a society does not run into a population explosion. Perhaps the extraordinary and seemingly contradictory history of sexual morality can be interpreted in part at least in these terms. The very widespread and persistent taboos against any form of sexual activity apart from that between men and women in some kind of family structure may stem from the survival value of fertility potential, which otherwise would be dissipated in nonprogenitive sexual activity. The widespread taboos against sexual activity outside the family structures designed for the rearing of children may also have survived because of the effect on fertility potential. Up to the last 100 years, of course, the effect on population growth through high infant mortality was so severe that the society which neglected fertility could easily die out. Adam Smith remarked, for instance, that, "It is not uncommon I have been frequently told in the Highlands of Scotland for a mother who has borne twenty children not to have two alive."[3] This was only 200 years ago. A society, whose moral principles do not foster the care of children, would clearly not have very good survival value under these circumstances.

The survival value of care for the aged is a little more puzzling. Those societies that live very close to the margins of existence, like the Eskimo and the nomadic tribes, are virtually forced to abandon their aged when they cease to be productive in order to survive at all. In societies with an easier environment and a larger surplus, however, the principle of respect for and care for the aged is very commonly given higher priority. This may have developed more out of the internal evolution of these moral principles rather than through their survival value for the total culture. We are all pretty sure that, if we do not die first, we will get old and that hence every person in the younger age groups has a personal interest in developing a long-term respect for the aged. The commandment—"Honor thy father and thy mother; that thy days may be long upon the land which the Lord thy God giveth thee" (Exodus 20:12)—may reflect a very common dynamic in societies that have the surplus to be able to do this.

Another very important factor in the survival of societies is the capacity for organization and community, especially for large-scale community. The European colonists in North America, as Adam Smith again observed, were able to expand against the Indians because they brought with them from Europe the "habit of subordination" (p. 259), and the ability to form large-scale organizations. Theft, dishonesty, lying, cheating, and other marks of selfish alienation tend to be subject to severe moral criticism whenever these characteristics destroy the community and organization of a society and hence diminish its survival value.

There is a curious paradox here that those moral qualities which make for internal harmony and may increase its survival from that point of view, may limit the society's capacity to deal with external enemies in the external environment. It is not surprising, therefore, that moral codes are frequently and almost universally ambivalent in this regard. They severely discourage murder, theft, cheating, lying, and so on at home while encouraging these things abroad. Christianity has tried to resolve this moral inconsistency by preaching the love of enemies, but even within nominally Christian societies this principle has been honored more in the breach than in the observance. Nevertheless, the tension between what might be called "internal morality" and "external morality" is real, and it has created pressure throughout human history for larger units in social organization. We now seem to be approaching the stage in the history of the human race when the union of the internal and the external ethic will have to be achieved; otherwise, the external ethic will destroy us all. Some form of world community, expressed perhaps in novel political institutions that have not yet been thought of, seems to be the only answer to the technical collapse of isolation, as we saw earlier (p. 154). Whether any of the existing ethical and religious systems can underpin the world community is a question for the future.

THE INTERACTION BETWEEN RELIGION AND ETHICS

The ecological and evolutionary interaction between religion and ethics is of immense complexity and cannot be resolved here. The interweaving is so subtle and pervasive that it is hard to perceive simple patterns in it. At first glance one might expect that mystical religion, with its emphasis on the immediate personal experience of the transcendent, would be self-contained and would not involve itself in interactions with the ethical dynamic, whereas religions of ritual, celebration, and community life would be integrated very closely into ethical systems and ethical change. The pattern is far more complex than this, however. Moses, for instance, as revealed in the Old Testament, was a man of charismatic mysticism, who was convinced he had met Transcendence face to face on Mount Sinai and by the burning bush. It was also Moses, however, who was the law giver, the community builder, the organizer, the moralist, and who forged the scattered slaves of Egypt into a vibrant community in the desert. George Fox, who was "come up in spirit through flaming sword into the paradise of God,"[4] also forged a scattered people into the "Spiritual Israel" of the Quakers, who crossed the desert of the Atlantic Ocean to found a "Holy Experiment" in Pennsylvania, and who made disproportionately large contributions to science and technology. The Wesley brothers—John, whose heart was strangely warmed, and Charles, who could write "Long my imprisoned spirit lay fast bound in sin and nature's night; thine eye diffused a quickening ray. I woke, the dungeon flamed with light; My chains fell off, my heart was free, I rose, went forth, and followed Thee"—created a movement that swept the working class of England and America into a powerful and well organized Methodist Church.

By contrast the ritualistic ethnic and community-bounded churches often seem to have produced a rather superficial impact on the ethical standards and behavior of their membership, perhaps because the more intense religious experience tended to be segregated in the religious orders and did not become part of the larger experience of the congregation. We also have the extraordinary experience of China in which the purely secular religion of Maoism, combining a militant dialecticism with a worldly wisdom rather like that of Benjamin Franklin plus a dash of the transcendental devotion of Saint Francis, has apparently succeeded in creating a remarkable transformation in the ethical principles and practice of hundreds of millions of people. There are many puzzling questions in this field that might be illuminated by further historical research.

THE ROLE OF REASON

A final question in this area is that of the role of reason in these long evolutionary processes of religion and ethics. The definition of reason is even more difficult than the definition of ethics. It includes those activities of the human mind that perceive identities and that are able to expose logical fallacies and contradictions and inconsistencies, and it edges over the vague boundary that separates it from evaluative processes of human judgment, which are the foundation of decision-making. The human reason that searches for models or patterns in the diffuse records of the past, as we have been doing in this volume, is itself an evolutionary product, however, not only in the sense that it emerges as a potentiality of the human nervous system in the biological sense, but also because it acquires an evolutionary record, a past of its own, a set of human artifacts in terms of books, documents, mathematical records, and so on, which cumulate as we come down through time. Reason is itself a species, perhaps a phylum, of human artifacts. It participates in ecological dynamics along with other species of biological and human artifacts.

The idea, which is not unknown to philosophers, that reason can give the final answer to puzzles of the pattern of human existence and that it dominates all other evolutionary processes within the framework of the human experience can be rejected as inconsistent with the pattern of evolution itself. Reasoning about the self and about society is likely to accelerate the patterns of evolutionary development; but we can be sure that reason as we know it today is not final. We now seem to be moving into a stage in which the prosthetic devices assisting the human reason, like computers, are becoming of increasing importance. In the future we may be able to perceive patterns and handle models of a complexity far beyond our present capability. Should this enable us to perceive the patterns underlying the human learning process itself, this might indeed constitute another gear change in the long process of evolution with a further acceleration of the evolutionary pattern through time.

NOTES

1. Henny Youngman, quoted in The Chicago Daily News, May 11-12, 1974, p. 22.

2. Garrett Hardin, "The Tragedy of the Commons," *Science,* 162 (1968), 1234-1248.

3. Adam Smith, *The Wealth of Nations* (New York: Modern Library Edition), 79.

4. "Now I was come up in spirit through the flaming sword, into the paradise of God. All things were new; and all the creation gave into me another smell than before, beyond what words can utter." *The Journal of George Fox* (New York: Capricorn Books, 1963), 97.

Chapter 16

Alternative Images of the Future

PATTERNS OF FUTURE PROJECTION

Mechanical Dynamics (Eclipses)

One of the major human purposes in attempting to perceive the patterns of space and time is to help in forming more accurate images of the future. We need to do this because, as we have seen, all decisions are about the future and all our experience and records are of the past. It is only as we see patterns in this past record that we have any hope of making projections of the future and of making decisions that will change the future in ways that we desire. To change the future, after all, is the object of any decision.

Our images of the future vary a great deal in clarity and certainty depending on the kind of system we are projecting. The projections of celestial mechanics are of great accuracy and certainty. We would be most surprised if an eclipse failed to show up on time to the split second. This is because fundamentally the solar system is in equilibrium (or very close to it), though a rather complex one, and we are simply perceiving its equilibrium patterns in space-time. Projections of equilibrium are very easy. If we have a book sitting on a table and nobody touches it, we will have a great deal of confidence that it will be there tomorrow. Even when a system is not in equilibrium we can predict with some confidence that, if there is a stable equilibrium, the system will move toward it, even though the path may be hard to predict in detail. We set a ball in motion at the top of a bowl and we are pretty sure that in a short time it will be settled in equilibrium at the bottom no matter by what path it traverses the bowl.

Turbulent Equilibrium Systems (Weather)

The next type of system is an equilibrium system subject to constant random shocks, in which case it never reaches the equilibrium and is always overshooting, going back to it and overshooting it again, oscillating back and forth around it. The earth's atmosphere, at least over moderate periods of time, seems to be a system of this sort, which is why meteorological preduction is so difficult. It is at least a temporary equilibrium system in the sense that it does not go on heating up or cooling off indefinitely, as its throughput of energy from the sun to earth's radiation is approximately constant. The overall amount of evaporation from the oceans and other bodies of water and the proportion of this which is precipitated in rain is also fairly constant over the earth. Nevertheless, the details of the system are in constant turmoil. It might be described as a "soap opera," a turbulent system in which random shocks are continually building up temporary disequilibria in explosive processes like storms, which eventually dissipate themselves as the equilibrium forces take over, but which constantly re-form.

A turbulent stream is another good example of a system of this kind. If we watch it, we see that the waves and splashes are never in the same place, but nevertheless there is an overall equilibrium pattern. In the case of the atmosphere we can detect turbulences of different sizes ranging from the wind devils of the dusty plains to tornadoes and hurricanes, and from thunderstorms to droughts and floods, from the long cycles, for instance, the 1000-year cycle, which is apparent in records of European weather, to the longer cycles, which produce the ice ages. We know virtually nothing about the mechanism of these longer cycles, but we have no reason to suppose, for instance, that what produced ice ages in the past no longer operates in this part of the universe.

Even in short run predictions meteorologists are not very successful. It has been stated that, if one says the weather tomorrow is going to be the same as it is today, one will predict about as well as a meteorologist. It may be indeed that with the new computer methods and modeling of the total world atmosphere we will be able to do better than this. This still remains for the future. The fact remains that meteorologists are dealing with a system of extreme complexity and they are not to be blamed if they find it very hard to reduce this to systems of predictable order

Planned Growth or Decay (Kittens)

As we move into biological systems, equilibrium systems become shorter in duration and less secure, so that prediction becomes more difficult. All living creatures exhibit homeostasis (Greek for equilibrium), as Cannon[1] called it. They have something like a dynamic equilibrium state, and divergences from this state produce cybernetic compensating· mechanisms to restore the original state. Thus, human beings have an equilibrium blood temperature of about 98.6° Fahrenheit, at which presumably the innumerable physical and chemical operations that constitute the machinery of the body operate most successfully. At lower temperatures than this both automatic and behavioral mechanisms get into play—our teeth chatter, pores contract, we stomp up and down, we seek clothing and warmth in the environment in order to restore the body temperature. If we go above 98.6° F, we perspire, we seek shade, refrain from activity, and so on. If the mechanism breaks down, we become sick. The fever, which is a breakdown of the homeostatic mechanism, is regarded up to a point as an unfailing sign of sickness and, if it rises beyond a certain point, it causes death.

Homeostatic equilibrium, however, is only temporary. With every day we age however imperceptibly. Both growth and aging are continuous failures of the homeostatic mechanism, but this too follows an equilibrium path or creode. The time pattern of the living organism from its fertilized egg to its final death has at least one general characteristic of the solar system in that it is a space-time structure that exhibits something like an equilibrium path. A kitten never turns into a hippopotamus and it is remarkably rare for little boys to turn into young ladies, though it can happen. We use creodes constantly in predicting the future of living creatures. In social systems, however, it is by no means easy to distinguish creodes and they are not particularly stable. Artifacts like automobiles age almost like horses in fairly regular patterns. Organizations also age, but in very irregular patterns, and they are capable of rejuvenation in a way that biological organisms and material artifacts are not.

As we move from the individual organism into the ecosystem we again find temporary equilibria, a little bit like homeostasis. In a climactic ecosystem each population, as we have seen, is at a level consistent with that of every other and for each population the birth rate equals the death rate, subject perhaps to certain fluctuations around this equilibrium. Mountains, rivers, forests, and prairies are all examples. Not even a climactic ecosystem, however, is permanent. It is constantly subject to slow, long-run changes, sometimes even to dramatic short-run changes resulting from climatic or geological shifts, biological mutation, or in the present era the intervention of the human race, which has turned many grasslands into deserts, prairies into farms, and oak and hickory forests into pine forests.

EVOLUTION AS UNCERTAIN DISEQUILIBRIUM

So we work our way up to evolution. Evolution has been a disequilibrium system from the very beginning. Whether it has some very long-run cyclical equilibrium between the alpha and omega points of de Chardin[2] we do not know, and there has not been time to find out. The record suggests that certainly for the last two or three billion years on restless earth the system has been in constant disequilibrium with tectonics and erosion in the rocks, with biological ecosystems changing all the time, and with old species be-

coming extinct and new species forming. The evolutionary pattern of mutation and selection has great interpretive power but remarkably little
predictive power. We do not really know what produces rapid evolutionary
change at one time and very slow change at another. We are trying to
interpret a record so fantastically imperfect that the details elude us. In
regard to biological evolution we are rather like an archeologist investigating a
city that has been reduced to completely fragmented rubble even without
foundations. He may be able to tell something about its general size and
outline, but what it was like and what really happened in it can only be a
subject of speculation.

When we come to social systems, which affect us most closely, again we
face a continuation of the evolutionary process with constant disequilibrium.
Here again there is something like climactic ecosystems among small tribes
that are fairly isolated and even among relatively elaborate civilizations, like
that of Mohenjo-Daro, which seem to have exhibited at least a quasi-
equilibrium for considerable periods. We can never be quite sure of this,
because the records again are very imperfect. No anthropologist has ever
followed a tribe for 500 years. The history of preliterate societies is very
dubious indeed. One suspects indeed that these societies change faster than
anthropologists think and that, if we could see them as they were 500 years
ago, we would find them very different. The mutability even of tribal
societies is suggested by the great variation found among them even under
similar circumstances. We already noted the case of two tribes in the Congo
separated only by a river and speaking approximately the same language that
are totally different in their cultures, although each obviously originated from
a common source. How long this divergence took we really do not know, but
it could have taken place in a couple of centuries. At Mohenjo-Daro many
artifacts at the bottom of the heap are almost indistinguishable from those at
the top, the only difference being about 900 years. This suggests technically
at least a society, in spite of the fact that it had cities and plumbing, that was
remarkably stable. What went on in terms of the social, behavioral, and belief
patterns we do not know. All the historical records of our own society
suggest that change takes place in all aspects—in artifacts, behavior, institutions, and beliefs. It is a little hard to believe that a society in which the
artifacts do not change is not also very stable in regard to these other things.
We can never be quite sure of this. We do not really know what can coexist in
the way of artifacts and the other aspects of social life. Mohenjo-Daro,
however, is a pretty exceptional case, perhaps because of its relative isolation,
which was eventually destroyed by the Aryan invaders or perhaps their
predecessors.

THE UNPREDICTABILITY OF KNOWLEDGE

Once we abandon equilibrium as a guide to the future in evolutionary
systems, there is a fundamental and irreducible obstacle to forecasting in any

detail. This is the fact that all evolutionary systems, both biological and societal, involve knowledge in some sense as an essential element. Evolution as we have seen is a process fundamentally in the field of knowledge or know-how structure both in the genosphere in biological evolution and in the noosphere in societal evolution. We quite clearly cannot predict the future of human knowledge. If we could predict what we are going to know say in the year 2000, we would not have to wait, because we would know it now. This is not to say we cannot speculate usefully about possible or even probable new knowledge and new discoveries, but we cannot predict them in any detail. Prediction of biological evolution is in a somewhat different category. In what might be called "ordinary" biological evolution, unaffected by the human race, the problem of prediction by humans may simply be the intolerable complexity of the system. If we knew more about the probabilities of mutation and the structure of selection, there might not be any fundamental obstacles to predicting at least the general patterns of future biological evolution. It does not surprise us, for instance, when the moths of smoky Manchester turn dark through natural selection, but these are extremely small systems. We really know very little in detail about biological evolution in the large. There is now, of course, the real possibility of large human intervention in biological evolution, not only through artificial selection, which has already produced the domesticated plants and animals, but also through direct genetic intervention. We seem to be close enough to this at least that the possibility is frightening; so much so indeed that there has been a call for a cessation of certain research in this area (p. 116). Once biological evolution becomes a function of human knowledge its predictability by humans becomes much less. It does not seem wholly impossible that we might re-create the dinosaur within a hundred years, but we certainly cannot predict how to do it.

FAILURES OF DEMOGRAPHIC PREDICTIONS

A good many attempts have been made in social systems to develop parallels to celestial mechanics in the form of models with constant parameters that may be projected into the future. Demographic projections, as we have seen (p. 57), are a classic example of these procedures. If we have an initial population and we can assume constant birth and death rates at different ages, or even if we can assume a function of regular change in these parameters, the population may be projected indefinitely. It is hardly an exaggeration, however, to say that all population projections have been wrong, simply because the parameters have stayed constant. Fertility is a particularly inconstant parameter. For instance, nobody expected the "baby boom" of the 1950s in the United States, or the enormous decline in infant mortality in the tropics after 1950. Nobody expected the great decline in fertility in the rich countries in the sixties. It is clear that all population projections have to be taken with a strong dose of disbelief; they are useful to do, but most dangerous to believe.

With the increasing posibility of intervention by governments into demographic processes, the uncertainty of population projections becomes even greater. The Romanian story is particularly instructive in this regard. In 1966 the Romanian government apparently learned that the decline in fertility was so dramatic under Communism that Romanians were no longer reproducing themselves. They went into what I have been calling "fertility shock" and overnight virtually prohibited abortion and severely limited birth control appliances. As a result Romania is the only country in human history I think to have doubled its crude birth rate in one year, from 14.3 in 1966 to 27.4 in 1967, and even though it is now declining again, when the population reaches equilibrium it will be much larger than it would have been without this episode. Today Romania with 20,000,000 people and about the agricultural resources of the state of Illinois could hardly be called underpopulated. Yet this was apparently the image held by the Communist government.[3]

With this one exception fertility seems to pay little attention to ideologies and religion. Catholics usually have higher birth rates than Protestants of the same class, income, and location. In Canada, however, the fertility of Catholic Quebec is now lower than that of the rest of the country. Once development proceeds to the point where people catch on to the cost of having children, they react accordingly and often with dramatic suddenness.

When one looks at the tropics the prospects for population control are very depressing. As we saw in Chapter 14, there was a dramatic decline in death rate due to malaria control more than anything else, which set off the current population explosion in the tropics. Previously with the birth rate at 40 per thousand and the death rate at 30 per thousand, the rate of growth was of the order of one percent per annum. Now with birth rates continuing around 40 and death rates now down to 10, the rate of increase in many countries has risen to 3 percent, even in some to 3 1/2 percent per annum. This means the population doubles every generation, placing an almost intolerable burden on the development of these countries. Just in order to stay where they are they have to build a whole new country every generation. With limited land and agricultural sources this may be impossible unless they can double agricultural productivity per acre. This can be done for a while, but there are severe limits to it. The "green revolution," which involves the introduction of new high-yield varieties, has been hailed as a solution to this problem, but it requires applications of fertilizer derived in large measure from oil, which may not long be available. It also has some undesirable side-effects in the way of increasing the inequality of income in rural areas. Only the richer farmers are able to take advantage of the new techniques, and hence become still richer, whereas the poor farmers may relapse into an even greater poverty. While the green revolution in the shape of high-yielding varieties of plants improves the potential for the solution of this problem, it by no means solves it automatically and, if it does not lead into population control, it may actually increase the sum of human misery in the end and create even greater catastrophes in the future.

There are factors in the world that might lead to very sudden changes in fertility in the tropical countries, however, which would give them a much better chance of surviving the next 50 or 100 years without catastrophe. A change in the status of women is perhaps the most hopeful sign here, as slow as it is. But changes like this can sometimes accelerate as ancient legitimacies are proven untenable and collapse. Just as the whole concept of empire collapsed in the mid-twentieth century, it may be that the age-long concept of the subjection of women will likewise collapse in its fourth quarter. The burden of childbearing has mainly fallen on women with the gains from it enjoyed by men. The possibility of revolt against childbearing on the part of women even in the tropics is by no means impossible. It is almost the only possibility that gives rise to much optimism.

ECONOMETRIC PROJECTIONS

Econometric projections are not different in principle from population projections. They again involve models with constant parameters, which rarely stay constant for very long. It is fairly easy to make projections in a period of relative stability such as we had, say, from about 1950 to 1973. The assumption that these stabilities will continue, however, is most dangerous. The great virtue of explicit model building is that models can be subjected to sensitivity analysis. That is, we can find out how much the projection will change if we change one of the parameters by a given amount. It is very dangerous, however, to do simple trend projections of complex indices, like gross national product, which depend on a great variety of underlying interactions and feedbacks.[4] The more structure we can put into our models, indeed, the less likely they are to be misleading, though of course the structure of the model must exhibit a strong correspondence to reality. The computer has had perhaps an unfortunate effect in permitting the construction of models with very large numbers of equations and parameters, in which we are apt to lose any sense of the significance of parametric change. The wise predictor will always look for potential instabilities in the parameters of his model and take into consideration the probability of improbable events, particularly in projecting over a long period of time. Over the next 100 years, for instance, events that have a low annual probability, like a great earthquake in San Francisco, the catastrophic explosion of a volcano in the Northwest, running out of oil and gas without finding any substitutes, or ecological collapse of American agriculture as a result of pests and blights winning the battle against research, are all things that might have to be taken into consideration.

SOCIAL PREDICTION: THE "ICEBERG EFFECT"

Social, political, and behavioral changes are often harder to predict than demographic and economic changes, although these are all interrelated. Prediction is particularly difficult when the movement is a result of two opposing forces, because it may even be that random elements will determine which of these is dominant and hence the whole direction of change. Lewis F. Richardson's analysis of "war moods"[5] is a good example of this kind of instability. He sees two moods existing simultaneously in the population, even in the individual, one of which involves willingness to undertake a war and to carry it on, the other involves unwillingness. The latter may either derive from a general predisposition toward peaceableness or be the result of war weariness as war proceeds. Each of these has a dynamic of its own. War willingness may rise in the light of perceived provocations, hostilities, a sense of insecurity, and so on, fed by arms races and mutual overestimations of hostility, and so on, until finally war willingness overcomes war unwillingness on the part of one of the parties and war is declared. Normally war ends when the rising cost of the war increases the war unwillingness, which eventually tops the willingness.

This might almost be called the "iceberg effect." As the lower part of an iceberg melts in warmer water, the iceberg's center of gravity rises until it overtops the center of gravity of the water displaced and good old Newtonian physics reverses the position of the iceberg and it overturns to find a new equilibrium. The more surprising changes in society are often the result of this kind of effect. The erosion of the invisible part of the consensus that assures social stability is often unseen and unnoticed until the equilibrium is destroyed and there is an unexpected, catastrophic overturn. Sometimes these overturns are relatively minor as in a coup d'etat in a military government, but at other times they might be quite catastrophic as in the French and Russian Revolutions.

Repressive regimes may ensure their stability for a while by pushing more and more people underground, as it were, rather as if an iceberg were to increase its density and settle lower in the water to compensate for the erosion of its underground mass (It may be that the metaphor is getting a bit out of hand!), but the catastrophe is often all the more overwhelming when it comes. The "sacrifice trap," which we noted earlier (p. 206), is an example of these processes, which sustain legitimacy for a time, even for a long time, but which eventually lead to sudden overturn, often with quite small forces like Cortez in Mexico or the Bolsheviks in Russia. These things are very unpredictable, however, especially because we have very little knowledge of the overturns that did not happen because dissatisfaction did not rise to the point where the overturn would have taken place, but instead simply drained away.

POLITICAL PREDICTION: THE BALANCE
BETWEEN SEPARATENESS AND UNION

Predictions about political change, therefore, are very wild guesses. One possible iceberg syndrome is that of separateness versus union. There is one dynamic that increases the desire for separateness and for religious, national, and racial identities. A group that has been forced into unity with others but not really absorbed into that unity is quite likely to develop separatism, particularly if it perceives itself in an inferior position. Things like the Black power movement in the United States, separatism in Quebec, Scotland, Wales by the Basques—the list is very large—rise and fall in a rather mysterious dynamic, and if it rises enough unions may be broken and smaller and more independent units established. We have seen this very many times in human history, as in the Protestant Reformation and its subsequent fissions into sects. The breakup of the empires, beginning perhaps with the American Revolution, followed by rebuilding and further breakup, is a striking pattern in human history. In opposition to the desire for separatism is the fact that very frequently union is strength, and up to a point the larger units are more efficient, have more power, have more to identify with, and so on.

The balance between separatism and union is often a very delicate one. In the British Isles, for instance, Ireland went for separatism; Wales and Scotland so far have gone for union. In this case it may have been religion that tipped the balance; Southern Ireland is Catholic while Wales and Scotland are Protestant like England. Canada has maintained a precarious balance with union so far winning out, but separatism in Quebec is strong and the balance could easily be tipped the other way. In this case probably the common fear and dislike of the United States have tipped the balance in favor of union in spite of the fact that culturally and religiously the two parts of Canada are very far apart. The European Common Market is an example of union of a rather limited kind overbalancing separatism, which has been the legacy of Europe for so long. Here again it may be the feeling of being in the middle between two very large powers—the United States and the Soviet Union—and in a very real sense of being the cultural ancestors of both that has brought Common Market countries together. Still, separatism triumphed in Norway. Sweden, Finland, and Austria are special cases of "buffer states" between the East and the West that find their survival value in separatism rather than in union. Switzerland, of course, is a very special case, having gotten away with separatism in relation to its neighbors and an extraordinary union of diverse languages, religions, and cultures internally for a long time, perhaps for geographical reasons.

The Soviet Union is a particularly interesting case. It is the last of the great nineteenth century empires, now that the Portuguese empire has been dismantled, and its boundaries follow very closely the boundaries of the Czar's empire. It contains a great diversity of nationalities. Up to now the union has predominated partly because of the police state of the Russians and partly because of some concessions to the nationalities in the way of local autonomy, a good deal of which seems to be more apparent than real. There is a certain "cognitive dissonance" here because of the existence of the "socialist camp," as the Communists call it. If Poland, part of which was part of Russia until World War I, can be an independent nation in the United Nations outside the Soviet Union and still be Communist, why cannot Lithuania, which is as old and legitimate a national unit as Poland? If Pakistan can be a nation, why cannot Uzbekistan, for the Uzbeks were civilized before the Russians had hardly emerged out of the woods? Georgia and Armenia, which are national entities, go back to at least the third century A.D. One would expect, especially if detente continues and the outside pressures are relaxed and, of course, if some kind of border settlement is made with China, that the separatist forces in the Soviet Union will turn out to be quite strong and it will not be at all surprising to see it break up in, let us say, the next 50 years.

India is another interesting case. It is a society of such great heterogeneity that one wonders if it can be governed centrally at all. As a nation it is mainly a creation of the British. Separatism began, of course, with Pakistan and continued with Bangladesh. If it ever starts in India, it will not be at all surprising to see India break up into ten or a dozen different states. This might not even be a bad thing for the Indian people, because smaller states might have a much better chance for good government and development than has the vast, unwieldy, and almost inevitably corrupt centralized government in Delhi.

A very interesting problem is what will happen to the divided countries— Korea, Germany, and China—divided by the ideological and military accidents that followed World War II? Historically the pressure for union is great; these are all countries that have shared a common history for a long time. Ideologically, however, where two parts have grown away from each other so drastically in the intervening generation, union would be a deeply traumatic experience for the part that had to make the major adjustment. Union always involves some sacrifice of power on the part of individuals who may very well have been enjoying it. We perceive this even in corporate mergers; it is particularly striking in states. Once people have tasted sovereignty they find it hard to go back to being a mere provincial, though sometimes they do, as apparently they have done in South Vietnam.

WORLD GOVERNMENT AND THE HUMAN IDENTITY

What then in the next period of human history are the chances for world government? At the moment they seem not very good. Each major war seems to produce a step toward it. The League of Nations was a little better than the Concert of Europe and the United Nations was a little better than the League of Nations, but even the United Nations is a very small organization.

Its whole budget barely exceeds that of the Ford Foundation. Its construction is almost designed to deprive it of power, the Assembly being dominated by the smaller and powerless countries and the powerful countries having only a veto in the Security Council. This is a sure design for not doing very much, even more so than the American government with its division of powers. In view of the fact that we put very little into the United Nations, it is surprising that it has done as much as it has. It does represent a tenuous new legitimacy drawn from the future rather than from the past, and however imperfectly it functions, it is the only visible symbol of the human race. It has had some success in moderating conflict in the Congo, in Cyprus, in Israel, and so on. It is hard to see, however, that it has a great deal of potential for growth. It has no tax power and is entirely dependent on its member states for finance. It has no threat power; any member can walk out at any time. The only power it has is integrative power, the power that rises from the desperate need for larger human organization.

The critical question for the next period of human history is whether the development of a world economy and world culture, which has already taken place, will create a sufficient world integrative system and a human identity, capable of creating the political unity so necessary in the midst of the separatism that is so rightly precious but also so frighteningly dangerous. The problem is more complicated than one of mere federalism. In a certain sense the world federalists are pointing toward a necessary future, but the parallel with the United States in 1789 is weak. The world is much more heterogeneous than the 13 colonies, and heterogeneity is hard to manage, as we see so clearly and disastrously in South Africa and in India and indeed in the United States of 1860. On the other hand, a world government would be very different from any national government because it would have no enemies except internal ones. Much of the activity of national governments centers around defense against external enemies. A government that has no external enemies is hard for us to visualize.

It may be indeed that we are looking for a political invention, which has not yet been made, that will satisfy the desperate need for world unity, for the liquidation of the world war industry and its conversion to civilian uses, and for a minimum capacity to deal with planetary problems such as atmospheric and oceanic pollution. In its early stages it is probable that the world political organization (one hesitates almost to call it a government) would have to shy away from the difficult problems of redistribution of wealth and power. These are difficult enough even in the national governments where there is a strong sense of national community. In the absence of a sence of a sense of world community, it is hard to visualize a very large grants economy from the rich to the poor either in wealth or in power. Ultimately this will have to be taken on as a function, but this will have to wait upon the growth of a world integrative system. It may be indeed that we will have to go through some major catastrophes before we can learn what must be learned. Perhaps a limited nuclear war and catastrophic local famines would, because of the present ease of communication, make a deep impression on human consciousness and force us toward a reconsideration of our values and institutions. One hopes this will not have to be the case, but one must also prepare for it.

THE FUTURE OF THE HOUSEHOLD

The future in regard to social institutions such as marriage, sexual customs, the arts, music, architecture, and religion is even more uncertain than in the case of politics. Like everything else all these things change; the human learning process sometimes produces irreversible changes, although from the historical record one would adduce that many of these changes are somewhat cyclical in nature. This makes one a little suspicious of perceiving irreversible changes too soon. There is a great deal of stability as well as change in these institutions. The same patterns often reappear under new names.

The nuclear family of at least one parent and children has been remarkably stable through all of human history from the very beginning. Indeed, it predates human history and reaches far back into biological evolution because it is an institution or behavior pattern that has obvious survival value for a species. There are no large signs that it is undergoing basic change even though in the developed countries there are signs of erosion of older, more rigid subcultures, perhaps as a result of increasing affluence. In the United States divorce rates have been rising over the last two or three generations, with a very sharp rise after World War II, a decline following it, and then a further rise. It is striking, however, that the rate of dissolution of marriage by divorce or death of one of the partners has not changed very much and that the rise in divorce is offset to some extent by the increase in the expectation of life and the decline in early deaths. A hundred years ago death came much earlier to either one or the other of the married partners. If people had lived longer, they might have had more divorce then.

The divorce problem is a little similar to the problem of the rise in the diseases of old age with increasing expectation of life. The last 100 years have seen an extraordinary decline in premature mortality before the age of 70. Yet there have been virtually no extensions of life beyond the 70s. We have no better chance of living to be a 100 today than we had a 100 years ago, though we have a much better chance of living to be 70. This in itself has produced important social changes and may produce more as the proportion of young people declines as we move toward an equilibrium population with low birth and death rates.

The nuclear family always exists in a hierarchy and network of larger, if less intense, communities. The extended family is, of course, such a larger community. This is a very old invention of the human race; no animal outside

of the human race is aware of grandparents. The development of consciousness of a complicated kinship network seems to come very early in human
development and is found even in the most primitive peoples. The extended
family may be suffering some erosion as a result of the increased mobility of
developed societies, which spreads the kinship group far afield whereas in the
old days all the kin were in the same locality. The mobility is a result of
improved transportation and communication, which also enables extended
families to keep in touch over long distances, however, so that it is by no
means clear that the extended family on the whole has been weakened.
Cultural distance may be more important here than physical distance. When
children move from the country to the city or when they rise into another
class the culture of the extended family often tends to be broken. The
most dramatic example of this is when light-colored members of the black
community "pass" into the white community, but only at the cost of cutting
off all communication with their kin.

Living communities (households) beyond the nuclear family are constantly
being tried in human history. They seem to be most long-lasting when they
are of a single sex like monasteries, nunneries or beguinages of the Middle
Ages. The United States has been particularly prolific in the founding of
utopian communities and this is still going on. It is only those with strong
religious bent and a considerable measure of isolation from the world outside,
like the Hutterites and the Society of Brothers, that seem to have very much
permanence. One strongly suspects, therefore, that the nuclear family will
continue for a long time, though there is always the chance that some
charismatic leader may create patterns of community living that are more
workable than those with which we are now familiar.

THE FUTURE OF SEX

Within the developed societies, and especially perhaps in the United States,
there has been a distinct shift in sexual customs and norms in the last
generation. Some of this is a change in talk rather than in practice; there is
some change in practice too. In part this is a result of increasing affluence.
The rich have always been able to afford greater sexual freedom than the
middle class and the respectable poor, though almost all societies have had a
"disreputable" poorer class that also practiced sexual freedom. Part of the
so-called sexual revolution of the last generation has been the result of what
might be called the aristocratization of the middle class as increasing affluence and the culture of the rich moves down the larger groups of the society.
That is not the whole story, however. There has been an erosion of the sacred
character of sex as a result of exposing it to scientific investigation. Psychologists and psychoanalysts began this process of desacralization. Freud opened
up sexuality for discussion at least in intellectual circles in the West in a way
it had never been discussed before. The sociologists and biologists like Kinsey

treated sexual behavior as a field of scientific observation and quantitative measurement.

Today sex is about as sacred as a common cold and about as mysterious as a gourmet cookbook. This may be an irreversible change, and not merely a phase of what might be called the licentiousness-puritan cycle, which is prominent in cultural history. The development of relatively easy methods of birth control such as birth control pills may represent an irreversible technical change, which can hardly fail to have a long-run impact on the sexual mores and practices. On the other hand, some element of sacredness in sex has characterized virtually every known human culture in one form or another and obviously has some basis in the dynamics of human interaction. Even in chimpanzees a great deal of sexual behavior is learned and it seems that in humans even more is learned than in chimpanzees. These learning processes depend on the institutions of childrearing, the transmission mechanisms of culture, and so on. The physiology of sex, however, which we inherit with our genetic structure, seems to link it very closely with deep emotion and passions. The view that sex is just another method of creating entertainment and pleasurable sensations hardly stands up to the evidence of human history or even of literature. I would not be surprised, therefore, to see a return of Puritanism as excessive sexuality produces either boredom or disgust, though it may be on a different level than before because of the certain irreversible changes like birth control.

THE FUTURE OF THE ARTS

The future of the arts is even more uncertain than that of the family. Virtually no human culture has ever been discovered that did not have art in some form. The human race clearly has a large potential in this direction. The fact that people in different cultures can easily learn to appreciate and enjoy the art of other cultures, as for instance the West enjoys Japanese paintings and the Japanese enjoy Western symphonies, suggests that the artistic expression of the human race is not purely a matter of individual whims or cultural training and transmission, and that it has some deep roots in the human nervous system. There are undoubtedly cyclical movements in tastes as there are in morals, which arise perhaps because of the tension between the constant desire for novelty and the exhaustion of certain kinds of artistic potential. There is a real problem in the constant accumulation of the artistic record. There seems to be a certain artistic law of entropy in that every particular form or style of artistic expression, whether in painting, sculpture, music, architecture, or dance, eventually exhausts its potential as time goes on. When this has happened further practice in this particular style will lead into degeneracy, overelaboration, imitativeness, and so on.

I suspect that even the constant desire to be up-to-date may actually limit potential creativity in the arts. A certain liberation from the fashion of the moment might release potentialities which otherwise would not be fulfilled. The poet who writes in the style of the Elizabethans or the Victorians, the painter who paints like the Dutch or Italian masters, the composer who composes in the style of Mozart or Beethoven, the architect who designs a Palladian or Gothic building is today despised as hopelessly old-fashioned and imitative. This, however, may be a mistake. Confining the artistic expression of the age to a single "modern" style has often led to dullness and artistic degeneracy. We may find in the future that artistic creativity will demand the freedom to practice in any of the styles of the past as well as to search for new styles. The assumption that all the potential of the old styles has been exhausted one suspects is premature.

In the socialist countries the arts have suffered a severe deterioration as a result of the enormous concentrations of power in the hands of the only patron, which is now the state. Art has been turned largely into propaganda and the creative individual expression of the artist is severely discouraged. Socialist art indeed is commercial art of the worst kind. It sells the policies and ideologies of the rulers of the socialist state. While good commercial art is certainly better than bad, there is no substitute for the fine arts in which the artist does his own thing, though even here the problem of patronage has always been an acute one. It is something the artist has had to transcend.

THE FUTURE OF RELIGION

The future of religion is again extremely hard to predict. Religion like the nuclear family seems to be a very fundamental part of human society and no society has been found without some sort of religious practices and beliefs. Even the specific forms of religion seem to have remarkable survival value, because it seems quite rare for a religion, once established, to become extinct. However, we do have cases such as the Aztec religion where the overthrow of a whole society and culture destroyed the religion along with it. There are deep historical connections that link religion with sex; both are part of the deep emotional layer of the human make-up.

It has been one of the paradoxes of the last 200 years that, while the rise in science and the movements in philosophy have created changes in our image of the world in many ways unfriendly to the established religions, in fact organized religion has shown extraordinary vitality and expansion. Here in the United States, for instance, church membership has risen from about 7 percent at the time of the Revolution to well over 60 percent today. Religions established by a state, as for instance in Scandinavia, are often weakened by this fact, as David Hume[6] had hoped. Where there has been separation of church and state, however, as in the United States, the churches have grown quite remarkably. Even in the socialist countries where the governments are officially hostile to religion because it is contrary to the official ideology of dialectical materialism, religion has exhibited a quite astonishing vigor, especially in the Eastern European countries where the Catholic Church in Poland, the Orthodox Church in Russia and Romania, and the Lutheran Church in Czechoslovakia have shown great vitality. By contrast, the churches in Britain, France and Scandinavia seem to have declined in the last couple of generations.

I am pretty sure religion will remain a major interest of the human race and new forms will arise and new prophets will attract a new generation of devotees in the endless search for meaning and goodness. What the content of these new sects will be one cannot, of course, predict. This is part of the symbolic system, the most wayward and unpredictable of all the systems with which we have to deal. Combining this with the inscrutable mysteries of the dynamics of authority and legitimacy, almost the only recipe for facing the future is to prepare to be surprised and enjoy the infinite variety that exists in the human potential. Perhaps, however, we can detect one possible trend—the movement from threats into exchange and on into integrative systems, which we noted earlier, may also apply to religion. The religions of fear of hell and of trading on the hope of heaven may give way to religions of grace and love.

THE NEXT 200 YEARS

The next 200 years will certainly represent the most profound transition the human race has ever had to pass through. Either we must solve the problem of producing a sustainable, high-level society on a world scale using solar energy for the throughput of recyclable materials to maintain an adequate artificial environment or we will collapse into a state much worse than what we have now. To express the full potential of the human organism we must sustain the dream of a world free from war, crushing poverty, and debilitating riches, in which every human being that comes into the world will have a reasonable chance of exploring the vast inner universe of human potential. If we fail in this—and we may—we are likely to fall back into a much more primitive economy, scratching a hard living once again from the woods and the fields and looking back on the present abundance of the affluent societies as a never-to-be-repeated Golden Age. This transition is going to require an immense effort of courage, intelligence, and love. Among the stranger delusions about the future was one prevalent a few years ago in which it was thought that we were going forward into a great age of abundance and leisure in which the main problem was going to be how to prevent boredom. It is a curious irony that the astrological symbol of the "Age of Aquarius" became the watchword of this supposed new age of abundance, because Aquarius is the only good Puritan among all the signs of the zodiac, trudging eternally with his waterpot around the heavens. Yet symbols have a way of being more true than their creators. It may be indeed that the earnest, hardworking Aquarius, bearing a little of the mysterious water of life, will symbolize what will carry us through into a better world for our descendents.

NOTES

1. Walter B. Cannon, *The Wisdom of the Body* (New York: W. W. Norton, 1939).

2. Pierre Teilhard de Chardin, *The Phenomenon of Man* (New York: Harper Torchbooks, 1965).

3. Michael S. Tertelbaum, "Fertility Effects of the Abolition of Legal Abortion in Romania," *Population Studies*, 26 (1972), 405.

4. Herman Kahn and Anthony J. Wiener, *The Year 2000* (New York: Macmillan, 1967) is an excellent example of the dangers of this approach.

5. Lewis F. Richardson, *Statistics of Deadly Quarrels* (Chicago: Quadrangle Books, 1960).

6. See Adam Smith, *The Wealth of Nations* (New York: Modern Library, 1937), 743.

Chapter 17

Alternative Patterns

THE UNIVERSE AS A JIGSAW PUZZLE

The human mind has a passion for pattern. Even the act of perception is a process by which we take the chaotic inputs that come into the senses and transcribe them into a pattern that we believe corresponds to an external reality. I look around me and see a room. The room that I see is an image, some kind of structure in my mind. I could imagine a very different room, but the room I believe I am perceiving has a very different quality from the one I am imagining, the strange quality that we call reality. What exactly we mean by this has puzzled philosophers for thousands of years. It does not seem to bother the ordinary person very much. If my image has the property of reality, I believe I can walk across the room and touch the opposite wall. If my image is a fantasy, I cannot do that. If I in fact get up, walk across the room, and touch the opposite wall, my image of reality is magnificently confirmed. I have an image of the future; in a few moments it becomes an image of the past. If I fit the image of the past over the image of the future and it corresponds, I am confirmed in my belief that what I experienced is reality.

This book is an attempt to outline a pattern for the whole universe and particularly for that tiny part of it which constitutes the environment in time and space of the human race. This is an absurdly ambitious project, which is bound in some sense to be a failure. In the first place, the pattern is far more elaborate and complex, by orders and orders of magnitude, than the pattern anybody can describe in a medium-size book. An immense amount of detail is missing. The very concept of "detail" suggests, however, that there are both larger patterns and smaller patterns within the larger patterns. What we are looking at in this book is the largest pattern. We cannot escape the question: "How do we know it is true?" But we cannot test its truth, in the way we test our image of the room we are in, by walking across the ten billion light years in space and ten billion years of time to touch the other side of the universe. We are trying to make a pattern out of a mystery, out of something of which we only have small biased samples in our perception. We are trying to perceive the picture in a jigsaw puzzle with most of the pieces missing. We have cues and clues—a piece of sky here, a piece of water there, a piece of tree here, a piece of building there—and we build up in our minds an image of what the picture must be; however, it is very easy to be wrong.

Doing a jigsaw puzzle, indeed, is in many ways a parable of a human being in the endless search for truth. We must start off with the faith that there is a pattern, that the pieces do in fact fit together. Nobody would ever start doing a jigsaw puzzle with a random collection of unrelated pieces. We look for cues and clues, straight edges, similar colors. We start off by sorting, classifying, segregating pieces that seem to have something in common, and we test and fit edge to edge to see if there is correspondence, and we sometimes have to be prepared for massive shifts, like Kuhn's scientific revolutions.[1] What we thought was sea turns out to be sky; what we thought was at the bottom turns out to be at the top. We have to achieve a queer combination of faith, humility, and pride. We must be willing to go on with our present images and hypotheses in the faith that what we now believe is going to work. Otherwise, we abandon the whole activity. We also have to be prepared to change, to reorganize, to shift large numbers of pieces to different places. Reorganizations, we should notice, often - take place as the puzzle approaches completion.

THE EVOLUTION OF IMAGES OF THE UNIVERSE

The pattern we have been describing in this book is by no means the only pattern the human race has perceived in the intricate complexities of the universe. We can perceive perhaps a pattern of patterns. Any pattern that has been perceived is part of the total pattern itself. We cannot simply reject and ignore it. All the patterns we perceive are only fragments of the larger pattern that we cannot perceive. All the patterns that have been perceived, therefore, deserve at least our critical respect. We may indeed perceive the pattern of patterns to be one of evolution and ecological succession. The earlier patterns may have become extinct species that left records, but do not presently exist in the minds of the present human race. Just because something is extinct, however, does not mean it ceases to be part of the total pattern. We see this, for instance, in the evolution of our image of the space and time configurations of the universe. Images of the ancient Hindus or the ancient Egyptians, the image of the flat earth covered with the great bowl of the heavens, the image of the round earth at the center of the universe with the heavens revolving around it, the Newtonian image, and the Einsteinian image certainly represent an ecological succession in the minds of some if not all human beings. We must remember, however, that in ecological succession and in evolution later species do not necessarily replace earlier species, but coexist with them. The amoeba coexists with the mammals and with man and may even outlast all the supposedly higher forms.

There is no proposition in evolution which says that what is later is necessarily better, though we sometimes have a strong suspicion that it may be. So it is with our images of the world. Different images that seem to be incompatible may coexist in the great ecosystem of the human mind simply because they occupy different niches. We watch the sun "rise." When we drive around town, we are operating essentially with the image of a flat earth covered with a bowl and this serves the purposes of getting around and of ordinary language perfectly well. In getting around town we can completely neglect the curvature of the earth. We can, if we like, imagine the sun as stationary with the eastern horizon dipping below it at dawn, even if this gives us a certain sense of vertigo; but from the point of view of relativity, this is not much more true than the image that the sun rises, which is much better for poetry and conversation. The niche of any image is limited by the human needs and activities that surround it. The image of a flat earth is fine for getting around town; it is of no use at all for the navigator or the astronaut.

We need to look, therefore, at other images of the larger pattern, even some that seem to be inconsistent with the evolutionary image that we have projected in this work. Inconsistency is a form of mental predation. Inconsistent images tend to eat up each other. Mutual predation is rare, of course, though by no means impossible. If one image becomes dominant, we have a predator-predatee relationship, but this, as we saw in Chapter 4, can be very stable, because the predator and predatee are each instruments in the survival of the other. It is not surprising, therefore, that we find inconsistent images coexisting and even dominant predator images unable to eliminate completely the images they think they dominate. Astrology, which was the father of astronomy, still coexists with it. It is very rare for the Oedipus scenario actually to be consummated.

ALTERNATIVE IMAGES

Animism

Let us look, therefore, at four images of the "larger pattern," which at present coexist with the evolutionary image presented in this book, that are in some respects inconsistent with it, but that have niches from which they are unlikely to be dislodged, and must be thought of as therefore part of the larger ecosystem of the noosphere. These alternative images are: animism, creationism, materialism, and revolutionism. No existing ideology can fall completely within one of these four categories, but this is what we should expect. Ideologies are not so much species as ecosystems of the mind and they are likely to have a good many varied constituents. The above four categories are not species either, but may be thought of perhaps as genera of images.

Animism is the view that the universe around us and its constituent parts is something like a human being. All humans grow up in an environment that consists partly, but very significantly of other human beings. There is evidence from the records of feral children growing up among animals, or children who have had no human contacts and have been shut away that the biological human cannot develop its genetic potentialities for humanity unless it is in the environment of other humans.

As children we soon learn as we observe them that other human beings are something like the self we observe from within. We have a world of inner experience that we can observe in ourselves, but cannot observe in others. This inner experience produces behavior in ourselves and we soon learn to interpret the behavior of others as similarly arising out of their inner experiences. Each human being is aware of an inner unit, say, the self as an actor and observer. We soon learn to deduce that other human beings have similar selves and we interpret their behavior as expressing these selves. It is not an unreasonable step of analogy to suppose that nonhuman objects likewise have selves, different and perhaps less complex from that which we perceive within our own body, but still capable of perception and behavior. Some are more active and like us, like the animals; some are more passive, like the vegetables; some very passive, like the rocks. Some seem more immediate, like the clouds and weather; some more remote, like the stars and planets.

Animism leads easily into fantasy and magic. We people the world with spirits—some benign, some malign—the kami of the Japanese waterfall, the nymphs, the dryads, the Olympian gods of the Greeks, the fairies and leprechauns of the Irish, the kachina of the Hopi; the list is innumerable. It is an easy step from this to the principle that just as other human beings can be affected by speech, entreaty, and persuasion, so can the other spirits of the environment. The rain gods and demons then give rise to incantations and rain dances, exorcism and blessing, idolatry and sacrifice. Animistic sentiment can lead into great poetry and drama. Linked with the darker human passions it can lead to Moloch and the valley of Rimmon and to the blood soaked pyramids of the Aztecs.

If anyone thinks that animism is extinct or a fossil relic of the past, all that is necessary to dispel that illusion is to open the newspaper. There is pretty sure to be an astrology column. I am not sure what the theory is behind astrology; if there is any, it almost has to be animistic, that somehow the planets and heavenly bodies are beings creating a personal climate around us, as do our human associates. Even if they are doing no more than weighting the dice of life, that is a pretty skillful operation for a planet and would seem to require a high degree of animistic thought.

We can perhaps dismiss astrology as superstition. If we turn to the sports pages, however, we will find creatures with strange names, like Red Sox and Dodgers, engaged in endless and elaborate rituals of conflict. If we turn to the political pages, we will find embodied spirits like Uncle Sam and John Bull, and animal totems in the shape of eagles, lions, and bears, exhibiting behavior and passions that are proper only to individual human beings. The tendency to be animistic about collectivities indeed goes very far back in the human race. Animism is weakest perhaps at the level of the corporation, which perhaps explains why, having neither a soul to be saved nor a body to be kicked, it constantly has the problem of keeping itself legitimate. The enormous legitimacy of the national state and its capacity to attract human sacrifice may be related to the fact that our image of it is highly animistic and that we think of it as a person.

It may be, indeed, that in some sense our animism is a necessity for human communication simply because, if we are to communicate about large and complex systems, there must be some way of reducing them to simplicity by abstraction. Our consciousness of the unity of the self in the middle of a vast complexity of images or material structures is at least a suitable metaphor for the unity of a group, organization, department, discipline, or science. If personification is only a metaphor, let us not despise metaphors—we might be one ourselves.

Creationism

Whether creationism is a stage beyond animism we do not really have to decide. It is, however, somewhat different. Animism comes by metaphor from introspection; creationism comes by metaphor from human activity. If we perceive something that is ordered, structured, and looks as if it might have a purpose, it is a very reasonable inference that somebody or something made it. The human race, as we have seen, is a fantastic producer of artifacts. We could well be described as Homo Faber. Again, as I look around the room, I see practically nothing that is not a human artifact. Even the plants have been modified by human beings. When I look out the window I am more likely to see objects that are not human artifacts, like trees, grass, sky, and clouds. It is at least not an unreasonable analogy to see these as artifacts too. Even if we have qualms about perceiving objects that are not human artifacts as artifacts of God, we are still likely to regard them as artifacts of at least a partly personified Nature. When we inquire into origins it is very easy to say that we understand how human artifacts came into being because we made them; when we find things around us that are not human artifacts it is a small step of analogy to say that somebody or something must have made these too.

The classic expression of creationism is, of course, the Old Testament of the Bible. Societies, whether Christian, Islamic, or Marxist, which have been profoundly influenced by Judaism, have creationism running very deeply through their modes of thought and in their metaphor and literature. Somewhat by contrast, the great Eastern stream of human experience coming out of India, China, and Japan is much less creationist, at least at the level of official religion. Brahma may breathe the universe in and out every ten billion years. Buddhism, apart from its concession to local animisms, is a virtually atheistic religion; Shinto is polytheistic even beyond the Greek imagination, though in some ways it is rather like Greek religion. But it was only the Lord God of Israel who made heaven and earth and all that therein is, and who at the same time could be mindful of man.[2]

Perhaps because creationism is so intimately linked to human creativity, it has produced an extraordinary universe of human creations—poetry, drama, ritual, architecture, sculpture, even clothing and jewelry—all designed to give glory through human creations to the creator of all things. It has also given rise to activities, in prayer and in worship, which transcend any secular ecstasy. For the physical ecstasy of rushing downhill in the snow on two long human artifacts people are prepared to sacrifice a certain amount of money, limb, and even occasionally life. But the ecstasy of skiing and the sacrifices made pales into insignificance beside the ecstasy of a St. Francis or a St. Theresa, the blood of the martyrs, and the vast economic sacrifice that produced the cathedrals as soaring monuments of worship. Add to this the fact that the belief in a benevolent providence is very frequently self-justified and will turn bad luck to advantage and guard against mistaking good luck for personal skill. Then we can see why perhaps agnostic evolutionism makes remarkably little dent on the niche of a vigorous creationism.

Nevertheless, there are severe strains between evolutionism and creationism, as we saw for instance in the Scopes' trial in Tennessee in the last generation and in the restrictive educational legislation in California at the present time. Darwin indeed is more of a threat to creationism than was either Newton or Laplace. Napoleon is supposed to have asked Laplace whether he found God in his equations of celestial mechanics, to which the astronomer replied: "I have no need of that hypothesis." His lack of need arises, however, because the solar system is an approximately finished work in a state of near-equilibrium, and the equations of celestial mechanics tell us very little about its creation. Consequently, Newtonian science was quite consistent, at least with deism, that is, the view of a creator that wound up the universe at the beginning and has presumably been standing by watching it unwind ever since. The eighteenth century Enlightenment on the whole was an enlightenment of deism. The French revolutionaries, it will be recalled, tried to set up a religion of the Goddess of Reason as a Supreme Being, which was remarkably unsuccessful in attracting adherents. The geologists on the other hand, even before Darwin, seemed to point to a universe in which nonhuman artifacts come into being as a result of blind randomness, governed only by the roll of nature's dice. It is not surprising that this view arouses anxiety and hostility among those for whom creationism is a sustaining and wholesome way of life.

Oddly enough, much the same problem has arisen in the Soviet Union in the Lysenko controversy. Lysenko was a fraudulent, but plausible biologist who claimed that the properties of plants could be changed by treatment of their seeds, thus in effect denying the fundamental principle of modern genetics, which is the stability of the genome in most environmental treatments outside perhaps of radiation. The outcome in the Soviet Union was much more tragic than it was in the United States. Mr. Scopes lived out a reasonably comfortable life after his trial, but dozens of Soviet geneticists were killed or sent to labor camps.

Genetics ran afoul of official Soviet ideology, perhaps because it was seen as a threat to what might be called "social creationism." Part of the appeal of Marxism is the belief that man can create not only his own societies and institutions, but also his own character. The idea of a genetic component to the world, totally unmalleable by present techniques at least, is highly unfriendly to the dream of socialist man as the conqueror of nature.

Whether the evolutionary perspective is ultimately inconsistent with creationism is a question that cannot really be answered in the present state of knowledge. There is certainly a creationist aspect to epigenesis or production, the formation of the phenotype from the genotype. The genotype is essentially know-how, a kind of structure of information and instructions that does in fact create a phenotype from the genotype by a process which is by no means dissimilar to that by which human beings create an automobile. When it comes to natural selection and the larger evolutionary process the problem is more severe. There is no "plan" as there is in the fertilized egg. Orthogenesis, that is, patterns of evolution from the simple to the complex, from man's simian ancestors to Homo sapiens or from that miserable little runt, eohippus, to the majestic horse, seems to suggest a direction of teleology in evolution. But these sequences may in fact simply be rare events, improbable sequences that actually came off. The real difficulty is that, until we have a theory of the evolution of niches—which we do not—all natural selection tells us is that the surviving survived, niches were filled, and new niches of some sort were developed. If new niches are more likely to be at the "top" of the scale of knowledge, know-how or complexity, whatever we call it, then selection itself becomes a learning process and it is not absurd to say with Tennyson, who agonized over these matters perhaps more than anyone else, "Yet I doubt not through the ages one increasing purpose runs, And the thoughts of men are widen'd with the process of the suns."[3] This could apply not only to the thoughts of men, but to the whole evolutionary process.

Materialism, Reductionism, Mechanomorphism

The word materialism covers a wide and confusing variety of ideas, but it does represent a family of views about the universe that exist in the ecosystem of the noosphere like the others. There is first philosophical and metaphysical materialism, which supposes that matter is the only reality and that psychological phenomenon, emotion, the mental world as we perceive it by introspection, are all in some sense illusion or "epiphenomena," whatever that may mean, produced by some arrangements or interaction of matter within the human body. This is somewhat related to the viewpoint of reductionism, which is the view that all nonphysical and nonchemical events can ultimately be reduced to events in physics and chemistry. This is a view of the world confined to a fairly small number of people. Nevertheless, it is by no means unknown in the scientific community. Whether it has had much impact in guiding research is a question.

The rise of molecular biology suggests that physical and chemical models can be very useful in interpreting the complex structures of biological organisms. Furthermore, what might be thought of as the opposite view to reductionism in biology, that is, vitalism, the theory that living organisms have some mysterious quality that sharply differentiates them from physical and chemical systems, did not prove to be a useful tool for the advancement of knowledge, whereas attempts to interpret the machinery of living objects in terms of physical and chemical mechanisms have been quite fruitful. In human medicine and physiology also the investigation of the physical and chemical machinery of the human body is very fruitful and has undoubtedly contributed to the extension of human life. Furthermore, we cannot doubt that drugs have proved to be valuable in the treatment of mental disease and that it would be of great advantage to us to know something about the machinery of human learning and formation of images, about which we really know very little.

There is a difference here between what might be called a "nothing-but" attitude and the "both-and" attitude. An evolutionary perspective I think is unfriendly to the "nothing-but" attitude and certainly unfriendly toward philosophical materialism in the sense that it sees the evolutionary process as primarily being a process in something like information or structure, and it regards material or matter either as a form of this or as its encodee, that is, the thing in which the information is encoded. Similarly, the evolutionary perspective is unfriendly toward a "nothing-but" reductionism. It perceives a hierarchy of complexity in the universe, and while the more complex systems always tend to incorporate the less complex ones, this does not mean that the more complex ones do not have peculiarities and structures that the less complex ones do not have. Thus, no one doubts that the human body is composed of chemical elements arranged in molecular patterns. The human body, however, is very different from a pile of chemicals and molecules. It is an organized structure containing and constantly processing enormous quantities of information, which the atoms and molecules serve to encode. Immediately after death the human body still contains much the same chemicals and molecules it did before, but they are no longer capable of encoding more complex systems, and indeed, their own structure will rapidly disintegrate when they are no longer part of a larger organization.

The "nothing-but" and "both-and" dichotomy applies also to another important view of the universe, which might be called mechanomorphism or mechanism, that it is very much like a machine. It was the success of human beings in fabricating machines that perhaps led to the mechanomorphic view of the universe that regards it as just one large machine of which we are a part. This is just as much a metaphor as creationism, and perhaps even less sustainable. The universe is certainly full of machinery and the attempt to understand it better is almost universally fruitful. This is true of the machinery of biological systems, as well as the machinery of social systems. The question whether the universe is "nothing but" a machine, however, cannot be answered by any means known to us and is not affected at all by the fact that increased knowledge of the machinery of the universe is not only interesting, but also useful to us.

THE "BOTTOM UP" AND "TOP DOWN" MODES OF HUMAN KNOWLEDGE

The situation is complicated by the fact that there are two modes of human knowledge. One is the "bottom up" mode, which is essentially mechanistic, and which starts with the understanding of simple components and works these up into the understanding of larger and more complex systems. Science on the whole falls into this mode, though in the course of its development incursions from the other mode, in the form of insight and intuition, are by no means uncommon or unimportant.

A second mode of human knowledge might be described as the "top down" method, which arises from the fact that we have inner experience of an extremely complex system, mainly ourselves, so that when it comes to knowledge about the human organism we have, as it were, an inside track that we do not have in studying other systems. A physicist has never been an atom or a chemist a molecule. No biologist has ever been an amoeba, although he has been a human being, a specimen of life. Every economist has made purchases; every sociologist has been in a family; every political scientist has been a member of a state, so that in the social sciences we do get a constant interaction and tension between the "bottom up" and the "top down" approach.

The "top down" approach tends, of course, to be folk knowledge. It tends to be knowledge of personal experience in the personal environment, and hence it can lead into serious errors when it is generalized to include larger systems, because our own personal experience and environment is a very small sample of the total. Within its own range of environment, however, a personal experience gives us very reliable knowledge about the world, often more reliable than our knowledge of the larger systems. For knowledge about the larger systems, however, we have to rely increasingly on the "bottom up" approach, as the system gets beyond our personal experience. And here mechanism is enormously useful.

Revolutionism

The fourth view of the world, revolutionism, is not perhaps on a par with the others, but it is an important component of many ideologies and it raises some questions perhaps not raised by the other three. As judged by the surviving records, the time structure of the universe seems to be divided into periods of no change or small, slow change, separated by periods of large, rapid, and significant change, which are of course the revolutions. The human race could almost be divided into revolutionaries and evolutionaries. Revolutionaries are those who conceive of change, and especially desirable change, as involving sudden, drastic, and large changes, which they are interested in promoting. Evolutionaries are that vast majority of the human race who jog along from day to day and do the ordinary work of the world, and who see change on the whole as proceeding slowly, gradually, steadily, and who look upon large and sudden changes as likely to be for the worse rather than for the better. This dichotomy might create some strange bedfellows. Among the revolutionaries, for instance, might come Billy Graham and the evangelicals, as well as Lenin and the Bolsheviks. The evolutionaries would be almost as heterogeneous as the human race itself. Nevertheless, the distinction has some interest.

The question of revolutionism breaks down into a number of others, particularly in light of the evolutionary perspective. It is a mistake to oppose revolution and evolution too sharply, although revolutionaries do seem to stand out as a category of persons. The question of the role of something like revolutions, however, in the total evolutionary process is an important one, and one that is actually not too easy to answer. The geological record suggests, of course, that there have been periods of relative stability represented by a particular geological era or deposition, and that these come to an end with some rather sudden dramatic changes and are followed by another era. These geological revolutions, if they may be so called, are often accompanied by great extinctions of species and genera of the previous period and the rather rapid development of a whole new set of species, as we have seen. It is still something of an open question whether these geologic revolutions actually took place or whether they are simply defects in the record. Unfortunately this is something we cannot resolve unless we discover better records.

THE IMPORTANCE OF RARE EVENTS

A critical problem here is the significance in the long evolutionary process of rare events. Events may be divided into two kinds, those which occur in regular or cyclical succession, like breaths, heartbeats, and sunrises, and those which occur at irregular intervals, like a flood, a new idea, or a genetic mutation. The rarity of irregular events can be measured roughly in what might be called a "period of probability," which is the reciprocal of their occurrence in a given time period. Thus, a 50-year flood is one with a probability of 1/50 in any one year, or what is the same thing, 1/600 in any one month, assuming no seasonality, and it has a period of probability of 50 years, or what is the same thing, 600 months. The period of probability is a useful measure because it is independent of the unit of time used. The probability of an event occurring within this period of probability is roughly two-thirds. The probability of its occurring in a period ten times the period of probability is very high indeed, .99995.[4]

This is a very important proposition for the theory of evolution. It means that over long enough periods of time, many improbable events are almost certain to occur. An event, for instance, with an annual probability of one in a billion and a period of probability of a billion years is almost certain to occur sometime within a period of ten billion years, which seems to be about the order of magnitude of the present universe. Laboratory science deals only with highly probable or repeatable events; it cannot deal with the highly improbable because it has simply not been around long enough. The length of life of the observer is too short. Not all rare events, of course, are revolutionary. Rare events are unusual; that is, they represent changes in the environment of a system. But these changes may not be very significant. They may for instance simply be like a blue moon, which would not affect anything very much on earth. On the other hand, they may be such things as a flood, draught, large earthquake, eruption, climatic change, or something that would indeed be dramatic and revolutionary. We could argue that large changes are likely to be rarer than small ones. It is not wholly clear but it is at least plausible to suppose that the corollary to this is that the rarer the event, the more important it is going to be. If the period of time is long enough in any evolutionary process, therefore, revolutionary changes are likely to occur.

Like the other categories, revolutionism can be very misleading and destructive if it is "nothing but," and the revolutionary often falls into this illusion. Most changes, and probably most important changes, and from the human point of view the most beneficial changes are not revolutionary in the sense that in themselves they do not imply large systems change, but emerge out of the ongoing evolutionary dynamic of the system itself. Revolutionary change is that which puts the system itself into a new gear, such as the development of DNA or the development of the human race. These are not to be ruled out of social systems either, although they are very rare, and even more rarely produced by revolutionaries.

A variety of revolutionism might be called "liberationism." That is a view of the world in which anything that is wrong is seen as some kind of oppression, the solution to which is to destroy the oppressors and liberate the oppressed. It would be fortunate if the world's problems could be solved so simply. That oppression in some form has existed and still exists nobody would deny, but that it is the major source of evil in the world is very doubtful indeed. Furthermore, the removal of one set of oppressors by revolution is all too likely to result in their replacement by another. Stalin in many ways was more oppressive than the Czar; Mao produced a spiritual tyranny worse than that of any Chinese emperor.

A BRIEF LOOK AT CURRENT IDEOLOGIES

Christianity

This is a very sketchy set of tools, but we can use it perhaps to take a brief look at the major ideological systems inhabiting the minds of mankind today, and to indulge in some speculations—they can be no more than that—about their evolutionary potential in the light of the human crisis of the next 100 or 200 years.

We look first at the three great phyla of human life, organization, and thought, which have a common genetic origin in Judaism. These are Christianity, Islam, and Marxist Communism. The persistence of Judaism as a genetic strain producing cultural offspring as well as an extraordinary culture within itself is one of the most remarkable phenomena of human history. Whether this is due to the survival value of what might be called ethical creationism I do not know. It is a phenomenon that defies simple explanation.

Christianity emerged out of Judaism some 2,000 years ago, developing into a much larger movement and again showing quite astonishing persistence and survival capacity in the face of severe challenges. In a sense it inherited the Roman Empire. It played an enormous role in forming the culture of medieval Europe. It survived the split between Rome and Avignon. It survived Luther, Calvin, and the Protestant Reformation. It colonized the whole of the Americas, survived the Enlightenment, and the American, French, and Russian Revolutions. It survived the rise of Islam, but only on the basis of territorial division. It is marginal in India and Japan and a total failure in China. Its world view is based on revelation. The early church, if we are to judge from the New Testament, which it produced, was a scattered community bound together by a common belief that a group of people had actually witnessed someone rise from the dead, not as a poetic fantasy but as a flesh and blood occurrence of daily life. Acceptance of this as fact seemed to give the Christians extraordinary power to love, to suffer, and to form communities. Over the centuries the church frequently became corrupt, power as usual turning out to be corrupting, and the faith often declined and was watered down and turned into metaphor, but just as constantly revived. Whether this constant renewal will continue who can say. We do not understand its conditions; we cannot say whether they have passed away.

The view of the world that has emerged out of science in many ways contradicts that of the Bible, both Jewish and Christian. A large part of the world can now be understood without the creationism so central to both Judaism and Christianity, but creationism still survives with great vitality as a language for the description of widespread religious experience. One suspects that the social system will continue to produce a niche that will be occupied by Christianity or something like it.

Islam

Islam can be regarded either as a mutant, partly out of Christianity, in part perhaps out of Judaism, coming out of a region that had been neglected and had then produced its own revelation and its own prophet, or it can be thought of initially perhaps as a reaction to a decayed Byzantine Christianity, particularly appropriate to arid climates. It gave rise to a great civilization stretching from Spain to the Philippines. It encouraged learning; in many places it exhibited the beginnings of science. For some reason I do not think we understand completely, it fossilized after about 1200 or 1300 A.D. After some 600 years of great vitality it lost the movement into science and developed sterile orthodoxy, even though its simple rituals and practices clearly satisfied religious and life needs of large numbers of people. Whether it was the destruction of Baghdad or the wastage of the Crusades that produced this fossilization I do not know. Whether it can revive, therefore, I also do not know. It is still a very live force in the world. It has obviously been sustainable. It may be due for revitalization in light of the pressures of the modern world, though its very decentralization oddly enough favors tradition and stagnation. While centralization has grave dangers, it also has great potential for change, as we saw in the Catholic Church under Pope John.

Marxism

The third great Judaic religion is Marxism. If it seems stretching the word to call a secular atheistic ideology a religion, so be it, but it is no more atheistic than classical Buddhism, though it is more secular. In a little more than 100 years, Marxism has had an extraordinary success. It has become the official doctrine of about a third of the human race, covering societies as diverse as the Soviet Union and China. It dominates Eastern Europe, it has a toehold in the Americas in Cuba, and it seems successfully to be seeking a hold in Africa.

With all the success of Marxism, its theoretical foundations are shaky, especially in light of evolutionary dynamics. The weakness of its social dynamic theory is suggested by its failures of prediction in such matters, for instance, as the distribution of income between labor income and nonlabor income. The proportion of national income going to labor went up in capitalist societies, not down as Marx predicted, and surplus value was widely distributed to the working class without any revolutionary change.

One basic fallacy of Marxism is the labor theory of value, not so much as a theory of relative prices, of which it is a crude first approximation and in which Marx made no advance on Ricardo,[5] but in the sense in which it is a theory of production. The essence of the Marxian theory is that labor produces everything, so that any income not derived from labor represents exploitation and is illegitimate. Under some circumstances the conclusion might have a certain measure of truth. The argument, however, is wholly fallacious. Production, as we have seen in this volume, does not come from labor, which is a concept so heterogeneous as to be almost worthless for scientific discussion. Production comes rather from knowledge or know-how, capturing energy to transform materials into more agreeable places, times, and forms.

Oddly enough, Marxism is much more accurate as a description of pre-capitalist societies than it is a description of capitalism. It fails hopelessly to come to grips with the complexities of the interrelationships involved. It is significant that it is only really in pre-capitalist societies or in incipient capitalist societies that Marxism has been successful. In a society where property is mainly in the form of land and tax capability, the theory of surplus value, that it is labor that produces all the food and the landlord and government simply take part of it without giving much in return, is by no means an unrealistic model. In developed capitalism, however, the class structure becomes so diffuse and surplus value, however defined, is so widely distributed that the Marxist model is of very little use as a guide to understanding or to policy.

In its political theory, Marxism must be described as either naive or hypocritical in thinking that revolution by a disciplined, organized party can conceivably produce a classless society. Communist revolutions have not "liberated the masses," and instead have subjected them to a tyrannical regime imposed by a small elite of ideological aristocrats. Communism represents the seizure of property for purposes of power by a small group of party leaders. The theory is that power is to be used for the benefit of the people. In practice, as always, it is used to perpetuate itself, to stifle dissent, and to channel the arts and literature into devices for legitimating and reinforcing the existing power structure. The experience of the last 50 years has demonstrated that at least in Western societies and those with a Christian heritage communist states have not liberated the human spirit, been oppressive to the working class, oppressed the arts, created secret police, sown widespread terror, used threats against their own dissident people, and even if they have produced modest economic development, it has been at a very high social cost.

The "Non-Judaic" World: India, China

When we look at the non-Judaic world, as we might call it—India, South Asia, Southeast Asia, China, and Africa—the picture is very different and complex. China is officially Marxist-Leninist, but in practice it has produced a mutation from communism so radical that its main enemy seems to be the Soviet Union. It seems to be another example of the unfortunate proposition that conflict between people of the same, slightly divergent ideologies is much more intense than conflict between people of different ideologies. The Christians fought the Moslems quite halfheartedly compared with the enthusiasm with which they slaughtered each other in the Thirty Years War or with the enthusiasm with which the Moslem sects slaughtered each other. It is not surprising that Russia gets along far better with the United States than it does with China.

The Chinese mutation is not only unique, however, it is very large. The evidence that a massive change has taken place in the conduct of the ordinary Chinese and in the principles that govern its ruling class seems almost incontrovertible, judging at least from the testimony of visitors. With the concentration of power that inevitably comes with communism has come, of course, the capacity to make serious mistakes. Both the Great Leap Forward of the late fifties and the Cultural Revolution of the late sixties were costly in terms of development, and one suspects in terms of many human values. On the other side, the development of a society of almost frightening integration and order and the abolition of extreme poverty are important items on the balance sheet. The future is hard to predict. The revolution created evolutionary potential, but the random elements in the realization of this potential create high uncertainty in the outcomes. About the most critical question for a society as close to the edge of its carrying capacity in terms of human population as is China, is whether population control can really be successful. Even with the smallest rate of population increase under the present regime, it will drift slowly but surely toward catastrophe.

In India, of course, the catastrophe seems much closer and it is hard to have any optimism at all. In regard to population it is a perfect example of the tragedy of the commons. As Mamdani[6] has shown, the only hope of the poor Indian cultivator is to have at least four sons so that he can expand his holding and perhaps send at least one son to the city to send back some remittances. It is precisely when what is rational for the individual is disastrous for the society that we have the tragedy of the commons. But how to change the institutions so that the interests of individuals and society coincide, especially in a country as diverse and heterogeneous as India, is a problem that will require an enormous amount of human effort, intelligence, and good will. Indonesia and many parts of Africa face essentially the same problem and it seems to be equally intractable everywhere. Even in those industrialized enclaves where fertility has declined, as in Singapore, Hong Kong, and to some extent Taiwan, it is still far above the reproduction rate and the alarming thing about population is that we are rapidly getting to the point where *any* rate of growth above zero leads to catastrophe. The only difference between rapid growth and slow growth is that slow growth takes longer and perhaps gives more time to adjust and to change, but the slowing of growth only postpones the inevitable catastrophe unless it turns into no-growth.

TOWARD A REALISTIC RADICALISM

Suppose one were to ask what changes in the noosphere in say the next 100 years or so, that is, in the totality of images of the world and the values placed on them and the emotions surrounding them, are most desirable from the point of view of the welfare of the human race? In my own view the answer would be a transformation of radical ideologies to realistic visions. There is no hope in a stand-pat conservatism and in a blind resistance to all change. We are in the midst of vast and largely irresistible change that cannot be stopped. We cannot freeze the world, except on a very temporary basis, any more than we can freeze prices and wages. If conservatism is an attempt to preserve some little island of order and wealth in the middle of the world going down to decay, disorder, and misery, it is an idle dream. There are no such islands.

With what might be called the radical passion one must have sympathy. The passion to eliminate poverty, misery, hunger, malnutrition, and avoidable ill health, and to create a world in which every human being born has a reasonable opportunity to fulfill the genetic potential for health and learning, love and joy, grief and resignation, is a passion in tune with the potential of the human race. But we have to admit, however unwillingly and unpleasantly, that passion is frequently but not necessarily the enemy of truth, and that passion distorts our image of the world often to the point where our illusions prevent fulfillment of the passion. It is the radical illusions, not the conservative coldness, that are the greatest enemies of the radical passion. If the radical passion is to be fulfilled, if we are indeed to move into a world that is better than what we have now, the radical illusions must be discarded and a realistic appraisal of the dynamic effects of human action must become widespread.

THE RADICAL ILLUSIONS: STATIC DISTRIBUTION, CLASS INTEREST, REVOLUTIONISM, MELIORISM

The first of the radical illusions might be called the illusion of static distribution; that the poor are poor because the rich are rich and there is only so much to go around, therefore, the answer is to redistribute the wealth and income by taking it away from the rich and giving it to the poor. No illusion is without some foundation of reality, and where the dynamics of society create increasing inequality institutions for equalization have to be created at some point to prevent inequality getting out of hand. We must think of this problem in dynamic terms, however, not simply in terms of "exploitation," which is a relatively small element in the distributional problem. Exploitation would be the situation where the poor produce a lot and the rich take it away from them. That exploitation exists and has been an element in human history cannot be denied, but that it is the major source of inequality, especially in the world today, is an illusion.

Inequality is primarily the result of differential development. The rich are richer than the poor because the rich have been getting richer faster than the poor. In this process exploitation has played a small role, but by far the greatest source of the differential is different rates of accumulation of knowledge, capital, and organization. These rates of accumulation are essentially internal properties of cultures. Nevertheless, exploitation is important as a psychological perception even where it is a minor element in terms of real transfers. Perception of past exploitation creates resentment, destroys community, and makes the solution of all problems more difficult. It may be necessary, therefore, sometimes to compensate for the feeling of exploitation, even though the objective realities may be different, in order to achieve a problem-solving community.

The second radical illusion may be called the illusion of class or group interest. This is the illusion that group behavior is explained by the interest of the group in some objective sense. It is almost a truism to say that individual behavior is guided by interest in the sense that everybody decides to do what he or she thinks is best at the time. This does not in any sense imply pure selfishness, which in fact is very rare. Our evaluation of what is "best" almost always depends on our images of the welfare of other people with whom we identify. Personal identity indeed is closely bound up with the group with which we identify. Identification groups, however, are not the same as interest groups. Any event or decision theoretically divides the human race into three interest groups: those who are favorably affected, those who are unfavorably affected, and those who are unaffected. These interest groups, however, practically never correspond to any identity groups, political, social, racial, religious, national, and so on.

The identity group most likely to be an interest group is the occupational group; something that raises the price of wheat is likely to benefit all the people in the wheat industry. One of the radical fallacies is to identify social class as both an identity group and an interest group. It is weak in both respects. Neither the workers of the world nor the capitalists unite. Even labor movements are loose federations of occupational groups. The working class or the capitalist class is not an interest group in the sense that there is practically no event or decision that will, for instance, affect all workers favorably and all capitalists unfavorably. All change affects some workers favorably and some unfavorably, some capitalists favorably and some unfavorably. The view of human history as a class struggle of interest groups, therefore, is totally unrealistic and can only lead to behavior that will have consequences utterly different from what is expected.

A third radical fallacy is the fallacy of revolutionism that, if only virtuous, right-thinking people can seize power, all will be well. Again, there is a small element of truth in this view. There are ruling classes in the sense that some babies have a much better chance of reaching positions of power than others. Ruling groups do deteriorate, become inefficient and oppressive, and prevent the evolutionary development of a society. Sometimes a new set of people in powerful roles sets off a new burst of evolutionary potential. On the other hand, power is nearly always less than people think. The decision-makers in powerful roles are quite limited in the decisions they can make. They have a limited agenda, though they can make catastrophic mistakes. Furthermore, the skills required in achieving power are not the same as those in exercising it, so the good revolutionary is usually a bad governor. There is a good deal to be said for the proposition that a high degree of randomness in the assignment of individuals to powerful roles gives survival value and is a safeguard at least against some of the traps of power. Another possible answer to the pathology of power is, of course, its wide distribution. Almost the only mechanism for achieving this is a market mechanism or some simulation of it in the political process, such as voting. It is another illusion to think that the revolution can produce a classless society. No matter who does it, revolution is a form of internal conquest and conquest always produces a stratified society. Communist countries today are a good example of this.

The fourth radical illusion might be called the illusion of meliorism, that it is easy to set up institutions in which things go from bad to better rather than from bad to worse. This is an illusion oddly enough that radicals tend to share with conservatives. They just favor a slightly different set of institutions. Because of this illusion, radicals tend to be insensitive to the "tragedy of the commons," in the famous phrase of Garrett Hardin,[7] a situation in which the short-run interest of the individual runs counter to the long-run interest of the group or even of the individual himself, so the commons get overgrazed, seas get overfished, forests get overcut, and so on.

The ultimate tragedy of the commons is of course the Malthusian tragedy, that the interest of the individual is to have more children than the society can ultimately afford. This principle, as we have seen, is relentless and devastating in its operation and unless institutional devices can be found to put the individual into a local and immediate environment in which what is best for the individual is also best for the society, a recurrent tragedy seems almost inevitable. It is perhaps part of the radical inability to think in dynamic terms that leads to such shocking irresponsibility in this matter. Garrett Hardin has suggested that pejorism, the view that things will go from bad to worse unless we organize to stop it and organize in the right way, understanding why things go from bad to worse, is a much more realistic view than meliorism. Meliorism is closely related to liberationism, the doctrine that all we have to do is to remove oppression and all will be well.

The fifth illusion of radicalism is hard to put a name to. It is the view that the hatred of evil is the same thing as the love of good, which unfortunately is not so, because the two attitudes produce very different consequences. This again perhaps goes back to meliorism and the view that, if we could only get rid of evil, the good will simply flower of itself, as over against the pejorist view that the good is a delicate plant that has to be cultivated.

Can there be a new radicalism that will reject the fallacies of the old and yet retain its passion? It will be all too easy for the perception of the fallacies of the old radicalism to lead to a decay of the passion for betterment, and to a withdrawal from the commitment to making a better world. Even fallacious passion would be better than this, for we cannot stop our ears to the cry of misery without losing the compassion that makes us human. But a realistic passion for betterment is not impossible, and it is to the hope of its fulfillment that this book is dedicated.

NOTES

1. Thomas S. Kuhn, *The Structure of Scientific Revolutions* (Chicago: University of Chicago Press, 1962).

2. When I consider thy heavens, the work of thy fingers, the moon and the stars, which thou hast ordained; What is man that thou art mindful of him? And the son of man, that thou visitest him? Psaml 8:3-4.

3. Alfred Lord Tennyson, "Locksley Hall."

4. Kenneth E. Boulding, "The Role of Catastrophe in Evolutionary Dynamics," paper presented at the American Association for the Advancement of Science Symposium on "Catastrophes: Analyses and Solutions," Boston, Feb. 21, 1976.

5. David Ricardo, *The Principles of Political Economy and Taxation* (London and New York: Everyman's Library, 1959).

6. Mahmood Mamdani, *The Myth of Population Control: Family, Caste, and Class in an Indian Village* (New York: Monthly Review Press, 1972).

7. Garrett Hardin, "The Tragedy of the Commons," *Science*, 7, 162 (1968), 1234-1248.

BIBLIOGRAPHY
SUGGESTIONS FOR FURTHER READING

In the enormous literature of this field it is hard to be selective. On the biological side, G. Evelyn Hutchinson, *The Ecological Theater and the Evolutionary Play* (New Haven: Yale University Press, 1965) is an excellent introduction. So is George G. Simpson, *The Meaning of Evolution: A Study of the History of Life and Its Significance for Man* (rev. ed.; New Haven: Yale University Press, 1967). Cyril D. Darlington, *The Evolution of Man and Society* (New York: Simon and Schuster, 1969) is a biologist's attempt to look at societal evolution. There is a lot to be said for going back to the classics. Darwin himself is well worth reading; Charles R. Darwin, *Origin of Species and Descent of Man* (New York: Modern Library Edition). An excellent introduction is Philip Appleman, ed., *Darwin* (New York: W. W. Norton, 1970). D'Arcy W. Thompson, *On Growth and Form* (2nd. ed.; New York: Cambridge University Press, 1952) is a great classic of biology and is a good background for evolutionary theory. Conrad H. Waddington, *The Ethical Animal* (Chicago: University of Chicago Press, 1967) is a sensitive account by a biologist of human evolution. The best introduction to sociobiology is David P. Barash, *Sociology and Behavior* (New York: Elsevier, 1977).

The philosophical literature is large. The outstanding work is P. Teilhard de Chardin, *The Phenomenon of Man* (New York: Harper and Row, 1959). The social and economic literature is meager. Richard Hofstadter's *Social Darwinism in American Thought* (rev. ed.; New York: Braziller, 1959) is a good introduction to an unfortunate episode. Again, there is much to be said for going back to the classics. I would defend Adam Smith, *The Wealth of Nations* (New York: Modern Library Edition), as the first evolutionary economist, especially his Book III. Thomas R. Malthus, *Population: The First Essay* (Ann Arbor: University of Michigan Press, 1959) was what inspired Darwin. Thorstein Veblen's *The Theory of the Leisure Class* (New York: Modern Library Edition), for its time, had important evolutionary insights. Among more recent works, Sir John Hicks, *A Theory of Economic History* (London: Oxford University Press, 1969) and Richard G. Wilkinson, *Poverty and Progress: An Ecological Perspective on Economic Development* (New York: Praeger Publishers, 1973) have the evolutionary perspective.

INDEX

absolute value, as illusion, 273
acculturation, **201***
adaptability vs. adaptation, 111
age, legitimacy of, 206
aged, care for, 319
aging, 12, 115, 279, 319
agreement, as scarce commodity, 22
agriculture, 137-139, 213, 226, 290
alcoholism, 314
alienation, 278
Allee, W. Clyde, 98n., 94
allocational efficiency, 245
allometry, **214**
alternative costs, 288
animism, 343
Appleman, Philip, 119n.
Ardrey, Robert, 154, 162n., 268n.
Aristotelian mean, 272
arms race, 148-150, 158-161, 202
arts, future of, 336
assets, financial, **178**
automobiles, 69, 73, 107, 125, 238
avoiders vs. approachers, 257
Ayres, Clarence, 249, 252n.

Baerwaldt, Nancy, 252n.
balance sheet, **178**
balloon pattern, **302**
Barash, David P., 24n.
Barnard, Chester, I., 196, 209n., 213
Bartlett, David F., 74n.
bathtub theorem, 47, 55, 57, 67, 70, 83, 170, 181
behavior, sequential, 107; theory of maximizing, 145, 233
beliefs, self-justified, 238
benevolence, **191**-193, 202-205, 208-210, 271, 277
Bertalanffy, Ludwig von, 231n.
biogenetics, **14**, 21, **122**
biological advantage, 179

---

*Boldface numbers indicate definitions.

biosphere, 29, 99-119, 154, 254, 258, 289
birth rate, **59**, 64, 72, 76, 298-300
bonding, 222-224, 228
Boserup, Ester, 290, 304n.
Boulding, Kenneth E., 52n., 98., 119n., 162n., 187n., 210n., 231n., 252n., 268n., 288n., 359n.
boundary of equal strength, 152, 161
Buridan's ass, 257
business savings, **179**

Calhoun, John B., 290, 304n.
Cannon, Walter, B., 324, 339n.
capability, **143, 146**
capital, **174**; market, **178**
Carlyle, Thomas, 218, 231n., 236
carpenter function, 108
catalysis, 12, 45, 49
catastrophe, 23, 82, 114, 137, 275, 299, 330, 355
celestial mechanics, 27, 36, 39, 253, 346
challenge, patterns of, 143-147
China, 352, 355
Chomsky, Noam, 130, 140n.
chromosomes, **101**-103, 117, 125, 199
class, **194**-196; struggle, 358
cleaning the market, **171**; 178, 184
cobweb theorem, 90, 183
coefficients of reactivity, 160
cohorts, **57**, 67, 74
commodities, as species, 170, 184
communication, 221, 225, 345
community, 249, 312, 334
competition, mutual, 80, 92, 254; not conflict, 256; of cultures, 318
competitive exclusion, 80, 93
complexification, 45
complexity, increase in, 104, 115
conditional viability, 161
conflict, 254-266, 271, 274; of interest, 246
conflictual behavior, 254
conservation, law of, 48

ABOUT THE AUTHOR

KENNETH E. BOULDING is truly one of the magisterial figures in the field of social science. He has served as president of five major scholarly societies (American Economics Association, International Studies Association, Peace Research Society, Society for General Systems Research, and Association for the Study of Grants Economy) and is currently President-Elect of the American Association for the Advancement of Science (1978). He has taught at universities in seven countries, authored over thirty books and hundreds of articles, pamphlets, and chapters on numerous topics (including a book of poetry), and is the recipient of twenty-four honorary degrees and a variety of other awards. He and his wife, Elise, are among the founders of the field of peace and conflict research, a primary interest over the years. Boulding is currently Distinguished Professor of Economics at the University of Colorado and Director of the Program of Research on General Social and Economic Dynamics in the University's Institute of Behavioral Science.